In this definitive work on parody Ma[...] [...]ry of theories and uses of parody from an[...] [...] new approach to the analysis and classification of modern, la[...] [...]odern theories of the subject. The author's earlier *Parody//Meta-Fiction* (1979) was influential in broadening awareness of parody as a double-coded device which could be used for more than mere ridicule, and her more recent *The Post-Modern and the Post-Industrial. A Critical Analysis* (1991) has provided a critical analysis of literary as well as of other concepts of post-modernism. In the present study she both expands and revises the introductory section of her 1979 text on ancient and modern definitions and uses of parody, adds substantial new sections on modern and post-modern theories and uses of parody and pastiche, and discusses in them the work of a variety of twentieth-century theorists and writers.

Parody: ancient, modern, and post-modern

Literature, Culture, Theory

General editors

RICHARD MACKSEY, *The Johns Hopkins University*
and MICHAEL SPRINKER, *State University of New York at Stony Brook*

The Cambridge *Literature, Culture, Theory* series is dedicated to theoretical studies in the human sciences that have literature and culture as their object of enquiry. Acknowledging the contemporary expansion of cultural studies and the redefinitions of literature that this has entailed, the series includes not only original works of literary theory but also monographs and essay collections on topics and seminal figures from the long history of theoretical speculation on the arts and human communication generally. The concept of theory embraced in the series is broad, including not only the classical disciplines of poetics and rhetoric, but also those of aesthetics, linguistics, psychoanalysis, semiotics, and other cognate sciences that have inflected the systematic study of literature during the past half century.

Titles published

Return to Freud: Jacques Lacan's dislocation of psychoanalysis
SAMUEL WEBER
(*translated from the German by Michael Levine*)

Wordsworth, dialogics, and the practice of criticism
DON H. BIALOSTOSKY

The subject of modernity
ANTHONY J. CASCARDI

Onomatopoetics: theory of language and literature
JOSEPH GRAHAM

Parody: ancient, modern, and post-modern
MARGARET A. ROSE

Parody: ancient, modern, and post-modern

MARGARET A. ROSE

CAMBRIDGE
UNIVERSITY PRESS

Published by the Press Syndicate of the University of Cambridge
The Pitt Building, Trumpington Street, Cambridge CB2 1RP
40 West 20th Street, New York, NY 10011-4211, USA
10 Stamford Road, Oakleigh, Victoria 3166, Australia

First published 1993

Printed in Great Britain at the University Press, Cambridge

A catalogue record for this book is available from the British Library

Library of Congress cataloging in publication data

Rose, Margaret, A.
Parody: ancient, modern and post-modern/Margaret A. Rose
p.   cm.– (Literature, culture, theory: 5)
Includes bibliographical references and index.
ISBN 0-521-41860-7 (hardback)—ISBN 0-521-42924-2 (paperback)
1 Parody 1 Title II Series
PN6149.P3R62   1993
801'.957–dc20 92–39133 CIP

ISBN 0 521 41860 7 hardback
ISBN 0 521 42924 2 paperback

Contents

vii

Contents

❖❖❖

Introduction

❖❖❖

When I first published on parody some twenty years ago now it was still being treated by many critics as a rather lowly comic form which had been of little real significance in the history of literature or of other arts. Not only was Dr Leavis said to have dismissed parody, but many of the structuralists and post-structuralists who were thought to have challenged his ideas had either described parody in negative terms or not deemed it or its examples important enough to warrant extensive or thorough analysis. It was also in part because of the latter attitude that the role played by parody in the development of terms favoured by structuralist and post structuralist theorists and critics, such as the term 'intertextuality', was not fully recognised or acknowledged. Since then, and with the rise of what has been called 'postmodernist' literature and theory, parody has seen something of a revival in contemporary theory and artistic practice, but on the basis of several different understandings, and misunderstandings, of its background, functions and structure.

In this new work on parody – 'ancient, modern, and post-modern' – an attempt has been made to clarify the modern, late-modern, and post-modern representations of parody which have dominated this century by reviewing the uses and meanings given the term from the ancients onwards and by analysing different aspects of a variety of works named parody in both ancient and modern times. These aspects of parody include the peculiarities of its structure, its comic character, the attitude of the parodist to the work parodied, the reader's reception of it, its meta-fictional and 'intertextual' aspects, and its relationship to other devices.

In addition to giving a critical review of past theories and uses of parody to the present with reference to these and other of its aspects, some new ways of designating the modern and post-modern uses of the term are suggested, and the concept of the post-modern explored and expanded further.

1

Of the chapters which follow, the first deals with the ancient meanings of the term parody as well as with the basic structure and functions of parody as used from the ancient mock-epics and the plays of Aristophanes onwards, while the second chapter discusses a variety of both ancient and modern terms with which parody has sometimes been confused, from burlesque and travesty, through pastiche and related forms, to satire, irony, and meta-fiction.[1]

The third chapter then discusses a variety of influential modern and late-modern theories and uses of parody, from those of the Russian formalists and M. M. Bakhtin, through extensions made to their theories by the reception theorists Hans Robert Jauss and Wolfgang Iser, to a variety of structuralist and post-structuralist comments on the subject.

The introductory section of the fourth chapter, on contemporary late-modern and post-modern uses and concepts of parody, begins with comments on the differences between the two major types of post-modernism which have dominated discussion of the subject in recent years and provides a summary of the many different definitions given the post-modern from the beginning of the twentieth century to its concluding decade. Following pages then discuss the various theories or uses of parody of Ihab Hassan, Jean Baudrillard, Fredric Jameson, Dick Hebdige, A. S. Byatt, Martin Amis, and others, before the chapter proceeds to a discussion of what can be called a 'post-modern' understanding of parody and to comments on the works and views of Charles Jencks, Umberto Eco, David Lodge, and Malcolm Bradbury.

The book ends with a general review and summary of the past uses and theories of parody, some concluding comments on its future, a bibliography of works referred to, and an index.

---

1 While this work is in all a new study of parody, chapters 1 and 2 also contain clarifications and extensions of arguments developed in my *Parody//Meta-Fiction. An Analysis of Parody as a Critical Mirror to the Writing and Reception of Fiction* (London, 1979).

❖❖❖❖❖❖❖❖❖❖❖❖❖❖❖❖❖❖❖❖❖❖❖❖❖❖❖❖❖❖❖❖❖❖❖❖❖❖❖

Defining parody from the Ancients onwards

❖❖❖❖❖❖❖❖❖❖❖❖❖❖❖❖❖❖❖❖❖❖❖❖❖❖❖❖❖❖❖❖❖❖❖❖❖❖❖

❖❖❖

Ways of defining parody

❖❖❖

Many definitions of parody have paid insufficient attention to its ancient heritage. Even the original *Oxford English Dictionary* entry on parody which describes it as deriving from the ancient Greek word παρῳδία ('parodia') can be said to have followed a largely eighteenth-century view of parody when defining it as a 'burlesque' poem or song. Several misunderstandings have been generated by the definition of parody as burlesque (the word 'burlesque' is not just a more modern word than 'parodia', but has been derived from quite different terms) and a more critical and historical approach seems necessary given both the repetition of the definition of parody referred to above in the new edition of the *OED*[1] and the advent of some new misunderstandings of the term.

Lack of attention to the historical background of the terms used to define parody has been but one of the problems of parody definition. One other problem has been the restriction of the description of parody to only one or two aspects of that term or its usage. In the past, parody has been defined by most of its lexicographers in terms of either

(1) its etymology,
(2) its comic aspects,
(3) the attitude of the parodist to the work parodied,
(4) the reader's reception of it,
(5) the texts in which parody is not just a specific technique but the 'general' mode of the work itself (one example is Cervantes' *Don Quixote*, where the parody of the works read by the hero is intimately related to the selection of adventures and characters and provides a textual background for Cervantes' work which can

---

1 See the new *Oxford English Dictionary*, 2nd edn (Oxford, 1989), vol. 11, p. 247. Liddell and Scott (eds.), *A Greek-English Lexicon*, revised edn (Oxford, 1983), p. 1344 also defines 'parodia' as meaning 'burlesque' as well as 'parody'.

also be used for 'meta-fictional' reflections on the writing of his own fiction or on the writing of fiction in general),

(6) its relationship to other comic or literary forms.

Several attempts have been made to clarify the concept of parody by expanding one or other of such categories, and some modern and post-modern theorists will be seen to have developed new criteria such as intertextuality from examples of general parody such as Cervantes' *Don Quixote* of 1605–15 or Sterne's *Tristram Shandy* of 1759–67. As the survey of modern and 'late-modern' theories of parody in chapter 3 will show, the complexity of great parody, as found in the works of Aristophanes, Cervantes, or Sterne, has rarely been acknowledged, however, as implying the necessity of investigating all of the above categories at once, and before the major modern theories of parody of the last century are reviewed the categories listed above will be discussed in greater detail so that some background is established for the understanding of both the problems and insights of those various theories.

The etymology of parody

Dispute and uncertainty have prevailed in descriptions of the ancient uses and meanings of words for parody. Of all the terms still used to describe comic quotation, imitation, or transformation, parody alone is named in the classical literature and poetics of the Greeks, and has gained some importance in the Western tradition from this fact. But it is also to some extent owing to its long history that the meaning of the term parody has become the subject of so much argument. This is so not just because the length of time involved has allowed dispute to propagate itself, but because it can be assumed that, in that time, records of its earliest uses and meanings have been lost.

One other factor which may need to be taken into account here is that some records were not made in the first place because the subject was not considered to be sufficiently 'serious' in the sense of either 'grave' or 'important' by all ancient scholars. Aristotle (384–322 BC) writes in chapter 5 of his *Poetics* that 'though the successive changes in Tragedy and their authors are not unknown, we cannot say the same of Comedy; its early stages passed unnoticed, because it was not as yet taken up in a serious way'.[2]

---

2 See Aristotle, *De Poetica*, translated by Ingram Bywater in *The Works of Aristotle*, edited by W. D. Ross, vol. 11 (Oxford, 1924), chapter 5, 1449a, and the Greek

Other problems for the historian of parody include the use of several different words by the ancient Greeks for that which modern languages have since accepted as meaning parody, and the way in which modern commentators on those terms have been limited by their vocabularies in their descriptions of the more ancient words.

Fred W. Householder Jr alludes to both of these issues in his article 'ΠΑΡΩΙΔΙΑ' of 1944 when rejecting the *OED* and Liddell and Scott definitions of 'parody' as being completely suitable for describing the more ancient words for that device.[3]

Householder's own definition of the term follows from his designation of Aristotle's use in chapter 2 of his *Poetics* of the word παρῳδία ('parodia'), to which most lexicons relate our word for 'parody', as the earliest found usage of that noun, and from the meaning given it by both Aristotle and a later commentator, Athenaeus of Naucratis (*c*.170–*c*.230 AD). After deriving the meaning of 'parodia' from its application by Aristotle in his *Poetics* to works written by Hegemon,[4] and from references to and quotations from Hegemon and other writers of 'parodia' in Athenaeus' *The Deipnosophists*,[5] Householder (p. 3) describes it as 'a narrative poem of moderate length, in epic meter, using epic vocabulary, and treating a light, satirical, or mock-heroic subject'.

Householder also connects this usage of 'parodia' to an earlier use of the term παρῳδός or 'parodos' (plural παρῳδοί or 'parodoi') to describe an 'imitating singer', or 'singing in imitation'[6] (which he suggests was made in contrast to a concept of the 'original singer'),[7]

---

text in Aristotle, *The Poetics*, translated by W. Hamilton Fyfe (Cambridge, Mass. and London, 1973), pp. 1–118; p. 20.

3 See Fred W. Householder, Jr, 'ΠΑΡΩΙΔΙΑ', *Journal of Classical Philology*, vol. 39, no.1 (January 1944), pp. 1–9.

4 Householder refers to the use of the noun παρῳδία in Aristotle, *Poetics*, chapter 2, 1448a.

5 See Athenaeus, *The Deipnosophists*, translated by Charles Burton Gulick, 7 vols. (London and Cambridge, Mass., 1941).

6 'Parodos' and 'parode' meaning the side entrance of the ancient theatre through which the chorus of the drama first entered, or their first song, are spelt πάροδος and πάροδή in Greek and derive from the words παρ/α 'by, by the side', and ὁδός 'way', not ᾠδή 'ode'.

7 See Householder, pp. 2 and 8, and see also F. J. Lelièvre, 'The Basis of Ancient Parody', *Greece and Rome*, Series 2, vol. 1, no. 2 (June, 1954), pp. 66–81; p. 79. Several studies have also been made of parody and music. See, for example, W. Steinecke, *Das Parodieverfahren in der Musik* (Kiel, 1934).

and to the derivation from those words of the noun παρῳδή or 'parode' and the idea of a song or 'ode' 'sung in imitation of another'.

After noting that Quintilian (Marcus Fabius Quintilianus, c.35 AD–d. after 96 AD) had described the word παρῳδή in Book 9.2.35 of his *Institutio Oratoria* as 'a name drawn from songs sung in imitation of others, but employed by an abuse of language to designate imitation in verse or prose',[8] Householder suggests that one difference between uses of παρῳδία and παρῳδή is that the latter can refer merely to 'close literary imitation',[9] but later implies that both could also refer to mock-epics.[10]

With reference to the derivation of the word παρῳδή from the word for 'ode' and the prefix 'para' Householder writes of the latter (p. 2): 'Excluding purely local uses, παρά in composition with verbs and verbal nouns, sometimes also with nouns and adjectives, quite commonly has the meaning "like, resembling, changing slightly, imitating, replacing, spurious".' Householder adds with reference to the use of παρά in words such as παρῳδός or 'parodos': 'Our basic sense, then, would seem to have been "singing in imitation, singing with a slight change" [e.g., of subject-matter].'

F. J. Lelièvre echoes this description when he defines παρῳδή or 'parode' in his article 'The Basis of Ancient Parody' of 1954 as 'singing after the style of an original but with a difference',[11] and also points to the ambiguity of the prefix 'para' and its ability to describe both nearness and opposition.[12] With reference to the many modern distortions of the ancient meaning of the term parody it is also significant that, despite Householder's concluding example of a change of subject-matter in words derived from παρῳδός, neither Householder nor Lelièvre restrict the ancient parody to the imitation of form with a change to subject-matter, as has been the practice in many other modern, post-seventeenth-century definitions of the term.[13]

---

8 See Householder, p. 7 and Quintilian, *Institutio Oratoria*, 4 vols., translated by H. E. Butler (London and Cambridge, Mass., 1960), vol. 3, p. 395.

9 See Householder, p. 4. Householder, however, admits to using only a few examples and at least one of these suggests that humour was also being described by the use of that term.   10 See, for instance, Householder, p. 8.

11 See Lelièvre, p. 72 and p. 66.

12 See Lelièvre, p. 66 and the following section on general parody.

13 This issue is discussed again both later in this chapter and in the account given in chapter 2 of the modern translation of parody into a form of the burlesque.

One of the earliest influential 'modern' (in the sense of post-Renaissance) discussions of parody, in J. C. Scaliger's *Poetices libri septem* of 1561,[14] further illustrates the dangers of translating the ancient Greek words and their connotations into other languages.[15] Scaliger had used the word 'ridiculus' in describing the basic meaning of parody as the singing of a song which 'inverted' or changed around the words of the songs sung by the Homeric 'rhapsodists' or bards and turned their sense into something 'ridiculous': 'Est igitur Parodia Rhapsodia inversa mutatis vocibus ad ridicula sensum retrahens.'[16] Scaliger's word 'ridicula' could be translated as 'laughable' in the sense of 'funny' or 'amusing' (it derives from 'rideo', 'to laugh', and had been used in Madius' *De ridiculis* of 1550 with relation to Aristotle's comments on the laughable), but had also been given the sense of 'to mock' by Horace and has more often been translated as to make 'ridiculous' in the sense of 'absurd', and as a mocking 'laughing at', rather than as a 'laughing with', by critics writing in English.[17] (Scaliger's *Poetices libri septem* also describes himself and some others as having composed during a carnival a parody of Virgil's *Aeneid* which reduced Virgil's heroic subject-matter to the subject of drink.[18])

Scaliger's discussion of parody was in its turn taken up by several other critics in their accounts of ancient parody, and while Scaliger cannot be held responsible for all of the negative connotations attributed to parody in recent centuries (one other reason is the relegation of parody to a sub-category of the burlesque in the eighteenth century), his use of the Latin word 'ridiculus' to describe the comic aspects of parody may be said to have led some English critics at least to view the latter in a more negative light than was necessary because of the associations of the word ridicule with

---

14 See the chapter on 'Parodia', in J. C. Scaliger, *Poetices libri septem* (Lyons, 1561), p. 46.

15 Scaliger's description of parody is also based on interpretations of Aristotle and Athenaeus.   16 See Scaliger, p. 46.

17 Egert Pöhlmann's claim in his 'ΠΑΡΩΙΔΙΑ', in *Glotta*, vol. 50, nos. 3–4 (1972), pp. 144–56; p. 144, that Scaliger understood 'para' in the sense of 'zuzüglich zu' (or as 'in addition to', rather than 'against') does not appear to have taken into account Scaliger's interpretation of the parodies as both inverting other songs and making them 'ridiculous'.

18 See Scaliger, p. 46. Th. Verweyen and G. Witting, *Die Parodie in der neueren deutschen Literatur. Eine systematische Einführung* (Darmstadt, 1979) also comment on this passage on their p. 11.

mockery in English, and to have thus made its eventual reduction to the burlesque more easy.

While John Florio's *Worlde of Wordes, Or Most Copious and exact Dictionarie in Italian and English* had followed some other classical scholars writing after Quintilian in defining parody in relatively neutral terms as 'a turning of a verse by altering some words' in 1598,[19] Ben Jonson's use of it in Act V, scene v of his *Every Man in his Humour*, to describe an imitation of popular verses which made them more 'absurd' than they were ('A Parodie! a parodie! with a kind of miraculous gift to make it absurder than it was'), had clearly emphasised the more 'ridiculous' aspects of the form,[20] and by the early nineteenth century Isaac D'Israeli could describe parody as including variations which stretched from the fanciful to the malignantly ridiculing.[21] Writing after both Scaliger's description of the Homeric rhapsodists as turning the sense of their models into the ridiculous and the reduction of parody to the burlesque by Joseph Addison and others,[22] D'Israeli had even gone on to describe the 'parodoi' who followed the Homeric rhapsodists as 'buffoons': 'When the rhapsodists, who strolled from town to town to chaunt different fragments of the poems of Homer, had recited, they were immediately followed by another set of strollers – buffoons, who made the same audience merry by the burlesque turn which they gave to the solemn strains which had just so deeply engaged their

---

19 Prior to Florio, Stephanus' *Thesaurus Graecae Linguae* (Geneva, 1572), vol. 1, column 119 g, had defined both 'parode' and 'parodia' as relating to 'parodeo' understood as 'canticum vel carmen ad alterius imitationem compono', while G. W. H. Lampe's *A Patristic Greek Lexicon* (Oxford, 1961–8), part 4 (Oxford, 1965), p. 1046 suggests that the fourth-century AD Gregory of Nyssa had also used 'parodeo' to mean to 'cite with alteration'.

20 Judith Priestman's doctoral dissertation, *The Age of Parody. Literary Parody and Some Nineteenth-Century Perspectives* (University of Kent at Canterbury, 1980), p. 245, n. 24 suggests that the *OED* is wrong in giving 1598 as the date for the first recorded use of parody in English deriving from this play since only the 1616 Folio version makes reference to it.

21 See Isaac D'Israeli, 'Parodies', in Isaac Disraeli, *Curiosities of Literature*, Second Series (1823) 14th edn (London, 1849), 3 vols.; vol. 2, pp. 504–11; p. 505. (Priestman, pp. 15 f. also notes how in the eighteenth century Dr Johnson had attributed to parody the functions of both alteration and degradation.)

22 See the section on the burlesque in chapter 2.

attention';[23] although he was also to agree with Fuzelier that parody was not simply 'buffoonery'.[24]

Whereas some, including Householder, have claimed that the 'parodoi' were amateurs who improvised imitations of the Homeric verses to create variety for the audiences of the more professional rhapsodists,[25] other commentators have attributed the 'parodes' to the Homeric rhapsodists themselves, or seen this particular question to be unresolved.[26]

Connections are also made between the earlier use of the word παρῳδός or 'parodos' to describe an imitating singer and the word παρῳδία or 'parodia' because both have been said to apply to the singing of songs in imitation of Homer which were of a 'mock-heroic' or 'mock-epic' nature.[27] As Householder has noted, Aristotle had applied the word παρῳδία in his *Poetics* to Hegemon of Thasos, a near contemporary of Aristophanes (*c*.450 BC–*c*.388 BC), and the author, according to Athenaeus' *The Deipnosophists*, of mock-epics such as the *Gigantomachia* or 'Battle of the Giants'. While Aristotle writes in chapter 2 of his *Poetics* on Hegemon simply that he was the first writer of parodies, and, like Nicochares, the author of the *Diliad*,[28] showed men in a bad light,[29] Athenaeus goes further by not only recording various anecdotes about Hegemon (such as that he had been dubbed 'Lentil Porridge' after being pelted with filth by his countrymen), but in describing him as a successful writer of epic parodies and in quoting

23 D'Israeli, 'Parodies', p. 505. D'Israeli, p. 506 n., names as sources the sixteenth-century Henry Stephen (Henricus Stephanus) and eighteenth-century Abbé Sallier, but fails explicitly to mention Scaliger's earlier, and not dissimilar, description of the rhapsodists.

24 See D'Israeli, p. 511, and the following discussion of Fuzelier's and D'Israeli's views.   25 See Householder, p. 8.

26 See, for example, Lelièvre, p. 79 on the openness of this question.

27 See Householder, p. 8 where he uses the term mock-epic. J. A. Cuddon's *A Dictionary of Literary Terms* (1977), revised edition (London, 1979), suggests, p. 398 that the term 'mock-heroic' may be described as a more general application of the term mock-epic and of its application of the heroic style and 'machinery' of the Homeric epics to more trivial subjects.

28 W. Hamilton Fyfe translates this in Aristotle, *The Poetics*, p. 11 as the 'Poltrooniad', but 'Diliad' preserves the Greek title of Δηλιάδα, and its probable mock-heroic character, better.

29 Aristotle's *Poetics*, chapter 2, also states after referring to Hegemon and others that comedy shows persons in a worse light than they are, while tragedy shows them to be better, but later specifies this, in its chapter 5, as relating not to every fault but to the 'ridiculous', or the 'laughable'. (See the phrase τὸ γελοῖον in *The Poetics*, 1449a, 34, p. 18.)

some of his work in the history of parody in Book 15. 697–9 of *The Deipnosophists*.[30]

After deducing, on the basis of Aristotle's and Athenaeus' applications of the word 'parodia' to the work of Hegemon, that the 'earliest attested sense' of 'parodia' may be inferred to be that 'it is a narrative poem of moderate length, in epic meter, using epic vocabulary, and treating a light, satirical, or mock-heroic subject', Householder adds that 'not only words but phrases and lines are borrowed from Homer' in such works, and that 'there seems to be no evidence that the names παρῳδή and παρῳδία were ever applied to such compositions in other metres or in prose, or to any imitating the language of other authors than Homer'.[31]

One extant example of an epic parody of the type associated with Hegemon is the 'mock-epic' known as the *Batrachomyomachia* or 'Battle of the Frogs and the Mice', which was attributed by some to Homer and by others to a 'Pigres'. Gilbert Murray's account of the *Batrachomyomachia* in the section entitled 'Comic Poems' in his *Ancient Greek Literature* of 1897 describes it as 'a rather good parody of the fighting epic', but questions the attribution to Pigres: 'An obvious fable – followed strangely enough by A. Ludwich in his large edition – gives it to one Pigres, a Carian chief, who fought in the Persian War.'[32] Later, F. J. Lelièvre points out that some attributions of the *Batrachomyomachia* to 'Pigres' following Suidas and Plutarch had also wrongly taken the Pigres who was brother to the Artemisia of Xerxes' time, in the fifth century BC, to be a brother of the Artemisia who was queen to Mausolus in the fourth century BC.[33]

Gilbert Murray's description of the *Batrachomyomachia* also gives

---

30 See Athenaeus (following Polemo), *The Deipnosophists*, vol. 7, pp. 243 f. (Athenaeus also quotes from Chamaeleon of Pontus on Hegemon in Book 9.406; vol. 4, p. 341.)

31 See Householder, p. 3. Householder, p. 4, suggests that the Liddell and Scott definition of 'parodia' should be changed to read '"parody or burlesque of Homer; mock-epic"', but also comments on the limits of the term burlesque to cover the ancient concepts of parody, as when he notes (p. 5) that 'the English term "burlesque" could not fit ... since burlesque does not require a specific literary model'.

32 See A. Ludwich, *Die Homerische Batrachomachia des Karers Pigres nebst Scholien und Paraphrase* (Leipzig, 1896). (The word *Batrachomachia* is from the version Ludwich prefers.)

33 See Lelièvre, pp. 80–1. One other suggestion regarding the date of the work is that its opening imitates Callimachus of Cyrene, and can, therefore, be no earlier than the third century BC. (See H. J. Rose, *A Handbook of Greek Literature. From*

some idea of its content: 'The battle began because a mouse named Psicharpax, flying from a weasel, came to a pond to quench his thirst. He was accosted by a frog of royal race, Physignathos, son of Peleus – (the hero of Mount Pelion has become "Mudman", and his son "Puff-cheek"!) – who persuaded him to have a ride on his back and see his kingdom. Unhappily a "Hydros" – usually a water-snake, here perhaps some otter-like animal – lifted its head above the water, and the frog instinctively dived. The mouse perished, but not unavenged. A kinsman saw him from the bank, and from the blood-feud arose a great war, in which the mice had the best of it. At last Athena besought Zeus to prevent the annihilation of the frogs. He tried first thunderbolts and then crabs, which latter were more than the mice could stand; they turned and the war ended.'[34]

After concluding this description of the *Batrachomyomachia*, Murray adds (p. 52) that there were many 'comic battle-pieces' and notes that 'we hear of a *Spider-fight*, a *Crane-fight*, a *Fieldfare-poem*'. Murray also states here that 'some of these were in iambics and consequently foreign to the Homeric style', so that they were, according to Householder's researches, not works which would have been termed parody by all ancient Greeks. .

Murray then goes on to discuss the comic poem the *Margites*, which was about an incompetent hero, and which some have attributed to Homer himself, although it was said to contain a mixture of iambic and 'heroic' metres. Murray adds with reference to its attribution to Homer by Aristotle that accounts of it as containing a mixture of heroic and iambic verse suggest 'a late metrical refurbishment of a traditional subject'. With regard to descriptions of the *Margites* as parody, which have implied that if Homer were the author then he had parodied his own work in it, Lelièvre asks whether it was not rather 'a comic picaresque epic' and adds that the word for parody was not applied to it in the ancient sources known to us.[35]

Murray concludes his section on 'Comic Poems' (p. 53) by questioning the general description of them as being by Homer:

Homer to the Age of Lucian (1934), 4th edn, revised, and corrected (London and New York, 1964), p. 56.)
34 See Gilbert Murray, *A History of Ancient Greek Literature* (1897), 3rd edn (London, 1907), pp. 51–2. Richmond P. Bond's *English Burlesque Poetry, 1700–1750* also contains a section on the *Batrachomyomachia*, and names several translations as well as imitations of it. (See Bond, chapter 7, pp. 176–88.)
35 See Lelièvre, p. 80.

'What is meant by calling these poems Homeric? Only that they date from a time when it was not thought worth while to record the author's name; and, perhaps, that if you mean to recite a mock epic battle, it slightly improves your joke to introduce it as the work of the immortal Homer.'

Paul Maas' article on 'Parodos (παρῳδός)' in *Paulys Real-Encyclopädie der classischen Altertumswissenschaft*,[36] which defines the παρῳδός as a writer of 'Homer-parodies' (or parodies of Homer),[37] also makes the point that both Hegemon's *Gigantomachia* and the *Batrachomyomachia* had 'concerned themselves' with the heroic subject-matter of the epics.[38] When Maas adds that 'most such parodies' had, by contrast, 'concerned themselves with the epic style',[39] he gives, however, no examples for the ancient parodies which he suggests had 'concerned themselves' with the form rather than with the content of the original, and the *Batrachomyomachia* which he has described as an exception to this rule remains the only complete example of an ancient parody of the epic of which we know.[40] (When Isaac D'Israeli claims in his 'Parodies' essay of 1823[41] that excerpts by the first-century BC Dionysius of Halicarnassus of · the verse of the third-century BC poet Sotades of Maroneia suggest that the latter had parodied the *Iliad* by changing its metre without altering its words, he omits to mention the fact that Dionysius had been speaking of a change to the order of the words as well as to metre and not specifically of parody.[42])

---

36 See Paul Maas, 'Parodos (παρῳδός)', in *Paulys Real-Encyclopädie der classischen Altertumswissenschaft*, neue Bearbeitung, edited by Konrat Ziegler (Stuttgart,1949), vol. XVIII/4, 1684–5. 37 See Maas, 1684.

38 See Maas, 1685. (Maas dates the *Batrachomyomachia* as deriving from *circa* the first century BC.)

39 See Maas, 1685 where he writes: 'Die Parodie erstreckt sich manchmal auf den heroischen Stoff (Hegemon Γιγαντομαχία, Batrachomyomachia), meist aber nur auf den epischen Stil, dessen Übertragung auf niedrige Verhältnisse schon an sich komisch wirkt.'

40 Maas is vague about what 'to parody' involves in terms of imitation or distortion, and his comment that those which concern themselves with the epic style apply the latter to low relationships in a comic manner even suggests such parody to be the comic contrast of a high style with low subject-matter, and with the addition of the latter, as in the *Batrachomyomachia* .

41 See D'Israeli, 'Parodies', pp. 505 f.

42 See Dionysius of Halicarnassus, 'On Literary Composition', in *Dionysius of Halicarnassus. The Critical Essays*, 2 vols., translated by Stephen Usher (Cambridge, Mass. and London, 1985), vol. 2, pp. 35–7.

Inferences which we can make for ourselves from the extant example of the *Batrachomyomachia*, and from accounts or fragments of works like it, about the meaning of the term 'parodia' for the Greeks when applied to such works[43] suggest that the 'parodia' could imitate both the form and subject-matter of the heroic epics, and create humour by then rewriting the plot or characters so that there was some comic contrast with the more 'serious' epic form of the work, and/or create comedy by mixing references to the more serious aspects and characters of the epic with comically lowly and inappropriate figures from the everyday or animal world.

As Householder points out (p. 5) when discussing the extension of the noun παρῳδία (parodia) and verb παρῳδέω (parodeo) by the Aristophanic scholiasts (commentators on the works of Aristophanes who wrote some time after him), to cover all sorts of comic literary quotation and allusion (Householder, p. 2, also describes this as the most frequent usage of the words for parody amongst the extant sources which he discusses), definitions which restrict parody to the imitation of form are clearly not adequate for that type of quotation either.

More will be said about the problems of defining parody of either an ancient or a modern kind as the 'imitation of form with a change to content' later in this chapter, in the discussion of the reader's understanding of the signals for parody. Other fragments of information provided by Householder about the ancients' use of parody words are that one other writer described by Athenaeus as a writer of parodies was Sopater, who was further described as a 'phlyakographer', or writer of comic dramatic sketches, and that Athenaeus had referred to other parodists including dramatists such as Epicharmus[44] and Cratinus in his brief history of parody in *The Deipnosophists*.[45]

A reading of Book 15.697–699 of Athenaeus' *The Deipnosophists*

---

43 Athenaeus also quotes some verses from a parody by Matro (who is also called Matron or Matreas), as well as from Hegemon's *Gigantomachia* and from Hipponax. Gulick's use of the word parody in his translation of Athenaeus, Book 14.621; vol. 6, p. 347, with reference to the 'hilarodia' and 'magodia', does not, however, relate to any use by Athenaeus of the word 'parodia' in those particular lines.

44 Epicharmus is also mentioned by Aristotle in his *Poetics*, chapter 3.

45 See Householder, p. 2, n. 4, where those discussed by Athenaeus in his Book 15 'history of parody' are listed, and Householder, p. 3 n. 8 on Athenaeus on Sopater and 'Oenopas' [Oenonas].

will show that as well as listing several other writers of παρῳδία mentioned by Householder, including Matro, Euboeus, Boeotus, and Hermippus, Athenaeus had quoted from Polemo's twelfth book of his *Address to Timaeus* where Polemo had named the sixth-century BC 'iambograph' Hipponax of Ephesus and not the fifth-century BC Hegemon as 'the inventor of this type'.[46] Athenaeus quotes Polemo's repetition of a few lines from Hipponax's *Hexameters* which follow a parodic evocation of other more serious epic openings such as Homer's call to the Muse in the opening of the *Odyssey* ('Tell me, O Muse, of the man of many devices, who wandered full many ways after he had sacked the sacred citadel of Troy'[47]) and with inappropriate metaphors and insults about Hipponax's 'hero': 'Tell me, Muse, of that maelstrom wide as the sea, that belly-knife, son of Eurymedon who eats indecently, how that he, miserable one, shall in miserable doom perish by stoning at the people's decree by the shore of the unharvested sea.'[48]

H. J. Rose writes with reference to this work in his *A Handbook of Greek Literature. From Homer to the Age of Lucian*, after referring to Polemo's description of Hipponax as the inventor of parody, that 'it is true that his [Hipponax's] fragments include the beginning of a poem in Homeric verse, making fun of one Eurymedontiades, a glutton, who seems to have been led through a mock-Odyssey of grotesque adventures'.[49] Rose adds that Hipponax had two decided merits, 'fidelity in his descriptions and concise vigour of style' which also brought him attention from later writers. Some years prior to H. J. Rose's history, Gilbert Murray had offered a somewhat less sympathetic portrait of Hipponax the 'iambicus' in describing him as being made out by tradition to be 'a beggar, lame and deformed himself, and inventor of the "halting iambic" or "scazon", a deformed trimeter which upsets all one's expectations by having a spondee or trochee in the last foot'.[50] Murray makes no specific mention of Hipponax's parodic *Hexameters*, but describes his works as all being abusive in some satirical manner.

Other forms related to the types of parody known to the ancients were what has been called the *cento* or *centones* (a string of quotations,

46 See Athenaeus, *The Deipnosophists*, vol. 7, pp. 242–3.
47 Homer, *The Odyssey*, translated by A. T. Murray (1919) (London and Cambridge, Mass., 1966), 2 vols., vol. 1, Book I, p. 3.
48 Athenaeus, *The Deipnosophists*, vol. 7, p. 243. Hipponax's original verses are on p. 242.   49 See H. J. Rose, p. 93.   50 See Gilbert Murray, p. 88.

also termed a 'quodlibet' after the Baroque), which may not necessarily be parodic or comic, but which can be used in parody or for parodic purposes,[51] and the σίλλοι, or *silloi* (from the singular, *sillos*). These *silloi* (or 'squint-eyed pieces' as they have also been called in English) were epic poems in mock-Homeric hexameters used to attack philosophical arguments. Examples have been attributed to both the sixth-century BC Xenophanes of Colophon and to the later Timon of Phlius (*c.*320 BC–*c.*230 BC), although F. J. Lelièvre for one has cast doubt on the application of the word *silloi* to the work of Xenophanes.[52]

Given that the second-century AD Aulus Gellius has described a work by Timon of Phlius, from which he quotes a fragment, as having been entitled Σίλλος ('Sillos'), the application of that word to his works is less controversial.[53] Isaac D'Israeli describes Timon's works as being 'levelled at the sophistical philosophers of his age; his invocation is grafted on the opening of the Iliad, to recount the evil-doings of those babblers, whom he compares to the bags in which Æolus deposited all his winds; balloons inflated with empty ideas!'[54] Dryden had also spoken of the *silloi* in his 'Discourse Concerning the Original and Progress of Satire' of 1693 as 'satyric poems, full of parodies; that is verses patched up from great poets, and turned into another sense than their author intended them'.[55]

In his comments on the *silloi*, in his 1954 article 'The Basis of Ancient Parody', F. J. Lelièvre concludes (p. 77) that 'this form of writing may employ parody but need not be purely parodic and the parody is not critical'. In addition to going on to take up some of the points made in Householder's 1944 article about the ancient words used to describe the parodic mock-epics,[56] Lelièvre agrees with Householder's suggestion that it is from the application of the word 'parodia' to the comic mock-epics that the word was applied to other

51 On this point see, for example, Wilhelm Horn, *Gebet und Gebetsparodie in den Komödien des Aristophanes* (Nuremberg, 1970), p. 56; Lelièvre, p. 76; and this book's passages on the cento in its chapter 2.   52 See Lelièvre, pp. 76–7.

53 See Aulus Gellius, *The Attic Nights of Aulus Gellius*, 3 vols., translated by John C. Rolfe (Cambridge, Mass. and London, 1961), vol. 1, p. 299; Book 3.17.1–6.

54 See D'Israeli, 'Parodies', p. 506 where he also refers in a note to Aulus Gellius' account of, and quotation from, Timon.

55 See 'A Discourse Concerning the Original and Progress of Satire' in John Dryden, *Of Dramatic Poesy and Other Critical Essays*, edited by George Watson (London and New York, 1962), 2 vols.; vol. 2, pp. 71–155; p. 103.

56 See Lelièvre, pp. 78 ff.

comic quotations in Aristophanes,[57] and also comments on how 'words of the παρῳδή-group are used to refer to humorous adaptations of an original' in Aristotle, Athenaeus, Diogenes Laertes and the Aristophanic scholiasts.[58] Lelièvre concludes his article by alluding to one of the meta-fictional aspects of the comic parody used by Aristophanes when he writes that 'with Aristophanes there develops the most advanced function of parody, that of selecting and illuminating the special characteristics of the author whose material is employed'.[59]

Many of the varieties of comic parodic quotation commented upon by the Aristophanic scholiasts may be found by the contemporary reader in extant 'paratragoedic' works such as Aristophanes' *Frogs* of 405 BC. The word 'paratragoedia', or 'paratragedy', from the Greek παρατραγῳδεῖν or 'paratragodein', which is defined as 'to mockingly imitate the style of tragedy' by Walther Kranz in his article 'Paratragödie', in *Paulys Real-Encyclopädie der classischen Altertums-wissenschaft*, has been used to describe those ancient Greek plays which involved the parody of tragedies.[60] This type of parody also involved the parody of conventions of the tragedy other than the style referred to by Kranz, and, as Augustus T. Murray has pointed out in his *On Parody and Paratragoedia in Aristophanes* of 1891, is sometimes difficult to separate from parody as such.[61]

That the parody of the conventions of the tragedy in the *paratragoedia* may take several different forms, and be used together with other types of parody, including those associated with the older mock-epics, is evident in Aristophanes' *Frogs*. In that work we not only have the creatures of the title arguing in 'mock-heroic' manner

---

57 Ibid., p. 73, footnote 1.   58 Ibid., p. 71.

59 Ibid., p. 81; and see also A. C. Schlesinger's 'Indications of Parody in Aristophanes', in *Transactions of the American Philological Association*, vol. 67 (1936), pp. 296–314 and 'Identification of Parodies in Aristophanes', in *American Journal of Philology*, vol. 58 (1937), pp. 294–305 for information on the 'clues' given by Aristophanes to his audience for the recognition of the targets of his parodies.

60 See Walther Kranz, 'Paratragödie', in *Paulys Real-Encyclopädie der classischen Altertumswissenschaft*, vol. XVIII/4, 1410–11. On the comic 'paratragoedia' and Aristophanes see also Augustus T. Murray, *On Parody and Paratragoedia in Aristophanes* (Berlin, 1891); Peter Rau, *Paratragödia, Untersuchungen einer komischen Form des Aristophanes* (Munich, 1967); and Wilhelm Horn, *Gebet und Gebetsparodie in den Komödien des Aristophanes* (Nuremberg, 1970), pp. 122 ff.

61 See Augustus T. Murray, pp. 4 ff.

with the god Dionysus who has masked himself (and with comic ineptitude) as the hero Hercules (the frogs win the 'battle' when Dionysus unwittingly begins speaking in their metre), but we also hear the character Aeschylus parodying the tragedian Euripides, and vice versa, and Aristophanes also parodying more general conventions of the tragedy such as the addresses of the chorus to the audience.

In addition to these and other 'meta-fictional' uses of parody,[62] Aristophanes uses the audience to his comedy and to its presentation of the Dionysian festival within it for some comic comments on the recipients of his parody:

DIONYSUS. Any sign of those murderers and perjurers he told us about?
XANTHIUS. Use your eyes, sir.
DIONYSUS. (*Seeing the audience*) By Jove, yes, I see them now. Well, what are we going to do?
XANTHIUS. We'd better be pushing on guvnor. The place is full of 'orrible monsters, or so the gentleman said.[63]

As noted previously, Fred W. Householder Jr's exposition of the uses made by the Aristophanic scholiasts of their words for parody shows that the use of the term 'parody' had been extended to apply to all sorts of comic quotation in Aristophanes' work by their time. Before looking further into Householder's analysis of the commentaries of the scholiasts and of their affirmation of the comic effect of the parody, his history of the ancient terms for parody, as described so far, may be summarised as having shown it to have developed from the 'mock-epic' song or parode (παρῳδή) of the 'parodos' or 'parodoi' (παρῳδός/παρῳδοί), through to the use of the noun 'parodia' (παρῳδία) for the mock-epics of Hegemon by Aristotle, and, then, to the application of the latter term and the verb 'parodeo' (παρῳδέω)[64] by the Aristophanic scholiasts and others to cover all sorts of comic quotation and textual re-arrangement.

---

62 One further example is given presently.
63 Aristophanes, *The Wasps, The Poet and the Women, The Frogs*, translated by David Barrett (Harmondsworth, 1971), p. 167. The Greek text can be found together with another translation in *Aristophanes*, 3 vols., translated by Benjamin Bickley Rogers (1924) (London and Cambridge, Mass., 1968), vol. 2, pp. 293–437.
64 Householder, p. 8 defines this as a verb meaning 'to sing, compose or write in the manner of mock-epic, to apply serious verses to humorous ends'.

Comic aspects of parody

Householder, as seen above, has not only defined the word παρῳδία, as used by Aristotle, as a 'narrative poem of moderate length, in epic metre, using epic vocabulary, and treating a light, satirical, or mock-heroic subject', but has also pointed to the extension made to this usage by the Aristophanic scholiasts' use of the word to describe a 'device for comic quotation'.[65] Householder, moreover, appears to mean by 'comic' both something that was used in ancient comedies such as the works of Aristophanes and something which produces the laughter associated with those works given the understanding by the audience of their comic nature.

These two senses of the word 'comic' are also suggested by the *OED* to be basic to the more modern English use of the term when it describes it as meaning (1) 'Of, proper, or belonging to comedy, in the dramatic sense, as distinguished from tragedy' and (2) 'Aiming at a humorous or ridiculous effect ... burlesque, funny.'[66] The adjective 'comical', the use of which includes a 1557 reference to Plautus as 'a comicall poet', is described in the *OED* as meaning (1) 'comic'; (2) 'trivial, mean, low; the opposite of *tragical*, or *elevated*, or *dignified*'; (3) 'like the conclusion of a comedy; happy or fortunate. (Opposed to *tragical*)'; (4) 'Resembling comedy, mirth-provoking; humorous, jocose, funny; ludicrous, laughable. (Of persons and things.) The ordinary sense (1685)'; (5) 'Queer, strange, odd. (*colloq.*)'.[67]

In addition to finding internal evidence in works such as *The Frogs* on the relationship of the comic (and of parody) to laughter in ancient literature, we can refer to the evidence provided by some of the masks used in ancient comedy, and to contemporary depictions of them, for another indication of how the comic was associated with the upturned mouth of the smile or the laugh by the ancients.[68] Further to this, Athenaeus has quoted Aristoxenus as saying with reference to parody that 'just as certain persons have made up parodies [παρῳδὰς] of hexameters to provoke laughter [γελοῖον], so also Oenônas introduced parodies of songs to the harp [κιθαρῳδίας], and he was imitated by Polyeuctus of Achia and Diocles of Cynaetha'.[69]

---

65 See Householder, p. 5, and Dübner's and Rutherford's editions of the Aristophanic scholia. 66 See the *OED*, 2nd edn, vol. 3, p. 536. 67 Ibid., p. 537.

68 Aristotle's *Poetics*, chapter 5, on comedy, also speaks of the mask that produces laughter. (See the Greek text in *The Poetics*, p. 20, or Ingram Bywater's translation.)

69 See Athenaeus, *The Deipnosophists*, vol. 6, p. 445; Book 14.638.

With reference to the application of the term parody to the ancient comedy, Householder also writes (p. 5) that the scholiasts 'apply the words παρῳδέω and παρῳδία to the insertion in comedy of a brief tragic, lyric, or epic passage, either (a) substantially unchanged, (b) with substitution of one or more words, (c) in paraphrased form, or (d) so changed as to be little more than an imitation of the grammar and rhythm of the original'.

While Householder himself does not comment on the fact, the insertion of an unchanged non-comic passage into the comic may itself create an incongruous contrast with the new context to produce a comic effect, and this might also be taken into account when assessing Householder's following reference to the grammarians (the previously referred to scholiasts) as being alone in using the words 'parodia' or 'parodeo' to refer to 'exact, verbatim quotation'.[70] (Not only, that is, may 'exact quotation' set up a comic discrepancy or incongruity between the quoted work and its new context, but such quotation may not ultimately be aimed at the complete replication of a work, but at a comic dislocation, through its contrast with the new and foreign context, of both, or either, its original form and meaning.[71])

With regard to the rhetoricians, and to the extension of the word parody from verse to either prose or colloquial speech, Householder adds (p. 6) that 'a writer may (1) quote verse with a metrical substitution of one or more words; (2) quote part of a sentence exactly, completing the grammatical structure with some different words of his own, either (a) altering the original sense or (b) keeping it, with partial paraphrase; (3) imitate (a) the sound and form of the original or (b) the general sense of the original, without preserving any essential words'. Householder continues· 'Under 1 we may again mention three possible subtypes: (a) the surprise anticlimax substitution, (b) the punning substitution, and (c) the identical pun, or substitution in sense only.'

Quintilian also discusses both the pun and the parody as a form of jest in Book 6 of his *Institutio Oratoria*,[72] and says in Book 6.3.96 of that

70 Ibid., p. 6. (Householder interchanges the terms grammarians and scholiasts.)
71 As elsewhere in this chapter, the comic effect will be taken as an indication of comic discrepancy in the parody, and the latter taken as the product of comic intentionality. If a comic effect is unintentional the work in question would be described as a 'pekoral' (see chapter 2) rather than as a parody.
72 See Quintilian, Book 6.3.53 ff. (vol. 2, p. 467) on the pun as jest and Book 6.3.96 ff. (vol. 2, pp. 491 f.) on parody as jest.

work that 'apt quotation of verse may add to the effect of wit'.[73] When speaking specifically of *parodia*, in Book 6.3.97, Quintilian additionally suggests that wit may be created by the 'invention of verses resembling well-known lines, a trick styled parody [παρῳ-δία]'.[74] While Householder has commented that Quintilian's use of the word παρῳδία here is not very different from his use of παρῳδή, he also notes in his following section that 1(b), 1(c) and 3(a) of the above were techniques which Quintilian was to associate with the production of a humorous (in the sense of witty and comic) effect.[75]

With regard to 3(a), the 'imitation of sound and form', Householder writes that 'it must be emphasized that this definition will not apply to any occurrences of these words in Greek and that it carefully excludes the one use which is most frequent'. (Householder does not elaborate on the nature of this frequent use at this point but had earlier described 'the use of quotation and allusion' as 'the most common' instance of the application of the parody words amongst known ancient authors.[76]) Householder adds after somewhat arbitrarily relating the definition of parody as the 'imitation of sound and form' to Quintilian's definition of it in 6.3.97 that 'if Quintilian were speaking of poetic composition rather than of the orator's use of verses, this definition might apply fairly well to the mock-epic variety of *parodia*, and even better to the modern conception of parody'.[77] As Householder had earlier criticised the modern understanding of parody for restricting it to 'style', this latter point is, however, not necessarily an endorsement of that particular usage.

Both Householder and Lelièvre have shown that the scholiasts and several others of the ancient critics have attributed a comic effect to parody. When Householder remarks in a footnote how 'some other word' was added to that for parody by the scholiasts 'when the presence of humor or ridicule is to be made plain',[78] and with relation to a claim made in his text that 'even by the grammarians, however,

73 See Quintilian, vol. 2, p. 491. (While Quintilian speaks specifically of 'urbanitas' here, the section as a whole deals with various types of jests and witticisms.)
74 Ibid., p. 493.
75 See Householder, p. 7 where he refers to Quintilian 6.3.97. (Householder's text says 4(a) rather than 3(a), but no 4(a) is listed and it was 3(a) which described the 'imitation of the sound and form of the original' to which Householder refers here.) 76 See Householder, p. 2. 77 Ibid., p. 7 n. 25.
78 See Householder, p. 8 n. 27. (Householder refers here to scholia on Lucian and others as well as on Aristophanes but uses words which do not derive directly from the Greek in speaking of 'humor or ridicule'.)

the notion of humor was not regarded as essentially present in the word',[79] it should be noted that the words referred to by him in his note in fact designate ridicule or its equivalent rather than humour alone. (Two of Householder's four examples of words added to parody to denote 'humor or ridicule' are 'skoptikos' and 'skopton', which are generally translated as describing ridicule or mockery,[80] while the others listed by him are words which do not necessarily designate humour or the comic rather than ridicule.)

One other way of interpreting the addition of words for ridicule to the term parody would be, moreover, that it describes a mis-usage or unusual usage of that device. Lelièvre comments on the above passages in Householder that 'Householder seems misleading in suggesting that both humour and ridicule are equally remote from the meaning of παρῳδή, &c.',[81] and adds that 'it is normally the second force only [ridicule] which requires an additional word ... to make itself felt'.[82] Although Lelièvre has also referred to Hermann Kleinknecht's suggestion in his *Die Gebetsparodie in der Antike* of 1937[83] that the passage in Athenaeus' *The Deipnosophists*, Book 14.638, in which the phrase τὸ γελοῖον ('to geloion') is used, explicitly suggests parody to be comic, and in contrast to those which specify it as ridicule, he is critical of Kleinknecht's generalisations from his chosen examples to the claim that the ancients distinguished between 'purely comic' and 'critical-ridiculing' parody, and the word γέλοιος has been translated by others from similar uses as designating the ridiculous as well as the humorous and the laughable.[84]

---

79 See Householder, p. 8. (Householder does not define humour here, but appears, as at some other points in his text, to be using the word to refer to aspects of the comic.)

80 See S. C. Woodhouse's *English-Greek Dictionary* (London, 1932), pp. 713 f. and Liddell and Scott, p. 1618. Woodhouse, p. 713 also notes that the word 'skoptein' is used in Euripides' *Cyclops*, 675, which is where Cyclops believes himself to have been made fun of by the chorus.

81 Lelièvre, p. 72, also describes Householder's p. 4 description of the παρῳδή discussed by Quintilian as 'a name drawn from songs sung in imitation of others, but employed by an abuse of language to designate imitation in verse or prose' as 'close literary imitation', as to make the word 'too colourless', and suggests that here too Householder has overlooked the centrality of the comic, of at least the ironic kind, to parody.

82 Lelièvre, p. 74 n. 2, and see also Lelièvre, p. 71 n. 1.

83 See Lelièvre, p. 74 n. 2 on Kleinknecht, *Die Gebetsparodie in der Antike* (Stuttgart and Berlin, 1937), p. 13.

84 See, for instance, Woodhouse, pp. 410, 479, and 714.

Yet one other way of interpreting the addition of the words mentioned by Householder and Lelièvre is that instead of adding something new or different to the idea of parody (whether correctly or incorrectly),[85] the words in question bring out or emphasise characteristics which were already implied in the term parody, but which needed to be brought out in certain instances in order to describe the especial nature of the usage made of it in certain works. Here too, however, the modern concept of ridicule as something negative and incompatible with more ambivalent forms of humour or comedy may not always be able to be used to translate all of the ancient words in question, some at least of which (such as 'to geloion') appear to describe the laughter associated with both ridicule and humour (in the sense of the comic), rather than mockery alone.[86]

With the modern designation of ridiculing parody as something negative or destructive in mind which Householder had questioned elsewhere in his article,[87] Lelièvre goes on to suggest that even when something like ridicule is used, it does not mean that the parodist is completely negative about a target. Although it further confuses the issue by appearing to admit ridicule to be a function of parody, Lelièvre adds with reference both to Gilbert Murray's point that Aristophanes was able to parody and admire Euripides at the same time[88] and to Mrs Richardson's argument that the parodist needs to be craftsman, critic, poet, and have the ability to combine admiration with laughter,[89] that it 'was, in fact, possible for Aristophanes to combine insight, criticism and ridicule without admitting malice just as it has been for many of the English parodists, especially those of the past century and a half from the Smiths to Sir Max Beerbohm'.[90]

85 Householder, pp. 8 and 9, also refers to one specialised depiction of parody as a pun or word-play in Hermogenes and suggests that this is a narrowing of the meaning of parody.

86 Words such as the Latin 'ridiculus', the English 'ridicule', the German 'lächerlich', and some Russian words for ridicule, all relate to words for laughter, but also have added negative associations.

87 See Lelièvre, p. 75 where he refers to Householder as suggesting that 'the connotations of ridicule and criticism in the modern English word "parody" have misled critics into assuming that Aristophanes regarded Euripides as an inferior poet'.

88 See Gilbert Murray, *Aristophanes. A Study* (Oxford, 1933). (Francis West's *Gilbert Murray. A Life* (London and New York, 1984), pp. 217 ff. also comments on how that 1933 work revises Murray's earlier views on Aristophanes.)

89 See Mrs Herbert Richardson, *Parody*, The English Association Pamphlet Number 92, August 1935 (London, 1935).   90 Lelièvre, p. 75.

The issue surveyed in the above passages, as to whether ancient parody was understood to be humorous, or ridiculing, or both, can be summed up in the following way:

(1) Given that the words quoted by him can be said to describe ridicule *rather* than humour, Householder has been misleading in arguing from the examples which he has given of words attached to parody that words for both humour and ridicule were often attached to that for parody when the presence of humour or ridicule was to be made plain, and that this suggests that humour was not always or necessarily present in the word parody.

(2) Although most of the words chosen by Householder designate ridicule rather than humour, other words attached to the description of parody (such as that found in Athenaeus 14.638), which have been translated as both ridicule and humour by some lexicographers, point to the problems of translating the ancient terms into modern equivalents, and especially given the modern understanding of ridicule and its laughter as something more negative or destructive than humour as such.

(3) The attachment of additional words to those for parody by the ancient scholiasts involves the attachment of words which must not only be carefully translated with both of the above points in mind, but which may then be interpreted, *depending upon the words, context, and work in question,* either as wrongly or rightly (or radically or conservatively) adding to the traditional meaning of the word for parody being used, or as bringing out meanings which were already there.

(4) The majority of works to which words for parody are attached by the ancients, and which are still known to us in whole or in part, suggest that parody *was* understood as being humorous in the sense of producing effects characteristic of the comic, and that if aspects of ridicule or mockery were present these were additional to its other functions and were co-existent with the parody's ambivalent renewal of its target or targets.

The following chapter will comment further on how the reduction of parody to a type of burlesque in modern literary criticism has associated it with mockery or ridicule for many modern critics, authors, and readers in both a more exclusive and a more negative manner.

While most associations of parody with the burlesque and its use of ridicule have seen parody criticised for the negativity or destructiveness of the burlesque, at least one other approach to parody as ridicule has attempted to define the element of ridicule as a positive characteristic.

This approach is to be found in Christopher Stone's *Parody* of 1914 where Stone writes that 'ridicule is society's most effective means of curing inelasticity. It explodes the pompous, corrects the well-meaning eccentric, cools the fanatical, and prevents the incompetent from achieving success. Truth will prevail over it, falsehood will cower under it.'[91] Despite the positive roles given parody by the above, Stone, however, is one of those modern writers on parody who sometimes identifies parody with the burlesque, and reduces the former to the latter and to its ridiculing functions where it might have been attributed some more complex or subtle uses, and may also be said to have confused rather than clarified the difference between parody as useful criticism and as destructive ridicule in introducing his concept of 'useful ridicule'.[92]

Stone had originally followed Sir Owen Seaman's view of the 'highest function' of parody as being its ability to criticise that which is false,[93] and Seaman's view may in its turn be taken back to a defence of parody made by the French critic and parodist Louis Fuzelier in 1738, which had been taken up by Isaac D'Israeli and other writers in English after that, and which had involved defending parody as a useful device for attacking falsity.

Fuzelier had made his defence of parody against an attack by the dramaturge Houdard de la Motte in an anonymous tract entitled 'Discours à l'occasion d'un discours de M[onsieur] D[e] L[a] M[otte] sur les Parodies', published in his *Les Parodies du Nouveau Théâtre Italien* of 1738,[94] by arguing both that parody did not attack an author personally, and that its main function was to unmask the vices which the tragedies had disguised as virtues.

In his 'Parodies' essay referred to previously, Isaac D'Israeli had quoted Fuzelier with approval as saying that '"far from converting virtue into a paradox, and degrading truth by ridicule, PARODY will only strike at what is chimerical and false; it is not a piece of buffoonery so much as a critical exposition. What do we parody but

91 See Christopher Stone, *Parody* (London, 1914), p. 8.
92 See, for example, Stone, p. 10 for his identification of parody and the burlesque.
93 See also Stone, p. 38.
94 Verweyen and Witting, p. 217, cite the reprint of Fuzelier's (4 volumed) work of 1738, published in 2 vols. (Geneva, 1970), vol. 1, pp. XIX-XXXV.

the absurdities of dramatic writers, who frequently make their heroes act against nature, common sense and truth?"'.[95]

Although he had earlier described the ancient rhapsodists as 'buffoons' D'Israeli can also be said to have echoed Fuzelier's defence of parody against Houdard de la Motte in suggesting even earlier in his essay that works such as Paul Scarron's travesty of Virgil had not been made 'in derision'.[96] Despite having made some criticisms of both Scarron and the burlesque style in the first edition of his *Curiosities of Literature*,[97] D'Israeli may even have taken up Scarron's own description, in the opening verses of the first book of his *Le Virgile Travesty en vers Burlesques* of 1648–53,[98] of the style of his *Typhon ou la Gigantomachie. Poëme Burlesque* as 'le style bouffon', in suggesting the parody of the ancient rhapsodists to be 'buffoonery'.[99] Given, however, both that Scarron's work cannot be regarded as an example of the most subtle parody, and that one other travesty of Virgil referred to by D'Israeli as not deriding its subject is that by C. Cotton, the author of *Scarronides: or, Virgile Travestie. A Mock-Poem. Being the First Book of Virgils Æneis in English, Burlésque*, in which the heroes and gods of the ancients are mercilessly reduced to the commonplace,[100] D'Israeli's concept of parody as buffoonery may still be criticised as being too reductive.[101] (The conclusion of Cotton's *Virgile Travestie* includes the verses: 'From *Dido* then a belch did fly, / 'Tis thought she meant it for a sigh, / And tears ran down her fair long Nose, / The Queen was *Maudlin* I suppose.'[102])

D'Israeli, as seen, had referred, nonetheless, to several different uses of parody in the earlier section of his essay, and to ones which ranged from the fanciful to the 'malignant'. The passage in question from D'Israeli's essay also begins with a definition of parody as a 'turning

---

95 See D'Israeli, 'Parodies', pp. 510–11. D'Israeli continues: '"Many tragedies", Fuzelier, with admirable truth, observes, "disguise vices into virtues, and PARODIES unmask them."' 96 See D'Israeli, 'Parodies', p. 504.

97 See Isaac D'Israeli, 'Scarron', in Isaac D'Israeli, *Curiosities of Literature*, 3 vols. (London, 1791–1817), vol. 2 (London, 1793), pp. 235–46.

98 See the beginning of Scarron's *Le Virgile Travesty en vers Burlesques* (Paris, 1653), p. 1.

99 D'Israeli also speaks of 'buffoonery' with reference to the burlesque in 'Scarron', p. 246.

100 See C. Cotton, *Scarronides: or, Virgile Travestie. A Mock-Poem. Being the First Book of Virgils Æneis in English, Burlésque* (London, 1664).

101 D'Israeli's 'Scarron', p. 246, is not quite as critical of Cotton as it is of Scarron.

102 See Cotton, p. 111.

of another' which is reminiscent of Florio's earlier, and relatively neutral definition of the term: 'Parodies were frequently practised by the ancients, and with them, like ourselves, consisted of a work grafted on another work, but which turned on a different subject by a slight change of the expressions. It might be a sport of fancy, the innocent child of mirth; or a satirical arrow drawn from the quiver of caustic criticism; or it was that malignant art which only studies to make the original of the parody, however beautiful, contemptible and rid-iculous.'[103] To D'Israeli this variety is, moreover, a result of the different uses made of parody by different individuals: 'Human nature thus enters into the composition of parodies, and their variable character originates in the purpose of their application.'

Although D'Israeli was correct in pointing to how parody has been used in a variety of different ways, problems have arisen when one or other of such applications have been singled out as the definitive use of parody.

While, for example, some other modern critics have reduced parody to the more modern concept of the burlesque and condemned it as trivial because of what they have seen to be the 'ridiculing' nature of its comedy, some more recent 'late-modern' writers on parody will be seen in later chapters to have denied the importance of its comic effect or structure altogether in order both to save parody from such denigration and to stretch its meaning and function to cover other fashionable meta-fictional and 'intertextual' forms.

Despite the problems created by such attempts to separate parody from the comic, it cannot be denied that the attribution of a comic effect or structure to parody which is also accompanied by a negative assessment of the worth of comedy has led some into seeing the parodist as merely a mocker of other texts and into condemning parody on moral grounds. (W. K. Wimsatt gives a brief survey of negative evaluations of the worth of comedy in his essay 'The Criticism of Comedy', in pp. 90–107 of his *Hateful Contraries. Studies in Literature and Criticism* of 1965.)

Whatever our attitude to comedy,[104] the complicated structure of the more sophisticated parody – in which the target text may not

---

103 D'Israeli, 'Parodies', p. 505.
104 More positive assessments of comedy are given by George Meredith in his 1877 'Essay on Comedy' and in the books listed in the bibliography by F. M. Cornford, George E. Duckworth, James K. Feibleman, L. J. Potts, and Leo Salingar.

only be satirised but also 'refunctioned'[105] – nonetheless demonstrates a more subtle (though still comic) use of other literary works
than is implied by the term burlesque, or even by the term 'mock-epic'
when the word 'mock' is used in the sense of 'mockery', 'ridicule', or
'spoof'. Even unambiguously comic works such as Aristophanes'
Frogs have shown how the use of parody may aim both at a comic
effect and at the transmission of both complex and serious messages,
and how the comic need not be eliminated from our definition of
parody when other such characteristics are being described. (The
argument between Euripides and Aeschylus in Aristophanes' *Frogs* has
much to say about the importance to the city of finding a responsible
voice and F. J. West, pp. 217 ff., points out that one reason for Gilbert
Murray's reassessment of Aristophanes in 1933 was Murray's
perception of the political relevance of Aristophanes' works to the
Europe of the 1930s.)

The ambiguity of the word 'mock' in terms such as 'mock-epic' or
'mock-heroic', where it can mean both spoof and *counterfeit* (as in
phrases such as 'mock-disbelief') is also often overlooked, and the
following section will consider the point that one of the chief sources
of the comic effect in parody has been the incongruous juxtaposition
of texts in which counterfeit may play a preparatory role in evoking
the reader's expectations for imitation before those expectations are
subverted or changed in some comic manner.

Imitation and incongruity in the comic parody

In his *Institutio Oratoria* (Book 6.3.85) Quintilian has described
'simulatio' and 'dissimulatio' as methods used in some forms of wit,
and both may be applied to at least some examples of parody.
Quintilian describes 'simulatio' or simulation 'as the pretence of
having a certain opinion of one's own' and 'dissimulatio' or
dissimulation as consisting in 'feigning that one does not understand
someone else's meaning'.[106] (The English word 'dissimulation' is now
defined as meaning 'dissembling' in a more general sense.)

---

105 The term 'to refunction' is used here to describe the new literary functions
gained by a text in the context of the parody.
106 See Quintilian, vol. 2, p. 485; Book 6.3.85. Quintilian, vol. 3, p. 391; Book 9.2.29
ff., also speaks of *prosopopoeia* or 'impersonation', the 'portrayal of character by
appropriate speeches' as being close to parody (παρῳδή) but this can relate only
to the imitative stage in parody or παρῳδία proper.

The 'simulation' of other styles, where the parodist pretends to be sharing the words and meaning of the object of parody, has been a technique used by many parodists to elicit the expectations of their audience for a text, before presenting another version or view of it, and a parody may also be said to be 'dissimulative', in the sense defined by Quintilian, when the parodist pretends not to understand the original meaning of a parodied author.

'Simulation' of an ironic kind may further be said to be practised when the parodist uses the text of a target as a 'word-mask' behind which to conceal his or her own intentions for a time. In such parody the target text may be the object of some reform or rewriting by the parodist, but may also be the object of satire, or a mask used to allow other targets to be attacked or reformed in an 'Aesopian' or covert manner.[107] Such disguises may be used by the parodist where direct criticism might run the danger of bringing down censorship or a libel suit onto the parodist, but the parodist may also imitate and then distort another text in order to imitate and criticise its reduction to unintended parody by other writers or 'poetasters' or by the misreadings of other readers or critics.

While none of the above cases of parodic imitation stop at imitation alone, Alfred Liede has argued in his article on parody in the second edition of the *Reallexikon der deutschen Literaturgeschichte*[108] that parody is but one special form of conscious imitation (which he sees as an age-old human activity) and that it is 'above all' an exercise in learning or perfecting a technique or style. This very basic stylistic approach to parody (which also revives older confusions of Quintilian's definition of *parode* with *parodia*) tells us something of the degree of skill needed by parodists to imitate the style they would parody, but despite Liede's division of the parody into several different types (Liede lists, for example, 'artistische', 'kritische', 'agitatorische' – or 'artistic', 'critical', 'agitatory' – parody), his approach runs into the danger of reducing most of its better (more 'artistic' and less 'critical' or 'agitatory') examples to a form of imitation while ignoring their other

107 I have discussed 'Aesopian' and political uses of parody in greater detail in *Reading the Young Marx and Engels. Poetry, Parody and the Censor* (London and Totowa N. J., 1978).
108 Alfred Liede, 'Parodie', in *Reallexikon der deutschen Literaturgeschichte*, 2nd edn (Berlin and New York, 1977), vol. 3, pp. 12–72; pp. 13 f.

refunctioning, and comic, aspects.[109] (Liede, p. 12, also criticises Paul Lehmann's division of parody into comic and critical, which H. Grellmann had used for his article on parody in the first edition of the *Reallexikon der deutschen Literaturgeschichte*, because of the difficulties of assessing a comic effect on different audiences, and says that the only thing that all parodies can be said to have in common is the 'conscious playing with a literary work'.) According to Liede (pp. 13 f.) the most wide-spread form of parody is, moreover, 'artistic parody', the ultimate goal of which is 'complete imitation', in which it is the success of the similarity of the parody to its model which determines its level of artistic quality. The questionable, if internally necessary, conclusion of this view to which Liede comes (p. 14) is that complete artistry in the writing of parody exists when it is not able to be distinguished from the original.

Given this conclusion and its lack of suitability for both ancient and modern examples of parody Liede's argument must be questioned as to its adequacy in defining 'artistic' parody, and as the most wide-spread form of parody. A history of parody will show, by contrast, that not only is the process of imitation only one of the factors involved in parody, but that some parody has been used to bring the concept of imitation itself into question, and that it is the structural use of comic incongruity which distinguishes the parody from other forms of quotation and literary imitation, and shows its function to be more than imitation alone.[110]

The creation of comic incongruity or discrepancy will be taken as a significant distinguishing factor in parody in the definitions given of it in this book and may also be said to explain both the production of the comic effect in the parody and how the parody may continue to be defined as comic even when, as Liede and others have suggested, not all readers may have the sense of humour or understanding to comprehend the intended comedy. To put this in other words, the incongruity between the parodied text and the parody which most parodies exploit in one intentionally comic way or another may be

---

109 Liede, p. 14, does write of artistic parody that its goal of complete imitation is carried out 'im Scherz oder Ernst' (as a joke or in seriousness), but does not explain how humour could arise from complete imitation where no discrepancy or incongruity is present.

110 Even when Liede, p. 14, writes that critical parody makes itself as dissimilar from its target as is possible, he still concentrates on the relationship of the parody to imitation at the expense of explaining its other characteristics.

said to produce the comic effects which act as an indication of the presence of comic parody to the reader or viewer, so that the parody may still be said to be 'comic' even when its comic aspects are not noticed or understood by a recipient. (Arguments which claim that the comedy of a work cannot be said to exist if the critic or reader in question cannot perceive it also seem to be all too similar to the argument that a table cannot be said to exist when you yourself cannot see it. The signals for comic parody which indicate its presence in a work can, however, be learned and their recipient made more aware of an author's comic intent by such means.)

Rather than restrict ourselves to post-eighteenth-century distinctions between ideal and reality or high and low in explaining the factors involved in the creation of comic discrepancy or incongruity in the parody, the comic in parody will be looked for in the creation of any type of comic incongruity, be it a dissimilarity or an inappropriate similarity between texts. This approach also allows for the classical understanding of parody as a device for comic quotation with a change to the original, without obscuring the changing historical nature of both the subject-matter of the parody and the variety of uses to which it can be put. In some parodic changes to other texts, the controlled discrepancy or incongruity between the parodied text and its new context is also one of the chief sources of the comic effect which distinguishes the parody from other types of literary criticism as well as from forgery and plagiarism.

For some students of comedy the essence of humour has resided in general in raising an expectation for X and giving Y or something else which is not entirely X. In paragraph 54 of the 'Analytic of the Sublime' of his *Critique of Aesthetic Judgement* of 1790 Immanuel Kant wrote, after stating that there must be something absurd in everything which excites laughter ('Es muß in allem, was ein lebhaftes, erschütterndes Lachen erregen soll, etwas Widersinniges sein') that '*laughter is an affect resulting from the sudden transformation of a tensed expectation into nothing*'[111] ('*das Lachen ist ein Affect aus der plötzlichen*

---

111 James Creed Meredith's translation of *Kant's Critique of Aesthetic Judgement* (Oxford, 1911) translates this on its p. 199 as '*Laughter is an affection arising from a strained expectation being suddenly reduced to nothing*'. D. H. Monro has also discussed this and other passages from Kant in his *Argument of Laughter* (Melbourne, 1951), pp. 147–61.

Verwandlung einer gespannten Erwartung in nichts'[112]). While Kant describes that which replaces the X as a 'nothing' in this passage, it is, however, still 'something' from the point of view of the humorist or parodist, and something which has been specifically chosen to create a comic rather than non-comic contrast. Kant himself suggests this to be the case when giving examples of humour in his *Critique of Aesthetic Judgement* where something new or unexpected does replace something else,[113] and when discussing in his *Anthropology* how parody as practised by such as Fielding in his *Jonathan Wild*, or Blumauer in his travesty of Virgil, may free the senses from conflicts created by the influence of false or damaging concepts by setting up a comic contrast to the expected.[114]

The dictum that the essence of humour has resided in raising an expectation for X and giving Y, or something else which is 'not entirely X', instead is also particularly well suited to describing the mechanism at work in parody when a text is quoted and the quotation then distorted or changed into something else; although here too a contrast will generally be made comic by a careful rather than by a haphazard selection of elements. (Simple difference or discrepancy alone, or its perception − as, say, in the perception of a discrepancy in an account − need not of course be parodic or comic.)

In parody the comic incongruity created in the parody may contrast the original text with its new form or context by the comic means of contrasting the serious with the absurd as well as the 'high' with the 'low', or the ancient with the modern, the pious with the impious, and so on. Here the expectations of the reader of the literary parody for a certain text may also be played upon, and direct and indirect comments made upon the reader and those expectations. In the case of parody more than one element may, moreover, be the subject of reader expectations. Because both the text of the parodist and the parodied work are the subject of the reader's attention, the latter may be surprised to see the parodied text offered in its new distorted form

112 See Kant's *Kritik der Urtheilskraft*, in *Kants Werke. Akademie-Textausgabe* (1902 ff.) (Berlin, 1968), vol. 5, p. 332.
113 I am grateful to Dr Mary A. McCloskey for discussions on this and related topics.
114 See Immanuel Kant, *Anthropology from a Pragmatic Point of View*, translated by Mary J. Gregor, The Hague 1974, pp. 40 (or Kant, *Anthropologie in pragmatischer Hinsicht*, erster Theil, erstes Hauptstück, dritter Abschnitt). The later section on 'productive Wit' (see Gregor pp. 90 ff.) also discusses both the playful and more serious uses of wit and its contrasts.

(X as Y), as when an imitation of Dickens appears in James Joyce's *Ulysses* in its 'Oxen of the Sun' set of parodies, but may also be surprised by a change of style in the work of the parodist (Y as X), or of Joyce writing in the style of Dickens.[115]

The sudden destruction of expectations which accompanies the perception of such incongruities has long been recognised as a basic ingredient of humour. In addition to Kant, the *Tractatus Coislinianus* which was published in 1839 from what was said to be a tenth-century manuscript in the De Coislin collection in Paris,[116] and which has been described by some commentators as belonging to a lost section of Aristotle's *Poetics*, and by others as an attempt to complete Aristotle's unfinished discussion of comedy,[117] also lists 'the unexpected' as one of the causes of laughter.[118]

In his edition of the *Tractatus Coislinianus* Lane Cooper further suggests that this point relates to the unexpected transformation of one expectation into another when he gives the example of Dionysus chosing Aeschylus instead of Euripides as his poet at the end of Aristophanes' *Frogs*.[119] In addition to this point and to Cooper's example, other causes of laughter listed in the *Tractatus Coislinianus*, such as 'deception', 'the impossible', 'the possible and inconsequent', 'debasing the personages', the choice of something worthless by one having power, and the lack of sequence in a story, may all be said to play with the subversion of audience expectations.[120]

Quintilian had also alluded in Book 6.3.84 of his *Institutio Oratoria* to the subversion of expectations in humour when he had written that 'there remains the prettiest of all forms of humor, namely the jest which depends for success on deceiving anticipations or taking another's words in a sense other than he intended. The unexpected element may be employed by the attacking party, as in the example

---

115 The 'Oxen of the Sun' passage in Joyce's *Ulysses* might also be described as an innovatory use of the nineteenth-century parody anthology's practice of lining up a series of authors to be parodied, and these formulae may be applied to the analysis of such works too.

116 Richard Janko's *Aristotle on Comedy. Towards a Reconstruction of Poetics II* (London, 1984), p. 5 takes the provenance of the *Tractatus Coislinianus* back to the thirteenth century AD, but suggests, p. 8, that it could even have come from the sixth century AD.

117 See Lane Cooper, *An Aristotelian Theory of Comedy with an Adaptation of the Poetics and a Translation of the 'Tractatus Coislinianus'* (Oxford, 1924), Preface and Introduction.   118 Ibid., p. 225.   119 Ibid., p. 249.

120 Ibid., p. 225. (And see also Aristotle's *Rhetorica*, Book 3.11.)

cited by Cicero, "What does this man lack save wealth and — virtue?"'.[121]

Quintilian's designation of the deception of anticipation as characteristic of the jest might also be kept in mind when reading Henry Fielding's *The Tragedy of Tragedies, or the Life and Death of Tom Thumb the Great. With the Annotations of H. Scriblerus Secundus* of 1731.[122] Here Fielding uses the device to present not only a parody of heroic tragedy but, in the annotations of H. Scriblerus Secundus (a name used by Fielding as a pseudonym for himself), a parody of commentaries on tragedy which also serves to explain (if through a veil of irony) details of the parody in which Fielding is indulging on the stage. So, for example, Doodle's opening conceit, in which expectations for the serious are deflated when he announces that nature is said to wear 'one universal grin', is explained by Scriblerus as deriving from a peculiar tradition of English tragedy and as a beautiful 'version' of phrases such as Lee's poetic lines which conclude 'All nature smiles'. In addition to the raising and deflating of expectations in Fielding's play on stage, Fielding's mock footnote in which Scriblerus Secundus gives his interpretation of Doodle's lines begins by raising and deflating expectations in saying that 'Corneille recommends some very remarkable day wherein to fix the action of a tragedy' and that 'this the very best of our tragical writers have understood to mean a day remarkable for the serenity of the sky, or what we generally call a fine summer's day'.

When Scriblerus Secundus writes in a comment to Tom Thumb's announcement of a secret in Act II, scene i, that 'this method of surprising an audience by raising their expectations to the highest pitch, and then balking it, hath been practised with great success by most of our tragical authors', he further unexpectedly juxtaposes Quintilian's description of a method of comedy with the methods of tragedy to suggest with some irony that the would-be tragedians in question had not produced the tragedy they had intended. Ironically he thus also describes his own function in Fielding's play as a tool of parody, and a function of the comic play to be to turn the conventions of the tragedies under attack upside down.

The controlled evocation and destruction of audience expectations was also basic to the ancient parody in which quotation or imitation

---

121 See Quintilian, *Institutio Oratoria* , Book 6.3.84, in Butler's translation, vol. 2, p. 485.
122 The play first appeared in 1730 without the 'Annotations'.

evoked other texts, and placed them in ironic conflict with the audience's perception of that which was happening in the parody as a whole. Act I, scene i of Aristophanes' comedy *The Frogs* begins with preparations being made for the Dionysian festival, a potential play-within-the-play. The slave Xanthias is arguing with Dionysus about the script:

XANTHIAS. Do you mean to say I've been lugging all these props around and now I'm not even allowed to get a laugh out of them? It's the regular thing I tell you. Phrynichus, Lysis, Ameipsias, all the popular writers do it. Comic porter Scene. There's one in every comedy.

DIONYSUS. Well there's not going to be one in this comedy.[123]

Ironically, 'this comedy' refers both to the Dionysian festival, the play-within-the-play, and to the Aristophanic comedy of which the characters are shown to be naively and ironically unaware. Thus, while Dionysus sees his statement as being true for his play, it is ironically not true for Aristophanes', in which we now derive humour from the parody of the popular comic porter scene referred to by Xanthias. Xanthias has unwittingly already played out a comic porter scene, while claiming he is not able to do so, and the baser forms of those scenes parodied in this more meta-fictional, and more ironic, treatment of them. Parody is in this case reflexive and 'meta-fictional' as well as comic and playful, and is also made distinct from the satire in which the author's statements are only directed outwards to the world of the reader.[124]

Further techniques and aspects of parody will be discussed when distinguishing it from satire and irony in the following chapter. Some techniques can also signal the parody to the reader, and it is from a consideration of these signals that the role of reader in both the composition and reception of the parody will be discussed.

Reader reception

As a basic premise it will be maintained during this discussion of the reader's reception of the signals for parody that a prime feature distinguishing the imitation (or the non-ironic, non-critical repro-

---

123 Aristophanes, *Frogs*, pp. 156 f. And see also Frances Muecke, 'Playing with the Play: Theatrical Self-Consciousness in Aristophanes', in *Antichton*, vol. 11, 1977, pp. 52–67 for further comment on this and other parodic passages in Aristophanes' works.

124 The subject of meta-fiction is discussed further in the concluding section of chapter 2.

duction of the whole or a part of another literary work in a text) from the literary parody is the establishment in the parody of comic discrepancy or incongruity between the original work and its 'imitation' and transformation. Even if some wish to believe that the reader cannot fully know the intention of the author, the experience of the parody text as comic[125] will mean that the reader can look for structural and other such reasons for that effect in the text in question.[126]

The most frequently found signals for parody can be broadly listed under the following categories.

I   *Changes to the coherency of the text quoted*

(1) Semantic changes:
(a) Apparently meaningless, absurd changes to the message or subject-matter of the original.
(b) Changes to the message or subject-matter of the original of a more meaningful, ironic, or satiric and comic character.
(2) Changes to the choice of words and/or to the literal and metaphoric functions of words taken from the original.
(3) Syntactic change (which may also affect the semantic level).
(4) Changes in tense, persons, or other 'sentence-grammatical' features.
(5) Juxtaposition of passages from within the parodied work, or with new passages.
(6) Changes to the associations of the imitated text made by the new context and other co-textual (and 'beyond the sentence') changes. (This might also include, for example, the transformation of criticism into the subject matter of fiction, as in Malcolm Bradbury's *Mensonge*.)
(7) Changes in sociolect, in idiolect, or in other elements of the lexicon.
(8) Changes to metre or rhyme in verse parodies, or to other such

---

125 As suggested, the 'sense of humour' associated with the recognition of a work as comic involves an at least partially learned ability to recognise and understand the signals for comedy, and this can explain some differences between individual reactions as well as between nations.
126 As also suggested in a previous note, such comic effects and their causes should be interpreted as intentional, or the parody renamed an unintentional parody or 'pekoral'.

'formal' elements in drama or prose works, as well as to subject-matter.

II *Direct statement*

(1) Comments on the parodied text or on the author of the parody, or on their readers.
(2) Comments on or to the reader of the parody.
(3) Comments on the author of the parody.
(4) Comments on the parody as a whole text.

III *Effects on the reader*

(1) Shock or surprise, and humour, from conflict with expectations about the text parodied.
(2) Change in the views of the reader of the parodied text.

IV *Changes to the 'normal' or expected style or subject-matter of the parodist.*

As suggested earlier, it may also be the case that the observation of an incongruous change in the style of the parodist will be as useful an indication of the presence of parody as the recognition of incongruity within the work being parodied, or between it and its new context. This occurs when the reader notices a significant contrast between the familiar style of the author of the parody and the style in which the parodist is writing in the parody (Y as X). That James Joyce did not normally write in the style of Dickens is but one indication of the parodic nature of the 'Dickens passage' in the 'Oxen of the Sun' parodies in Joyce's *Ulysses*, and a change in the expected subject-matter of 'Y' may also signal parody.

In addition to being the object of reception by an outside reader, the parody can play upon the expectations of an imagined reader or recipient in the construction of its parody. In this sense the discussion of the reader and parody has to be concerned not only with the external reader's reception or recognition of a parody, but with the parody's own internal evocation of the expectations of the reader. While in most cases of parody the internal evocation of the expectations of the reader will be achieved by the quotation or imitation of the work to be parodied, in some cases the parody will also be found to have created and used a fictional reader as a mirror to some of those readers outside it, as, in, for example, Miguel de Cervantes' depiction of Don Quixote as a reader of the romance in his parodic *The Adventures of Don Quixote*.

The existence of such different uses of the reader in a parody will also make the reception of it and the understanding of its signals by the external reader even more complex than suggested previously.

To begin the process of unravelling the role played by the reader in the production and reception of the typical parody, the latter may first of all be said to contain at least two connected models of communication. The first of these is between the parodist and the author of the parodied text, and the second between the parodist and the reader of the parody, who may also be assumed to be a reader of the parodied text in either its original and/or its parodied form in the parody of which they are a reader.

In brief, the work to be parodied is 'decoded' by the parodist and offered again (or 'encoded') in a 'distorted' or changed form to another decoder, the reader of the parody, whose expectations for the original of the parodied work may also be played upon and evoked and then transformed by the parodist as a part of the parody work. If the reader of the parody already knows and has previously decoded the parodied target, they will be in a good position to compare it with its new form in the parody, but if they do not already know the target text of the parodist, they may come to know it through its evocation in the parody itself, and to understand the discrepancy between it and the parody text through the latter.

As will be seen again in the chapter on modern theories of parody, this last point is one which has often been overlooked in this century by theorists and editors of parody alike. When, for instance, Walter Jerrold and R. M. Leonard write in the 'Prefatory Note' to their *A Century of Parody and Imitation* of 1913 that 'Isaac D'Israeli asserted that "unless the prototype is familiar to us a parody is nothing"', and then add that 'as a matter of fact some of the best work is that of which the originals have been forgotten long since', but without explaining how this can be so,[127] they, like many others before and after them, fail to note how the parodist's embedding of the parodied work in the parody means that even readers not well acquainted with the work in

---

127 See *A Century of Parody and Imitation*, edited by Walter Jerrold and R. M. Leonard (Oxford, 1913), p. v.

question can come to know it in the parody work, and even while it is being treated in a parodic manner. As the following chapters on modern and post-modern parody will show, it is, moreover, only when this fact is recognised that the multiplicity of encodings and decodings which are present in most parodies, and their role in the evocation and transformation of the expectations of the external reader, can be fully appreciated.

There are also several different sets of terms available for analysing the external reader's reception of the parody and the way in which the parody both shows us the parodist's decoding of the parodied work and uses that decoding to raise and transform the expectations of its external reader. One set of terms which allows all of these parodic decodings and encodings to be depicted at once can be derived from the 'text-linguistic' studies of S. J. Schmidt which have concentrated on the analysis of the reception of texts by the reader, on the expectations of the reader, and on the author's awareness in encoding a work of the factors involved in reader reception.[128] Using the terminology suggested by Schmidt, the reception of a text can be described in basic terms as the reception of a text-world, TW, in a reader's world, RW, at X time and place. If we apply these categories to the description of the reception of parody, we have, however, to speak of the parody as consisting of at least two text-worlds − that of the parodist and that of the target as reproduced by the parodist, or TW1 and TW2 respectively. While both of these texts may be described as being received by the external reader at X time and place, the author of the parody in which the two texts are to be found (or TW1) can also be described as a reader of TW2, and TW2 as having a readership separate from the readership of the parody text as a whole. The advantage of using such a terminology is that one distinctive role of parody within literature, of offering at least two texts within one work, can be clearly depicted, together with the fact that the texts in question may be accompanied by their own 'worlds' of authors and readers and their expectations.

Although it cannot explain all that occurs in the more complex parody, this description of the parody as containing at least two texts

128 See Siegfried J. Schmidt, *Texttheorie* (Munich, 1973), and *Literaturwissenschaft als argumentierende Wissenschaft* (Munich, 1975) and my *Die Parodie: eine Funktion der biblischen Sprache in Heines Lyrik* (Meisenheim on Glan, 1976), pp. 112 ff. Where non-literary parody is to be discussed some appropriate alternatives for the terms text and reader can be substituted.

and their 'worlds' can be applied to most parodies, and from the basic to the complex. Hence just as in the many verse parodies which have flourished in the last centuries, parts of one or more texts have been embedded in the parody which has then added, subtracted, or changed its 'target' to set up a contrast of some comic kind to it, so Cervantes' more complex *Don Quixote* encodes the world of the romance through the enthusiasms and imitative heroic actions of its 'hero', and does so from within the text-world of Cervantes' novel where reality is set up as an antidote to the hero's illusions.

In the cases of verse parodies known as 'double parody', as practised, for example, by Sir John Squire, where one poet is rewritten in the style of another poet by a third, we have what might even be called three text-worlds, and some other examples of parody can also be said to contain more than just two text-worlds. Most examples of parody will further demonstrate, however, that all of the text-worlds in question have been constructed, or at least reconstructed, by the parodist to some extent.

As suggested previously, the reception of the parody by its external reader will depend upon the latter's reading of the 'signals' given in the parody text which relate to or indicate the relationship between the parody and the parodied text and its associations. While many commentators on parody have claimed that a parody will not be recognised as such once its target, the parodied work, has been forgotten, the embedding of the parodied text within the text of the parody both contributes to the ambivalence of the parody which derives from its ability to criticise and renew its target as a part of its own structure and ensures some continued form of existence for the parodied work. Not only, moreover, does the embedding of the latter in the parody give some opportunity for the external reader to recognise it to at least some degree in their reception of its parody, but it also enables the parodist to raise the external reader's expectations for a particular work before introducing the changes which will surprise those expectations and produce the parody's comic effects.

Some of the most common signals for parody have been listed previously. As the understanding of most of those signals is related to the reader's perception of the variety of texts in the parody work, a few of the most common reactions of modern readers to those signals as the signals of a parody can also be listed with reference to their perception or not of the plurality of text-worlds in the parody:

(1) The reader does not recognise the presence of parody, or

understand the signals created in it, because he or she does not
recognise TW2, the parodied text, as a quotation from another
work, but reads it only as a part of TW1.

(2) The reader recognises the presence of two (or more) text-worlds,
but does not comprehend the parodistic intention of the author or
the objective parodic relationship between the two (or more)
texts. He or she may believe, for instance, that the author is
unintentionally misquoting. One other reason for this reaction
may be that readers do not notice the signals of parody because
their sympathy for a parodied text is so strong that their
assumptions about it have not been affected by the parody.

(3) The friend to the parodied text recognises its place in the parody
as a target of the latter and feels both themself and the parodied
text and its author to be the targets of satire.

(4) The reader recognises the parody from the comic discrepancy, or
comic incongruity, between TW1 and TW2 and enjoys the
recognition of the hidden irony of this construction (and the way
in which the parody has both borrowed from and renewed the
parodied work) as well as any satire against or humour about the
parodied text and the reader sympathetic to it. This might also be
regarded as an 'ideal' reader reaction to a parody.

More specific reactions than the above could also be given with
reference to the earlier more detailed list of signals for more specific
examples of parody, but as the different types and examples of parody
are numerous, such general guidelines have had to be given so that the
readers of this work may apply them, and other relevant pieces of
information, to the analysis of such examples for themselves.

In describing the most common signals for parody, both here and
in earlier passages, I have also tried to avoid the distinctions between
form and content made in many modern definitions of parody. As seen
previously, the ancient usage of parody words cannot adequately be
summed up by this distinction, and Fred W. Householder, Jr has
explicitly criticised the application of 'the English terms "parody" and
"burlesque"' to the ancient scholiasts' use of the words 'parodia' and
'parodeo' to describe comic quotation because the English terms have
come to restrict parody to the 'style of composition'.[129]

Christopher Stone's 'Parody' of 1914 had also had to add 'sense-
rendering' to the other two types of 'form-rendering' and 'word-

---

129 See Householder, p. 5, and pp. 1–2.

rendering' which he had found in examples of burlesque verse parody before moving on to discuss works of prose parody,[130] but even in cases of comic imitation of particular genres, or of the form of verse works, the popular definition of parody as the 'imitation of the form of a work with a change to its content' is not very useful or meaningful. This is so because, even when wishing to 'parody' a work by imitating its form and changing its content, the parodist, as shown by Hipponax's ironic evocation of the 'Muse' in his *Hexameters*, will often imitate or evoke both the form and content of a work in some manner before introducing the changes which the reader will be able to recognise as such and appreciate as parody.

Yet one other problem with the description of parody as the imitation of form with a change to content is that this overlooks the fact that in some cases, and especially in cases of prose parody, the parody of a work may entail the changing, as well as the imitation, of both the 'form' and 'content', or 'style' and 'subject-matter', of the original. Laurence Sterne's classic prose parody *Tristram Shandy*, with its apparently chaotic juxtapositions of the normal beginnings, endings, and even printed end-pages of the book, and comic discussion and transformation of the expected content of the 'life-story', can be taken as one example of a prose work which imitates and then changes both the form and content of the more straightforward autobiography, and many other more or less similar examples could be cited.

A passage from Heinrich Heine's 1824 prose piece *Ideen. Das Buch le Grand*, chapter 14, also illustrates how difficult it is to separate the imitation and changing of form from the imitation and changing of content in prose parodies where the parody of a genre is not necessarily involved. When speaking of a physically and financially well-endowed 'Millionarr' ('Million-Narr', or 'millionaire fool')[131] Heine parodies the biblical parable of the camel which could not pass through the eye of the needle, that had served to illustrate the position of the rich man who could not pass into Heaven, by juxtaposing lexical elements from within the parable which contribute to both its 'form' and 'content'. (In this case it can be argued that these elements can also be described in terms of semantic and syntactic components.) Cutting through the original metaphysical lesson of the Bible (as in, for

130 See Stone, p. 38.
131 Sigmund Freud discusses this and Heine's 'famillionär' pun in chapter 2 of his *Der Witz und seine Beziehung zum Unbewußten* of 1905.

example, Matthew 19, 24: 'it is easier for a camel to go through the eye of a needle than for a rich man to enter into the kingdom of God'), Heine parodies it so that its English 'post-biblical' equivalent becomes: 'a camel will find it easier to enter the kingdom of heaven, than this man to go through the eye of a needle'.[132] Here lexical elements within a single story are rearranged to bring about semantic change and a discrepancy with the original biblical passage which is also made comic because of both the substitution of camel for rich man as candidate for heaven and the suggestion that the bulk of the well-fed rich man will make it even more difficult for him than for the camel to pass through the eye of a needle. As in many other cases of so-called 'form and content' relationships, semantic–syntactic dependency means here that a change to one aspect is accompanied by a change to the other, and that the description of parody as 'the imitation of form with a change to content' is again inadequate as a generalisation which may cover all instances.

Tom Sharpe's comic use of the parable of the camel and the rich man in his novel *Porterhouse Blue*, in a sermon by Porterhouse's hearing-impaired chaplain, is less of a direct parody of it than is Heine's, but also works by transposing elements in the biblical story in an unexpected and comic manner, and without apparent concern for maintaining either its original 'form' or 'content'. The Dean, who has been concerned about the threatened changes to the college's kitchens and to their exotic fare, has just been awoken from a day-dream about partridges which had been brought on by the Chaplain's opening reading of a parable from Jeremiah in which their nesting habits are compared to the unproductive harbouring of ill-gotten riches: 'He awoke from his reverie towards the end of the sermon to find the Chaplain in a strangely outspoken way criticizing the college for admitting undergraduates whose only merit was that they belonged to wealthy families. "Let us remember the Lord's words, 'It is easier for a camel to go through the eye of a needle, than for a rich man to enter into the Kingdom of God'", shouted the Chaplain. "We have too many camels in Porterhouse."'[133] Like Heine's parodistic rewriting of

132 Heine's parody of the Luther Bible reads: 'ein Kamel kommt eher ins Himmelreich, als daß dieser Mann durch ein Nadelöhr geht.' See Heinrich Heine, *Ideen. Das Buch le Grand*, chapter 14, in *Reisebilder II* of Ernst Elster (ed.), *Heinrich Heines Sämtliche Werke* in 7 vols., vol. 3, rev. edn (Leipzig and Vienna, 1893), p. 178.
133 See Tom Sharpe, *Porterhouse Blue* (1974) (London, 1983), p. 194.

the parable, the Chaplain's substitution of camel for rich man as the figure from the parable with which most of his audience would identify themselves or their neighbours exchanges elements from the biblical text in an unexpected manner, and is doubly comic because of the suggestion that this may not have been intended by its clerical perpetrator. Whether a discussion of the passage which insisted on describing it as parody because it imitated the form of the Bible 'but with a change to its content' would be entirely satisfactory is questionable. Reasons for this include the fact that such a distinction would overlook not only the way in which both the form and the content of the Bible have had to be evoked and imitated before it could be changed in a parodistic manner, but that the parodistic addition made to the Bible's comparison of camel and rich man has implicitly changed the 'form' of the original biblical story as well as its content when incongruously juxtaposing elements which the Bible had kept separate.

To summarise the above discussion, parody in its broadest sense and application may be described as first imitating and then changing either, and sometimes both, the 'form' and 'content', or style and subject-matter, or syntax and meaning of another work, or, most simply, its vocabulary. In addition to, and at the same time as the preceding, most successful parodies may be said to produce from the comic incongruity between the original and its parody some comic, amusing, or humorous effect, which, together with the changes made by the parodist to the original by the rewriting of the old text, or juxtaposition of it with the new text in which it is embedded, may act as 'signals' of the parodic nature of the parody work for its reader.

The above description of parody has been given with reference largely to the more traditional application of it to works of literature. A briefer, and more general, definition of parody which may be used to describe the uses of parody in both literature and other artistic forms will be offered later in this chapter after the following, further aspects of its definition have been discussed.

Attitudes of the parodist

There have been, in brief, two main theories about the nature of the attitude of the parodist to the text quoted. The first maintains that the imitation by the parodist of a chosen text has the purpose of mocking it and that the motivation in parodying it is contempt. The second holds that the parodist imitates a text in order to write in the style of that text and is motivated by sympathy with the imitated text. The first view often sees parody as an unambivalent form of comic and ridiculing imitation, while the second acknowledges that the parodist has an admiring attitude of some kind to the 'target' or 'model' which has been made a part of the parody text. Support for this second theory may also be found in interpretations of 'parody' as meaning both a song sung 'against' or 'in opposition' to another and a song sung 'beside' or 'near to' another which have been made by some critics on the basis of the ambiguous meaning of the root term 'para' as designating both 'beside' and 'opposite'.

Lutz Röhrich also indicates that there exist two major concepts of the nature of the attitude of the parodist to the parodied work.[134] The first which Röhrich mentions describes parody as deriving from the desire to imitate a favourite style. The second sees parody as mockery born of the poet's realisation that his age is 'epigonal'. Röhrich writes that the second opinion is more widely held: 'The widely spread belief that one can only parody that which one loves is only partially true. Parody is much more frequently the symptom of satiation. Parodies are determined by a negative tendency towards the transmitted text. They have a tendency towards opposition. A protest is made against that which has been transmitted. Boredom, satiation, or lack of belief unburden themselves in laughter.'[135]

The view that the parodist's attitude is sympathetic (as expressed, for example, by Thomas Mann in his novel *Doktor Faustus*) is dismissed by Röhrich as being a minority opinion. As Röhrich himself points out later, parody, however, is not only destructive (as the second, more popular, opinion would have it), but is also reconstructive: 'Parodistic changes of pre-given traditions need not only be viewed negatively as a destruction of that which has been sung or spoken. They reveal at the same time a process of linguistic re-formation and new-formation.'[136]

One other suggestion which can be made here is that the love of a parodist for the object of the parody need not exclude a desire to change and modernise it, and yet one more that the love of a work can help the parodist know and reproduce it better in the parody. Further

---

134 See L. Röhrich, *Gebärde–Metapher–Parodie* (Düsseldorf, 1967), p. 215 ff. Röhrich also writes p. 217 that parody can proceed from either the form or the content of a work ('Parodie kann von der Form oder vom Inhalt ausgehen').

135 Translated from Röhrich, p. 215.   136 Ibid., p. 221.

to this, the desire of a parodist to change another text can lead to the production of something new from it, the love of which may lead the parodist to view the target text, and its contribution to the parody in question, with some sympathy. The parodist need not, moreover, be attracted only to the style of a work as Röhrich suggests, for, as argued previously, parody is not necessarily restricted to the imitation of the style or 'form' of a work.

It has also been argued that history proves that only parodies of well-known and powerfully poetic works survive. While it has been seen already that several of those maintaining this argument have overlooked the fact that the parody itself keeps its target alive to at least some extent by quoting or imitating something of it within itself, the parody should also have something new to say about these works for it to survive independently as a parody.

Despite the fact that parodies may be *both* critical of *and* sympathetic to their 'targets', many critics have continued to describe parody as being *only* critical, or *only* sympathetic, or playful, or agitatory, or engagé, or blasphemous, or ironic, or imitative, or counter-imitative, and so on. In addition to being a device which is able, because of its peculiar dual structure, to have an ambivalent, or ambiguous, relationship to its 'target', parody is able to be used to demonstrate several of the above characteristics at once, if, or when, an author chooses.

General parody

The later sections of this study on modern and late-modern theories of parody will show that some critics who have praised works of general parody such as *Don Quixote*, *Tristram Shandy*, or Joyce's *Ulysses*, in which parody has been used to create the structure and stories of the works as a whole, have also condemned specific parody as a minor literary form, or refrained from describing those larger and more complex works as works of comic parody. As suggested below, both specific and general parody may, however, be both comic and ambivalent, and parody be described as such as a whole.

The ambivalence of both specific and general parody

It has already been seen that while parody is accompanied by a comic effect it need not necessarily ridicule the work of its target or 'parodee'. Both Lelièvre and Householder[137] cite Aristophanes'

---

137 Householder, p. 6.

47

admiration for Euripides to make this point, and several other commentators have made it with reference to either parody or to related aspects of the ancient comedy. In 'general parody' where the author has used parody to set up the plot and characters of a work, and/or to reflect upon the processes of fiction in general, as in, for instance, Cervantes' *Don Quixote*, some ambivalence towards the parodied text or texts which have contributed to the plot or characters of the parody may be central to the complexity of the parody as a whole.[138] In other more specific, and satiric, uses of parody, a parodist may also use the parodied work in an ambivalent manner as a contributing part of the parody, and, if using parody to mock a poetaster or a distortion of a text, need not attack the parodied text itself.

As F. J. Lelièvre has argued in his article 'The Basis of Ancient Parody' of 1954 (p. 66), an ambiguity exists in the word 'parodia' in that its prefix 'para' can be translated to mean both nearness and opposition.[139] Lelièvre writes that '"παρά" may be said to develop two trends of meaning, being used to express such ideas as nearness, consonance and derivation as well as transgression, opposition, or difference', and that 'in compounds a synthesis of these two forces may sometimes be found'. Lelièvre continues: 'On this analogy our word would indicate that parody is something sung – or composed – conformably to an original but with a difference, and this idea can also be seen to lie behind the two main techniques used by the ancient parodists.'

Fred W. Householder, Jr has already been seen to have described 'para' as an ambiguous word. Despite its definition of parody as burlesque, the *OED* also describes 'para' as having had the sense as a preposition of 'by the side of', 'beside', 'whence alongside of, by, past, beyond etc.', while in composition it had the same senses with

138 The 'general parody' spoken of here does not necessarily entail the 'general irony' which D. C. Muecke, p. 120 defines as 'life itself or any general aspect of life seen as fundamentally and inescapably an ironic state of affairs', although the latter is comparable to the 'parodic realism' found in some of the contemporary works mentioned in chapter 4.

139 I previously discussed this point in my *Parody//Meta-Fiction* of 1979, pp. 33 ff., and with reference both to the double-coded nature of parody and to the ambivalence of parody as both *Beigesang* and *Gegengesang*. Some references to the ambiguity of the word 'para' have already been made in this work, on its pp. 8, 9, and 46. Other references to 'para' and to its various meanings can be found in the Index.

such cognate adverbial ones as 'to one side, aside, amiss, faulty, irregular, disordered, improper, wrong', also expressing 'subsidiary relation, alteration, perversion, simulation', which are also the senses which are said to be found in English derivatives including parody.[140]

Most commentators on the classical etymology of the word parody have been aware of the ambiguity of its prefix 'para'. One modern commentator on the classical texts who translates the word 'para' with relationship to parody as only meaning 'opposite' is Hermann Koller in his article 'Die Parodie' of 1956,[141] although his purpose in doing so is to illustrate what he sees to be the close relationship of parody to the singing of one song against another, and he does write later that parody was not primarily meant to mock its target.[142]

The ambivalence of great parody – from Aristophanes to today – of apparent empathy with and distance from the text imitated – can be said to be implied in the classical understanding of it as a song sung 'in imitation of', and as both 'next to' and 'different from' another, as it has been described by both Householder and Lelièvre. Yet the root term 'para' in the word parody was not always translated as meaning *both* opposition to its object *and* nearness by post-Renaissance critics: more usually it became *either* opposition *or* consonance – and in German, for example, parody became either *Gegengesang* (a song sung in opposition to another) or *Beigesang* (a song sung alongside another).

Just as these more one-dimensional views of parody as either satire or imitation have been in part responsible for the relegation of the type of specific parody used in popular verse or prose works to a lower literary form, so they have also led to the relegation of authors associated with general and sophisticated uses of parody such as Cervantes to canons of lesser importance.[143] The story of the rises and falls in popularity of Cervantes and other such authors over the

---

140 See the *OED* , 2nd edn, vol. 11, p. 172. Other 'para' words in English listed there include 'parabaptism', 'paradox', and 'parallel'. And see also Liddell and Scott, *A Greek-English Lexicon*, pp. 1302 ff. for further information on the uses of 'para'.

141 See Hermann Koller, 'Die Parodie', *Glotta*, vol. 35, nos 1–2 (1956), pp. 17–32; p. 19.

142 See Koller, p. 22. For a critical reaction to Koller's article see Wilhelm Horn's *Gebet und Gebetsparodie in den Komödien des Aristophanes* (Nuremberg, 1970) p. 35 n.53 and for some further discussion of it see Pöhlmann, pp. 145 f.

143 See also the account in chapter 2 of Addison's description of *Don Quixote* as burlesque.

centuries cannot be told in detail here, but there are several instances where the relegation of parody to the burlesque can be connected to the fall from grace of those authors as mere parodists, and where the separation of their works from those terms has taken place when they were to be rehabilitated as 'serious' writers.[144]

While it also involved separating parody from the 'merely comic', although not from the comic as such,[145] one exception to this may be said to have occurred in Germany when the early Romantic critics August Wilhelm and Friedrich Schlegel encouraged both the positive use of the word 'Parodie' and the study of Cervantes.[146] August Wilhelm Schlegel also emphasised the ambivalence of parody towards its target, and spoke of it, when commenting on the ancient comedy in the eleventh of his 'Vorlesungen über dramatische Kunst and Literatur' of 1809–11, as being both 'dependent on and independent of' its object.[147]

Even when the Grimms' nineteenth-century *Deutsches Wörterbuch* defines παρῳδία as 'neben-, gegengesang' it makes, however, no mention of the positive uses of the term by the Schlegels and other early Romantics,[148] or by others such as Kant, and goes on to describe parody as the refunctioning of a serious work into a 'comic or mocking' one in a much more negative and less complex manner.[149]

---

144 And see also Dorothy Van Ghent's comments on this and other aspects of *Don Quixote* in her *The English Novel. Form and Function* (New York, 1953).

145 When Friedrich Schlegel describes Cervantes as a great artist in the *Athenaeum* of 1799's 'Notizen' (see A. W. and Fr. Schlegel (eds.), *Athenaeum*. 1798–1800 (Stuttgart, 1960), pp. 324–7) he also suggests, p. 326, that Cervantes was 'not merely' a 'Spaßmacher' or 'joker'.

146 August Wilhelm Schlegel praises Cervantes in, for instance, his *Geschichte der klassischen Literatur* and in the 35th lecture of his *Vorlesungen über dramatische Kunst und Literatur* of 1809–11. (See his *Kritische Schriften und Briefe*, ed. E. Lohner (Stuttgart, Berlin, Cologne, Mainz, 1962–74), vol. 3, pp. 193–4 and vol. 6, pp. 251 ff. respectively.)

147 See A. W. Schlegel, *Kritische Schriften und Briefe*, vol. 5, p. 132. A. W. Schlegel also refers to Plato's admiration for Aristophanes in the following lecture, pp. 139 f.

148 Friedrich Schlegel's 1799 praise of Cervantes had been made in a review of Ludwig Tieck's translation of *Don Quixote*, and Ingrid Strohschneider-Kohrs' *Romantische Ironie in Theorie und Gestaltung* (Tübingen, 1960), p. 135 also refers to an essay by Tieck of 1828 in which he praises *Don Quixote* for mixing seriousness and parody.

149 See the Grimms' *Deutsches Wörterbuch*, vol. 7 (Leipzig, 1889), p. 1464. Goethe's 'Über die Parodie bei den Alten' (1824), in Goethe, *Sämtliche Werke*, Jubiläums-Ausgabe, 40 vols., ed. E. v. d. Hellen *et al.* (Stuttgart and Berlin, 1902–7), vol. 37,

General and specific parody: conclusion

Despite the fact that it was the use of specific and satiric parody which often led to a work being dubbed burlesque and banned from the canon of more serious literary forms,[150] the concept or use of general parody need not exclude that of specific parody, and especially as it is the techniques of the latter which serve to create the ambivalent dependence of general parody on its target as found in works such as *Don Quixote*. Jorge Luis Borges might also be said to have alluded to the way in which the target contributes to the constitution of both the basic and the complex parody in writing that 'Cervantes has created for us the poetry of seventeenth-century Spain, but neither the century nor that Spain were poetic for him ... The plan of his book precluded the marvellous; the latter, however, had to figure in the novel, at least indirectly, just as crimes and a mystery in a parody of a detective story.'[151]

In both its general and specific forms, parody, unlike forms of satire or burlesque which do not make their target a significant part of themselves, is ambivalently dependent upon the object of its criticism for its own reception. In addition to making the target of parody a part of the parody text, the parodist may also choose to unmask and deflate other writers by using their works ironically as a temporary 'word-mask' for the parodist. Even explicitly critical parody can make the comic discrepancy between the parodist's style and that of the target text into a weapon against the latter and at the same time refunction the target's work for a new and positive purpose within the parody in a manner which must make the parody's criticisms of the parodied text to some extent ambivalent.

Both by definition (through the meaning of its prefix 'para') and structurally (through the inclusion within its own structure of the work it parodies), most parody worthy of the name is ambivalent towards its target. This ambivalence may entail not only a mixture of criticism and sympathy for the parodied text, but also the creative expansion of it into something new. Most other of the specific characteristics of

pp. 290–3, also gives a negative assessment of the term when it claims it is inadequate for the description of ancient literature.

150 One other German critic of parody at the end of the eighteenth century was J. C. Gottsched.

151 See Jorge Luis Borges, 'Partial Magic in the *Quixote*', in *Labyrinths* (Harmondsworth, 1976), p. 228.

parody, including its creation of comic incongruity between the original and the parody, and the way in which its comedy can laugh both at and with its target, may be traced to the way in which the parodist makes the object of the parody a part of the parody's structure.

In much meta-fictional parody familiar literary structures may also be deliberately 'foregrounded', or brought into the 'foreground' of a work from its background structure, by being made more obvious, more complex, or confusing through the contrast of works in the parody. Here the structural role assumed by the parodied text in the parody may also be made more complex and ambivalent than in other less obviously meta-fictional parodies. The parodied work may not only function, for instance, as the target of the parodist's criticism or 'refunctioning', and contribute to the structure and effect of the parody by lending it its 'preformed' linguistic material, but may also serve to bring into the 'foreground' of the parody work aspects of the writing of literature and of its reception in general.

In all of these specific and general uses parody may be defined in general terms as *the comic refunctioning of preformed linguistic or artistic material*.

The term 'refunctioning' has been explained previously as referring to the new set of functions given to parodied material in the parody and may also entail some criticism of the parodied work. The term 'preformed material' is used in the above definition in order to describe the way in which the materials targetted in a parody have been previously formed into a work or statement of some kind by another, and is used in place of the terms 'form' and 'content' which have been seen to have been used in misleading ways in many modern definitions of parody.

Both the phrase 'preformed material' and the word 'refunctioning' may also be used to describe the modern and 'post-modern' parody of non-linguistic, musical, visual, architectural, or film works, as well as cases of cross-parody between these different media, and some of these modern and post-modern uses of parody and pastiche will be mentioned or discussed further in following chapters.

In this chapter, it has been seen, amongst other things, that by incorporating parts of the target text into the parody, parodists can both ensure the closeness to a target necessary for an accurate firing of their critical arrows and preserve the essential features of the target which will make the parody outlive the demise of the parodied work's readership. In doing this parody will also be seen in the following chapter to differ not only from satire, but from the travesty, persiflage, and other forms of criticism or imitation of literary or artistic works which have sometimes been confused with parody, or used, in anachronistic manner, as a part of its definition.

❖❖

Distinguishing parody from related forms

❖❖

This chapter isolates some of the terms which have been confused or contrasted with parody during the modern period and gives some brief but basic descriptions of their distinguishing characteristics, together with some further analysis of the distinguishing features and functions of parody.

Burlesque and travesty

The modern reduction of parody to a type of burlesque in descriptions given of it in the eighteenth century and after has already been seen to have limited the meaning of the more ancient definitions and uses of parody. Not only is the term burlesque of more recent origin than the Greek words for parody, but it is usually described as being derived from the Italian *burla*, meaning a joke or a trick,[1] rather than from equivalents for the words from which the term parody is derived, and is for this reason, and the meanings given to it by its early users, less able to describe the way in which the parody (or '*para*-ode') imitates and then comically transforms other works in ambiguous and often complex meta-fictional ways. As Householder has pointed out, some burlesque does not even require a specific literary model,[2] and the word has been used to describe a variety of types of comic and even non-comic entertainments.

On the history of the term burlesque Henryk Markiewicz states that the word for it was imported from Italy, where it had been in use in the sixteenth century, to France, where, in the seventeenth century, it 'acquired more diverse meanings, sometimes of a pejorative colouring'.[3] Richmond P. Bond writes in his *English Burlesque Poetry*,

---

1 'Burlesque' has also been described in some modern Italian dictionaries as 'va mettere in burla'.   2 See Householder, 'ΠΑΡΩΙΔΙΑ', p. 5.
3 See Henryk Markiewicz, 'On the Definitions of Literary Parody', in *To Honor Roman Jakobson. Essays on the Occasion of his Seventieth Birthday*, 3 vols., vol. 2 (The Hague, 1967), pp. 1264–72; p. 1266.

1700–1750 of *1932* that Blount's *Glossographia* of *1656* had described burlesque as meaning 'drolish, merry, pleasant',[4] but 'le burlesque', according to Markiewicz, could also mean at the time 'grotesque, rank or flat comicality, extravagance of imagination or style (especially using vulgar or extraordinary language), no matter to what literary genre the work belonged'.[5] Markiewicz adds that 'in its more narrow sense, the word was applied to travesty' (a term of similar vintage used by Giovambattista Lalli in his *Eneide travestita* of *1634* and by Paul Scarron in his *Le Virgile Travesty en vers Burlesques* of *1648–53*, and derived from 'travestire' meaning 'to disguise' or 'to change clothing'), 'or to the mock-heroic poem, or as the name for a category including these last two'.[6]

As observed previously, a term for parody, παρῳδία , had been applied by the ancients to what is now called the 'mock-heroic' poem, as well as to other, related, devices of comic quotation. The introduction into common critical usage of the terms burlesque and travesty in the eighteenth century was, however, to see those more modern terms take over this role from parody in following centuries, and even though neither modern term had originally described the especial devices or peculiarities of parody involved in its comic imitation and transformation of other works.

Many twentieth-century works of criticism have not only defined parody as burlesque but have attributed to burlesque some of the characteristics and history of the more ancient form of parody. E. Bradlee Watson's articles on the burlesque of the 1940s suggest burlesque is parody 'when the imitation humorously parallels the style or mannerisms of a particular work or author or school, but with a trivial or ludicrous purpose'.[7] W. J. MacQueen-Pope's article 'Burlesque' in *Cassell's Encyclopaedia of Literature* of *1953* claims it can be said that Aristophanes used burlesque,[8] and John Jump has introduced

4 Richmond P. Bond, *English Burlesque Poetry, 1700–1750* (Cambridge, Mass., 1932), p. 19. 5 See Markiewicz, p. 1266.

6 Ibid. C. Cotton uses the term in the last sense in his *Scarronides: or, Virgile Travestie. A Mock-Poem. Being the First Book of Virgils Æneis in English, Burlésque* of 1664.

7 See E. Bradlee Watson, 'Burlesque' in *Dictionary of World Literature. Criticism, Forms, Technique*, edited by Joseph T. Shipley (London, 1945), p. 79 and 'Burlesque' in *Dictionary of World Literary Terms. Forms, Techniques, Criticism* (1943), new enlarged and completely revised edn, edited by Joseph T. Shipley (London, 1970), p. 35.

8 See W. J. MacQueen-Pope, 'Burlesque', in *Cassell's Encyclopaedia of Literature*, edited by S. H. Steinberg (London, 1953), 2 vols., vol. 1, pp. 72–3; p. 72.

the chapter on 'The Mock-Poem' in his *Burlesque* of 1972 with the statement that 'high burlesque flourished in the Classical literature of Greece and Rome'.[9] Although Jump's conclusion to his book (p. 72) shows him to have been aware that the word burlesque was not classical, but derived from a word which had had a comparatively short history, Jump has also followed Richmond P. Bond's 1932 study of *English Burlesque Poetry, 1700–1750* in relegating the more ancient concept of parody to one other species of 'high burlesque'.[10]

Richmond Bond had divided the burlesque into both high and low and specific and general in his book of 1932, and had claimed (p. 4) that 'all burlesque may generally be called diminishing or magnifying, degrading or elevating, low or high'. Bond continues: 'More definite names for the component divisions of burlesque are possible. The travesty lowers a particular work by applying a jocular, familiar, undignified treatment, and the Hudibrastic poem uses the same procedure on more general matter, the difference being one of particular and general. The parody mimics the manner of an individual author or poem by substituting an unworthy or less worthy subject, and the mock poem copies the manner of a general class of poetry without specific reference to a poet or poem, again the difference being one of strictness of imitation. Thus the travesty and the parody imitate some definite work or style; the Hudibrastic and the mock poem are more general in their approach.' Bond then adds (pp. 4–5) that 'the low burlesque places the subject above the style and consists of the travesty and the Hudibrastic, with the distinction between the two species that of degree of closeness of imitation; the high burlesque fixes the style above the subject and consists of the parody and the mock poem, with the same distinction of degree. Parody and travesty have in common closeness of satirical representation, mock-heroic and Hudibrastic lack of closeness, parody and mock-heroic elevation of a trifling subject in a higher style, travesty and Hudibrastic degradation of a serious subject in a lower style; parody is not connected with the Hudibrastic, nor travesty with the mock-heroic, except in the sharing of the general burlesque incongruity.'

John Jump's other species of the burlesque are based on those outlined by Bond and include the 'low burlesque' forms of 'travesty'

9 See John Jump, *Burlesque*, (London, 1972), p. 37.
10 Bond suggests that the use of *burlesque* does not preclude the use of more specific terms, such as parody (see Bond, p. 11), but nonetheless discusses the latter as a sub-category of burlesque.

and 'hudibrastic' as well as the 'high burlesque' of the 'mock-poem'. Jump (p. 2) also defines parody in similar terms to Bond as the 'high burlesque of a particular work (or author), achieved by applying the style of that work (or author) to a less worthy subject'. Jump gives the example of Fielding's *Shamela* as an example of such parody, and echoes Bond in describing the mock-epic (such as Pope's *Rape of the Lock*) as a form of high burlesque which lavishes 'the style characteristic of the class upon a trifling subject'. Travesty is then defined by Jump as 'the low burlesque of a particular work achieved by treating the subject of that work in an aggressively familiar style', and Byron's *Vision of Judgement* given as an example, while 'hudibrastic' (such as is found in Butler's *Hudibras*) is described as 'the low burlesque of a less confined material'.

Bond's, and Jump's, definitions of parody as high burlesque not only apply a term dating from only the sixteenth century, and associated with ridicule,[11] to the more ancient concept and practice of parody,[12] but also utilise an eighteenth-century distinction between two different kinds of burlesque made popular by Joseph Addison in number 249 of *The Spectator* of 15 December 1711. There Addison had written: 'The two great Branches of Ridicule in Writing are Comedy and Burlesque. The first ridicules Persons by drawing them in their proper Characters, the other by drawing them quite unlike themselves. Burlesque is therefore of two kinds, the first represents mean Persons in the Accoutrements of Heroes, the other describes great Persons acting and speaking like the basest among the People. *Don Quixote* is an Instance of the first, and *Lucian's* Gods of the second.'[13]

In dividing burlesque into two types in this passage, Addison has applied the term burlesque to both an ancient and a modern example of parody, and has described both types of burlesque as belonging to a form of ridiculing caricature which is different from comedy. While describing both comedy and burlesque as forms of ridicule, Addison's contrast of comedy and burlesque in the above quotation also gives a different account of comedy from Aristotle's *Poetics*, chapter 2, where

---

11 See also Jump's definition of 'burla' on his p. 72 and Bond, p. 18.

12 Bond, p. 19 also refers to John Kersey's 1706 edition of Edward Phillips' *New World of English Words* of 1658 as defining *parody* as 'a Poetick Sport, which consists in putting some serious Pieces into Burlesk, and affecting as much as is possible, the same Words, Rhymes and Cadences'.

13 Bond quotes this passage on his p. 40, and see also Joseph Addison, *The Spectator*, edited by D. F. Bond, 5 vols.; vol. 2 (Oxford, 1965), pp. 467–8.

comedy is described as showing persons to be worse than they are, and projects something like its description of comedy as showing people to be worse than they are onto the burlesque.[14]

As seen previously, Aristotle had been referring to 'the first parodist' (or writer of 'burlesques' in Addison's terminology), Hegemon of Thasos, as well as to 'Nicochares, the author of the *Diliad*', just prior to making his more general point about comedy that it shows persons to be worse than they are, and had later explained in his *Poetics*, chapter 5, 1449a that comedy shows men to be worse than they are as regards the ridiculous [or the laughable], 'which is a species of the ugly'.[15] Addison's distinctions between the burlesque and comedy, and application of the term burlesque to examples of parody, not only distinguishes the latter from the more ancient form of comedy while reducing it to the more modern term of the burlesque, but may also be said to have encouraged others such as Bond and Jump to reduce parody to one of the two sub-categories of the latter which are described in Addison's text.

Other distinctions between two types of burlesque had been made prior to Addison's, but without using the examples of parody chosen by Addison. Bond's *English Burlesque Poetry, 1700–1750* of 1932 itself describes a similar distinction made by John Ozell in the 1708 dedication to his translation of Nicolas Boileau's *Le Lutrin* of 1667 with reference to Boileau's work and to Butler's *Hudibras*: 'If I distinguish right, there are two sorts of *Burlesque*; the first where things of mean Figure and Slight Concern appear in all the Pomp and Bustle of an *Epic* poem; such is this of the *Lutrin*. The second sort is where great Events are made Ridiculous by the meanness of the Character, and the oddness of the Numbers, such is the *Hudibras* of our Excellent Butler.'[16]

Of these descriptions of the types of burlesque Addison's is of particular significance in the history of the replacement of the term

14 While Addison speaks of the burlesque as drawing persons 'unlike' themselves rather than 'worse', his description of the two types of burlesque as comparing the base or the mean to the great involves showing the great to be worse than they are in at least one of those types.

15 Ingram Bywater translates Aristotle as saying there that 'as for Comedy, it is ... an imitation of men worse than the average; worse, however, not as regards any and every sort of fault, but only as regards one particular kind, the Ridiculous, which is a species of the Ugly'.

16 See Bond, *English Burlesque Poetry*, p. 37. Judith Priestman's dissertation, *The Age of Parody. Literary Parody and Some Nineteenth-Century Perspectives* (University of

parody by that of the burlesque because it reduced both a type of ancient parody and an important example of modern parody in the novel, Cervantes' *Don Quixote*, to its examples of the burlesque,[17] and because of the way it reached a wide public.

Addison's reduction of *Don Quixote* to another form of burlesque in which 'mean persons' are depicted in the 'Accoutrements of Heroes' tells us little, however, about either the varieties of literary parody to be found in that work, or about the nature of parody itself. Cervantes' novel may, for instance, be described as parody because of its depiction of a 'mean person' who imagines himself to be a hero from a romance, but not just because of its comic contrast of low to high, but because that device allows Cervantes parodistically to quote and analyse the chivalric romances which have influenced his 'hero', and from that point to reflect in ironic and meta-fictional manner on the writing and reading of books in general.

In addition to reducing Cervantes' work of parody to the burlesque, Addison had separated an ancient form of parody from Cervantes' parody in describing Lucian's gods as an example of the second type of burlesque in which great persons are shown as 'acting and speaking like the basest among the People'. While Addison had described Lucian's work as burlesque, and others following his divisions of burlesque were to describe it as travesty, Lucian's treatment of the gods had not, in fact, been very different from Aristophanes' parodistic treatment of the god Dionysus in his *Frogs*.

Addison's description of Lucian's parodistic treatment of the gods as a different type of burlesque from that used by Cervantes not only separates the ancient type of parody used by Aristophanes and his like from the modern use of parody by Cervantes without convincing argument, but also fails to acknowledge that each of the types of 'burlesque' described in Addison's article may be found in the ancient as well as the modern parody and that this fact still does not exhaust all the possible meanings or applications of the latter term.[18]

Kent at Canterbury, 1980), pp. 12–13, also discusses this quotation and gives a good account of other eighteenth- and nineteenth-century uses of the words burlesque and parody in English.

17 Works such as Scarron's *Virgile Travesty* and Cotton's *Scarronides* can more easily be named 'burlesque', because of their authors' choice to use that word and the way it describes their less complex uses of parody, though even here it cannot wholly cover the latter.

18 All of Bond's, and Jump's, four types of burlesque are covered by the ancient use of the term parody to describe the parody of the Homeric epic, but they still do

Despite its limitations in adequately describing either the parody used in Cervantes' *Don Quixote* or ancient parody, Addison's division of the burlesque into two different types, and application of one of these to Cervantes' novel, has been used by several modern critics to provide a definition of parody as 'high burlesque' in which the low is compared to an high ideal, and one of travesty as 'low burlesque' in which the high is compared to something low.

David Worcester's *The Art of Satire* of 1940 is but one other work which uses Richmond Bond's post-eighteenth-century division of the burlesque into high and low to speak of burlesque in terms of high and low burlesque with reference to forms which have otherwise been termed parody or travesty.[19] Worcester (p. 44) first of all defines the low burlesque as creating a standard below its victim and as making the reader measure him against that standard, and the high burlesque as placing a standard above the victim to spotlight his faults. In his section entitled 'High and Low Burlesque' Worcester then describes the low burlesque as 'inviting the reader to compare its subject with what is base and sordid', and goes on to say that 'a satirist might, for example, represent Aeneas as a vagabond and Dido as a fishwife'.[20] After describing the high burlesque as depending 'not on noticing similarities but on noticing differences' (p. 46), Worcester adds (p. 47), just prior to making mention of Richmond Bond's distinctions, that 'conventionally, high burlesque treats a trivial subject in an elevated manner' (the example of the story of the battle of the frogs and mice in the *Batrachomyomachia* could fit this), and that low burlesque (Cotton's treatment of Dido in his *Scarronides* could serve as an example) 'treats an elevated subject in a trivial manner'.

As Worcester himself goes on to suggest (p. 48), it is, however, not always possible to apply this typology to all examples with equal success, and it can say little about the specific treatment given the Homeric epics in the mock-epic parodies of which works such as the *Batrachomyomachia* are an example.

Worcester's example of Dido compared to a fishwife is reminiscent, moreover, of Bond's account of Boileau's description of his *Le Lutrin* as

not tell us everything about the structure, comic techniques, or subtlety of the more ancient form.

19 See David Worcester, *The Art of Satire* (1940), (New York, 1960). Worcester refers to Bond's divisions on his pp. 47–8.

20 See Worcester, p. 46 where he also describes the low burlesque as the 'half-brother to invective-satire'.

an experiment in a 'new type' of burlesque, where Boileau writes that 'whereas, in the other Burlesque, *Dido* and *Æneas* talk like Oyster-Women and Porters; [21] in this, a Watch-maker and his Wife speak like *Dido* and *Æneas*'.[22] While this description by Boileau of his *Le Lutrin* would, according to Worcester's criteria, bring it close to parodies such as the *Batrachomyomachia*, to which it has been said to be similar in its contrast of an epic style with a trivial subject-matter,[23] Worcester's characterisation of the high burlesque as being based on such a contrast also cannot tell us all there is to know about the parodic character of Boileau's work.[24]

Worcester's distinctions between low and high burlesque which describe low burlesque as involving comparisons of the high to the low, and high burlesque as involving a contrast of the trivial to the high, break down, furthermore, if both categories are applied to the extant examples of ancient parody. Hence, when Homer's heroes are replaced by 'anti-heroes' in the fragment of Hipponax's *Hexameters* which Athenaeus has left us, or by animals in the *Batrachomyomachia*, we have the anti-heroes or animals raised ironically to the level of 'heroes' at the same time as Homer's heroes are ironically reduced to, and compared with, the 'lower' levels of the 'anti-heroes' by the latter's imitations of them. In addition to the above, parody, as seen previously, may change another work, and produce a comic effect, by a variety of small or large changes to the parodied text other than either of those just described.

Bond's description of parody as 'high burlesque' and of travesty as a form of 'low burlesque' has not only repeated many of the problems found in Addison's divisions of burlesque, and in his application of them to what both we and the ancients could call parody, but has taken up and added to those divisions an equally modern division between form and content which is not to be found in most ancient applications of words for parody. Bond begins his 1932 book by arguing: 'The essence of humour lies in incongruity, and when imitation is added, burlesque is the result. Burlesque consists, then, in

---

21 See again the quotation from Cotton's *Scarronides* in chapter 1.
22 See Bond, p. 203.
23 See also chapter 7, 'The Non-English Burlesque in England', in Bond, pp. 176 ff., on the *Batrachomyomachia* and its imitations.
24 Bond, pp. 200 ff. also comments on the mixture of parody and satire in Boileau's *Le Lutrin*, and Worcester admits on his p. 48 that 'seldom is a burlesque poem true to type throughout'.

the use or imitation of serious matter or manner, made amusing by the creation of an incongruity between style and subject. This inconsistency between form and content, this opposition between what is said and the way it is said, is the necessary qualification of the burlesque.'[25]

Bond's subsequent (pp. 4 ff.) division of burlesque into high and low types which involve a contrast of high and low style and subject-matter also echoes several seventeenth- and eighteenth-century descriptions of the burlesque in which parody is relegated to one of its forms. Bond was well aware of these definitions,[26] and both he and Jump have quoted Dryden's earlier comments on Boileau's *Le Lutrin* in his *Discourse concerning the Original and Progress of Satire* of 1693 that 'his subject is trivial, but his verse is noble',[27] in which a contrast between style and content is found by Dryden in Boileau's work.[28]

Wolfgang Karrer suggests in his *Parodie, Travestie, Pastiche* of 1977 that many of the eighteenth-century descriptions of parody in terms of style versus content and of other such oppositions had reached a culmination in a passage in Henry Home's (Lord Kames') *Elements of Criticism* and that this was used as a model for other descriptions of parody well into this century.[29] Home had written, if with explicit reference to burlesque rather than to parody,[30] although he later speaks of the two as the same in another section of his text:[31] 'A grave subject in which there is no impropriety, may be brought down by a

---

25 Bond, p. 3. (Bond follows Christopher Stone when he writes on his p. 13 that 'the parody must keep its attention fixed on the poem to be imitated. Word-rendering, form-rendering, and sense-rendering are the usual methods', but also describes parody as the creation of a subject similar to but unsuitable for that of the parodied work.)

26 Bond, p. 4 refers to Heinrich Schneegans' definitions of parody and travesty in terms of form and content in his *Geschichte der grotesken Satire* (Strassburg, 1894), pp. 34 and 36, and later mentions earlier discussions of the burlesque in which similar form/content distinctions are made.

27 See Dryden, ed. George Watson, vol. 2, p. 148, Jump, p. 38, and Bond, p. 193.

28 Dryden does not, however, call Boileau's work burlesque here, and later describes the burlesque as 'the serious words of the author perverted into a ridiculous meaning'. (See Dryden, p. 103.)

29 See Wolfgang Karrer, *Parodie, Travestie, Pastiche* (Munich, 1977), p. 53. (Karrer gives 1824 as the date of Home's work, but it had appeared first in 1762.)

30 Home begins this paragraph: 'Burlesque, though a great engine of ridicule, is not confined to that subject; for it is clearly distinguishable into burlesque that excites laughter merely, and burlesque that provokes derision or ridicule.' See Henry Home, (Lord Kames), *Elements of Criticism* (1762), 3rd edn (Edinburgh and London, 1765), 2 vols.; vol. 1, p. 350.   31 See Home, vol. 1, pp. 442–3 n.

certain colouring so as to be risible; which is the case of the *Virgil Travestie*; and also the case of the *Secchia Rapita*: the authors laugh first at every turn, in order to make their readers laugh. The *Lutrin* is a burlesque poem of the other sort, laying hold of a low and trifling incident, to expose the luxury, indolence, and contentious spirit of a set of monks. Boileau the author turns the subject into ridicule, by dressing it in the heroic style,[32] and affecting to consider it as of the utmost dignity and importance; and though ridicule is the poet's aim, he himself carries all along a grave face, and never once bewrays a smile: the opposition between the subject and the manner of handling it, is what produces the ridicule; and therefore, in a composition of this kind, no image professedly ludicrous ought to have quarter; because such images destroy the contrast.'[33]

Home (p. 351) continues by stating in summary that 'the burlesque that aims at ridicule, produces its effect by elevating the style far above the subject', and then warns of taking this too far, as in the ancient *Batrachomyomachia*.[34] Despite having referred to this ancient example of parody in his discussion of the burlesque in this way, Home (p. 359) makes some specific comments on parody in which he distinguishes it from 'every species of ridicule', and writes that 'it inlivens a gay subject by imitating some important incident that is serious: it is ludicrous, and may be risible; but ridicule is not a necessary ingredient'. Later, however, Home adds (p. 360) that 'though ridicule, as observed above, is no necessary ingredient in a parody, yet there is no opposition between them: ridicule may be successfully employ'd in a parody; and a parody not less successfully to promote ridicule.'

Bond does not criticise Home's discussion of the burlesque in terms of style and subject-matter,[35] and he and his followers have not been alone in their use of distinctions between form and content in their definitions of high and low burlesque in this century. Given the inclusion of parody in the forms of burlesque spoken of by Bond and his followers, and the description of parody in terms of form and content by them as well as by others following the seventeenth- and

32 Karrer, who is referring to Home's *Elements of Criticism* (London, 1824), pp. 167 f., ends his quotation at this point.   33 Home, vol. 1, p. 351.
34 Ibid., p. 352. Home adds here that 'it is beyond the power of imagination, to form a clear and lively image of frogs and mice, acting with the dignity of the highest of our species'.
35 See Bond, p. 57 where Bond also notes that Home 'makes his division of burlesque depend on the excitation of mere laughter or of ridicule'.

eighteenth-century traditions which have been described previously,[36] the point must again be made that while some parodists have changed the content of a work while imitating its form, others have changed both the form and the content of their target and created incongruities from it which did not rely upon a contrast of those two elements alone.

This last point has been seen to be true of both modern and ancient parody. The extension of the term 'parodia' to all sorts of parodic quotation by the Aristophanic scholiasts had meant that even the ancient words for parody were not just applied to the parody of generic works with a recognisable form. The subject of the Aristophanic scholiasts, Aristophanes himself, may also be said to have changed other works with comic effect by using a variety of different parodistic methods: from the imitation and comic transformation of a variety of tragic forms and subjects to the parodistic quotation of a variety of different statements. Several examples, of varying kinds, could be given, and, as seen previously, the ancient terms for parody were in general not defined, or used, on the basis of any hard and fast distinction between form and content as assumed in the previously given distinctions between parody and travesty.

Other students of the ancient forms of parody apart from those mentioned previously, such as Householder and Lelièvre, have recognised this point. Wilhelm Horn, for instance, has suggested when quoting Grellmann's definition of parody as something which differs from travesty because it retains the formal elements of the original while changing the content in an unsuitable manner, where travesty retains the content of the original while clothing it in a new and unsuitable form, that such a description of parody limits the definition of parody which we might give on the basis of its known ancient forms.[37] Yet another critic of Grellmann's influential article on parody, Alfred Liede, has also criticised the distinction between parody and travesty, in his article on parody in the second edition of the *Reallexikon der deutschen Literaturgeschichte* which replaces Grellmann's contribution to the first edition, when writing that travesties can

36 See, for instance, H. Grellmann, 'Parodie', in *Reallexikon der deutschen Literaturgeschichte*, vol. 2, edited by P. Merker and W. Stammler (Berlin, 1926/28), pp. 630–53; p. 630. As previously seen, Paul Maas' article in *Paulys Real-Encyclopädie der classischen Altertumswissenschaft* also applies a distinction between style and content to the description of parody.
37 See Wilhelm Horn, *Gebet und Gebetsparodie in den Komödien des Aristophanes* (Nuremberg, 1970), p. 36 and following pages.

contain parodies and that parodies can contain the elements ascribed to travesty.[38]

Despite the truth of this statement by Liede, most applications of the modern terms 'burlesque' and 'travesty' to parody have applied characteristics to the parody which are not only not as old as that ancient term or the works which it was used to describe, but not as suitable for, or as explanatory of, all the possible meanings and functions of the older term. When the ancient Greek mock-epics, or even Roman Menippean satires such as Seneca's 'Apocolocyntosis', are described as using both parody and travesty in the same text, the application of the word travesty to such works, and separation of its characteristics from parody, is also less historically accurate than the application of the word parody to them.

The use of the term 'high burlesque' to describe parodies of both the ancient and the modern period, and the use of the term 'low burlesque' to describe other aspects of the ancient parody as travesty, have not only applied an eighteenth-century concept of burlesque, and division between form and content, to ancient parody in an anachronistic and divisive manner, but have also led to a modern distinction between heroism and baseness, the high and the low, being applied to all types of works. This is particularly inappropriate, however, where authors have used parody and other such devices not just in order to bring a high work low, but to reduce the very distinctions between high and low upon which such canonisations are based,[39] or where they have simply ignored such distinctions.

As suggested previously, the largely negative character of the reception of parody as a form of little literary seriousness in the last few centuries may also be related to its ahistorical association with the less literary and more *buffo* characteristics of the burlesque, and with what were seen to be the more ridiculing 'levelling' uses of the latter.

After seeing his satiric and parodic play *The Historical Register for the Year 1736* followed by the Licensing Act of 1737 which gave the Lord Chamberlain powers to veto the performance of such works, Henry Fielding had made a clear distinction between the burlesque and the more ancient comedy in the Preface to his parodic novel *Joseph Andrews* of 1742, and, after describing it on its title page as having

---

38 See Liede, p.13.
39 And see also Ian Donaldson, *The World Upside Down. Comedy from Jonson to Fielding* (Oxford, 1970), pp. 7 ff. on the topic of levelling.

been 'written in imitation of the manner of Cervantes' (its full title was *The History of the Adventures of Joseph Andrews and of his Friend Mr. Abraham Adams. Written in Imitation of the Manner of CERVANTES, Author of Don Quixote*) had explicitly aligned his work with the more ancient form of the comedy as something less distortive than the burlesque.[40]

As with Joseph Addison's contrast of the comedy to the burlesque, this distinction was also based, however, on a radical reinterpretation, or avoidance, of the Aristotelian understanding of the nature of comedy as showing people to be worse than they are with regard to the ridiculous or the laughable. Without explicitly referring to this comment by Aristotle, Fielding wrote in his Preface of 1742 in line with Addison's division between the comic and the burlesque: 'Indeed, no two Species of Writing can differ more widely than the Comic and the Burlesque: for as the latter is ever the Exhibition of what is monstrous and unnatural, and where our Delight, if we examine it, arises from the surprizing Absurdity, as in appropriating the Manners of the highest to the lowest, or *è converso*; so in the former, we should ever confine ourselves strictly to Nature from the just Imitation of which, will flow all the Pleasure we can this way convey to a sensible Reader.'[41]

Later in his Preface to *Joseph Andrews* Fielding does refer to Aristotle as claiming that villainy is not the object of the ridiculous in comedy[42] (Aristotle has been translated as writing in his *Poetics*, chapter 5, that 'the Ridiculous may be defined as a mistake or deformity not productive of pain or harm to others'[43]), but again does not explicitly refer to Aristotle's prior comment that comedy shows men to be worse than they are with regard to the ridiculous,[44] and criticises Aristotle for not saying what the object of the ridiculous might in fact be.

For Fielding the answer to this last question of what the object of the ridiculous might be is 'affectation', and this is an answer which also brings him closer to Plato than to Aristotle. This is so not only because affectation is preferred by Fielding as the chief characteristic of the ridiculous to the 'ugliness' to which Aristotle had related 'the

40 See Henry Fielding, *Joseph Andrews*, edited Martin C. Battestin (Oxford, 1967), pp. 3–11.   41 Ibid., p. 4.   42 Ibid., p. 7.
43 See Ingram Bywater's translation of Aristotle, *De Poetica*, chapter 5.
44 Fielding, *Joseph Andrews*, p. 7 does, however, refer to Aristotle as describing 'the Ridiculous' as being 'proper to Comedy'.

ridiculous', to use the word chosen by both Addison and Fielding (Fielding's Preface also goes on to criticise those 'who can look on Ugliness, Infirmity, or Poverty, as ridiculous in themselves'[45]), but because it recalls Plato's suggestion in the dialogue between Protarchus and Socrates in the *Philebus* that the ridiculous can be defined as a failure of self-knowledge, and that this is made the object of laughter in the comedy when a character fails to live up to a false self-image of wealth, appearance, or virtue.[46]

Fielding had also been working in 1742 on a translation with the Reverend Mr Young of Aristophanes' *Plutus*, which they published as *'Plutus, the God of Riches. A Comedy'* from Aristophanes with a Dedication which recommended Aristophanes, and with a Preface which described him as 'one of the oldest Professors of the Comic Art' and as beloved of Plato.[47] Plato was, in addition, a philosopher admired by the third Earl of Shaftesbury, and it is the latter's suggestion that hardly any burlesque was to be found in the writings of the Ancients to which Fielding also refers in his 1742 Preface to *Joseph Andrews* when aligning his work with the more ancient form of the comedy.[48]

The rest of Lord Shaftesbury's statement on the burlesque had further suggested, in a contrast to Aristotle's description of comedy as developing together with democracy,[49] that it could not have been practised by the ancients because it was a form more typical of countries where tyranny prohibits the free expression of serious thought.[50] The use of the term burlesque to cover parody by many of his and Fielding's contemporaries (Fielding himself uses the two terms interchangeably at one point in his Preface to *Joseph Andrews* when he speaks of 'those Parodies or Burlesque Imitations'[51]) was, however, to enable some criticisms of the burlesque to help banish the name of comic parody from the canon of 'serious' and 'acceptable' literature at that time, and despite the parody's more ancient, comedic, and democratic, uses.

45 Ibid., p. 9.
46 See Plato, *Philebus*, translated by Harold N. Fowler (1925), (London and Cambridge, Mass., 1962), pp. 197–399; pp. 333 ff.
47 See Henry Fielding, *'Plutus, the God of Riches. A Comedy'* from *Aristophanes* (London, 1742). The Preface describes Plato as having had a copy of Aristophanes with him on his death bed.   48 See Fielding, *Joseph Andrews*, p. 5.
49 See Aristotle's *Poetics*, chapter 3, 1448a.
50 See Fielding, *Joseph Andrews*, p. 5, n.1.   51 Ibid., p. 4.

As will be seen again in the following sections on modern and late-modern theories and uses of parody, effects of this relegation of parody to the burlesque have included the development of a modern view of it as an inferior literary form, incapable of either complexity or seriousness, as well as of modern and 'late-modern' attempts to separate parody from both the burlesque and the comic in order to treat it as a more serious meta-fictional or 'intertextual' form. As will be seen in the paragraphs which follow, the identification of parody with other literary forms and devices has also led to misunderstandings about both its history and character, and many of the terms which are described below are so described in order that their differences from parody, as well as their similarities to it, may become more obvious.

Persiflage, 'pekoral', plagiarism, and hoax

The term *persiflage*, which is derived from the French, is defined in the *OED* as 'light banter or raillery; bantering, frivolous talk', or as a 'frivolous manner of treating any subject'.[52] It has also been used to describe the light satirical mocking of another's work and like some applications of the word 'burlesque' can also denote a comic or mocking 'mimicry'. When applied to something parodic the term 'persiflage' is, however, usually more descriptive of the attitude of the parodist than of the structure or techniques of the parody, and, while it may sometimes be used to describe mimicry, is not necessarily concerned with the comic quotation and transformation of literary works, as is the literary parody.

In his article 'Was parodiert die Parodie?', Hans Kuhn has introduced the term *pekoral* from the Swedish, where it can designate an unintentionally comic or stylistically incompetent piece of writing by a 'would-be' but untalented poet or writer.[53] Given this meaning, the word pekoral may also be applied to unintentional parodies written by incompetent authors, or *poetasters*, who have unsuccessfully imitated another style or work.

Kuhn further defines the pekoral as implying a certain naiveté on the part of the author, a discrepancy between intention and capacity, and a lack of stylistic sensitivity and judgement as to which devices are

52 See the *OED*, 2nd edn (Oxford, 1989), volume 11, p. 595.
53 See Hans Kuhn, 'Was parodiert die Parodie?', in *Neue Rundschau*, vol. 85 (1974), pp. 600–18; p. 604.

suited to which subject, but also suggests that the perception of the 'pekoral' character of a work may vary depending upon the education of the reader and the literary norms of their time.

Definitions of *bathos* which describe it as the product of an unsuccessful and therefore ludicrous attempt to portray pathos in art further suggest that its examples might be described more broadly as examples of the 'pekoral',[54] and several of the works collected together in Charles Lee's and D. B. Wyndham Lewis' *The Stuffed Owl. An Anthology of Bad Verse* of 1930 could also be described by that last word.[55] As the play of Snug the Joiner in Shakespeare's *A Midsummer Night's Dream* attests, the 'pekoral' or the 'poetastic' or 'bathetic' work has long been made the subject of more sophisticated parodies,[56] while Ben Jonson's parody of other writers in his play *The Poetaster*[57] also gives some idea of how parody may be used to present another work as an unintended farce or failure.[58]

The term *plagiarism* has sometimes been used to characterise as literary theft the close imitation or quotation of other literary texts which can occur in the initial stages of parody. Plagiarism itself, however, is usually much more concerned to conceal or destroy its sources than is the parody, and does not intentionally set out to reveal its purpose by the use of comic incongruity as does the parody in its later stages.

The literary *hoax* is also more concerned to conceal its intentions than is the parody, and may be described as an ironic simulation of another work where there is an intention to deceive another into thinking that that which they are reading is something other than what it is. (Y is intentionally made to look like X in order to trick the reader into thinking that they are reading X.) Parody cannot normally

---

54 See, for example, *The New Encyclopædia Britannica*, 15th edn of 1974 (Chicago etc., 1991), Micropædia, vol. 1, p. 958. By contrast, the *OED*, 2nd edn, vol. 1, p. 1001 describes *bathos* with less emphasis on a lack of intentional humour as the 'ludicrous descent from the elevated to the commonplace in writing or speech; anticlimax'.

55 See Charles Lee and D. B. Wyndham Lewis, *The Stuffed Owl. An Anthology of Bad Verse* (London, 1930).

56 George Kitchin suggests in his *A Survey of Burlesque and Parody in English* (London, 1931) , p. 63 that this 'play-within-a-play' may also have served to parody an actual work.

57 See *The Complete Plays of Ben Jonson*, ed. G. A. Wilkes, vol. 2 (Oxford, 1981), pp. 119–228.

58 Some of the parodic elements in Jonson's *The Poetaster* are discussed by Kitchin, pp. 57 ff.

be equated with the hoax as the parodist will usually aim to create a comic or surprise effect by letting readers or viewers realise that they are receiving something different from the work which is being parodistically imitated. (Y is suddenly given instead of X.) The literary hoax may, however, also involve the imitation of another's work, when Y is being made to look like X, in a way which is similar to the imitation made of work X in a parody prior to its unexpected and comic transformation into something else, and may even conceal some parody proper within itself.

Quintilian also speaks in Book 9.2.35 of his *Institutio Oratoria* of fictional letters which may sound like parody, although this is where he speaks of parody simply as παρῳδή, and as 'a name drawn from songs sung in imitation of others, but employed by an abuse of language to designate imitation in verse or prose'. The *Letters of Obscure Men* of 1516, by Ulrich von Hutten and others,[59] may, however, be taken as an example of a collection of fictional letters which imitates the style of those it is attacking in the manner of both the literary hoax and of the preliminary stages of the parody and which uses parody proper to make an added attack on its target and to signal its differences from the latter to its initiated audience. Such parody-hoaxes further establish for themselves at least two audiences, of those who will be deceived by the imitation of another work, and of those who will understand its parodic and satiric purposes, and in doing this are usually both satiric and ironic.

'Counterfeited' letters of the type of the *Letters of Obscure Men* have also been popular amongst parodists seeking to insinuate themselves into the camp of their target whilst using that target's style as their disguise. The parodistic wearing of the mask of a target has, however, sometimes led to confusion amongst readers and critics as to the intentions of the parodist in question, and, occasionally, to the misfiring of an intended hoax. In the case of 'Ern Malley', a fictitious Australian poet, motor mechanic and insurance salesman, who was invented by the poets James McAuley and Harold Stewart to trick the modernists of their literary world into accepting a parodistic imitation of their modernist ideals as the work of a great modern poet, the acclaim given McAuley's and Stewart's parody as a great modern

---

59 See, for instance, the edition, *Epistolæ Obscurorum Virorum*. The Latin text with an English rendering, notes, and an historical introduction by Francis Griffin Stokes (London, 1909).

work of art by some may be seen not only as a reflection on the poetic dexterity of the hoaxers, but also as an unintended consequence of the modernity of both parody and its 'intertextual' techniques and of the related forms used by the hoaxers to create their modernist verses.[60]

James Joyce was one modernist who was both a parodist and a writer of literary hoaxes. While Joyce's *Ulysses* may be taken as a classic example of a modernist, and even 'pre-post-modernist',[61] use of parody in prose, a different kind of parody, and one which might even be said to have ironically imitated that used in some parodic hoaxes, is to be found in Joyce's work of the 1920s entitled 'Litter to Mr James Joyce'.[62] This 'pseudo' or 'fictitious' letter bears the signature of Vladimir Dixon, and, in the tradition of the *Letters of Obscure Men*, sets out to parody the ignorance and antipathy of Joyce's critics by imitating, and exaggerating, the ignorance of their style and prejudices.

Other examples of works which have used the persona of another, fictitious author to parody certain other literary genres for comic effect include Frederick Crews' parodies of the critical article in his *The Pooh Perplex. A Freshman Casebook* of 1963, Jorge Luis Borges' and Adolfo Bioy-Casares' *Six Problems for Don Isidoro Parodi* of 1942 and *Chronicles of Bustos Domecq* of 1967,[63] and Malcolm Bradbury's *My Strange Quest for Mensonge. Structuralism's Hidden Hero. With a Foreword/Afterword by Michel Tardieu (Professor of Structuralist Narratology, University of Paris) translated by David Lodge* of 1987.

Not all literary hoaxes have been as comic, or have been intended to be so easily discovered as those referred to above, but those using parody have, as suggested previously, both imitated the style of their victim in the manner of the hoax and then distorted that which is being imitated in order to reveal their own ironic or satiric purpose.[64]

---

60 See *Ern Malley's Poems*, edited by Max Harris (Adelaide, 1971). One recent description of the poems as potential early examples of the post-modernist technique of bricolage also overlooks the fact, despite the cautious nature of its wording, that that which it describes as post-modernist bricolage is simply a modernistic, if also ironic, use of pastiche.

61 This latter designation is discussed further in chapter 4.

62 See *Our Exagmination round his Factification for Incamination of Work in Progress* by Samuel Beckett and others (1929), (London, 1972), pp. 193–4.

63 I am particularly grateful to Miranda Hughes for drawing my attention to these works, and for discussions on them and others.

64 See also W. L. Renwick's Introduction, in W. E. Aytoun, *Stories and Verses* (Edinburgh, 1964), p. xvii, to W. E. Aytoun's *Firmilian* and its parody of the

Pastiche

Pastiche has also been described as a type of literary *forgery* by some, although it has not always been associated with the intention to forge, or to hoax, and need not be so associated. Peter and Linda Murray's *A Dictionary of Art and Artists* is but one work which defines pastiche as forgery. It describes 'PASTICHE, PASTICCIO' as 'an imitation or forgery which consists of a number of motives taken from several genuine works by any one artist recombined in such a way as to give the impression of being an independent original creation by that artist'.[65] Yet not only may pastiche describe the combination of elements from one or more works in another where the intention to forge is not to be found, but the recombination of different elements which is described as being characteristic of pastiche may be found in many of the so-called 'original creations' to which pastiche is contrasted in such definitions.

Despite its more recent history and differences from parody, pastiche has also been used as a synonym for parody, and especially in French literature, where it has, for example, been used to describe both conscious and unconscious parody.[66] Pastiche, however, is not only a much more recent term than parody, but differs from the latter in describing a more neutral practice of compilation which is neither necessarily critical of its sources, nor necessarily comic.

While the even more modern form of *montage* may be distinguished from parody because it does not necessarily involve the comic contrast of works found in parody, it can also be distinguished from pastiche in works of art when objects are mounted together with less of the integration than is usual in the pastiche. Since both 'montage' and 'pastiche' have been applied to other, extra-artistic forms in recent years, these differences between them have, however, become less sharp, and 'montage' (from the French '*monter*', 'to mount') has been able to be defined in the *OED* as meaning figuratively, 'the process of

Scottish 'Spasmodics', a 'Storm and Stress' group of writers of the second half of the nineteenth century, and on the hoaxing of their readers.

65 See Peter and Linda Murray, *A Dictionary of Art and Artists* (1959) (Harmondsworth, 1960), p. 234.

66 See also the discussion of Proust and parody in Valerie Minogue's 'The Uses of Parody: Parody in Proust and Robbe-Grillet', in *Parody. A Symposium*, edited by Margaret A. Rose, in *Southern Review*, 13/1, 1980, pp. 53–65.

making a mixture, blend, or medley of various elements; a pastiche; a sequence, miscellany'.[67]

One authority on the subject of pastiche, Leif Ludwig Albertsen, has further distinguished pastiche from parody by describing both parody and travesty as being different from pastiche in polemically reforming their models.[68] For Albertsen pastiche also involves the reproduction of both the form and the content of a work,[69] and such pastiche will be seen to differ from parody by those who have defined the latter as the imitation of the form of a work involving a change to its content. Because it has already been seen that such a definition of parody has its problems, the pastiche which is not also parody is, however, best distinguished from the latter because its compilation – or 'double-coding' – of different works does not usually have the comically incongruous structure or comic effect of the parody. As with several other of the forms discussed here, pastiche may nonetheless be used by a parodist as a part of a parody, or some parodic elements included in the pastiche as a whole.

The term pastiche as applied to the arts today derives from the Italian word 'pasticcio', and means in general terms (from the translation of the Italian *pasticcio* as a 'pasty' or 'pie' dish containing several different ingredients, and from the application of that word to certain paintings) the compilation of motives from several works. Such a definition is also suggested in the *Oxford English Dictionary* where the word 'pastiche' is described as deriving from the Italian *pasticcio* and where the latter is defined as meaning a 'medley of various ingredients; a hotchpotch, farrago, jumble'.[70] For the *OED* the word 'pasticcio', which it uses to cover 'pastiche', can describe more specifically: '**a**. In the original It. sense, a pie containing numerous ingredients, of which macaroni and some form of meat are the chief constituents. **b**. An opera, cantata, or other composition, made up of various pieces from different authors or sources, a pot-pourri. **c**. A picture or design made up of fragments pieced together or copied with modification from an

---

67 See the *OED*, 2nd edn, vol. 9, p. 1039. (And see also the discussion in chapter 4 of 'bricolage' for another example of a word which has sometimes been used to describe pastiche.)

68 See Leif Ludwig Albertsen, 'Der Begriff des Pastiche', *Orbis Litterarum*, vol. 26, no. 1, 1971, pp. 1–8; p. 2.

69 See Albertsen, pp. 5–6, and see also Wolfgang Karrer on Albertsen in Karrer, p. 49.

70 See the *OED*, 2nd edn, 1989, vol. 11, p. 321, where Florio is also quoted as defining *pasticcio* as 'any manner of pastie or pie'.

original, or in professed imitation of the style of another artist; also, the style of a picture, etc.'[71] Examples of the use of the term *pasticcio* given in the *OED* include a statement dated 1706 on the art of painting which describes 'those pictures that are neither originals nor copies, which the Italians call *Pastici* ... because as the several things that season a pasty are reduc'd to one taste, so counterfeits that compose a *pastici* tend only to effect one truth'.[72]

Although the use of the word 'counterfeit' in the above quotation does not necessarily imply a moral condemnation of the use of pastiche from that particular author, but describes, more simply, an imitation, many later uses of the term pastiche in English have implied such moral evaluation, and without the moral or negative colouring of their usage being explained as something which has been added to the term. HRH the Prince of Wales' *A Vision of Britain* alludes to the existence of this problem in the use of the word pastiche when it refers to people using the word 'pastiche' disparagingly with respect to architecture and adds: 'They mean "fake" or a direct copy, something utterly unimaginative. But there's nothing "fake" about building in an established tradition, or in trying to revive one.'[73]

In addition to the fact that pastiche may be used in imaginative rather than derivative ways, it is clearly not the case that an eighteenth- or nineteenth-century architect imitating a classical style in a building made with contemporary materials, or a post-modern architect who 'double-codes' an ancient with a modern style, are offering us fakes or forgeries of the works which they have compiled in theirs with the aim of having us believe that their work is really classical, or ancient. As such examples indicate, the description of pastiche as meaning a fake or a forgery cannot easily, or sensibly, be used for architectural pastiche in which a compilation of different styles is deliberately used to constitute a new historicistic style,[74] and is also not appropriate for those works of art in other media in which a compilation of different styles or motifs is used deliberately, and without the concealment which is characteristic of both the forgery and the more serious hoax.

71 Ibid.
72 Ibid. And see also Wido Hempel, 'Parodie, Travestie und Pastiche', in *Germanisch-Romanische Monatsschrift*, Neue Folge, vol. 15 (1965), pp. 150–76; p. 167.
73 See HRH the Prince of Wales, *A Vision of Britain* (London, 1989), p. 73.
74 That is, a style which deliberately includes references to other now historical styles.

Despite its initial explanation of the more mechanical and neutral meanings of the term, the *OED* goes on to list several applications of the term pastiche which use it in a condemnatory way as well as some others which use it to praise the 'pasticheur', but without explaining that all of these uses have added a value judgement to the more neutral technique of compilation which the word describes. Even Edward Lucie-Smith's *Dictionary of Art Terms*, which describes *pastiche* (French) and *pasticcio* (Italian) in largely neutral terms as 'a work of art using a borrowed style and usually made up of borrowed elements, but not necessarily a direct copy', adds with some condemnation of the form that 'a pastiche often verges on conscious or unconscious caricature, through its exaggeration of what seems most typical in the original model'.[75]

Some evaluations of pastiche have also stressed its positive potential in order to counteract the more negative descriptions given of it or of its related forms by others. Leif Ludwig Albertsen's article on the concept of pastiche which was referred to previously suggests, for example, not only that pastiche should now be dissociated from such negative terms as 'counterfeit',[76] but that it is a way of reviving things from the past for the pasticheur's age[77] which indicates the presence of some sympathy for the elements borrowed by it.

Some critics who have described the term as neutral have also felt the need to defend it against accusations of being a derivative or lesser literary form. D. S. Raven, for example, writes in the Preface to his *Poetastery and Pastiche. A Miscellany* of 1966, that he has used the term pastiche in his title 'because that word, as it seems to me, is associated relatively little with the *moral* judgements passed on derivative art'.[78] After noting that most critics have no high opinion of derivative art and that 'at best, such critics call it *parody*, conceding a degree of (rather naughty) skill to the imitator, and implying a certain fault, maybe, in the original author who has left himself open to it', and that 'at worst they call it *plagiarism*', Raven (pp. 5 ff.) goes on to argue that 'little enough writing is wholly underivative', that 'imitation has not always been regarded in this unfavourable light', and that 'the great Roman poets, for instance, were nearly all imitators to a remarkable extent'. Raven also appears to feel the need to defend such writing

75 See Edward Lucie-Smith, *The Thames and Hudson Dictionary of Art Terms* (London, 1984), p. 141.
76 See Albertsen, pp. 2–3.   77 Ibid., p. 8.
78 See D. S. Raven, *Poetastery and Pastiche. A Miscellany* (Oxford, 1966), p. 5.

when he adds (p. 6) that 'admitted that derivative writing is less "worthy" than what is strictly "original", it still need not be regarded as positively vicious, and may carry amusement and even instruction with it'.

As will be seen later, in the sections on post-modern parody and pastiche in chapter 4, the view that pastiche may have some positive aesthetic and other functions has also been expressed in the pastiche of a pluralism of styles in some recent post-modern architecture, and despite, if not in direct reaction to, the attempts of some other critics to give post-modern pastiche a bad name. Although it has been attacked by some literary and cultural critics in recent years for its use of pastiche, post-modern architecture has differed from many other media in which pastiche has been used in that it has been able to extend an architectural tradition of using pastiche in which a more neutral understanding and description of it as a device for the transference of a design from one work or medium to another had been allowed to develop in earlier centuries. This was also to some extent in contrast to the condemnation of pastiche as derivative which was to be found in the more individually author-based and originality-orientated painterly and literary arts.

While the history of architecture demonstrates the existence of a variety of different uses of pastiche in that field, and assessments of them, Russell Sturgis' *A Dictionary of Architecture and Building* of 1902[79] is but one work which reflects the way in which pastiche has previously been used by at least some contributors to architectural history with less moral condemnation of its derivativeness than in other arts, and especially in those in which the importance of individual original genius has been stressed.

Sturgis' dictionary defines pastiche in largely neutral terms which are still applicable to the use of pastiche in post-modern architecture today: '*Pasticcio*, pastiche: 'A. A work of art produced in deliberate imitation of another or several others, as of the works of a master taken together' and 'B. Especially, in decorative art, the modification for transference to another medium, of any design. Thus, the cover of a book may be the *pasticcio* of a mosaic pavement.'[80]

79 See Russell Sturgis, *A Dictionary of Architecture and Building* (London and New York, 1902), 3 vols., vol. 3, p. 73.

80 Ibid., p. 73. One other dictionary which places some emphasis on architecture, J. W. Mollett's *An Illustrated Dictionary of Words used in Art and Archaeology* (London, 1883) also defines pastiche without condemning it as derivative when it

One other example of pastiche in which designs from one medium have been transferred into another may be found in the neo-classical furniture designs of Robert Adam or Thomas Chippendale in which the façades or decorations of classical stone and marble architecture have been reduced and then imitated in wood. One more recent example of pastiche in architecture which has even been described as translating Chippendale's furniture designs back into architecture is Philip Johnson's 'post-modern' *AT&T* building.

There are, moreover, many more examples of post-modern pastiche which could be named,[81] and these and other aspects of pastiche will be discussed further in chapter 4.

Quotation, 'cross-reading', cento, and contrafact

While the non-parodic quotation found in some pastiche may be described as leading a reader or viewer to make associations between two contingent and usually compatible works, the function of the quotation in the parody can be said to be to connect and contrast disparate texts so that either their concealed identity or lack of identity will be brought into the foreground with some comic effect. This technique of parodic quotation could also be compared to the game of 'cross-reading' described below, which forces the reader to make associations between texts not normally placed together. Here too, however, the result, as in the pastiche, may not always be comic, while the creation of comedy when it is created must be attributed largely to the reader rather than to any comic author.

In his 'Nachahmung der englischen *Cross-readings*' ('Imitation of the English *Cross-readings*') the Enlightenment scholar and satirist Georg Christoph Lichtenberg describes the game of 'cross-readings' as one in which connections are made between unconnected subjects in a newspaper of mixed contents by the 'player' reading one line of a vertically set newspaper article column horizontally into another across the page.[82] In this way, as Lichtenberg's own various examples

describes 'Pasticcio' on its p. 245 as 'an imitation of the style of another painter in an independent design'.

81 See, for example, Charles Jencks, *The Language of Post-Modern Architecture* (1977) 6th revised enlarged edn (London and New York, 1991). (Post-modern pastiche is also usually more than mere 'façadism', or the pasting of a façade on to the front of a building.)

82 See Lichtenberg's 'Nachahmung der englischen Cross-Readings', in *Georg Christoph Lichtenbergs Vermischte Schriften. Neue vermehrte, von dessen Söhnen*

show, unexpected and incongruous associations may eventuate, and the seriousness of each article be undermined. (One example of Lichtenberg's 'imitations' of this game from the personal columns reads: 'On the 12th a man died in his 104th year / and was christened Friderica Sophia.'[83]) While the comic effects of such 'cross-readings' are to some degree dependent upon the placement of words in a column which neither the writers nor the readers themselves have controlled, as well as on the reader's ability to make something new from them from their choice of lines, such incongruous associations and 'collages'[84] have often served a parodic and comic function when simulated in literary works, and may be found in some cases to be similar to the *parodistic use of the cento,* in which many different quotations may be strung together without obvious rhyme or reason other than that different quotations are mixed incongruously and humorously where they would not necessarily have been so mixed by another author.

Lelièvre, in speaking of the closeness of the *cento* itself to parody, writes: 'Certainly *centones* involve the manipulation of an original work and the application of an author's verses to a situation not intended by him with the contrast which is part of the essence of parody. On the other hand the element of literary criticism which is sometimes found in parody is rare in the cento.'[85] In addition to there being a lack of criticism in the cento form, there is a lack of comic effect in most of its examples, save when they are used for satiric or parodic purposes. As with many other forms of quotation, the ambivalence of artistic parody is also generally lacking in the cento.

Parodic quotations are also unlike the authoritative quotation in that they usually do not relate contingent texts to reinforce or support the authority of an author, but to connect humorously unlike subjects in order to make ironic or startling comments on them which may be

veranstaltete Original-Ausgabe (Göttingen, 1844–53), vol. 2 (Göttingen, 1844), pp. 63 ff.

83 See Lichtenberg, vol. 2, p. 65, and see also the discussion of Lichtenberg's game of cross-readings in Karl Riha, *Cross-Reading und Cross-Talking. Zitat-Collagen als poetische und satirische Technik* (Stuttgart, 1971), pp. 6 ff.

84 'Collage' (from the French 'coller', 'to stick') describes the application of one material onto another (such as, as in some works by Picasso, fragments of newspaper onto a painting), and usually produces a dislocation of the elements of the whole. See also Edward Lucie-Smith, *The Thames and Hudson Dictionary of Art Terms* (London, 1984), p. 52.

85 F. J. Lelièvre, 'The Basis of Ancient Parody', p. 76.

of a humorous and/or critical nature. This has the effect of both making the quoted text appear 'strange', as produced by the device described by the Russian formalists as *priyom ostranneniya*,[86] and of associating it with the work of the parodist in a manner in which it was not previously associated. As in other forms of parody, parodic cross-reading may see a 'semantic shift' or change in meaning accompany the structural changes resulting from the comparison and contrast of the two texts.

The basic technique used by literary parody in the quotation of parts or of the whole of another text is also important in establishing the ambivalence of the parodist's attitude to the object of criticism in the structure of the parody text. Unlike satire, the parody makes the 'victim', or object, of its attack a part of its own structure, and its reception is thus to some extent influenced by the reception of the object of its criticism, the text which is made a part of the parodist's text.

The function of the specific techniques used by parody in refunctioning a quoted text can only be properly analysed in the context of the parodic works in which they are used. Common types of techniques have, however, been given labels now in general use. Erwin Rotermund, for example, has listed total or partial caricature, substitution, addition, and subtraction,[87] and to these may be added exaggeration, condensation, contrast, as well as the creation of discrepancy or incongruity. The overall function of these devices used by the parodist is to assimilate 'Text B' into 'Text A' as its second code, and (after fulfilling other functions, such as the evocation of the expectations of the reader) to ironise, criticise, or refunction Text B in some comic fashion. In the course of the parody, Text B can also be used as a mask for the parodist or for the target and/or its readership, as well as as an important structural part of the parodist's own text.

The use of quotation to establish comic discrepancy or incongruity as well as contingency between texts distinguishes parodic quotation from most other forms of quotation and literary imitation and often suggests the presence of a more critical attitude on the part of the parodist to the naive imitation or reception of other texts.

86 See, for example, Viktor Shklovsky's 'Art as Technique', in Lee T. Lemon and Marion J. Reis (eds.), *Russian Formalist Criticism: Four Essays* (Lincoln, Nebraska, 1965), pp. 3–24; p. 12, and the discussion of the Russian formalists in chapter 3.
87 See Erwin Rotermund, *Die Parodie in der modernen deutschen Lyrik* (Munich, 1963), p. 9.

One other form of imitation which should be distinguished from parody because of the absence of the comic from its traditional forms is the *contrafact* or *contrafactum* (from the Latin *contrafacere*, meaning 'to counterfeit' in the sense of 'to make against') which is a word applied in mediaeval and Renaissance musicology to the substitution of one sung text for another where the same music is used.[88]

Satire

Parody has often been used for what have been described as satiric purposes, but the following section will point first of all to the more significant differences between satire and parody.[89]

As with several other older terms, including parody, some dispute has surrounded the definition of satire. The *Oxford English Dictionary* notes, for example, that formerly the word satire was often confused or associated with 'SATYR' and that this confusion was based on the notion that the Latin *satira* (from which our word for satire is said to derive) came from the Greek *satyr*.[90] Now, however, suggests the *OED*, the word *satira* is to be regarded as a later form of *satura*, meaning 'medley', from the phrase *lanx satura*, meaning a 'full dish' and, by extension, 'a medley of ingredients'.[91]

In addition to describing satire as deriving from the word 'satura' the *OED* goes on to define satire as meaning in both ancient and modern usage a poem (or, in modern use, 'sometimes a prose composition') in which 'prevailing vices or follies are held up to ridicule'. While the derivation of this meaning is not explained by the etymology given in the *OED*, others have pointed to the role played by the association of 'satire' with 'satyr' in our understanding of the meaning of the former as ridicule.[92] Yet others have questioned the

88 The *OED*, vol. 3, p. 840 adds to its description of *contrafactum* the phrase 'as the substitution of a sacred text for a secular one or vice versa', but also quotes descriptions of it which confuse it with parody. And see also Th. Verweyen and G. Witting, *Die Kontrafaktur: Vorlage und Verarbeitung in Literatur, bildender Kunst, Werbung und politischem Plakat* (Constance, 1987) for a more extensive discussion of the 'contrafact' and criticism of confusions of it with parody.

89 Contrary to Linda Hutcheon's 1985 account of my *Parody//Meta-Fiction* of 1979, it also distinguished parody from satire. (See, for example, its section 'Satire and Parody'.)   90 See the *OED*, 2nd edn, vol. 14, p. 500.

91 See also Michael Coffey, *Roman Satire* (London, 1976), pp. 11 ff. for an extended discussion of *satura* and the definition of satire.

92 See, for example, John Burke Shipley's article 'Satire' in *Dictionary of World Literary Terms. Forms, Techniques, Criticism* (1943), new enlarged and completely

extension of the word 'satura' to cover all satire, and Keith Aldrich has suggested that 'satura' is 'represented by the extant writings of only three poets: Horace, Persius, and Juvenal' and designates there a 'liberality of thematic invention and a degree of looseness of style within a poem that make it a kind of poetic medley'.[93]

As will be seen presently from the case of Menippean satire, the two aspects of *satire* of medley and ridicule have been associated with forms which have since been called satire, however, from at least the time of Menippus, in the mid-third century BC. In English letters, John Dryden's *Discourse Concerning the Original and Progress of Satire* of 1693 had also referred to the derivation of satire from *satura* and had both described the latter as meaning a 'full dish' or a 'hotchpotch' and referred to the critical functions of satire.[94]

A few decades later Henry Fielding's play *The Historical Register for the Year 1736* also presented the character of a satirical playwright called 'Medley', whose purpose was to ridicule the 'vicious and the foolish'. When Medley is asked in Act I, scene i of Fielding's play to describe his 'Design', he replies that it is 'to ridicule the vicious and foolish Customs of the Age, and that in a fair manner, without Fear, Favour or Ill-nature, and without Scurrility, ill Manners, or common Place'.[95] Medley further suggests his purpose to be one of a comic catharsis of sorts when he adds that he hopes 'to expose the reigning Follies in such a manner, that men shall laugh themselves out of them before they feel they are touch'd'.[96]

Despite the fact that some parody may appear to treat its target in a manner similar to satire in making it the object of laughter, one major factor which distinguishes the parody from satire is, as already noted, the parody's use of the preformed material of its 'target' as a constituent part of its own structure. Satire, on the other hand, need not be restricted to the imitation, distortion, or quotation of other literary texts or preformed artistic materials, and when it does deal

revised edition, edited by Joseph T. Shipley (London, 1970), pp. 286–90; pp. 286 ff.

93 See Keith Aldrich, 'The imitative nature of Roman satire', in *Proceedings of the 4th Congress of the International Comparative Literature Association 1964*, edited by François Jost, 2 vols., vol. 2 (The Hague, 1966), pp. 789–96; p. 792.

94 See John Dryden, ed. George Watson, vol. 2, p. 105.

95 See Henry Fielding, *The Historical Register for the Year 1736* (London, 1737), p. 4.

96 Ibid. And see Act III, scene i of Fielding's play for a description of Medley as a satirist.

with such preformed material, need not make itself as dependent upon it for its own character as does the parody, but may simply make fun of it as a target external to itself.

Tuvia Shlonsky also writes in an article entitled 'Literary Parody. Remarks on its Method and Function'[97] that 'to subordinate parody to satire is to undermine its literary exclusiveness in which resides its particular power, function and effect'. Shlonsky's additional claim that while parody is not indifferent to the extra-literary (social, religious, or philosophical) norms essential to satire, 'the norms with which it deals are strictly literary', tends, however, to restrict even the literary parody too much to the literary, so that, for example, the use made of parody by such as Cervantes to depict the relationship of other literary works to external truths or realities cannot easily be explained by it. In refunctioning the preformed language material of other texts and discourses literary parody has often created allusions to another author, another reader, and their 'norms', as well as to the relationship between the text, or discourse, and its social context. While literary parody may be distinguished from other forms of satire as a form dealing with the refunctioning of preformed literary and linguistic material, such a distinction should not imply that literary parody is therefore only concerned with literary norms.

Further differences between the satire and the parody are that the satirist may be concerned with attacking either that which is considered normative or distortions of the norms which they wish to protect, but that the parodist may also recreate or imitate certain norms or their distortions in order to attack or defend them in the parody text. If the perspective of some parodists may seem to be anti-normative and distortive, much parody has served to renew norms by recreating them in a new context before making them the subject of a new critique and analysis.

Shlonsky also concentrates on the more reductive uses of parody as a 'device to lay bare other devices', as the Russian formalists sometimes described parody, when he writes (p. 797) that 'in so far as parody is an imitation, it simply takes its generic characteristics from a specific original and since each parody may have a different genre for

97 Tuvia Shlonsky, 'Literary Parody. Remarks on its Method and Function', in *Proceedings of the 4th Congress of the International Comparative Literature Association 1964*, edited by François Jost, 2 vols., vol. 2 (The Hague, 1966), pp. 797–801; p. 797.

a model, in itself is generically neutral. In so far as it is not a simple imitation but a distortion of the original the method of parody is to disrealize the norms which the original tries to realize, that is to say, to reduce what is of normative status in the original to a convention or a mere device.'

Shlonsky even reveals the derivation of some of his understanding of parody to be from the Russian formalist reduction of it to a device for 'laying bare the device' later in his article when he discusses (p. 800) the analysis which can be made by the parodist of the fictional nature of literature: 'Non-parodic works which attempt to convince the reader of their truth and reality strive to blur the awareness of the reader as to the presence of a medium by the employment of various devices while effacing them as far as possible. Parody, on the other hand, can operate only when awareness of the reader is at its peak. Moreover, since it aims at sharpening the reader's awareness of the literary medium, parody employs the devices of its original while laying them bare, to use the term coined by the Russian Formalists. In general the parodic method is the extension, in various directions and to various degrees, of the device of laying bare the device. In its attempt to expose that illusion which it originally tries to conceal, parody has a close affinity with irony.'

The relationship between parody and irony will be returned to presently, while the problematic character of the Russian formalists' understanding of parody will be discussed in greater detail in chapter 3. To summarise some of the mechanics of specific parody which distinguish it from satire, it can be said that such parody works by juxtaposition, omission, addition, condensation and by discontinuance of the original structure and/or content of the literary or artistic context which it quotes, imitates, or alludes to in order comically to refunction it, and that it is hence to at least some extent ambivalently constructed from the target which it refunctions. While parody is in general a much more ambivalent form than satire, in that it makes its 'target' a part of its own work, when parody has been used in satire it has usually given the latter some of the ambivalence characteristic of parody, and helped to make new and multi-layered works of art from the process of satiric reduction.

The use of parody in literary satire has been popular since ancient times. In addition to works by Aristophanes and his followers, more 'modern', post-Renaissance satirical critiques of contemporary writers, such as the Duke of Buckingham's play *The Rehearsal* of 1665 (first published 1672) or Sheridan's *The Critic* of 1779, have all put parody to use in their invectives against bad writing or bad criticism, and this has been carried on into this century by both writers and critics.

Such parody has taken many different forms, and some contemporary examples will be referred to later. One earlier example of a work in which both irony and parody are used in a satire of other writers is Alexander Pope's 'Receipt to make an Epick Poem', which was first published in June 1713 and later used in chapter 15 of *The Art of Sinking in Poetry* of 1728.[98] In it Pope mocks those poetasters who had borrowed their poetic machinery from the Ancients, but who had used it without genius. To Pope their use of others' inventions could be seen as a type of home cooking for which the best cure might be a parodic receipt or recipe which would ironically mirror the faults of the cooks in question. As with Swift's *A Modest Proposal* for curing hunger in an overpopulated Ireland, Pope's recipe demanded wit enough in the reader to divine the crucial pinches of irony: 'For the *Fable. Take out of any old Poem, History-books, Romance, or Legend, (for instance* Geffry of Monmouth or Don Belianis of Greece) *those Parts of Story which afford most Scope for long Descriptions: Put these Pieces together, and throw all the Adventures you fancy into one Tale. Then take a Hero, whom you may chuse for the Sound of his Name, and put him into the midst of these Adventures: There let him work for twelve Books; at the end of which you may take him out, ready prepared to conquer or to marry; it being necessary that the Conclusion of an Epick Poem be fortunate.'*[99]

Many other examples of satire using parody and irony in both fiction and non-fiction as well as in mixtures of these forms might be given, and further comparisons and contrasts of satire and parody will be found in the following section on irony and parody. Firstly, however, something must be said about the case of Menippean satire, a genre named after Menippus of Gadara, a Cynic writing in the midthird century BC, in which use of parody with satire also shows how those different forms have long been used together.[100]

As will be seen in later sections of this work, Menippean satire has

---

98 See J. S. Cunningham (ed.), *Pope, The Rape of the Lock* (Oxford, 1966), pp. 100–3. Cunningham, p. 7 also comments on how Pope's *The Art of Sinking in Poetry* had parodistically 'inverted' Longinus' *On the Sublime*.

99 See Pope's 'Receipt to make an Epick Poem' of 1713, in Cunningham, pp. 101–2.

100 The 'Menippean satirist' Varro (116–27 BC) is said to have used the words 'saturae menippeae' for the genre and the latter is sometimes dated from the first century BC.

been attributed a role in the development of several writers who are discussed in this book as parodists. Eugene P. Kirk's *Menippean Satire: An Annotated Catalogue of Texts and Criticism* of 1980 refers, for instance, to Menippean satire living on in Swift, Fielding and Sterne,[101] and to how Menippean satire was 'an often-used form of humorous polemic over the history of [intellectual and theological] disputes up to the eighteenth century'.[102]

Kirk's page xi summary of the genre also shows it to have utilised a number of different other genres and forms, and to have understood satire as being both an instrument of criticism and a 'medley' of forms: 'The chief mark of the Menippean satire was unconventional diction. Neologisms, portmanteau words, macaronics, preciosity, coarse vulgarity, catalogues, bombast, mixed languages, and protracted sentences were typical of the genre, sometimes appearing all together in the same work. In outward structure Menippean satire was a medley – usually a medley of alternating prose and verse, sometimes a jumble of flagrantly digressive narrative, or again a potpourri of tales, songs, dialogues, orations, letters, lists and other brief forms, mixed together. Menippean topical elements included outlandish fictions (*i.e* fantastic voyages, dreams, visions, talking beasts) and extreme distortions of argument (often "paradoxes"). In theme, Menippean satire was essentially concerned with right learning or right belief. That theme often called for ridicule or caricature of some sham-intellectual or theological fraud. Yet sometimes the theme demanded exhortation to learning when books and studies had fallen into disuse and neglect.'

Kirk also names many different practitioners of Menippean satire, from Menippus himself to Varro, Petronius, Lucian, Seneca, Erasmus, Swift, Fielding, Rabelais, Cervantes, and Sterne, and emphasises that all are different. (Kirk even writes on his page xiv that 'there never was "one kind" of Menippean satire, not even in the writings of Menippus himself – for Menippus parodied broadly the different ancient forms of learned discourse'.) Kirk (p. xiv) adds with reference to Menippus' now lost parody that he 'chose to parody the established genres of philosophic discourse – the dialogue, symposium, epistle, treatise, testament and cosmography – by exaggerating their fictions and arguments, pushing their logic to an absurd extreme simply by taking

---

101 See Eugene P. Kirk, *Menippean Satire: An Annotated Catalogue of Texts and Criticism* (New York, 1980), p. ix.

102 Ibid., p. x. I am also grateful to Cathy Curtis for discussions on this topic.

the sages completely literally (*e.g.* Epicurus was born when some atoms fortunately collided), and by thrusting in verses, songs, iambics, curses and other unexpected and rambunctious material upon the formal learned genres.'

Parody, according to Kirk's Introduction and following bibliographic annotations, was also present in varying degrees in the works of other Menippean satirists. Indeed, ancient parody, such as that found in the works of Aristophanes, may have been one of their sources, in that several of the early examples of Menippean satire not only echo the comic and parodic dialogues of Aristophanes' plays – and the way in which those dialogues can interrupt the main action of the piece as well as the way in which they can be used to bring the gods or a hero down to earth – but also make reference to Aristophanes and his works.[103] Lucian of Samosata, of the second century AD, whose works were described by Joseph Addison as an example of the burlesque in which the gods are made to speak in the manner of mean persons, not only uses some of Aristophanes' parodic techniques, but also makes mention of Aristophanes in some of his satires,[104] and uses Menippus as a character in his *Conversations in the Underworld*, and as a character who carries on the satirist's unmasking of the pretentious after death.[105]

To summarise this section it may be said that there are several distinct differences between parody and satire – such as the way in which the parody may make its target contribute to its own text – but that parody may be used by the satirist to attack an author or reader through the evocation and mockery of a particular work with which they may be associated, and that the parody may sometimes have the satiric aim of using a target text or other preformed work to attack its author or audience.[106]

---

103 See also Kirk, p. 12 on Seneca and Petronius; Kirk, pp. 228–9 on J. Bompaire on Lucian; and Kirk p. 268 on Philip Pinkus on 'The New Satire of Augustan England' for references to the relationship of Menippean satire to Aristophanes.

104 Paul Turner also makes reference to the importance of allusion to literary tradition in the work of Lucian and other writers of the 'Second Sophistic' in his introduction to his translation of Lucian, in Lucian, *Satirical Sketches*, translated by Paul Turner (Harmondsworth, 1961), pp. 12 ff.

105 See Lucian, pp. 65 ff.

106 Some differences between parody and satire will also be summarised in diagrammatic form in the following section on parody and irony.

Irony

Both irony and parody may be said to confuse the normal processes of communication by offering more than one message to be decoded by the reader and this duplication of messages can be used, in either case, to conceal the author's intended meaning from immediate interpretation.

The term irony generally describes a statement of an ambiguous character, which includes a code containing at least two messages, one of which is the concealed message of the ironist to an 'initiated' audience, and the other the more readily perceived but 'ironically meant' message of the code. One example of irony in speech which can also illustrate the structure of at least some literary irony is that when one person looks out through a window at some unpleasant weather and passes the comment to another viewer of 'oh, what a lovely day!' he or she may be understood to be meaning something different to that which their statement says and appears to mean. (Saying such a statement when the weather is fine would not usually be received as irony, and neither would it be possible to have a statement received as ironic if there was no chance for its receiver to perceive the contrast between the statement and its subject which would show the former to be meaning something other than what it says.) The more common definitions of irony which describe it as 'saying what one does not mean', or as 'meaning something different from what one says', are also more easily understood when the duality of messages given in an ironic statement or code is spelt out.

In the parody the complex function of the dual meaning of the irony is matched by that of the dual text or code when the parodied text is used as a 'word-mask' or 'decoy-code' to conceal or complicate the message of the parodist. (X appears to be saying Y but is in fact saying something different.) While the ironist may also use parody to confuse a meaning, the parodist may use irony in the treatment of the parodied work and its messages in a variety of different ways – from, for example, the ironic use of the parodied text to conceal the parodist's identity or meaning to the use of irony in meta-linguistic or meta-fictional comments about that text and its place in the parodist's work.[107]

---

107 D. C. Muecke's *The Compass of Irony* (London, 1969) and later works analyse a variety of forms of irony. Other books on irony listed in the bibliography

Irony alone, however, is usually more 'cryptic' than most parody, which – though ambiguously containing a mixture of messages – usually also contains at least two distinct codes with two distinct sets of messages from more than the one author, in contrast to the combination of messages in the single code of the ironist.

Whereas, moreover, the difference between the 'apparent' message of the ironist's code and its 'real' message is generally left concealed for the recipient of the irony to decipher, the parodist usually combines and then comically (and, thus, noticeably) contrasts a quoted text or work with a new context, contrasting Code B of the parodied text with Code A of the parody text, and with the aim of producing laughter from the recognition of their incongruity. The author of the parody may also posit a reader who is assumed to have been the decoder of the parodied work as the object of satire, as Cervantes has done with his Don Quixote. Although parody may in these ways be more specific, and satiric, in its criticism than is irony, and may be more easily understood because of its presentation of two codes as well as messages, the parodied text generally also remains in the ambivalent position of belonging both to the work of the parodist and to the author and reading public attacked by the parodist.

Some modern discussions of irony and satire have criticised satire for lacking the subtlety of irony, and while parody has been seen to have shared and contained elements of both satire and irony, as well as the ambivalence towards its target indicated above, its associations with satire have led it to be criticised as being too destructive by some. By contrast, when Friedrich Schlegel wrote that Romantic irony was of a 'higher' (that is, more reflexive) form than satire, he had also asked whether irony might not be called 'self-parody',[108] and the previously noted importance attributed to Cervantes by the early Romantics may also be taken as an indication of the respect shown by them to the reflexivity of literary parody as they understood it.

The variety of definitions given parody as ironic or satiric over the centuries also reflects on how it has been used in several more or less ironic and satiric ways, and on how some of its characteristics have been compatible with those of both irony and satire. Parody can nonetheless be distinguished from irony and satire proper by virtue of

include those by Wayne C. Booth, D. H. Green, and Ingrid Strohschneider-Kohrs.

108 See Ingrid Strohschneider-Kohrs, *Romantische Ironie in Theorie und Gestaltung* (Tübingen, 1960), pp. 35 f. and p. 77.

several of its defining characteristics, and all of these three forms shown as differing in some essential aspects.

Briefly to review these forms and their differences, it can again be said that the object of the author's criticism in the satire is distinguished from the object of irony and parody in being separated from the author's sympathies and in being made the object of the latter's criticism but not an otherwise integral aesthetic part of the satirist's message. While the parodied text may be both 'victim' and model for the parodist, the object of the satirist's attack remains distinct from the satirist and generally plays a comparatively minimal role in adding to the structure or aesthetic reception of the satirist's work.

While most irony may be said to work with one code which conceals two messages, and most satire be described as sending one largely unequivocal message about its target to the reader through a single code,[109] parody not only contains at least two codes, but is potentially both ironic and satiric in that the object of its attack is both made a part of the parody and of its potentially ironic multiple messages and may be more specifically defined as a separate target than the object of the irony. Parody, moreover, may be said to differ from both satire and irony (as well as from other devices) in its comic juxtaposition of specific preformed linguistic or artistic materials.

The relationships between the author and the object of criticism or contrast in irony, parody, and satire, may be summarised in the following diagrammatic manner, as:

if A is the code of the author, B the code of the quoted text or work, C the object of criticism or contrast within the code of the author, $\rightarrow$ the direction of criticism or refunctioning from the message or messages of the code, and $\leftarrow$ the direction of reflection back to the meaning of the author, then:

IRONY $= A \leftarrow \rightarrow C$;

PARODY $= A + B \leftarrow \rightarrow B = C$;

SATIRE $= A \rightarrow C$.

This, like any schema, is only a model dealing with certain common characteristics, which does not describe all differences, including differences in the type of comic effect produced in each, but which can be varied or expanded according to which of the above elements needs to be explained further. Parody, as has been suggested, may also

---

109 Menippean satire or any other example of satire which uses parody or quotation is obviously a different case in this instance.

identify its target text with a certain reader (R) or with the attitude of a particular group of readers, and make the latter a target of its critical analysis and comedy, or $A + B \longleftrightarrow B = R = C$.

Two other uses of parody can be summarised as:

(1) The use of parody as a mask for the author, through which the latter is ironically identified with their target for some time, or $A = B \longleftrightarrow B = C$.

(2) Parody used as a mask to describe the object of the parodist's satire (as in the criticism of other poets as unwitting parodists), or $A + B \longleftrightarrow B(= X) = C$.

Although some satire may be described as 'utopian' as well as critical when its criticism is used to clear a path for the propagation of new myths and plans, parody may not only be generally more ambivalent towards its target in using the object of its criticism as a part of a 'reformed work' itself, but may also complicate the satirist's more straightforward contrast of reality to an ideal by showing a variety of conflicting ideals or representations of reality.

The unique multiplicity of codes which is to be found in the parody also explains the ability of the parodist to be not only both satiric and ironic, but, in some instances, to combine both 'engaged' and imaginative literature in the one work. In its most sophisticated forms, the parody, moreover, is both synthetic and analytic and diachronic and synchronic in its analysis of the work it quotes, in that it is able to evoke a past work and its reception and link it with other analyses and audiences.

In reflecting upon another literary work from within a literary form, literary parody is also able to act not only as an 'archaeological' analysis of another literary form and its background, but as a form of 'strong reading' of another work or set of works, to quote the term used by Harold Bloom. In making its target a part of its own structure the parody, however, will not simply break away from its preceding texts, as other 'strong readings' have been described as doing, but will transform them and recreate them within itself. In acting in this and other ways as a commentary upon other literary works, parody is also able to be used as 'meta-fiction', and it is this application of parody which will be seen in later chapters to have been concentrated upon in many recent modern and 'post-modern' analyses of parody.[110]

---

110 Other, related, criteria such as 'intertextuality' will also be discussed in the following chapters on modern and post-modern theories of parody.

Meta-fiction

The use made of parody by ancient authors such as Aristophanes as well as by more modern authors from Cervantes onwards has shown it to have been used in ancient as well as modern times to reflect in both 'meta-fictional' and comic fashion on other authors as well as on the composition and audience of the parody work itself.[111]

Even before Cervantes' *Don Quixote* we have in the 'Tale of Sir Thopas', in Chaucer's fourteenth-century *Canterbury Tales*, one of the most complete literary portraits of the author as parodist, self-parodist, and reader satirist. When Chaucer himself is asked by the 'Hooste' to 'Telle us a tale of myrthe, and that anon',[112] he gives us one and a half cantos of parody of the clichés of earlier romances before allowing himself to be interrupted by the host's plea for him to stop his rhymed 'dogerel'.[113] Ironically, it is then also implied in the host's assumption that Chaucer the character is the poetastic perpetrator of the clichés in question, rather than their parodist, that the tale told by the author as character shows less literary talent than those of his other characters.

In addition to these comic and complex games with the roles of author and characters, Chaucer's more critical readers may be said to have been mirrored ironically in the character of the host, the critical but also naive decoder, or interpreter, of the tale within the text. Unlike the host the external reader, however, is put into the position of being able to recognise the irony inherent in both this trick and in the author's depiction of himself in the role of artless storyteller, as well as the ironic suitability of such 'meta-fictional' parody for the tale of the author. For if it can be said that each pilgrim's tale reflects his or her standing or profession in some manner, as does, for instance, the Knight's tale of ancient heroes and 'knights', so it can be suggested that one of the most appropriate literary forms for the author would be the meta-fictional self-parody, in which is reflected not only his literary models, but his own more ironic and sophisticated style, and, in the interruption by the host, the role of the reader as interpreter of the text.

---

111 See, for example, the scenes between Xanthias and Dionysus in Aristophanes' *The Frogs*, in Aristophanes, *The Wasps, The Poet and the Women, The Frogs*, translated by David Barrett (Harmondsworth, 1971), p. 167 and pp.156 f.

112 Quoted from *The Complete Poetry and Prose of Geoffrey Chaucer*, edited by John H. Fisher (New York etc., 1977), p. 247.   113 Ibid., p. 252.

Like Cervantes' *Don Quixote*, Chaucer's parodic 'Tale of Sir Thopas' is, together with its frame, both meta-fictional and comic. Despite the fact that all meta-fictional parody will be comic if it is truly parodic, many recent discussions of parody as meta-fiction have run the dual risks of reducing parody to meta-fiction at the expense of acknowledging the other traditionally defining characteristics of parody such as its comic structure and effect, and (after having eliminated the comic from parody) of even suggesting that all meta-fiction is parody.[114]

Some awareness of the differences between parody and meta-fiction must be maintained, however, if these terms are to be used in any meaningful fashion. While the term meta-fiction when used by itself may describe a reflection by an author on their activity as author, or on that of others, or on the structure or composition of another text, or on its audience, the parody of a literary work, as suggested previously, can be attended not only by such meta-fictional reflections, but by other characteristics of parody such as its comic refunctioning of the work's preformed material.

One classic meta-fictional statement to be found in 'modern' literature, which may also be interpreted as being part of a parody of the use of the 'self-conscious narrator' in fiction,[115] is the ironic reflection by Laurence Sterne's fictional author/narrator in volume IV, chapter 13 of *Tristram Shandy* on the difficulties of ever completing an autobiography. When Tristram states 'write as I will ... I shall never overtake myself'[116] he is being both more self-conscious than most other autobiographers and more parodistic of their genre. Tristram's statement may be read as a meta-fictional comment on the impossibility of an author ever describing all of their life, because they will never be able to complete their description of their present

---

114 Although Patricia Waugh acknowledges the comic character of parody she also speaks of it and meta-fictionality as interchangeable, as on p. 77 of her *Metafiction. The Theory and Practice of Self-Conscious Fiction* (London and New York, 1984): 'This release function is central to parody, and therefore to metafiction.' (My *Parody//Meta-Fiction* makes distinctions on, e.g., its p. 65.)

115 Mark Loveridge, *Laurence Sterne and the Argument against Design* (London, 1982), pp. 9 f. refers to Sterne's choice of the self-conscious narrator as being of a form which was 'almost hackneyed' by the time he wrote *Tristram Shandy*. And see also Wayne C. Booth, 'The Self-Conscious Narrator in Comic Fiction before *Tristram Shandy*', *PMLA*, 67 (March 1952), pp. 163–85.

116 See Laurence Sterne, *The Life and Opinions of Tristram Shandy, Gentleman*, edited by Graham Petrie (Harmondsworth, 1967), p. 286.

description, but its function in Sterne's novel as a parodistic reflection on the realism of other pseudo-autobiographical works makes it more than meta-fiction and a comic, parodic comment on the more naive 'autobiography' and its readers.[117]

Parodies of statements which have not been made in other works of fiction, but in speeches or in pamphlets, such as P. G. Wodehouse's parodistic references to the slogans and practices of British fascism in his descriptions of Roderick Spode's band of 'Black Shorts' in *The Code of the Woosters* of 1937 and other works, or his parodies of school speeches, as in chapter 17 of his *Right Ho, Jeeves*, or the parody of the academic public lecture in Kingsley Amis' *Lucky Jim* of 1954, are less likely to be meta-fictional,[118] and such works also provide examples of how some parody need not be self-consciously meta-fictional even when it occurs within a fictional context and in works which use some meta-fictional tricks.[119]

Meta-fictional statements of both an ironic and parodic nature which allude to the processes of writing in general may be found in other 'Cervantean' authors such as Henry Fielding, as when, for example, the author interrupts the story of Joseph Andrews in his *The History of the Adventures of Joseph Andrews and of his Friend Mr. Abraham Adams. Written in Imitation of the Manner of* CERVANTES, *Author of Don Quixote* of 1742, in chapter 1 of book II, with a digression entitled 'Of divisions in authors' on the manner and purpose of dividing a book into chapters. The creation of interruptions to the narrative flow by such parodic 'meta-fictional' interpolations and the ensuing 'foregrounding' of the author's construction of the narrative and its component parts have also been of particular interest to twentieth-century critics such as the Russian formalists and have constituted one reason for their selection of meta-fictional parody texts as paradigms of the literary work in general. Before turning to this last issue, it must, however, again be stressed that not all meta-fiction may be parodic in the traditional, comic sense of parody, just as

117 Volume IX, chapter 24 of *Tristram Shandy* also invokes the 'Gentle Spirit of sweetest humour, who erst did sit upon the easy pen of my beloved CERVANTES'.
118 See P. G. Wodehouse, *The Code of the Woosters* of 1937 (London, 1990), p. 54; *Jeeves and the Feudal Spirit* of 1954 (London, 1990), p. 25; *Right Ho, Jeeves* (London, 1922), chapter 17; Kingsley Amis, *Lucky Jim* (Harmondsworth, 1977), pp. 221–7; and the references to the last work in chapter 4 of this book.
119 See, for instance, the comically meta-fictional opening of Wodehouse's *Right Ho, Jeeves*.

not all parody may be meta-fictional, or concerned, that is, with the imitation and transformation of other fictional works. In addition to the preceding, some meta-fiction may be comic without being parodic, by virtue of the presence in it of forms of comedy other than parody, such as irony.

For an example of a meta-fiction which is not predominantly parodic, one may even look to works such as John Fowles' *The French Lieutenant's Woman* where 'meta-fictional' references to other texts outside of the novel's fictional world are not part of any clearly comic parodic game, and even when they serve to reflect upon the fictional nature of the story in hand and its relationship to its historical setting as perceived by the author, or contribute to its irony. Descriptions of Fowles' novel as parody often rely, moreover, upon separating parody from the comic in a manner which has come to be characteristic of some 'late-modern' understandings of parody,[120] and then equating parody with the more general, and sometimes also subsidiary, characteristics of meta-fiction such as the direct address to the reader, or the introduction of self-reflection into areas of the novel where it is not normally to be found.

Robert Burden's *John Fowles, John Hawkes, Claude Simon: Problems of Self and Form in the Post-Modernist Novel; a Comparative Study* of 1980 is but one work which translates parody into meta-fiction in such a manner when speaking of Fowles' novel.[121] Burden writes, for instance, on his page 284 that 'in *The French Lieutenant's Woman*, parody, manipulating the expectations of the reader, and also utilizing elements of pastiche, transcends the comic playfulness of burlesque for more serious intentions'. Having separated parody from the comic as well as from the burlesque, and the 'serious' from the comic, Burden continues: 'In Fowles's novel we may locate the parody of a past convention in the disruption of expectations exemplified in all the various intrusions of hindsight, the direct addresses to the reader on the confrontation of traditional and modern theories of the novel, and the intentional rescissions of expected endings (the Victorian and the modern happy-ever-after situations). The parody in this self-conscious narrative fiction is located in the oscillation between implicit and explicit critiques of a literary convention and its founding world-view

120 This subject is discussed further in following chapters.
121 See Robert Burden, *John Fowles, John Hawkes, Claude Simon: Problems of Self and Form in the Post-Modernist Novel; a Comparative Study* (Würzburg, 1980), pp. 283–4.

(ideological substructure). It is a critique of a view of life already articulated in art, and is then also a critique of that art.'

Burden also discusses parody elsewhere in his book in a 'late-modern' manner as critique or disruption,[122] and again without consistent reference to the peculiarly comic characteristics of parody, so that the term is both widened to cover forms of criticism or transformation which can be effected by means other than by parody understood in its traditional sense as a device for the comic rewriting of other works and the parody's own particular comic ability to practise meta-fiction overlooked.[123]

As with some other recent attempts to separate parody from the comic, there is an underlying lack of recognition in such statements of the potentially complex as well as 'serious' nature of some of parody's comic functions, as well as of the way in which the application of those functions to the comic imitation and transformation of other texts distinguishes the meta-fictional parody from meta-fiction as such, or from the meta-fiction which uses other forms of comedy. Many parodies also foreground the techniques used in the construction of other works in their parody of them in a manner which is similar to other non-parodic meta-fictional works, but do so as a part of their comic (and complex) reconstruction of the other work, or with some comic juxtaposition of elements of that work to which their comic undermining of reader expectations for it is related.

One example of comic meta-fictional parody in which parody gives new life to other literary works and devices by making them a part of a 'meta-fictional' reflection on the author's own literary practices is to be found in David Lodge's *Changing Places* when his character Hilary Swallow writes a letter to her husband Philip asking if he still wants her to send his copy of *Let's Write a Novel* and is made to add with unconscious irony: 'What a funny little book it is. There's a whole chapter on how to write an epistolary novel, but surely nobody's done that since the eighteenth century?'[124] Even if the exact model for *Let's Write a Novel* is not known by the reader, its title and the descriptions

---

122 See, for example, Burden, p. 303 on John Hawkes' *The Lime Twig* of 1961.
123 Inger Christensen's *The Meaning of Metafiction. A Critical Study of Selected Novels by Sterne, Nabokov, Barth and Beckett* (Bergen, Oslo, Tromsø, 1981), p. 154 acknowledges the comic character of the parodic meta-fictions it discusses but also suggests, p. 155 that 'the metafictive novel has necessarily a satirical aspect'.
124 See David Lodge, *Changing Places. A Tale of Two Campuses* (1975), (Harmondsworth, 1987), p. 130.

given of it clearly evoke a type of 'do-it-yourself' guide to novel-writing which Lodge's ironic interpolation of it into an imitation of the 'epistolary novel' parodistically, and comically, uses for its own new purposes. When *Let's Write a Novel* finally reaches Philip Swallow via sea-post during a flash-back in which he recalls Désirée Zapp as saying '"You can't go back, once you've started. You can only go forwards"',
it is used both for some further irony and for some further renewal of the device being parodied: 'The spine was missing and the pages were stuck together. He managed to prise it open in the middle, however, and read: "Flash-backs should be used sparingly, if at all. They slow down the progress of the story and confuse the reader. Life, after all, goes forwards, not backwards."'[125]

Lodge's novel is a good example of how a meta-fictional parody can be comic and of how it can use satire and irony together because the targets of the parody have been made into a part of the parody text itself. The use of both irony and satire to compare and contrast fiction and reality in such meta-fictional parodies also suggests that the use of meta-fiction need not necessarily designate scepticism about the ability of the fiction to describe or evoke external reality in any realistic or meaningful manner, as has been claimed by some recent commentators on meta-fiction. Lodge himself has written that 'it would be false to oppose metafiction to realism',[126] and many other meta-fictional parodies have followed the example of Cervantes in setting up comparisons and contrasts between fiction and reality which allow the author both to have fun in showing a reader where other authors or readers have confused the two 'realms' and to create a more 'realistic' type of fiction.

Although a few recent theorists have suggested that fiction can only ever be meta-fictional and talk about itself, some parodists such as Sterne have also shown us the limits of such talk (as with reference, for instance, to the task of writing a completely accurate auto-biography), and have used their knowledge of those limits both to make fun of those who have not understood them and to show their readers an author who is in control of the distinctions between the fact and fiction and truth and falsity described in the novel. As such writers have been aware, it is, moreover, the understanding of those

125 Ibid., p. 186.
126 See David Lodge, *After Bakhtin. Essays on Fiction and Criticism* (London 1990), p. 19.

distinctions which will allow the reader to take on the role of a Cervantes rather than that of a Don Quixote in interpreting their works.

Some more recent uses of parody have continued to play with a confusion of fiction and reality, and with added side-references to modern theories about both, which require the reader to keep some track of their differences, and of the author's manipulations of them. One example is to be found in Malcolm Bradbury's parody of the 'Author's Note' in his *The History Man*: 'This fiction is for Beamish, whom, while en route for some conference or other, I last saw at Frankfurt airport, enquiring from desk to desk about his luggage, unhappily not loaded onto the same plane as he. It is a total invention with delusory approximations to historical reality, just as history itself. Not only does the University of Watermouth, which appears here, bear no relation to the real University of Watermouth (which does not exist) or to any other university; the year 1972, which also appears, bears no relation to the real 1972, which was a fiction anyway; and so on. As for the characters, so called, no one but the characters in this book knows them, and they not well; they are pure inventions, as is the plot in which they more than participate. Nor did I fly to a conference the other day; and if I did, there was no one on the plane named Beamish, who certainly did not lose his luggage. The rest, of course, is true.'[127]

Even to understand the humour of Bradbury's statement about 'the real University of Watermouth (which does not exist)' we have to have some idea about the real existence in the past of other 'Author's Notes' which have tried to dissociate their fictions from real places, the tradition of which Bradbury's 'Author's Note' is parodistically imitating. Bradbury's own *Stepping Westward* of 1965 had also begun with such a note, if with some irony: 'Note. The characters in this fiction are total inventions; the university where part of the action takes place is much too improbable to resemble any existing institution; the American state to which the university belongs does not exist, though it has of necessity been set down in an area occupied by other states; and the America of the novel differs in many details of geography, politics, law and customs from the real, as it were original, America.'[128]

127 See Malcolm Bradbury, *The History Man* (1975), (London, 1977), 'Author's Note'.   128 See Bradbury, *Stepping Westward* (London, 1979), 'Note'.

In addition, we have to have some idea that (1) there is no known university called Watermouth, (2) there are ones which are still not identical with the satirist's fiction but which approximate that which is being described in his novel to the extent that they may be assumed to have provided some material for his satire, and (3) that literary humour of the type used in the 'Author's Note' to Bradbury's *The History Man* relies upon turning our normal expectations (which are based on past events and writings including its own) 'upside-down' or 'inside-out', but not necessarily by making any real change to the normal relationships of up and down, or outside and inside, or fact and fiction. This last point does not mean that a statement made in fiction may not be able to affect the world outside it through the effects it may have on its readers, but that it will remain fiction, while the world 'outside' it (and its reader/agents) will remain distinguishable from it. Even when these distinctions are described as not holding by an author, and the world outside is shown as moving 'inside' (as in, for example, the disturbed head of Elias Canetti's Peter Kien in the novel *Die Blendung*[129]), a reader must still be able to know the two are separable to understand the point of such fictions.

Much of the recent theory which has claimed with more seriousness than Bradbury's 'Author's Note' that history is like fiction in being but a discourse or a collection of signs,[130] or that we cannot use it to . know any hard-and-fast facts or truths about the 'real' past, has blurred these distinctions between fiction, history and reality in a way which would seem to make it hard for their followers to understand the point of such works, or of works such as Cervantes' *Don Quixote*.

Rather than say that meta-fiction of either a parodic or a non-parodic kind must necessarily offer a relativistic view of both the world and its writing in which no distinctions between illusion and reality, history or fiction, or truth and falsity can be made, works such as Cervantes' meta-fictional parody have demonstrated that meta-fictional statements may show us both where and when other fictional statements have created illusion or falsity, and how they have done so.

---

129 This novel was translated into English as *Auto-da-Fé* and was analysed in depth in David Roberts' *Kopf und Welt*, trans. Helge und Fred Wagner (Munich and Vienna, 1975).

130 Linda Hutcheon, for instance, writes on p. 112 of her *A Poetics of Postmodernism. History, Theory, Fiction* (New York and London, 1988) that 'both history and fiction are cultural sign systems, ideological constructions whose ideology includes their appearance of being autonomous and self-contained'.

One function of meta-fiction, to use a distinction suggested by Gilbert Ryle in his *The Concept of Mind*, is not only to show (in the sense of to describe or to assert) 'that' (as is the case with most 'true or false' statements), but to show 'how' the fictional work, and its depictions of truth and reality, are constructed. Such meta-fictional statements can also be put to use in showing how an illusion has been made, and may, in this manner, serve to illustrate a distinction between truth and illusion in the work in which they have been stated. When pointing to the creation of illusion in another work, their comments on the 'realism' or not of a certain fiction need not undermine, moreover, the ability of themselves or the works of another writer to give a more realistic account, or of agents in the world outside the fiction to make statements of fact about that external world which are true rather than false. As suggested earlier, meta-fictional parodies such as Cervantes' *Don Quixote* not only illustrate some of these more general points, but also show how the parodist may use them in several different and comic ways to criticise and refunction less self-reflective works of fiction; to educate their own readers to a greater awareness of both the possibilities and limitations of fiction; and to create new works from old.

Several of the above issues will be returned to in the following chapters on modern and post-modern theories of parody, where some further criteria for the description of parody – such as intertextuality and textual discontinuity – will be seen to have been derived from its more meta-fictional examples,[131] but where some effects of the modern reduction of parody to the burlesque will also be found to have lived on in attempts either to separate meta-fictional or intertextual parody from the comic or to describe its 'intertextual' examples as something other than parody.

131 While meta-fiction can be defined as a work of fiction which comments or reflects upon another text, its 'intertextual' element can be described as the presence in its text of the words, passages, or messages of others.

Modern parody

❖❖

Modern and late-modern theories and uses of parody

❖❖

This chapter analyses both the problems and achievements created by some of the early modern and 'late-modern' literary theorists of this century who have either explicitly dealt with parody or based their theories on predominantly parody texts. As suggested in the conclusion of the preceding chapter, this and the following chapter also deal with the derivation of the concept of intertextuality from some of those parody texts and describe several of the ways in which the use of that concept has both helped to make some of parody's more complex functions better appreciated and obscured their specifically parodic nature.

Russian formalists

Amongst the most influential of modern theorists who have built their theories of the literary text on examples of general parody such as *Don Quixote* and *Tristram Shandy* are the Russian formalists whose major works were published in the first two decades of the twentieth century. One of the best known of these theorists is Viktor Shklovsky (1893–1984), whose extrapolations of general literary characteristics from parody texts such as *Tristram Shandy* have contributed to the application to literature in general of characteristics of meta-fictional parody since described as 'discontinuity' and 'intertextuality'.[1]

One reason for the acceptance by some critics of Shklovsky's generalisations from works of parody as being relevant to all literature may be, moreover, that in the pages of his now famous essay of 1921 on Sterne's *Tristram Shandy* Shklovsky had neither stressed the word parody, nor stressed how many of the characteristics which he had chosen as being significant were peculiar to Sterne's parodic, and

---

1 This issue was also touched upon in my *Parody//Meta-Fiction* (London, 1979), but is explored in greater detail and depth in the material which follows.

'Menippean', novel. When Shklovsky first published his essay on *Tristram Shandy* in Petrograd in 1921 it was entitled '*Tristram Shendi' Sterna i Teoriya Romana* (*Sterne's 'Tristram Shandy' and the Theory of the Novel*) and its first page contained no reference to parody, in being entitled '*Sterne's Tristram Shandy*. Stylistic Commentary'. Only when the essay was reprinted in Shklovsky's collection of essays entitled *O Teorii Prozy* ('Of the Theory of Prose') of 1925[2] was it called 'Parodiini Roman. "Tristram Shendi" Sterna', or, to quote one of its translations into English, 'A Parodying Novel. Sterne's *Tristram Shandy*'.[3] In Shklovsky's *O Teorii Prozy* of 1925 the index also referred to one passage in the essay on *Tristram Shandy* as being about parody, although the term parody was not used on that page itself, and 'parody' in the form of the word '*parodirovaniye*' was defined in the index as '*priyom ostranneniya*', or 'device for alienation'.[4] (The passage of the 1925 essay on *Tristram Shandy* to which the index entry for parody referred[5] was on the peculiar 'unrolling' of the plot in Sterne's novel,[6] but parodies of Cervantes and motivation are also noted.)

While Shklovsky had begun his essay by discussing *Tristram Shandy* as a formalistically 'revolutionary' novel which was very different from 'the ordinary kind of novel'[7] (Shklovsky bases this contrast on a comparison of 'ordinary poetry with its phonetic instrumentation and the poetry of the Futurists, written in obscure language'), he had ended by claiming that '*Tristram Shandy* is the most typical novel in world literature',[8] and it is this claim which others after

---

2 See Viktor Shklovsky, *O Teorii Prozy* (Moscow and Leningrad, 1925), pp. 139–61.

3 See the (partial) translation of Shklovsky's essay from the 1929 edition of his *O Teorii Prozy* by W. George Isaak, in John Traugott (ed.), *Laurence Sterne. A Collection of Critical Essays* (Englewood Cliffs, N. J., 1968), pp. 66–89.

4 See Shklovsky, *O Teorii Prozy*, 1925, p. 185. 'Alienation' is replaced by 'estrangement' in some translations, but see also Sher, in Viktor Shklovsky, *Theory of Prose* (1929), translated by Benjamin Sher (Illinois, 1990), pp. xviii f., on the problems of translating 'ostranneniya'.

5 See Shklovsky, *O Teorii Prozy*, 1925, pp. 142–3 and Sher pp. 150–1.

6 See also Tzvetan Todorov, 'Some Approaches to Russian Formalism', translated by Bruce Merry in Stephen Bann and John E. Bowlt (eds.), *Russian Formalism: A Collection of Articles and Texts in Translation* (Edinburgh, 1973), pp. 6–19; pp. 12–13 on this topic.

7 See Shklovsky, *O Teorii Prozy*, 1925, p. 139 and Victor Shklovsky, 'Sterne's *Tristram Shandy*: Stylistic Commentary' (1921), in Lee T. Lemon and Marion J. Reis (eds.), *Russian Formalist Criticism: Four Essays* (Lincoln Nebraska, 1965), pp. 25–57; p. 27.

8 See Shklovsky, *O Teorii Prozy*, 1925, p. 161 and Lemon and Reis, p. 57.

him such as Robert Alter and some of his readers have quoted most. (Alter, whose *Fielding and the Nature of the Novel* of 1968 had criticised F. R. Leavis' assessments of Fielding as too negative,[9] and whose *Partial Magic. The Novel as a Self-Conscious Genre* of 1975 had criticised Leavis' criticisms of parodists such as Sterne and Joyce,[10] begins the chapter on Sterne in his later work with Shklovsky's concluding phrase.[11])

In apparent contrast, as noted previously, to its concluding, more frequently quoted claim, Shklovsky's essay begins with Shklovsky saying that in it he does 'not propose to analyze Laurence Sterne's novel, but rather to illustrate general laws of plot' and that 'formalistically, Sterne was an extreme revolutionary; it was characteristic of him to "lay bare" his technique'.[12] Shklovsky then continues to speak of the 'chaos' which can be found in *Tristram Shandy* and of how the action is continually interrupted or transposed, but in a 'strictly regulated way', 'like a picture by Picasso'.[13]

As in the rest of his essay, Shklovsky, however, makes no analysis of the use made by Sterne of the discontinuous form of the Menippean satire which others known to Sterne had used before him, and, unlike Shklovsky, earlier commentators on Sterne who had been aware of this tradition had not seen the author of *Tristram Shandy* as a revolutionary but as an imitator.[14]

Eugene P. Kirk's *Menippean Satire: An Annotated Catalogue of Texts and Criticism* of 1980 (p. 153) has even shown how connections may be made between the discontinuous style of Sterne's *Tristram Shandy* and the 'Menippean' style of the 'Bruscambille' (*Les Fantasies de Bruscambille. Contenant plusiers Discours, Paradoxes, Harangues et Prologues facecieux*, Paris, 1615) which Walter Shandy buys for three crowns in Sterne's novel: 'Sterne's Walter Shandy gladly paid three

---

9 See Robert Alter, *Fielding and the Nature of the Novel* (Cambridge Mass., 1968), p. 3. Leavis' *The Great Tradition* (1948) (Harmondsworth, 1967), p. 12, does, however, at least say of Fielding that 'what he *can* do appears to best advantage in *Joseph Andrews*'.

10 See Robert Alter, *Partial Magic. The Novel as a Self-Conscious Genre* (Berkeley, Los Angeles and London, 1975), p. ix.

11 See Alter, *Partial Magic*, p. 30. Leavis' *The Great Tradition*, p. 11 criticises Sterne for his 'irresponsible and (nasty) trifling' as well as the overvaluation of it by others.

12 See Shklovsky, *O Teorii Prozy*, 1925, p. 139 and Lemon and Reis, p. 27.

13 See Shklovsky, *O Teorii Prozy*, 1925, pp. 139 f. and Lemon and Reis, pp. 27 f.

14 As an imitator, that is, of other 'Menippean', not 'typical' novels.

half-crowns for this eccentric *schrift* of mock-encomia, in which the customary order of book-parts was quite jumbled: unlike Beroalde de Verville, who had begun with *"Conclusion"*, "Bruscambille" joins prologue to prologue, never getting past his introductory matter, while straying from prose to verse. The prologue on noses, the main attraction for Shandy, is at pp. 190–2; there are also laudatory prologues on nothing, on the utility of cuckolding, on the ass, and similarly momentous topics. Three mock-disquisitions (pp. 112–26) analyze the flatus, as to whether it is corporal, spiritual, and beneficial.'

Kirk (p. 237) has further pointed out that Wilbur D. Cross' *The Life and Times of Laurence Sterne* of 1925 has discussed Sterne as a plagiarist – if as 'a brilliant and honest one'. According to this view, Sterne was much indebted for the 'Shandean' manner to such authors as John Dunton and the Renaissance wits mentioned by John Ferriar, the 1812 edition of whose *Illustrations of Sterne, with Other Essays and Verses* of 1798 Kirk (p. 243) describes as discussing Sterne's debts to Burton, Swift, Thomas D'Urfey, Bouchet, Gaspar Ens, Beroalde de Verville, Agrippa d'Aubigne, and the 'Bruscambille' 'with the clear suggestion that "Shandeanism" is derived from them'.

D. W. Jefferson's essay '*Tristram Shandy* and the Tradition of Learned Wit' of 1955 is also described by Kirk (p. 253) as 'explaining Sterne's manner not as adherence to any single genre but to a broad current of Renaissance mock-intellectualism', while his own '*Tristram Shandy*, Digression, and the Menippean Tradition'[15] is described by him (pp. 257–8) as attempting to survey all other critical explanations for the genesis of the 'Shandean style'; as seeking to show that imitation of earlier Menippean satires which used conspicuous, flagrant and self-conscious digression was most of Sterne's enterprise; and as discussing Sterne's development of Menippean satire to illustrate 'themes of life's and language's discontinuity and ineffability through digression'.[16]

As suggested previously, Shklovsky's failure to discuss the issue of Sterne's relationship to other Menippean works is accompanied by his description of Sterne's use of discontinuity and other such devices as revolutionary rather than as plagiaristic or imitative. Given, however,

---

15 This was published under the name of Eugene Korkowski in *Scholia Satyrica*, vol. I, no. 4 (1975), pp. 3–15.
16 Kirk also notes that the variety implicit in the term *satura* agrees with the special Menippean emphasis on digression.

both that Shklovsky's view is difficult to hold when the information about Sterne's predecessors referred to by Kirk is acknowledged, and that the description of Sterne as plagiarist overlooks his particular use of parody, some middle path between these two views of Sterne as revolutionary innovator and as plagiarist would seem to be necessary.

Such a middle way would allow us to see Sterne as one who used works of the Menippean tradition such as the 'Bruscambille' as both a model for his own games with the discontinuity of thought and language and as objects for those games. Unlike most (if not all) plagiarists, Sterne has given us the name of the 'Bruscambille' in his own work, and has also made it an object of fun by his association of it with the character of Walter Shandy. If Sterne then imitates some of its discontinuity it is with the irony of the parodist who is using it as the basis of a new work – and of one which will foreground the techniques of the less reflective novelist.

Had Shklovsky been more aware of the associations of Sterne with the Menippean tradition when he wrote his essay on *Tristram Shandy* he might still have chosen to call Sterne an innovator, but it would have been more difficult to have claimed this on the basis of Sterne's use of discontinuity and transpositions of plot. That this change in Shklovsky's approach to Sterne's use of discontinuity might also have affected the history of recent literature and its canonisation of such forms is yet another interesting question to consider. Shklovsky, however, like so many of the structuralists and post-structuralists who have continued his interest in discontinuity and 'intertextuality', to use their words, had much less interest in the history of the forms used by the parodist than in their formal functions. While some may think that Shklovsky's analyses and their popularisations have been for the best, despite their critical shortcomings, others may be justified in suggesting that the twentieth-century popularisation of intertextuality and discontinuity as something new has now reached the stage where, even if some thought it 'modern' in the beginning (and have recently sought to continue its life by calling it 'postmodern'), it is itself in need of some of the 'defamiliarisation' of which Shklovsky himself had spoken as being necessary for the introduction of literary change.

Shklovsky has also been criticised by the historian of Russian formalism Victor Erlich, in the latter's *Russian Formalism. History – Doctrine* of 1955, for generalising from *Tristram Shandy* to the novel in general. Erlich writes, for instance, on Shklovsky's claim that '*Tristram Shandy* is the most typical novel in world literature', that 'the adjective "typical" in Sklovskij's [Shklovsky's] eulogy of *Tristram Shandy* is characteristically misapplied' and that 'the use of this term betrayed the Formalist's "modern" bias in favor of non-objective art, his tendency to mistake the extreme for the representative, the "pure" for the "superior"'.[17]

In contrast to Erlich, Lee T. Lemon and Marion J. Reis are not so critical of Shklovsky when they suggest in their introduction to Shklovsky's essay on *Tristram Shandy* that 'Shklovsky can logically conclude his essay with the apparent exaggeration that "*Tristram Shandy* is the most typical novel in world literature"', because what he means 'is that it is the most plotted, the least "storied", of any major novel'.[18] Perhaps if Shklovsky had said the most 'essential', rather than the most 'typical', his sentence might have been more easy to accept by others such as Erlich. As it is, the use of the word 'typical' is confusing in suggesting, as it does, that all other novels are like *Tristram Shandy*, rather than that Sterne's novel contains (as Shklovsky's argument as a whole has suggested) a revolutionary and largely 'untypical' 'foregrounding' of that which Shklovsky has seen to be the essence of the novel.[19] Despite this point, which both makes some sense of the apparent contradiction between Shklovsky's opening and concluding statements and shows how some have been misled unnecessarily into the faulty argument that the parodic *Tristram Shandy* is like all other literature, it would, however, again need to be pointed out with reference to Shklovsky's argument as a whole that some of the revolutionary 'foregrounding' found in Sterne's novel can in fact be found in other earlier 'Menippean' and parodic works. Shklovsky himself, moreover, appears to at least implicitly acknowledge the existence of precedents for Sterne's 'revolutionary' practices when he repeats some of his points about *Tristram Shandy* in other passages in his *O Teorii Prozy* on the discontinuous and intertextual structure of works such as Cervantes' parodic *Don Quixote*.[20]

---

17 See Victor Erlich, *Russian Formalism. History – Doctrine* (1955), 3rd edn (New Haven and London, 1981), p. 194.   18 See Lemon and Reis, p. 26.

19 Richard Sheldon suggests in his *Viktor Borisovic Shklovsky: Literary Theory and Practice, 1914–1930* (University of Michigan Dissertation, 1966), pp. 135–6 that Shklovsky was being whimsical in setting up his contradictory opening and conclusion, but also points elsewhere in his thesis to Shklovsky's sometimes arbitrary, and misapplied, use of terms.

20 See, for example, Shklovsky's essay 'Kak sdelan *Don Quixote*', ('How *Don Quixote* is Made'), in Shklovsky, *O Teorii Prozy*, 1925, pp.70–96. (It is translated from the 1929 edition by Sher, pp. 72–100 under the title 'The Making of *Don Quixote*'.)

In chapter 11 of his *Russian Formalism. History – Doctrine* (pp. 192–3) Victor Erlich criticises the Russian formalists in general for overstressing the novelty of works in which literary conventions are 'laid bare' as well as for their emphasis on form: 'The Formalists were quick to accord preferential treatment to cases where the conventional nature of literary art was, to use the *Opojaz* term, "laid bare"; they consistently played up those literary works the only content of which was form. In their assessments of contemporary Russian literature they praised "naked" verbal play in verse and encouraged techniques of indirection in prose fiction, e.g. parody, stylization, whimsical toying with the plot.' Erlich adds (p. 193) that it was significant that Shklovsky used *Tristram Shandy* as a touchstone of the novelist's art', and that 'what endeared Sterne' to him was 'his adeptness at parody and his mockery of conventional narrative schemes'.

Later (p. 196) Erlich describes Shklovsky's formalist methods as suiting *Tristram Shandy* because it was 'the most non-objective and form-conscious of the famous novels', but as not suiting very much else. After criticising Shklovsky's formalistic analysis of *Don Quixote*, Erlich writes (p. 197): 'If *Don Quixote*, a novel making lavish use of the devices of parody and irony, does not lend itself too well to ultra-Formalist operations, one shudders at the thought of applying Sklovskij's [Shklovsky's] scheme to, say, *The Divine Comedy*. Could any one seriously maintain that Dante's theology was merely a "motivation" of a heterogeneous plot, an ideological pretext for the fictional exploration of various planes of existence?'

One of the problems with the formalist reduction of parody to a device of alienation for 'laying bare' the artifice of a work of art is also touched upon by Erlich when he writes (p. 198) that 'the concern with the idiosyncratic, the purely literary, gave rise to the tendency to equate literature with literariness, to reduce art to its distinguishing feature'. Some of Erlich's other comments on the suitability of *Tristram Shandy* for formalist analysis (such as that 'the Formalist students were at their best in dealing with what might be called quotation mark techniques – with parody and stylization, "laying bare" the artifice and destroying the illusion of reality'[21]) suggest that his own view of parody might not have recognised all of its dimensions, yet his criticisms of the reductionist character of the formalist approach to art

21 See Erlich, p. 248. Erlich also mentions Eikhenbaum's interest in the parodic stories of 'O. Henry' (the pseudonym of William Sydney Porter) here.

and its devices still help to show that the formalist view of parody was also one which could have been more complex.

Many of Shklovsky's other statements on parody are, moreover, brief and not always consistently developed. Shklovsky's essay 'How *Don Quixote* is Made'[22] is similar to his essay on *Tristram Shandy* in looking at the way in which interpolations and discontinuity in the appearance of characters 'motivate' the action of the novel, but lacks explicit reference to the role played by parody in such formal features. Some references to parody can be found in Shklovsky's other works, as in his study of the 'classical English novel' which includes discussions of both Sterne and Dickens,[23] but these are not extensive. Shklovsky's other references to parody in his *O Teorii Prozy* essays include ones made towards the end of an essay entitled 'Roman tayn' or 'The Mystery Novel', in which he also spends some time analysing Dickens' *Little Dorrit*, to how Fielding had 'parodied the old novel in his *Tom Jones*',[24] and to the 'laying bare' of a Dickensian device by the author V. Kaverin.[25] Here parody again appears to be understood as making something new from an old or dead form by 'laying bare' its devices, but is again not discussed at any length.

Shklovsky had further suggested in an essay published in his *O Teorii Prozy* on the connection between devices of plot construction and general stylistic devices[26] both that parody could re-use 'used-up' stylistic devices[27] (as he had suggested in other of his writings) and that not only parody but every work is created as both a parallel and contrast to some model.[28] Shklovsky had also claimed the

22 See Shklovsky, 'Kak sdelan *Don Quixote*', in *O Teorii Prozy*, 1925, pp. 70–96, and Sher, pp. 72–100.
23 See Viktor Shklovsky, *Khudozhestvennaya Prosa. Razmishleniya i Razbori* (Moscow, 1959), pp. 261–394; p. 276.
24 See Shklovsky, *O Teorii Prozy*, 1925, p. 137, and Sher's translation of the 1929 edition, p. 145.
25 See Shklovsky, *O Teorii Prozy*, 1925, p. 138, and Sher, p. 146.
26 See Shklovsky, *O Teorii Prozy* , 1925, pp. 21–55. Parts of this essay are translated by Jane Knox in Shklovsky, 'The Connection between Devices of *Syuzhet* Construction and General Stylistic Devices (1919)', in Stephen Bann and John E. Bowlt (eds.) *Russian Formalism: A Collection of Articles and Texts in Translation* (Edinburgh, 1973), pp. 48–72, while the 1929 edition is translated in full in Sher, pp. 15–51.
27 See Shklovsky, *O Teorii Prozy*, 1925, p. 42, Bann and Bowlt, p. 66, and Sher, p. 38.
28 See Shklovsky, *O Teorii Prozy*, 1925, p. 26, Bann and Bowlt, p. 53, and Sher, p. 20. (Shklovsky adds here that a new form does not arise to give voice to a new content, but to replace an old form which has lost its artistic value.)

'intertextual' point earlier in this passage that it could be stated as a general rule that a work of art is generally perceived against a background of other works, and in connection with them, and that the form of a work is determined by its relationship to other forms which have preceded it.

In a passage not translated in the 1973 translation of this essay into English, but which is of some importance in understanding the intellectual background to Shklovsky's interest in devices which can be used to create difference and discontinuity, Shklovsky goes on to refer to Broder Christiansen's *Philosophie der Kunst* as speaking of 'Differenzempfindungen', or 'perceptions of difference', as themselves being different from, but as important as, sensual perception in the reception of works of art, and as being formed when an artist creates differences from other works or canons.[29] In a move which is repeated by Shklovsky in his eventual merging of parody with devices of contrast and discontinuity in general,[30] Christiansen had given as examples of such creations of 'difference' a poem by Rilke in which prosaic words mix with the poetic[31] and the caricaturing of ideals by Ibsen,[32] but had not then differentiated the caricature from his other example by reference to its normally comic nature, and had even referred to Ibsen's caricatures as being 'bitterly serious'. (When Christiansen does discuss caricature as a form of the comic in a later section of his book, in its pages 176–7, he criticises Kant's definition of the comic as replacing the expected with 'nothing', by arguing that the latter is always something new to be interpreted, but concludes that the liberation which is said to be given by the comic is like the flapping of wings of a chicken which, despite everything, remains grounded.)

When, after discussing the way in which parody can revitalise old devices, Shklovsky refers to parodic stories by Boccaccio, and to one from which Cervantes in particular had derived some fun (to Boccaccio's story of how a Babylonian Sultan sent one of his

---

29 See Shklovsky, *O Teorii Prozy*, 1925, p. 27 and Broder Christiansen, *Philosophie der Kunst* (Hanau, 1909), pp. 117–25.

30 Christiansen, p. 308 also speaks of 'the modern', as represented in Impressionism, as 'the avoidance of the continuous', and elsewhere, as on his p. 310, uses the word 'discontinuous' to describe the same phenomenon.

31 Ibid., p. 119. (Christiansen's description of this particular example of difference also suggests another reason why Shklovsky concentrated on works which others have described as typically 'Menippean' in their mixture of forms.)

32 Ibid., p. 122.

daughters to a certain king to be his wife and how, due to a series of incidents, the princess passes through four years and ten other men before she reaches her goal, and as a virgin[33]), he too makes no specific investigation of the particularly comic character of the parody, although he knows that he is using the term parody to describe stories which have changed other texts in a manner which other readers, and writers, have perceived to be comic.[34]

In the expanded conclusion of the first part of another essay from *O Teorii Prozy*, on 'the structure of the story and the novel', published in the second edition of that work of 1929, Shklovsky also refers to Chekhov's stories as being notable for their surprise ending changes to the 'salon' stories of the time, as well as for treating the 'epigones' of such stories with irony and for laying bare the artistic devices hidden in those works.[35] In Shklovsky's description of Chekhov's story 'To bila ona' ('It Was She'), the term parody is also used to describe the comic imitation and rejuvenation of worn-out devices, although the particularly comic character of parody is again not explicitly investigated.[36] Shklovsky concludes this section of his essay by suggesting that whereas the stories of Chekhov had not previously been treated as his best work, such games with the devices of fiction show that they are important.[37]

In yet another essay in the first edition of his *O Teorii Prozy*, on 'literature without *suzhet*',[38] Shklovsky discusses again the subjects of discontinuity and intertextuality, if in a variety of terms other than these,[39] and suggests that both Lev Tolstoy's *War and Peace* and

33 See Shklovsky, *O Teorii Prozy*, 1925, pp. 42–3; Bann and Bowlt, p. 66; and Sher, p. 38.
34 Shklovsky (ibid., p. 43) refers, for instance, to Cervantes as laughing at Boccaccio's story.
35 See Shklovsky, 'Stroyeniye Rasskaza i Romana', in *O Teorii Prozy*, 2nd edn (Moscow, 1929), pp. 68–90; pp. 74 ff., and Sher, pp. 52–71; pp. 57 ff.
36 See Shklovsky, *O Teorii Prozy*, 1929, p. 77, and Sher, pp. 59 f.
37 See Shklovsky, *O Teorii Prozy*, 1929, p. 79, and Sher, p. 61.
38 See Shklovsky, *O Teorii Prozy*, 1925, pp. 162–78 and Sher's translation of the 1929 edition, pp. 189–205. (Sheldon, while pointing to a lack of consistency in Shklovsky's use of terms, suggests, p. 87, that the word 'suzhet' is largely used by him to describe 'the arrangement of events within the work', but the word can be translated more simply as 'plot'.)
39 An essay of 1917, in Shklovsky's *O Teorii Prozy*, 1925, pp. 7–20 (translated as 'Art as Technique' in Lemon and Reis, pp. 3–24, and as 'Art as Device' by Sher, pp. 1–14), had also spoken of the ways in which art is able to make us notice how it is constructed.

Laurence Sterne's *Tristram Shandy* could best be called novels because they 'violate ... the laws of the novel'.[40] Shklovsky also claims that the 'canon' of the novel as genre can be parodied and changed better than any other canon, and refers next to Fielding's *Joseph Andrews* and to diversions from the structure of the novel in it such as its Book III, chapter x, 'A discourse between the poet and the player; of no other use in this history but to divert the reader', but again without specific investigation of their comic aspects.

To Shklovsky the 'digressions' which he finds in Fielding and other such novelists serve three different purposes. The first is that they allow the author to interpolate new material into the novel. The speeches of Don Quixote, for example, allowed Cervantes to weave critical judgements, philosophical material, and the like into his work. The second, to which Shklovsky attributes greater importance, is that they retard the action, and Shklovsky adds that Sterne has used this device especially often, and to create tension in the expectations of the audience for the continuation of the main action. Finally, the third role of these digressions for Shklovsky is that they create contrasts, and here Shklovsky quotes Fielding himself on contrast as saying that it runs through all the works of creation.[41]

In addition to discussing implicitly functions of parody in Cervantes, Sterne, and Fielding without specific reference to its comic character in the above summary, Shklovsky turns in the second part of this essay to the Russian writer Rozanov and writes of his collection of biographical details, literary opinions, and images, that although these works look to be lacking in form they represent for him 'a new genre', which could best of all be compared to 'a novel of the parodic type'; have an only weakly expressed novelistic plot (*suzhet*); and are 'without a comic hue'.[42] Although Shklovsky has not explicitly separated the comic from parody itself in this passage, other formalists will use similar language to do so, and will thus also lay a basis for the 'late-modern' separation of parody from its more ancient comic functions and structure, and the reduction of it to but yet another meta-fictional or intertextual form.[43]

---

40 See Shklovsky, *O Teorii Prozy*, 1925, p. 165, and Sher, p. 192.
41 See Shklovsky, *O Teorii Prozy*, 1925, pp. 165–6, and Sher, pp. 192–3.
42 See Shklovsky, *O Teorii Prozy*, 1925, p. 166, and Sher, p. 193.
43 The term 'late-modern' is used here because the theories in question are both from a 'late-modern' period (from the 1960s onwards) and extend the modern separation of the comic from the complex in parody.

One other statement made by Shklovsky, in his 1923 essay 'Pushkin and Sterne: *Eugene Onegin*', also argues that a work may be interpreted as comic in one age and as tragic in another, and in a way which suggests that parody, as a literary device, might be subject to a variety of comic and non-comic reactions.[44] Shklovsky had also written towards the end of this essay of the way in which parody may give life to old devices without specific reference to its comic character: 'It is an interesting question, why particularly *Eugene Onegin* was made in the form of a parodic Sternean novel. The appearance of *Tristram Shandy* was due to the petrification of the devices of the old *roman d'aventure*. All its techniques had become totally ineffectual. Parody was the only way to give them a new lease on life ... '[45]

Even though Shklovsky's treatment of parody as an 'alienation effect' for the 'laying bare' of outworn devices was useful in pointing to how it can give a 'new lease of life' to outworn forms, his reduction of it to such a device in his various essays created the problem that, as with other theories which equate parody with only the intertextual, the meta-fictional, or the discontinuous, parody cannot then be distinguished from other instances of those forms in the same way as can parody when understood in its fuller, and more traditional sense, as the comic refunctioning of other works.

Other formalists have echoed Shklovsky's views of parody. Boris Tomashevsky, for example, speaks in his *Teoriya Literatury*, or 'Theory of Literature', of 1925 of how the plot where all the characters of a drama turn out to be related in the last act (as in Molière's *The Miser*) is parodied in works such as Beaumarchais' comic *The Marriage of Figaro* when that plot is 'dead'.[46] Tomashevsky had also spoken earlier in his 1925 text of parody as developing an incongruous split of style and subject-matter, and as being, at times, a means for comic contrast,[47] but had reduced the comic to ridicule when speaking of

---

44 See Shklovsky, '*Evgenii Onegin*' (*Pushkin i Stern*), in *Ocherki po Poetike Pushkina*, Berlin, 1923, pp. 199–220; p. 199, translated by M. Holquist, in Victor Erlich (ed.), *Twentieth-Century Russian Literary Criticism* (New Haven and London, 1975), pp. 63–80; p. 63.

45 See Shklovsky, '*Evgenii Onegin*' (*Pushkin i Stern*), p. 219, and Erlich, 1975, p. 79.

46 See Boris Viktorovich Tomashevsky, *Teoriya Literatury* (Leningrad, 1925), pp. 149 f., and 'Thematics', excerpted and translated from *Teoriya Literatury*, 1925, in Lemon and Reis, pp. 61–95; pp. 81–2.

47 See Tomashevsky, *Teoriya Literatury*, p. 26. Contrast is also emphasised in Tomashevsky's later (p. 209) description of parody as either the discussion of a

parody as both comic and as ridiculing and destructive with reference to its 'laying bare of the device' in a later part of his work: 'If the laying bare of another's literary devices is realised through a comic interpretation we have parody. The functions of parody are many, but its usual function is to ridicule an opposing literary group, destroying its aesthetic system and exposing it.'[48] (In later editions of his *Teoriya Literatury*,[49] Tomashevsky adds 'grotesque' comic distortion to the list of parody's characteristics, and elsewhere mentions some of its more 'vulgar' forms.[50])

Tomashevsky echoes Shklovsky more closely when he writes after stating that 'parodies are quite widespread; they were traditional in dramatic literature, when any more or less significant work called for an immediate parody', that 'parody always assumes as the background from which it takes off, another literary work (or a whole group of works)',[51] and that 'some parodies, not primarily satiric, are developed as the free art of laying bare techniques'.[52] Tomashevsky also refers to Shklovsky's beloved Sterne: 'Thus the followers of Laurence Sterne at the start of the nineteenth century formed their own school, which had developed out of parody, into a school which pursued parody as an art in its own right. In contemporary literature, Sterne's techniques have been revived and widely disseminated (the transposition of chapters, excessive and casual digressions, the slowing of the action, and so on, are typical).'[53]

Tomashevsky further appears to agree with Shklovsky when he writes that 'a significant number of parodies may be found among the tales of Chekhov',[54] but again demonstrates a more problematical view of the comic when he adds after stating that 'devices are laid bare

high subject in low language, as in the burlesque 'or travesty', or as the use of a high style for a low subject.
48 See Tomashevsky, *Teoriya Literatury*, 1925, p. 161, and Lemon and Reis, p. 94. (As in some of the following quotations, I have made the English translation match Tomashevsky's meaning more closely where necessary.)
49 See, for example, the second edition, *Teoriya Literatury. Poetika* (Moscow and Leningrad, 1927), p. 22.
50 See, for example, Tomashevsky, *Teoriya Literatury. Poetika*, 1927, p. 24.
51 See Tomashevsky, *Teoriya Literatury*, 1925, p. 161, and Lemon and Reis, p. 94.
52 See Tomashevsky, *Teoriya Literatury*, 1925, p. 161, and Lemon and Reis, p. 95. (Tomashevsky, p. 26 had also spoken of there being elements of parody which mix with satire in the stories of N. S. Leskov.)
53 Tomashevsky, *Teoriya Literatury*, 1925, p. 161, and Lemon and Reis, p. 95.
54 See Tomashevsky, *Teoriya Literatury*, 1925, p. 161, and Lemon and Reis, pp. 94–5.

because a perceptible device is permissible only when it is consciously made noticeable', that 'when a device is noticed despite the author's attempt to conceal it, it produces a comic effect detrimental to the work', and that 'to prevent this the author deliberately lays bare the device'.[55] How these sentences knit with Tomashevsky's previous, Shklovskian suggestion that parody too is a device for laying bare the device, and his added suggestions that such parody is comic as well as ridiculing, is not explained, and even though some distinction could have been made here between the unintentional comedy of the instance being described and that of the parody.

When Tomashevsky continues he again appears to be describing parody as Shklovsky had done, as a device for giving new function and meaning to older texts, although no specific mention is made of parody, and its functions (as described by both Shklovsky and himself) seem now to be attributed to the renewal of literary devices in general, and to forms in which the comic and the comically incongruous are not necessarily present: 'Thus devices are born, live, grow old, and die. To the extent that their use becomes automatic, they lose their efficacy and cease to be included on the list of acceptable techniques. Renovated devices with new functions and new meanings are required to prevent techniques from becoming mechanical. Such renovation is like the use of a quotation from an old author in a new application and with a new meaning.'

As with several of the theories discussed in the following sections, it is clear that not all modern or 'postmodern' theories of parody have dealt with it in an entirely consistent manner. Some of the inconsistencies to be found in theories like those above (such as that parody is sometimes described as comic and sometimes not) will also be found to have been continued in theories developed after them which are still in vogue today. Despite these problems, many of which reflect the problems some critics still have with treating a comic form like parody as a 'serious', in the sense of an important, or meaning-bearing, literary device, it could be said that at least some of what Shklovsky has said has been of use in pointing to functions of comic parody in renewing dying or overused literary forms which had been overlooked by others because of the lack of 'seriousness' attributed to parody as a comic device.

For all their interest in parody as a device for laying bare other

---

55 See Tomashevsky, *Teoriya Literatury*, 1925, p. 161, and Lemon and Reis, p. 95.

devices, the Russian formalists themselves were largely to remain victims of the denigration of parody as a comic form, and to fail to acknowledge adequately the difference between parody and other forms which lay in its use of comic devices and the importance of those comic devices themselves. Because of this some were also to confuse or merge parody with other intertextual devices and to fail to comment explicitly on how many of the texts from which they derived their central literary characteristics of discontinuous plot development and intertextual reference were in fact works of comic parody, and not the same, for that reason, as works which were not parodic.

Strangely enough, given their avowed interest in form – but perhaps again because they had not treated parody sufficiently thoroughly as something different from other devices for alienation and the like – many of the Russian formalists were also not to delve very far into the structure of parody itself, or into how its own particular and comic 'double-coding' of one text with another was to enable it to create something new from its destruction of old forms. Although Shklovsky refers to the ability of parody to create new literature from its destruction of old devices, his statements about this are generally made in gnomic rather than analytic sentences. (Shklovsky also writes in such a fashion in his *A Sentimental Journey. Memoirs, 1917–1922* of 1923 when he states that 'art is fundamentally ironic and destructive. It revitalizes the world. Its function is to create inequalities which it does by means of contrasts.'[56])

Taking a lead from a suggestion made by Jurij Striedter that it was Yuriy Tynyanov rather than Shklovsky who understood best how parody was able to achieve its renewal of literary forms,[57] one can, however, turn to Tynyanov to find at least some understanding of the peculiarly dualistic, or 'double-coded', structure of the parody which is basic both to its structure and to its ability to give new life to older works.

Tynyanov's most influential statement on parody is generally

56 See Shklovsky, *A Sentimental Journey. Memoirs, 1917–1922* (1923), translated by Richard Sheldon (Ithaca and London, 1970), p. 232.
57 See Jurij Striedter's introduction to his *Texte der Russischen Formalisten*, vol. I (Munich, 1969), 'Zur formalistischen Theorie der Prosa und der literarischen Evolution', pp. IX-LXXXIII; p. XLII, where he suggests that Shklovsky's view of parody as a largely mocking or playful tool for the alienation and revelation of automatised forms did not explain as well as Tynyanov's work how such destructive parody could create new forms.

acknowledged to have been made in his *Dostoyevsky i Gogol'* (*k Teorii Parodii*) or *Dostoyevsky and Gogol* (*Towards a Theory of Parody*) of 1921. (Tynyanov's 1924 book *The Problem of Verse Language* also refers to parody, and, in particular, to the dynamics of its 'deformation' of other forms, but discusses it largely as one form of new verse construction amongst others, while his *O Parodii*, or 'On Parody', essay of 1929, on the use of parody by a variety of Russian writers, was published only after his death, in 1977.) In his comments on Tynyanov's 1921 work in his 1927 essay 'The Theory of the "Formal Method"', Boris Eikhenbaum writes that Tynyanov's treatment of the question of parody in Dostoyevsky's *The Village of Stepanchikovo* of Gogol's *Correspondence with Friends* was overshadowed by a whole theory of parody as both 'a stylistic device (stylized parody)',[58] and 'as one of the manifestations (having great historical-literary significance) of the dialectical development of literary groups'.[59] Eikhenbaum adds: 'With this arose the problem of "succession" and "tradition" and, hence, the basic problems of literary evolution were posed [as part of the study of style] ... "Literary evolution" was complicated by the notion of struggle, of periodic uprisings, and so lost its old suggestion of peaceful and gradual development. Against this background, the literary relationship between Dostoevsky and Gogol was shown to be that of a complicated struggle.'[60]

Eikhenbaum notes further that Shklovsky too, in his *Rozanov* of 1921, had shown that 'literature moves forward in a broken line'. (Shklovsky's previously discussed essay from his *O Teorii Prozy* of 1925 on 'literature without *suzhet*' is based on his *Rozanov* of 1921, but omits the last six pages of the latter.) Eikhenbaum also quotes Shklovsky as saying in his *Rozanov* that '"in each literary epoch there is not one literary school, but several. They exist simultaneously, with one of them representing the high point of the current orthodoxy. The

---

58 Eikhenbaum's interest in parody is also evident in his 'O. Genri i Teoriya Novelli' of 1925, in Eikhenbaum, *Literatura: Teoriya, Kritika, Polemika* (Leningrad, 1927), pp. 166–209; translated by I. R. Titunik as 'O. Henry and the Theory of the Short Story', in *Readings in Russian Poetics: Formalist and Structuralist Views*, edited by L. Matejka and K. Pomorska (Cambridge, Mass., 1971), pp. 227–70, although Erlich, 1955, p. 248 complains that Eikhenbaum's essay has made O. Henry sound as if he had been an 'honorary Formalist'.

59 See Boris Eikhenbaum, 'The Theory of the "Formal Method"', in Lemon and Reis, pp. 99–139 (from Eikhenbaum, *Literatura*, pp. 116–48); p. 134.

60 From Lemon and Reis, p. 134.

others exist uncanonized, mutely"'.[61] Eikhenbaum continues: 'The
moment the old art is canonized, new forms are created on a lower
level', and again quotes Shklovsky: '"Each new literary school heralds
a revolution, something like the appearance of a new class. But, of
course, this is only an analogy. The vanquished line is not obliterated,
it does not cease to exist. It is only knocked from the crest; it lies
dormant and may again rise as a perennial pretender to the throne.
Moreover, in reality the matter is complicated by the fact that the new
hegemony is usually not a pure revival of previous forms but is made
more complex by the presence of features of the younger schools and
with features, now secondary, inherited from its predecessors on the
throne."'[62]

In addition to sharing some of Shklovsky's views on the
development of literature, and on the role played by parody in that
development, Tynyanov echoes Shklovsky when speaking of parody
as the 'mechanisation' of a device in his *Dostoyevsky and Gogol*: 'The
essence of parody lies in the mechanisation of a specific device,
whereby the mechanisation is of course only noticeable when the
device which it mechanises is known. In this way the parody fulfills a
double function: (1) the mechanisation of a specific device, and (2) the
organisation of new material, to which the mechanised old device also
belongs.'[63]

Tynyanov, however, goes further than Shklovsky in characterising
some other aspects of the structure and peculiarities of parody in this
text. Not only, for instance, has Tynyanov discussed the idea of the
'word-mask' with reference to parody in it,[64] but he has also
recognised, as suggested previously, the peculiarly 'double' structure
of parody which results from its 'wearing' of the refunctioned words

---

61 Ibid., p. 135.
62 Ibid. Eikhenbaum, on Lemon and Reis, p. 136, also describes Russian formalism in
    general as understanding literary evolution 'as the dialectical change of forms'.
63 See Tynyanov's 'Dostoyevsky i Gogol'', in his *Arkhaisty i Novatory* of 1929
    (Munich, 1967), pp. 412–55; p. 430. (The passage is not in the translation of the
    essay given in *Twentieth-Century Russian Literary Criticism*, edited by Victor Erlich
    (New Haven and London, 1975), pp. 102–116.) (The 1929 Russian text is largely
    the same as that of 1921.)
64 See Tynyanov, *Arkhaisty i Novatory*, pp. 428 ff. (Erlich, 1975, does not translate
    the first half of Tynyanov's essay in which the subject of the 'word-mask' is
    treated more fully, and his p. 115 also eliminates reference to the phrase used on
    Tynyanov p. 453 to describe an instance of parody by Dostoyevsky as a 'word-
    mask'.)

of others.[65] In line with this understanding of the ambiguous, dual structure of the parody Tynyanov was also able to suggest that parody can be sympathetic to its target and that the material for it can be both respected and admired. As evidence for this claim Tynyanov points out that parodies of the Old Testament were popular with orthodox Jews and that Pushkin was able both to have a high regard for Karamzin's *History of the Russian State* and to parody it in his 'Chronicle of the Village Goryukhino', as well as both to admire and parody the style of *The Iliad* and its Russian translation. Tynyanov concludes this argument by summarising the concept behind it: 'The fact is that the very essence of parody, its dual planes, is a definite, valuable device.'[66]

This recognition of the dual 'planes', or structure,[67] of parody also goes beyond Shklovsky's view of it as an alienation device for the laying bare of others, for although Shklovsky had suggested that such parody could both create and destroy, he had not fully shown how these two things could go together, or how the 'dual-planed', or 'dual-texted',[68] structure of the parody was to make such dual relationships possible. (Later, in an essay entitled 'Ornamental Prose', in the second edition of his *O Teorii Prozy* of 1929, Shklovsky speaks of a 'many-planed' [*mnogoplannoy*] work planned by Bely being reduced to ornamental prose, but while referring to Bely's sometimes 'humorous' view of the resulting 'collision' of his planes does not apply the concept or phrase specifically to parody.[69])

Like the early Shklovsky Tynyanov nonetheless continues to value the way in which a parodist may use parody as a device for renewing the outworn devices of another, as when he comments on how

---

65 As will be seen presently, Tynyanov specifically describes the structure of parody as 'dual-planed'.

66 See Tynyanov, p. 436 and Erlich, 1975, p. 104, although Erlich's translation of this last sentence is freer than that given here.

67 Tynyanov's word 'plan', meaning 'plane', or 'level', is translated by Erlich as 'structure'. Although not incorrect this does not make Tynyanov's word as recognisable as does the more literal translation of it as 'plane'.

68 Tynyanov also uses his description of parody as 'dual-planed' to refer to the fact that the parody consists of at least two texts.

69 See the second edition of Shklovsky's *O Teorii Prozy* of 1929, pp. 205–25; pp. 206 f. Sher's translation of Shklovsky's 'Ornamental Prose' essay (see Sher, pp. 171–88; pp. 172 f.) translates 'mnogoplannoy' as 'multi-levelled' rather than as 'multi-planed' but does allow Shklovsky to speak elsewhere in his essay of the different 'planes' of the work.

Dostoyevsky parodies not only the late Gogol's overall rhetorical thrust but also his individual stylistic devices when he parodies the latter's crescendo technique 'by repeating insistently one or another word'.[70]

Tynyanov even explicitly refers to Shklovsky when he writes that 'Dostoyevsky's heroes often parody each other, just as Sancho Panza parodies Don Quixote in his conversations with the latter (V. Shklovsky). But in Dostoyevsky expressions first used by his heroes are placed between authorial quotes and become portable parodic clichés.'[71] Tynyanov, however, raises new problems with regard to the understanding of parody when he concludes by not only stressing his earlier Shklovskian definition of parody as a game with the device, but by separating parody from its comic elements in an even more explicit manner than Shklovsky: 'The fact that the parodic character of *The Manor of Stepanchikovo* has hitherto escaped the critics' attention is curious, but not unique. Parodies of plots often are deeply concealed. It is doubtful that anyone would have realised that "Count Nulin" is a parody, had Pushkin not testified to that effect. And how many of such unrevealed parodies are there? When the parody is not revealed, the work changes. So changes every literary work taken out of the plane to which it was assigned. Even the parody, the main element of which lies in stylistic details, naturally loses its parodic character when torn away from its second plane (which can simply be forgotten). This is an important measure for resolving the question about parody as a comic genre. The comic is usually the colouring which accompanies parody, but is by no means the colouring of the parodic itself. The parodic character of the work may fade away while its comic colouring remains. Parody lies wholly in a dialectical play with the device. If a parody of tragedy becomes a comedy, a comedy parodied may be a tragedy.'[72]

While Tynyanov's point that the comic may live on after the disappearance of the parodic function of a work separates the comic from the parody in an even more precise manner than when Shklovsky

70 See Tynyanov, p. 448 and Erlich, 1975, p. 112.
71 See Tynyanov, p. 454 and Erlich, 1975, pp. 115–16.
72 See Tynyanov, p. 455 and Erlich, 1975, p. 116. (Erlich's translation is, however, again rather free, and his translation of the penultimate sentence as describing 'the essence of parody' is misleading in that Tynyanov had not only *not* used that particular phrase here, but had previously used it to describe the 'dual planes' of the parody.)

speaks of the absence of a 'comic hue' with reference to the 'parody-like' works of Rozanov,[73] it suggests, nonetheless, that the two may be found together.

Like other of his statements, Tynyanov's point that the demise of the parody's target and purpose may leave it with a comic 'hue' but no parodic function, underestimates, however, the way in which the dual structure of the parody allows it to keep both its target and its own parodic function alive.[74] Stella Gibbons' *Cold Comfort Farm* of 1932, for instance, is still comic even if one does not know the specific works it parodies, because its parody of those works has evoked them for the reader of the parody before or while making fun of them by exaggerating their peculiarities. Even if not all readers will now be able to put a name like Mary Webb to the 'primitivist' works parodied by Stella Gibbons,[75] many are at least able, because of the evocation of those works in Gibbons' parody of them, to recognise from her text the types of work being parodied, as well as to appreciate the comedy of the incongruity set up by her between the original and the parody.

Tynyanov's very last lines are also as problematical as are some of his other concluding statements. Tynyanov had earlier used the phrase 'if a parody of tragedy becomes a comedy, a comedy parodied may be a tragedy' in a section in which he had discussed the close relationship between stylisation and parody. There he had written, and with some suggestion of how the parody may be differentiated from the stylisation because of the comic nature of the parody: 'The stylisation stands close to the parody. Both live a double life: behind the plane of a composed work stands another plane, stylised or parodied. In the parody, however, the lack of consonance between the two planes dislocates them; the parody of a tragedy becomes a comedy (it is all the same whether this occurs through the underscoring of the tragic or through an expedient exchange with the comic), the parody of a comedy may be a tragedy. In the stylisation this lack of consonance is missing; there is, on the contrary, a matching of the planes with each

---

73 Both Tynyanov and Shklovsky use the word 'okraska' to describe the comic 'colouring' or 'hue' of parody in their 1921 texts.

74 Other instances of Tynyanov's underestimation of the power of the parody to evoke its target are to be found in the previously quoted passages from his p. 430 on the mechanisation of the device and in his statement on the way in which the second plane of the parody work is forgotten, p. 455.

75 See also the entry on parody in J. A. Cuddon, *A Dictionary of Literary Terms* (1977), revised edition (London, 1979), pp. 483–5; pp. 484–5 on these works.

other: of the stylised and that which glimmers through it. Nonetheless, it is only a short step from the stylisation to the parody; the comically motivated or stressed stylisation becomes parody.'[76]

Following his previously quoted discussion of parody as a 'mechanisation of the device', Tynyanov had added, in the conclusion of the first part of his essay, that parody is present in a work when the second parodied plane 'glimmers through the work', and that 'the more narrow, defined, and limited is this plane, and the more clearly do all the details of the work contain a double nuance, and are perceived from a double view-point, so is the parodic character of the work more sharply stamped on it'.[77] While the original point of Tynyanov's phrase that 'if a parody of tragedy results in a comedy, a comedy parodied may turn out to be a tragedy' becomes clearer when one can read the whole of his essay, and see that one thing he was trying to say with that phrase when he first used it was that the parody will always contain a contrast between its two levels, his statement here that a parody of a comedy may become tragedy is problematic in not only separating parody from the comic, but in again underestimating the power of the parody to evoke and retain its target and its particular comic or tragic 'colouring'.

This last view might also be said to be present in Tynyanov's statement in his essay 'On Literary Evolution' of 1927 that 'parody is viable only in so far as what is being parodied is still alive',[78] which contrasts to some extent with both Tomashevsky's 1925 suggestion that parodies attack devices which are already dead, and with Shklovsky's prior suggestions that parody is often used to revitalise used-up devices. As seen previously, even when Tynyanov echoes Shklovsky's descriptions of parody as the mechanisation of used-up devices he insists that these devices must still be known.[79] Perhaps some of this confusion might have been resolved had Shklovsky also commented upon the point made in Broder Christiansen's *Philosophie der Kunst* of 1909 that when differences are established *within* a work

76 See Tynyanov, p. 416.   77 See Tynyanov, p. 433.

78 See Tynyanov's 'O Literaturnoi Evolutsii' of 1927, dedicated to Boris Eikhenbaum, in Tynyanov's *Arkhaisty i Novatory* of 1929 (Munich, 1967), pp. 30–47; p. 36 or the translation by C. A. Luplow, in *Readings in Russian Poetics: Formalist and Structuralist Views*, edited by L. Matejka and K. Pomorska (Cambridge, Mass., 1971), pp. 66–78; p. 70.

79 See the previous reference to Tynyanov's 'Dostoyevsky i Gogol'', in Tynyanov, *Arkhaisty i Novatory*, p. 430.

the contrast between them lasts much longer than when contrasts are made with external rules or canons.[80] But although this point might have been used by Shklovsky to explain how the parody can preserve and even re-vivify both its target and its differences from it by internalising the parodied work within its own text, it was not.[81]

The evocation by the parody of its target which Tynyanov overlooks in his statements on parody also makes it difficult to think of examples of the parody of a comedy producing a tragedy. Tynyanov himself gives no examples of such a transformation, and, as suggested previously, does not investigate further the implications for this matter which may be derived from his recognition of the dual-planed structure of the parody and of the way in which the parody contains and re-presents its target. Even when we can say that a parodied phrase has been re-used in a more tragic context, it will be difficult to claim that none of its previous comic associations are not evoked with it to give at least a bitter-sweet taste to its new appearance, while the use of parody itself, with its incongruous juxtapositions of the unexpected, should also produce at least some comic reaction from its audience.

Although it is above all a comic work,[82] one can even refer here to the way in which David Lodge has parodied post-structuralist terminology in his *Small World* of 1984 with Morris Zapp's use of the phrase '*every decoding is another encoding*'.[83] When this phrase suddenly turns up again on a badge Zapp has had made for another congress (p. 194) we have what might be called a comic refunctioning of its first use by Zapp, some of the comedy of which derives from the juxtaposition of the expected with the unexpected use of the phrase. When Zapp uses the phrase again (p.282) in more serious, and potentially 'tragic', circumstances, when kidnapped by the political

80 See Christiansen, pp. 122 ff.
81 M. M. Bakhtin also fails to acknowledge the above aspects of Christiansen's argument in calling Christiansen's aesthetics 'monologic' in his *Problemy Poetiki Dostoyevskogo* (1963), (Moscow, 1979), p. 24. (See also Bakhtin, *Problems of Dostoevsky's Poetics* (1963), edited and translated by Caryl Emerson (Manchester and Minnesota, 1984), p. 21.)
82 Parody, and the comedy that attends it, pervade Lodge's *Small World* with its parodic refunctionings of the plot of the romance, the Grail legend, and of more modern (and already parodic) works such as Oscar Wilde's *The Importance of Being Earnest*.
83 See David Lodge, *Small World. An Academic Romance* (Harmondsworth, 1986), p. 25.

friends of the millionaire Marxist critic Fulvia Morgana, it brings with it memories of its earlier, more comic uses, and the creation of an at least bitter-sweet or tragic-comic tinge to the seriousness of the scene.

The question of the evocation of the associations of a parodied work in parody will be returned to in a later section of this chapter, while David Lodge's fictions and criticism will be discussed in greater detail in the following chapter with reference to his 'post-modern' understanding and uses of parody. Prior to those sections, the next will both deal again with some of the issues raised by the Russian formalists, and with their influence, and investigate the works of another influential modern theorist who has been of interest to both 'late-modern' and 'post-modern' authors and theorists, the critic Mikhail Mikhailovich Bakhtin (1895–1975).

M. M. Bakhtin

Some critics have described Mikhail Bakhtin as having been critical of the Russian formalists because of a claim made by V. V. Ivanov in 1973 that Bakhtin was the author of books by both V. N. Volosinov and P. N. Medvedev, and, more specifically, of the latter's *The Formal Method in Literary Scholarship. A Critical Introduction to Sociological Poetics* which contains criticisms of Russian formalism.[84] Others, however, have criticised Ivanov's claim,[85] and differences between Bakhtin's published ideas and those in the above named book by Medvedev suggest that caution should be taken in accepting Ivanov's statement.

As will be seen in following pages, several of Bakhtin's points about parody have both echoed the Russian formalists' choice of parody texts and developed further some of their analyses and characterisations of parody. (Katerina Clark and Michael Holquist comment in their *Mikhail Bakhtin* of 1984 on how Bakhtin has both taken up ideas from the formalists about the role played by parody in the evolution

---

84 See *The Formal Method in Literary Scholarship. A Critical Introduction to Sociological Poetics* by P. N. Medvedev/M. M. Bakhtin, translated by Albert J. Wehrle (Baltimore and London, 1978).

85 See, for instance, Tzvetan Todorov's *Mikhail Bakhtin. The Dialogical Principle*, translated by Wlad Godzich (Minneapolis, 1984), pp. 6 ff., and the Preface to V. N. Volosinov, *Freudianism. A Marxist Critique* (1927), by I. R. Titunik and Neal H. Bruss (New York, San Francisco, London, 1976), pp. xii ff.

of the novel and about the 'laying bare of the device' and echoed the formalists' choice of literary works by Sterne, Cervantes and Dickens,[86] but other points of contact between their theories of parody will also be made below.)

One of the ways in which Bakhtin may be seen to have developed Tynyanov's view of parody as 'dual-planed', in which, in contrast to stylisation, a lack of consonance prevails, is, for instance, in the development in his study of Dostoyevsky's 'polyphony' in his *Problems of Dostoyevsky's Art* of 1929,[87] on which his later *Problems of Dostoyevsky's Poetics* of 1963 is based,[88] of his concept of parody as both a 'double-voiced' form and one which is based on contrast and dissonance.[89]

In a chapter published in both of the above books,[90] and translated into English in the translation of the latter,[91] Bakhtin first of all speaks of parody together with stylisation, *skaz*, and dialogue as 'artistic-speech phenomena' which are 'two-ways directed':[92] 'All these phenomena, despite very real differences among them, share one common trait: discourse in them has a twofold direction – it is directed both toward the referential object of speech, as in ordinary discourse, and toward *another's discourse,* toward *someone else's speech.* If we do not recognize the existence of this second context of someone else's speech and begin to perceive stylization or parody in the same

86 See Clark and Holquist, *Mikhail Bakhtin* (Cambridge, Mass. and London, 1984), p. 269. (While they exclude Rabelais from their list of the authors discussed by both Bakhtin and the formalists, Shklovsky has mentioned him in his *O Teorii Prozy* essays.)

87 This is the English title usually given to Bakhtin's *Problemy Tvorchestva Dostoyevskogo* (Leningrad, 1929), henceforth referred to as 'Problemy, 1929'.

88 Bakhtin's *Problemy Poetiki Dostoyevskogo* of 1963, or 'Problemy, 1963', was translated into English by R. W. Rotsel in 1973, but the translation which will be referred to here, and henceforth abbreviated as 'Problems', is Mikhail Bakhtin, *Problems of Dostoevsky's Poetics*, edited and translated by Caryl Emerson (Manchester and Minnesota, 1984).

89 As will be seen later in this section, Bakhtin also uses Tynyanov's term 'dual-planed' in a description of the carnival square in his *Problems, 1963*.

90 See Bakhtin, *Problemy*, 1929, pp. 105 ff. and Bakhtin, *Problemy*, 1963, pp. 210 ff.

91 See Bakhtin, *Problems*, pp. 181 ff., chapter 5, 'Discourse in Dostoevsky'. (Because of lack of space specific reference is not made to Bakhtin's Russian texts save when the original words are of particular importance to points made in the text above or there is a translation problem.)

92 Bakhtin, *Problemy*, 1929, p. 106 speaks of 'dvoyako-napravlennikh slov' and Bakhtin, *Problemy*, 1963, p. 215 of 'dvoyakaya napravlennost' slova'.

way ordinary speech is perceived, that is, as speech directed only at its referential object, then we will not grasp these phenomena in their essence: stylization will be taken for style, parody simply for a poor work of art.'[93]

In his following discussion of *skaz* Bakhtin goes on to acknowledge the Russian formalist Boris Eikhenbaum as being the first 'to bring the problem of *skaz* to the fore in our scholarship',[94] and while he makes no explicit reference to Tynyanov's differentiations of the double planes to be found in parody and stylisation, may also be said to have echoed these in his following distinction of parody and stylisation: 'The situation is different with parody. Here, as in stylization, the author again speaks in someone else's discourse, but in contrast to stylization parody introduces into that discourse a semantic intention that is directly opposed to the original one.'[95]

This is not unlike Tynyanov's distinction between stylisation and parody which he makes on the basis of the consonance and dissonance between their dual planes. Bakhtin's discussion of this subject differs from Tynyanov's, however, in not only stressing the hostility of the 'clash' of voices in the parody, but in failing to mention the comic 'colouring' of the parody which Tynyanov had explicitly separated from the parody in his 1921 text but had not eliminated altogether from its description:[96] 'The second voice, once having made its home in the other's discourse, clashes hostilely with its primordial host and forces him to serve directly opposing aims. Discourse becomes an arena of battle between two voices. In parody, therefore, there cannot be that fusion of voices possible in stylization or in the narration of a narrator (as in Turgenev, for example); the voices are not only isolated from one another, separated by a distance, but are also hostilely opposed. Thus in parody the deliberate palpability of the other's discourse must be particularly sharp and clearly marked. Likewise, the author's intentions must be more individualized and filled with specific content. The other's style can be parodied in various directions and may have new accents introduced into it, but it can be stylized essentially only in one direction – in the direction of its own particular task.'[97]

93 See Bakhtin, *Problems*, p. 185.   94 Ibid., p. 191.   95 Ibid., p. 193.
96 Tynyanov's *The Problem of Verse Language* of 1924 and 'O Parodii' essay of 1929 also refer to the comic aspects of parody.
97 See Bakhtin, *Problems*, pp. 193–4.

Bakhtin then points to the different types of parody which may exist, but without revising their previously defined basis: 'Parodistic discourse can be extremely diverse. One can parody another person's style as a style; one can parody another's socially typical or individually characterological manner of seeing, thinking, and speaking. The depth of the parody may also vary: one can parody merely superficial verbal forms, but one can also parody the very deepest principles governing another's discourse. Moreover, parodistic discourse itself may be used in various ways by the author: the parody may be an end in itself (for example, literary parody as a genre), but it may also serve to further other positive goals (Ariosto's parodic style, for example, or Pushkin's). But in all possible varieties of parodistic discourse the relationship between the author's and the other person's aspirations remains the same: these aspirations pull in different directions, in contrast to the unidirectional aspirations of stylization, narrated story and analogous forms.'[98]

After adding that 'inherent in most cases of contemporary *skaz* is a slight parodic overtone', Bakhtin continues with reference to other, similar forms: 'Analogous to parodistic discourse is ironic, or any other [ambiguous],[99] use of someone else's words; in those instances too another's discourse is used for conveying aspirations that are hostile to it. In the ordinary speech of our everyday life such a use of another's words is extremely widespread, especially in dialogue, where one speaker very often literally repeats the statement of the other speaker, investing it with new value and accenting it in his own way – with expressions of doubt, indignation, irony, mockery, ridicule, and the like.'[100]

Bakhtin also suggests that in both stylisation and parody 'the author makes use precisely of other people's words for the expression of his own particular intentions', but notes that in parody 'the specific actual parodied discourse is only implied', and that 'authorial discourse itself either poses as someone else's, or claims someone else's discourse as its own'.[101] Bakhtin then goes on to speak of varieties of tension

98 Ibid., p. 194. Bakhtin also refers, pp. 194–5, to Leo Spitzer's point that the words of another always sound strange and can even sound mocking in our own mouths.
99 The English translation (*Problems*, p. 194) says 'double-voiced' and not 'ambiguous' here, but Bakhtin's *Problemy*, 1929, p. 119 and *Problemy*, 1963, p. 225 both use the word 'dvusmislenniy' (meaning 'double-meaning' or 'ambiguous') and not their word for 'double-voiced' ('dvugolosoye') in this instance.
100 See Bakhtin, *Problems*, p. 194.   101 Ibid., p. 195.

between the parodist and the parodied text, if with perhaps too much animation, or anthropomorphisation, of the latter: 'When parody senses a fundamental resistance, a certain strength and depth to the parodied words of the other, the parody becomes complicated by tones of hidden polemic. Such parody already has a different sound to it. The parodied discourse rings out more actively, exerts a counterforce against the author's intentions. There takes place an internal dialogization of the parodistic discourse. Similar processes occur whenever the hidden polemic is coupled with a narrated story, and in general in all examples of the third type when there is a divergence in direction between the author's and the other person's aspirations.'[102] Bakhtin adds at the end of his following paragraph: 'Such [vari-directional] discourse is not only double-voiced[103] but also double-accented; it is difficult to speak it aloud, for loud and living intonation excessively monologizes discourse and cannot do justice to the other person's voice present in it.'[104] In his summary of this discussion Bakhtin classifies parody as 'III.2', 'Vari-directional double-voiced discourse', the second type in class iii 'Discourse with an orientation toward someone else's discourse (double-voiced discourse)'.[105]

Later Bakhtin refers to Dostoyevsky's 'sharp and unexpected transitions from parody to internal polemic, from polemic to hidden dialogue, from hidden dialogue to stylization ... then back again to parodistic narration and finally to an extremely intense open dialogue',[106] and adds that 'what is important here ... is not only the diversity and abrupt shift of discursive types, nor the predominance among them of double-voiced, internally dialogized discourses.' The uniqueness of Dostoyevsky, Bakhtin continues, 'lies in his special distribution of these discursive types and varieties among the basic compositional elements of a given work'.[107]

---

102 Ibid., p. 198.
103 In this instance, and in the table which follows, Bakhtin does himself use the word 'dvugolosoye', meaning 'double-voiced'. See Bakhtin, *Problemy*, 1929, pp. 125 ff. and *Problemy*, 1963, pp. 230 f.
104 See Bakhtin, *Problems*, p. 198.
105 Ibid., p. 199. The first type of the third class is entitled 'Unidirectional double-voiced [*dvugolosoye*] discourse' and includes 'stylisation'; the third 'active type' (reflected discourse of another)' includes forms such as hidden internal polemic and dialogue.   106 Ibid., p. 203.
107 Ibid. Bakhtin speaks of 'dvugolosoye' or 'double-voiced' discourse in these passages. (See also Bakhtin, *Problemy*, 1929, p. 133 and *Problemy*, 1963, p. 236.)

While Bakhtin's classification of parody as a 'double-voiced' form lends it some ambivalence in his discussion of Dostoyevsky's polyphonic novel, his stress on the hostility between the voices present in the parody[108] is indicative of the fact that he – like some of the Russian formalists – had continued to view it in the modern manner as a largely destructive device. Despite emphasising its 'dialogicity' and 'ambiguity' in both his 1929 and 1963 texts Bakhtin also depicts parody as a device which reduces the complex to the simple or to a distortion of its basic characteristics when he writes in both his 1929 and 1963 works of the treatment of Golyadkin in Dostoyevsky's *The Double* that 'as in any parodic stylization, there is an obvious and crude emphasis upon the basic characteristics and tendencies of Golyadkin's discourse'.[109]

Bakhtin's echoes of the ideas of the Russian formalists on both parody and other matters are also to be found in essays of the 1930s and after in which he discusses the carnivalistic and Menippean traditions, such as his 'Discourse in the Novel' of 1934–5, 'Forms of Time and of the Chronotope in the Novel. Notes toward a Historical Poetics' of 1937–8, 'From the Prehistory of Novelistic Discourse' of 1940, and 'Epic and Novel. Toward a Methodology for the Study of the Novel' of 1941.[110]

Bakhtin's early essay entitled 'Discourse in the Novel' of 1934–5,[111] for instance, takes up both his earlier 'formalistic' analysis of parody as 'double-voiced' and returns to some of the subjects and themes of the Russian formalists themselves. With reference to the latter, Bakhtin speaks in his section headed 'Heteroglossia in the Novel' of how in

108 See Bakhtin, *Problems*, pp. 193–4; *Problemy*, 1929, p. 118; and *Problemy*, 1963, p. 224.

109 Bakhtin, *Problems*, p. 211; *Problemy*, 1929, p. 146; and *Problemy*, 1963, p. 245. Bakhtin's 'The Problem of the Text in Linguistics, Philology, and Other Humanities Sciences' of 1959–61 also describes parody as a 'crude' form of dialogism. See Bakhtin, *Estetika Slovesnogo Tvorchestva* (*Aesthetics of Verbal Creativity*), edited by Sergey Averintsev and Sergey Bocharov (Moscow, 1979), p. 300 and *Speech Genres and Other Late Essays*, translated by Vern W. McGee and edited by Caryl Emerson and Michael Holquist (Austin, 1986), p. 121.

110 See *The Dialogic Imagination: Four Essays*, translated by Caryl Emerson and Michael Holquist and edited by Michael Holquist (Austin and London, 1981) from Bakhtin, *Voprosy Literatury i Estetiki* (*Questions of Literature and Aesthetics*) (Moscow, 1975), henceforth referred to as *Voprosy*.

111 See Bakhtin, *The Dialogic Imagination*, pp. 259–422, and *Voprosy*, pp. 72–233. says discussed here in chronological order are printed in the reverse order rson's and Holquist's translation.)

the English comic novel 'we find a comic-parodic re-processing of almost all the levels of literary language, both conversational and written, that were current at the time'. Here Bakhtin also writes of parodic stylisation: 'This usually parodic stylization of generic, professional and other strata of language is sometimes interrupted by the direct authorial word (usually an expression of pathos, of Sentimental or idyllic sensibility), which directly embodies (without any refracting) semantic and axiological intentions of the author. But the primary source of language usage in the comic novel is a highly specific treatment of "common language".'[112] Further to this, Bakhtin treats *Little Dorrit*, one of Shklovsky's favourite Dickens texts, with relation to both the comic and to what he describes, in yet another echo of Tynyanov's description of the dual-planed character of parody, as its 'typical double-accented, double-styled *hybrid construction*'.[113]

Shklovsky had discussed Dickens' *Little Dorrit* with reference to parody in both his study of the English classical novel and in his essay on the mystery novel in his *O Teorii Prozy*,[114] and Bakhtin goes on to write of other authors of the English comic novel of whom Shklovsky has made mention that 'in Dickens' predecessors, Fielding, Smollett and Sterne, the men who founded the English comic novel, we find the same parodic stylization of various levels and genres of literary language, but the distance between these levels and genres is greater than it is in Dickens and the exaggeration is stronger (especially in Sterne)'.[115]

While he will write in his later essay on the chronotope on how Rabelais' laughter is less radical and more soft in Sterne,[116] Bakhtin goes on in this essay to describe Sterne's parody as being 'almost as radical': 'The parodic and objectivized incorporation into their work of various types of literary language (especially in Sterne) penetrates the deepest levels of literary and ideological thought itself, resulting in a parody of the logical and expressive structure of any ideological

112 See Bakhtin, *The Dialogic Imagination*, p. 301.
113 Ibid., p. 304 and see also Bakhtin, *Voprosy*, p. 117.
114 See Shklovsky, *O Teorii Prozy*, 1925, pp. 112–38; the translated excerpts from that essay in Matejka and Pomorska, pp. 220–6; and Sher's complete translation of the 1929 edition of the essay, in Sher, pp. 117–46.
115 See Bakhtin, *The Dialogic Imagination*, p. 308.
116 Ibid., p. 237.

discourse as such (scholarly, moral and rhetorical, poetic) that is almost as radical as the parody we find in Rabelais.'[117]

Bakhtin also refers us to what he sees to be the specific and general roles of parody in the comic English novel, and via an argument which can be contrasted with one put in P. N. Medvedev's *The Formal Method in Literary Scholarship. A Critical Introduction to Sociological Poetics* against Shklovsky that Sterne's parody in *Tristram Shandy* revealed only the distortions of good novels and not the 'typical':[118] 'Literary parody understood in the narrow sense plays a fundamental role in the way language is structured in Fielding, Smollett and Sterne (the Richardsonian novel is parodied by the first two, and almost all contemporary novel-types are parodied by Sterne). Literary parody serves to distance the author still further from language, to complicate still further his relationship to the literary language of his time, especially in the novel's own territory. The novelistic discourse dominating a given epoch is itself turned into an object and itself becomes a means for refracting new authorial intentions.'[119]

Like both Shklovsky and Tynyanov, Bakhtin further attributes a role to parody in the evolution of the novel: 'Literary parody of dominant novel-types plays a large role in the history of the European novel. One could even say that the most important novelistic models and novel-types arose precisely during this parodic destruction of preceding novelistic worlds. This is true of the work of Cervantes, Mendoza, Grimmelshausen, Rabelais, Lesage and many others.' For Rabelais, Bakhtin adds, 'a parodic attitude toward almost all forms of ideological discourse – philosophical, moral, scholarly, rhetorical, poetic and in particular the pathos-charged forms of discourse ... was intensified to the point where it became a parody of the very act of conceptualizing anything in language'.[120]

Such comments by Bakhtin on the importance of Rabelais for the history of the comic novel are largely orientated towards the role played in his work, and in that of similar spirits such as Cervantes and Sterne, of what Bakhtin terms the 'various forms and degrees of parodic stylization of incorporated languages'. In later writings,

117 Ibid., p. 308.
118 See Medvedev, *The Formal Method in Literary Scholarship. A Critical Introduction to Sociological Poetics*, pp. 114–16.
119 See Bakhtin, *The Dialogic Imagination*, p. 309.
120 Ibid. Bakhtin, *The Dialogic Imagination*, p. 310 also describes Sterne's *Tristram Shandy* as following Rabelais' 'philosophy of the word'.

however, Bakhtin will develop his concept of carnivalistic parody further from the examples provided by Rabelais (as well as from studies of both carnival and the grotesque[121]) and speak of his parody, and that of other 'carnivalistic' works, as 'grotesque parody'.[122]

Bakhtin goes on to say in his early essay that parodic stylisation is a stylisation 'that, in the most radical, most Rabelaisian representatives of this novel-type (Sterne and Jean Paul), verges on a rejection of any straightforward and unmediated seriousness' and 'limits itself to a principled criticism of the word as such'.[123] For Bakhtin such parody is also a 'comic form' for the incorporation and organisation of 'heteroglossia' in the novel, and while the comic itself is not analysed further the 'play with a posited author' in the comic novel descended from Cervantes is contrasted with other forms of heteroglossia which are 'defined by their use of a personified and concretely posited author (written speech) or teller (oral speech)'.

Bakhtin's summary of what he has said on heteroglossia in the novel returns us to Cervantes' *Don Quixote*, and to some of the features which had made it of interest to Shklovsky: 'We have touched upon only those major forms typical of the most important variants of the European novel, but in themselves they do not, of course, exhaust all the possible means for incorporating and organizing heteroglossia in the novel. A combination of all these forms in separate given novels, and consequently in various generic types generated by these novels, is also possible. Of such a sort is the classic and purest model of the novel as genre – Cervantes' *Don Quixote*, which realizes in itself, in extraordinary depth and breadth, all the artistic possibilities of heteroglot and internally dialogized novelistic discourse.'[124]

Bakhtin's following comments on heteroglossia repeat some of his statements on the 'double-voiced' character of parody in his 1929 book on Dostoyevsky but also contain some new terms and insights: 'Heteroglossia, once incorporated into the novel (whatever the forms for its incorporation), is *another's speech in another's language*, serving to express authorial intentions, but in a refracted way. Such speech

---

121 Bakhtin mentions, for example, both Heinrich Schneegans' and Wolfgang Kayser's works on the grotesque in his *Rabelais and his World* of 1965.

122 As noted previously, Tomashevsky had also spoken briefly of 'grotesque parody' in later editions of his *Teoriya Literatury*, but without the praise for it given by Bakhtin in his works.

123 See Bakhtin, *The Dialogic Imagination*, p. 312.   124 Ibid., p. 324.

constitutes a special type of *double-voiced discourse*. It serves two speakers at the same time and expresses simultaneously two different intentions: the direct intention of the character who is speaking, and the refracted intention of the author. In such discourse there are two voices, two meanings and two expressions. And all the while these two voices are dialogically interrelated, they – as it were – know about each other (just as two exchanges in a dialogue know of each other and are structured in this mutual knowledge of each other); it is as if they actually hold a conversation with each other. Double-voiced discourse is always internally dialogized. Examples of this would be comic, ironic or parodic discourse, the refracting discourse of a narrator, refracting discourse in the language of a character and finally the discourse of a whole incorporated genre – all these discourses are double-voiced and internally dialogized. A potential dialogue is embedded in them, one as yet unfolded, a concentrated dialogue of two voices, two world views, two languages.'[125]

To describe parody as 'double-voiced' is, however, only to describe one of its aspects, and one which, as the above quotation shows, it shares with several other forms. Although some other more recent critics may be said to have overlooked this latter fact, Bakhtin himself reminds us of it after analysing the *skaz*: 'All such phenomena (stylization, parody, *skaz*) are also, as has been shown above, double-voiced and double-languaged phenomena.'[126]

Bakhtin's identification of parody and hybridisation also attributes the role he has given parody in literary evolution to other hybrid forms when he suggests that 'we may even say that language and languages change historically primarily by means of hybridization, by means of a mixing of various "languages" co-existing within the boundaries of a single dialect'.[127] Bakhtin also depicts the 'novelistic hybrid' as '*an artistically organized system for bringing different languages in contact with one another*, a system having as its goal the illumination of one language by means of another, the carving-out of a living image of another language'.[128] When Bakhtin returns to the example of comic and parodic novels such as *Don Quixote* and *Tristram Shandy* to illustrate a following point that 'where hybridization occurs, the language being used to illuminate another language ... is reified to the point where it itself becomes an image of a language', he is, however,

125 Ibid., pp. 324–5.   126 Ibid., p. 337.   127 Ibid., pp. 358–9.
128 Ibid., p. 361.

using examples of the parodic reification of language to illustrate a general point about hybridisation in a way which underplays the specifically comic functions of the parodies in question.

Having suggested some links between dialogic and hybrid forms (and through his use of parody texts as examples for the latter) Bakhtin goes on to distinguish between hybridisation and dialogisation: 'Hybridization, in the strict sense, differs from internally dialogized, interillumination of language systems taken as a whole. In the former case there is no direct mixing of two languages within the boundaries of a single utterance – rather, only one language is actually present in the utterance, but it is rendered *in the light of another language*. This second language is not, however, actualized and remains outside the utterance.'[129] Bakhtin adds that 'the clearest and most characteristic form of an internally dialogized mutual illumination of languages is *stylization*'.

Bakhtin writes next of parodic stylisation with a reduced stress on the ambivalence of parody and an increased stress on its tensions and destructiveness: 'In another type of internally dialogized inter-illumination of languages, the intentions of the representing discourse are at odds with the intentions of the represented discourse; they fight against them, they depict a real world of objects not by using the represented language as a productive point of view, but rather by using it as an exposé to destroy the represented language. This is the nature of *parodic stylization*.'[130]

Bakhtin continues by re-introducing the possibility of a more ambivalent and creative stance for the parodist, and by relegating the more destructive attitude which he has begun to describe above to what he terms 'rhetorical parody': 'Such a parodic stylization can, however, create an image of language and a world corresponding to it only on condition that the stylization not function as a gross and superficial destruction of the other's language, as happens in rhetorical parody. In order to be authentic and productive, parody must be precisely a parodic *stylization*, that is, it must re-create the parodied language as an authentic whole, giving it its due as a language possessing its own internal logic and one capable of revealing its own world inextricably bound up with the parodied language.'[131]

Bakhtin then writes of stylisation and parody, but without reference to the way in which parody may be separated from stylisation because

---

129 Ibid., p. 362.   130 Ibid., pp. 363–4.   131 Ibid., p. 364.

of its comic elements: 'Between stylization and parody, as between two extremes, are distributed the most varied forms for languages to mutually illuminate each other and for direct hybrids, forms that are themselves determined by the most varied interactions among languages, the most varied wills to language and to speech, that encounter one another within the limits of a single utterance. The struggle going on within discourse, the degree of resistance that the parodied language offers to the parodying language, the degree to which the represented social languages are fully formed entities and the degree to which they are individualized representation and finally the surrounding heteroglossia (which always serves as a dialogizing background and resonator) – all these create a multitude of devices for representing another's language.'

In addition to echoing Tynyanov's distinctions between stylisation and parody to at least some extent here, Bakhtin appears to follow Shklovsky when he suggests that 'parodic stylization' can be suspected through the interruption of a story such as Sterne's *Tristram Shandy*.[132] Bakhtin also takes on Tynyanov's problems with the identification of parody, and lack of acknowledgement of the power of the parody to evoke and preserve its target text, when he states that 'except in those cases where it is grossly apparent, the presence of parody is in general very difficult to identify (that is, difficult to identify precisely in literary prose, where it rarely is gross), without knowing the background of alien discourse against which it is projected, that is, without knowing its second context'.[133]

In this essay Bakhtin does, however, broaden his description of heteroglossia to encompass the role played by popular or folk characters or fools in the parody, and this is a move which may be said to have been of some significance in forging the link with the carnivalistic which was both to dominate his later work and to differentiate it further from that of the formalists.

Even when he echoes Tynyanov's and Shklovsky's depictions of Sancho Panza as parodying Don Quixote in his conversations with the latter, Bakhtin puts greater stress on the lower region of life represented by Sancho and his discourse than either Tynyanov or Shklovsky had done when discussing Cervantes' novel: 'In *Don*

---

132 Ibid., p. 374.
133 Ibid. Bakhtin also goes on here to refer to the presence of parodic stylisation and other variants of double-voiced discourse in the Sophistic novel.

Quixote the internally polemical orientation of "respectable" discourse vis-à-vis heteroglossia unfolds in novelistic dialogues with Sancho, with other representatives of the heteroglot and coarse realities of life and in the movement of the novel's plot as well. The internal dialogue potential embedded in respectable discourse is thus actualized and brought to the surface – in dialogues and in plot movement – but, like every authentic manifestation of the dialogic principle in language – it does not exhaust itself completely in them, and is not resolved dramatically.'[134]

To Bakhtin both Cervantes and Rabelais are representative for such reasons of what he terms a 'Second Stylistic Line': 'For the Second Stylistic Line, the respectable language of the chivalric romance – with all its polemical abstractness – becomes only one of the participants in a dialogue of languages, it becomes the prosaic image of a language – most profoundly and fully instanced in Cervantes – capable of internally dialogic resistance to new authorial intentions; it is an image that is agitatedly double-voiced.'[135]

Bakhtin adds later that 'the one-sided dialogism that is present in embedded form in Sentimental novels is made explicit in novels of the Second Stylistic Line, where Sentimental pathos, as one language among other languages, as one of many sides in the dialogue of languages surrounding a man and his world, takes on a parodic ring.'[136] (A foot-note to this also refers to Fielding, Smollett and Sterne and to others in Germany such as Musäus and Wieland as examples and adds: 'In their artistic handling of the problem of Sentimental pathos (and the didactic approach) in its relationship to actual experience, all these authors follow the lead of *Don Quixote*, whose influence is decisively important.')

Later still Bakhtin refers again to *Don Quixote* as an exemplar of the Second Stylistic Line and writes of the latter as containing works in which parody is not merely polemical but is part of a broader artistic purpose: 'In these great and seminal works the novelistic genre becomes what it really is, it unfolds in its fullest potential. In such works authentic double-voiced novelistic images fully ripen, now

134 Ibid., p. 384.
135 Ibid., p. 386. Bakhtin, pp. 385–6, had also described such works as dragging high styles down to the low so that 'heteroglossia avenges itself for having been excluded and made abstract' (as in, for example, the chivalric romance).
136 Ibid., p. 398.

profoundly differentiated from poetic symbols, and become the unique thing they ultimately are ... Languages cease to be merely the object of a purely polemical or autotelic parodying: without losing their parodic coloration completely, they begin to assume the function of artistic representation, of a representation with value in its own right.'[137]

Bakhtin then speaks again of the 'dialogic resistance' put up by the parodied text to the parodying intentions of the other and of how 'an unresolved conversation begins to sound in the image itself', and goes on to suggest that later developments from *Don Quixote* were part of the process of trying to resolve the unresolved arguments embedded in it.[138] Following these points Bakhtin suggests how the embedding of different genres in novels of the Second Stylistic Line introduce heteroglossia into the novel,[139] and adds that 'as a counterweight to "literariness", novels of the Second Line foreground a critique of literary discourse as such, and primarily novelistic discourse'.[140] Bakhtin continues by echoing both Shklovsky's and his own comments on how the novel in general is characterised by self-criticism (though without explaining how the novels of the 'First Line' fit into this claim): 'The *auto-criticism of discourse* is one of the primary distinguishing features of the novel as a genre. Discourse is criticized in its relationship to reality: its attempt to faithfully reflect reality, to manage reality and to transpose it (the utopian pretences of discourse), even to replace reality as a surrogate for it (the dream and the fantasy that replace life).' Bakhtin adds with reference to Cervantes' parody: 'Already in *Don Quixote* we have a literary, novelistic discourse being treated by life, by reality. And in its further development, the novel of the Second Line remains in large measure a novel that tests literary discourse.' Bakhtin then divides this testing of literary discourse into two types and writes that the first type 'concentrates the critique and trial of literary discourse around the hero – a "literary man", who looks at life through the eyes of literature and who tries to live "according to literature".'[141]

The formalist concept of the 'laying bare of the device' is also used

137 Ibid., p. 409. (Bakhtin also contrasts the novels of the 'Second Line' to other 'picaresque or comic parodic prose' here.)   138 Ibid., pp. 409 f.
139 Ibid., p. 411.   140 Ibid., p. 412.
141 Ibid., p. 413. Bakhtin names *Don Quixote* and *Madame Bovary* as the best-known exemplars of this type but then says this can be found in 'almost every major novel'.

by Bakhtin to describe some types of meta-fictional works when he applies his second type of testing to 'an author who is in the process of writing the novel (a "laying bare of the device", in the terminology of the Formalists), not however in the capacity of a character, but rather as the real author of the given work'. Bakhtin again echoes Shklovsky when he relates this type of testing to Sterne's parodistic treatment of the novel and notes that 'alongside the apparent novel there are fragments of a "novel about the novel"' (the classic exemplar is, of course, *Tristram Shandy*)'. As Bakhtin himself goes on to say, and as Shklovsky too had shown, this second type may, however, also be found in *Don Quixote*: 'Both these types of testing literary discourse may, moreover, be blended into one. Thus as early as *Don Quixote* we already have elements of a novel about a novel (the polemic of the author against the author of the projected second part). And the forms of testing literary discourse may be highly diverse (variations on the second type are especially numerous).'

Bakhtin continues with especial reference to parody, and makes a distinction between that which he terms an 'external and crude literary parody', where attack on the target seems to dominate, and a second kind of parody, where the parodist is in 'solidarity with the parodied discourse': 'Finally, we must emphasise in particular the varying degrees of parodying to which literary discourse is subjected. As a rule, the testing of discourse is coupled with its being parodied – but the degree of parody, as well as the degree of dialogic resistance of the parodied discourse, may be highly varied: from external and crude literary parody (where nothing more than parody is intended) to an almost complete solidarity with the parodied discourse ("romantic irony"); midway between these two extremes, that is, somewhere between literary parody and "romantic irony" stands *Don Quixote*, with its profound but cunningly balanced dialogism of parodying discourse.'

While the first of these types of parody appears to understand parody as a song sung in opposition, or as 'Gegengesang', the second kind – which Bakhtin ends up describing as 'romantic irony' rather than as parody – stresses the consonance of parody with its target, as is assumed to be the case in parody understood as 'Beigesang'. Bakhtin's designation of *Don Quixote* as standing midway between these two extremes 'with its profound but cunningly balanced dialogism of parodying discourse' brings parody back to the position where it should have been from the beginning as *both* 'Gegengesang' *and* 'Beigesang', rather than as *either* 'Gegengesang' *or* 'Beigesang', although Bakhtin himself does not make this point, and again leaves his own theoretical depiction of parody divided between a more simple, negative, ridiculing form and a more stylistically complex one in what can be described as a still modern manner.

One other point which Bakhtin does make explicit in this part of his work (and in some contrast to Shklovsky) is, however, that not all types of literary meta-fiction or self-questioning are parody. Bakhtin notes with reference to this point that 'we do find testing of literary discourse in the novel that completely lacks this parodying intention', and gives a work by M. Prishvin as an example of a novel about a novel which does not use parody.[142] Bakhtin also appears to contradict his and Shklovsky's earlier claims that the novel in general is characterised by self-criticism when he writes that 'the category of literariness characteristic of the First Line, with its dogmatic pretensions to lead a real life, is replaced, in novels of the Second Line, by a trial and self-critique of novelistic discourse'.[143] These distinctions are, however, again swept away when Bakhtin goes on to make the point that 'toward the beginning of the nineteenth century this sharp opposition between two stylistic lines in the novel [such as the romance and its parody] comes to an end ... Any novel of any significance in the nineteenth and twentieth centuries is of a mixed character, although of course the Second Line dominates.'[144]

The section of Bakhtin's essay 'Forms of Time and of the Chronotope in the Novel. Notes toward a Historical Poetics' of 1937–8[145] which is entitled '*The Functions of the Rogue, Clown and Fool in the Novel*'[146] differs more clearly from the work of the formalists in reflecting Bakhtin's increasing interest, in the 1930s and after, in the folkloric and carnivalistic forms of parody,[147] although here too there

---

142 Ibid., pp. 413–14. 143 Ibid., p. 414.
144 Ibid. Bakhtin also goes on in conclusion to this (p. 422) to speak of how different ages accentuate and reaccentuate certain characteristics of these novelistic traditions and of how this is important for understanding literary history.
145 Ibid., pp. 84–258, and *Voprosy*, pp. 234–407.
146 See Bakhtin, *The Dialogic Imagination*, pp. 158 ff. One other study of the fool from this time is Enid Welsford's *The Fool. His Social and Literary History* of 1935.
147 One reason for this may have been the demands made in the edicts on socialist realism for more interest to be shown in popular subjects and forms, as suggested, for instance, by Clark and Holquist, pp. 271–2, although Bakhtin also developed his interest along the lines of seeing carnival as a challenge to orthodoxy in a way which did not sit entirely well with those edicts.

is some recourse both to his own and their earlier stylistic interests and beliefs.

Bakhtin not only refers here to the role of satire and parody in the mediaeval carnival where the figures of the rogue, clown and fool dominate proceedings, but, as in his 1963 study of Dostoyevsky, to the carnival square in which they appear: 'Their laughter bears the stamp of the public square where the folk gather. They reestablish the public nature of the human figure; ... their entire function consists in externalizing things. ... This creates that distinctive means for externalizing a human being, via parodic laughter.'[148] Bakhtin then goes on to describe Cervantes' *Don Quixote* as the 'parodied hybridization of the "alien, miraculous world" chronotope of chivalric romances, with the "high road winding through one's native land" chronotope that is typical of the picaresque novel',[149] and suggests (though again without analysis of its contribution to the comedy of Cervantes' novel) that this hybridisation of the two chronotopes 'radically changes their character; both of them take on metaphoric significance and enter into completely new relations with the real world'.[150]

Bakhtin even seems to move closer to those who would prefer to analyse parody as 'double-voiced' *rather* than as comic (and to reflect the understanding of others of comic parody as something limited) when he goes on to suggest in this essay that terms like 'parody' and 'joke' are but 'narrowly restrictive labels' for the 'heterogeneity and subtlety' of the idea of prosaic allegorisation introduced by figures such as the rogue.[151] Despite this, Bakhtin again spends much time on an analysis of laughter which includes some reference back to parodic and comic forms of carnivalised literature,[152] and gives a statement about the 'freedom' of the latter: 'Of all aspects of the ancient complex, only laughter never underwent sublimation of any sort — neither religious, mystical nor philosophical. It never took on an

---

148 See Bakhtin, *The Dialogic Imagination*, pp. 159–60.

149 Ibid., p. 165 (Bakhtin, p. 84, explains the term chronotope is derived from the 'Einstinian connection of time and space'.)   150 Ibid., p. 165.

151 Ibid., p. 166. Bakhtin also appears to separate parody from the more complex meta-fictionality of *Tristram Shandy* when he refers to Sterne's use of the concept of 'Shandyism' for this 'prosaic allegorization', and to the complexity of his work.

152 Bakhtin also discusses the importance of laughter in other essays in his *Voprosy*; in *Problems*, 1963; *Rabelais and his World*, 1965; and *Speech Genres and Other Late Essays*, translated by Vern W. McGee and edited by Caryl Emerson and Michael Holquist (Austin, 1986), p. 135.

official character, and even in literature the comic genres were the most free, the least regimented.'[153]

Following the above comment on laughter Bakhtin notes that no systematic classification of irony, parody, humour, or the joke yet existed in his time,[154] and adds in another echo of Tynyanov, as well as of many other commentators on parody, that one cannot understand parody 'without reference to the parodied material', 'without exceeding the boundaries of the given context'. As in his more extended analyses of the dual structure of the parody, which could have been expanded to show how the parody uses the parodied text as part of its structure and can remind the reader of the parodied work by such means, Bakhtin (like Tynyanov) again omits to mention that a parody may establish the identity of its target and its world for the reader of the parody within the parody text, and as a part of its 'double-voicedness'.

Bakhtin's essay 'From the Prehistory of Novelistic Discourse' of 1940[155] has also echoed Shklovsky on modern literature in claiming that one of the characteristics of the novel is its constant self-criticism: 'The stylistic structure of *Evgenij Onegin* is typical of all authentic novels. To a greater or lesser extent, every novel is a dialogized system made up of the images of "languages", styles and consciousnesses that are concrete and inseparable from language. Language in the novel not only represents, but itself serves as the object of representation. Novelistic discourse is always criticizing itself.'[156]

From this point Bakhtin moves on to describe the role of laughter in the development of the novelistic genre but speaks of its ancient, 'ridiculing' forms as a separate force from that of the 'polyglossia' and 'interanimation of languages' which 'elevated' those forms 'to a new and ideological level, which made possible the genre of the novel'.[157]

Bakhtin continues in the following section of his essay to comment

---

153 See Bakhtin, *The Dialogic Imagination*, p. 236. On p. 220 Bakhtin had referred to the influence of Aristophanes on the works of Rabelais and on p. 221 to that of Lucian on Rabelais, and also adds p. 236 on Rabelais: 'In the world of Rabelais, more decisively significant than any other way of reworking the ancient complex we have considered (with the exception of the Aristophanic and Lucianic types) is *laughter*.'

154 See Bakhtin, *The Dialogic Imagination*, p. 237.

155 Ibid., pp. 41–83; *Voprosy*, pp. 408–446.

156 See Bakhtin, *The Dialogic Imagination*, p. 49.

157 Ibid., pp. 50 f. Bakhtin's word for ridicule here (see *Voprosy*, p. 417) is 'osmeyaniye'.

specifically on parody as 'one of the most ancient and widespread forms for representing the direct word of another',[158] but also turns to a somewhat narrow understanding of even its more sophisticated examples as ridicule:[159] 'One of the most ancient and widespread forms for representing the direct word of another is *parody*. What is distinctive about parody as a form? Take, for example, the parodic *sonnets* with which *Don Quixote* begins. Although they are impeccably structured as sonnets, we could never possibly assign them to the sonnet genre. In *Don Quixote* they appear as part of a novel – but even the isolated parodic sonnet (outside the novel) could not be classified generically as a sonnet. In a parodied sonnet, the sonnet form is not a genre at all; that is, it is not the form of a whole but is rather *the object of representation*: the sonnet here is the *hero of the parody*. In a parody on the sonnet, we must first of all recognize a sonnet, recognize its form, its specific style, its manner of seeing, its manner of selecting from and evaluating the world – the world view of the sonnet as it were. A parody may represent and ridicule these distinctive features of the sonnet well or badly, profoundly or superficially. But in any case, what results is not a sonnet, but rather the *image of a sonnet*.'[160]

Much else of what Bakhtin says here about parody and its treatment of distinctive generic features may be agreed with in the case of those parodies, such as the 'mock epic', which attempt to refunction the generic characteristics of their targets. (Bakhtin goes on to say after the above passage that 'for the same reasons one could not under any circumstances assign to the genre of "epic poem" the parodic epic "War between the Mice and the Frogs" (*sic.*),[161] and adds that 'we would also have to say the same of Scarron's *Virgil travesti*'.[162]) Parody, as seen in chapter 1, and as Bakhtin himself suggests elsewhere, need not, however, only imitate and then attack the formal or generic characteristics of a work.

Bakhtin continues by again associating parody with ridicule, and

158 See Bakhtin, *The Dialogic Imagination*, p. 51.
159 Bakhtin (*Voprosy*, p. 418) uses another, but related word for ridicule here, of 'vismeyat''.   160 Bakhtin, *The Dialogic Imagination*, p. 51.
161 Bakhtin's inversion of the usual title of the 'Batrachomyomachia', or 'Battle of the Frogs and the Mice', may be an error, but also appears on one of the versions discussed by Ludwich.
162 A note to Bakhtin's *Rabelais and his World* (1965), translated by Helene Iswolsky (Cambridge, Mass. and London, 1968), p. 200, also describes Scarron as following 'the Rabelaisian line'.

with the ridicule of largely serious works: 'All these parodies on genres and generic styles ("languages") enter the great and diverse world of verbal forms that ridicule the straightforward, serious word in all its generic disguises.'[163] Despite describing parody as ridicule, on the basis of older carnivalistic forms, but also on the basis of what has been seen in preceding chapters to be a modern, post-seventeenth-century reduction of parody to the burlesque and to its ridiculing functions,[164] Bakhtin's text goes on to criticise those who have extrapolated from these more modern forms of parody to the older: 'The nature and methods available for ridiculing something are highly varied, and not exhausted by parodying and travestying in a strict sense. These methods for making fun of the straightforward word have as yet received little scholarly attention. Our general conceptions of parody and travesty in literature were formed as a scholarly discipline solely by studying very late forms of literary parody, forms of the type represented by Scarron's *Énéide travestie*,[165] or Platen's "Verhängnisvolle Gabel", that is, the impoverished, superficial and historically least significant forms. These impoverished and limited conceptions of the nature of the parodying and travestying word were then retroactively applied to the supremely rich and varied world of parody and travesty in previous ages.'[166]

Bakhtin also seems unaware of the similarity of his own concept of parody as ridicule to these modern concepts of parody as burlesque when he continues to speak not only of parody and travesty in the same breath but of 'the parodic-travestying forms in world literature'. While Bakhtin's use of the term 'parodic-travestying' may be said to take parody back to the variety of types to which the word was applied by the ancients, before its reduction to a type of 'high' burlesque and the introduction of the word travesty to describe the 'low burlesque' in the seventeenth century and after, it brings with it the other reductive features of the more modern term 'travesty'. Bakhtin goes on to refer to several classical accounts of these 'parodic-travestying forms' from ancient times onwards,[167] and adds: 'It is our

163 See Bakhtin, *The Dialogic Imagination*, p. 52 and Bakhtin, *Voprosy*, pp. 418 f.
164 Bakhtin's words here again include forms of the word for ridicule, 'osmeyaniye'.
165 See Paul Scarron's *Le Virgile Travesty* of 1648–53. (Bakhtin simply writes a Russian transliteration of 'Énéide' here.)
166 See Bakhtin, *The Dialogic Imagination*, p. 52.
167 Ibid., pp. 52–3 names his sources for the ancient period as Aulus Gellius, Plutarch, Ambrosius Theodosius Macrobius, and Athenaeus, and also refers to

conviction that there never was a strictly straightforward genre, no single type of direct discourse – artistic, rhetorical, philosophical, religious, ordinary everyday – that did not have its own parodying and travestying double, its own comic-ironic *contre-partie*. What is more, these parodic doubles and laughing reflections of the direct word were, in some cases, just as sanctioned by tradition and just as canonized as their elevated models.'[168]

The 'doubling' of which Bakhtin is speaking here is, moreover, of a different kind to the doubling of which he had spoken earlier with reference to the 'dialogical' or 'double-voiced' character of the parody text. Here we have, in addition to that more twentieth-century stylistic analysis of the double structure within the parody, a description of the parody (or 'travesty') work itself as a parodying double to that which it is 'ridiculing' which revives the description given by Scaliger and others of the ridiculing imitation of the Homeric rhapsodists by the ancient 'parodoi'. (The possibility that Dostoyevsky's *The Double* had influenced Bakhtin's use of the term 'parodic double' in some way might, however, also be taken into account here, and especially given both the parodic character of the 'double' described in Dostoyevsky's story, and Bakhtin's reference to Dostoyevsky's 'parodying double' in the section of his *Problems of Dostoyevsky's Poetics* in which parody is described as a 'laughing aspect'.[169])

Bakhtin goes on to apply this concept of the 'parodic double' to what has been seen as ridiculing parody in both ancient and later times, and suggests that these parodic doubles also indicate 'that the literary consciousness of the Greeks did not view the parodic-travestying reworkings of national myth as any particular profanation or blasphemy. It is characteristic that the Greeks were not at all embarrassed to attribute the authorship of the parodic work "War between the Mice and the Frogs" [sic] to Homer himself.'[170] Where

the more modern scholarly works of A. Dietrich, Hermann Reich (an author of a work on the mime) and F. M. Cornford.
168 Ibid., p. 53. Bakhtin also goes on to briefly discuss the 'fourth drama' or satyr play vis-à-vis the tragedy.
169 See Bakhtin, *Problems*, pp. 127 f., quoted in the following discussion of Bakhtin's 1963 text. (Like Dostoyevsky's 'double' Bakhtin's 'parodying double' does not represent a complete duplication of the work it parodies but entails a distortion and 'destruction' of the latter.) And see Freidenberg on old and new parody.
170 See Bakhtin, *The Dialogic Imagination*, p. 55.

Tynyanov had explained the tolerance by orthodox groups of parodies of their canonic works to rest in the ambivalent dual-planed structure of the parody, Bakhtin now suggests that ridiculing parodies or travesties were allowed because they were corrective 'doubles' to their more 'straightforward' targets: 'For any and every straight-forward genre, any and every direct discourse − epic, tragic, lyric, philosophical − may and indeed must itself become the object of representation, the object of a parodic travestying "mimicry". It is as if such mimicry rips the word away from its object, disunifies the two, shows that a given straightforward generic word − epic or tragic − is one-sided, bounded, incapable of exhausting the object; the process of parodying forces us to experience those sides of the object that are not otherwise included in a given genre or a given style.' Bakhtin adds: 'Parodic-travestying literature introduces the permanent corrective of laughter, of a critique on the one-sided seriousness of the lofty direct word, the corrective of reality that is always richer, more fundamental and most importantly *too contradictory and heteroglot* to be fit into a high and straightforward genre. The high genres are monotonic, while the "fourth drama" [the satyr play] and genres akin to it retain the ancient binary tone of the word.'

Despite his previous descriptions of such 'corrective' parody as ridicule, Bakhtin also states here that 'ancient parody was free of any nihilistic denial'. Bakhtin's reasons for stating this are, however, to take us back to his description of parody as the ridicule of the form of the genre in which the ancient heroes were celebrated: 'It was not after all, the heroes who were parodied, nor the Trojan War and its participants; what was parodied was only its epic heroization; not Hercules and his exploits but their tragic heroization.' Bakhtin continues along this track, if with some further reduction of his previous emphases on ridicule: 'The genre itself, the style, the language are all put into cheerfully irreverent quotation marks, and they are perceived against a backdrop of a contradictory reality that cannot be confined within their narrow frames. The direct and serious word was revealed, in all its limitations and insufficiency, only after it had become the laughing image of that word − but it was by no means discredited in the process.'[171] Bakhtin concludes: 'Thus it did not bother the Greeks to think that Homer himself wrote a parody of Homeric style.'[172]

171 Ibid., pp. 55–6.   172 Ibid., p. 56.

Bakhtin's descriptions of ancient parody, both here and elsewhere, may also represent at least some projection of his studies of mediaeval sacred parody and of the rationales for its allowance of the parody of sacred texts onto parody in general. Bakhtin's following discussion of mediaeval parody goes on to connect the mediaeval carnival to that of the Roman saturnalia,[173] and to reveal one of his sources for his account of the mediaeval *parodia sacra* and its legitimisation to be the work of the German scholar Paul Lehmann: 'One of the best authorities on medieval parody, Paul Lehmann, states outright that the history of medieval literature and its Latin literature in particular "is the history of the appropriation, re-working and imitation of someone else's property" ... – or as we would say, of another's language, another's style, another's word.'[174] While Bakhtin will follow Lehmann in several ways, he adds the term 'parodic-travestying' literature to Lehmann's analyses when he continues by noting that 'here a whole spectrum of possible relationships toward this word comes to light, beginning at one pole with the pious and inert quotation that is isolated and set off like an icon, and ending at the other pole with the most ambiguous, disrespectful, parodic-travestying use of a quotation.'[175]

Paul Lehmann's *Die Parodie im Mittelalter* of 1922[176] (p. 11) had itself said of parody that it was 'a special kind of imitation', but that to call it just imitation was to make it meaningless, and that (p. 13) it must also be described as having carried out its distortions and transformations of other works with the intention of producing comedy. Having said this Lehmann had added (p. 14) that the mediaeval parody could be comical without serious ridicule and that when the mediaeval parodists did mock something it was generally not the holy text but some misuser of it. After defining his use of parody in this way, Lehmann (p. 25) had gone on to give as an example of such mediaeval parody the 'Cena Cypriani' (or 'Feast of Cyprian'), which he first describes as 'an old Christian parody of large dimensions inherited and renewed in the ninth century'. It began, as Lehmann writes, and as can

---

173 Ibid., pp. 68 ff.

174 Ibid., p. 69. Bakhtin is referring to Lehmann, 1922, p. 10.

175 See Bakhtin, *The Dialogic Imagination*, p. 69. Bakhtin does not state towards what the parody might be disrespectful here and even continues, p. 70, to say that with regard to the parodic playing with a work that 'it is often difficult to determine the degree of license permitted in that play'.

176 See Paul Lehmann, *Die Parodie im Mittelalter* (Munich, 1922).

be seen from the versions given in the *Monumenta Germaniae* to which he refers,[177] with the lines that 'once upon a time there was a King of the East named Johel, who wished to give a great feast at Cana in Galilee'. Lehmann adds (p. 26) that the story of the work was that after dining at the table in the manner appropriate to the biblical attributes or stories (Adam seats himself in the centre, Eve sits on an enormous fig-leaf, Cain on his plough, Abel on a milk pail, Noah on his ark and Samson on the pillars of the temple etc.), and being affected by the feast in appropriate manner (Adam lies down to sleep, Noah gets drunk, Pilate brings water to the table for the guests to wash their hands, David reaches for his harp, and Pharaoh chases after the guests and falls in the water), the guests had to bring the king gifts – including Christ a lamb and Moses two tablets. But then there comes a conflict when the king discovers that all sorts of things have been stolen, and martyrs the guests until Agar is killed for the sins of all of them and is buried with great ceremony.

Lehmann (pp. 26–7) comments on this echo of the Bible, and on other biblical references in it, that its treatment of them is so comic that we sometimes forget their original seriousness. Lehmann then adds (p. 27) that as late as 1904 a Jesuit had described the function of the *Cena Cypriani* to be that of a mnemonic and had referred to a treatise by Zeno of Verona as an authority, but that a contrary view is given by Lapôtre, who tried to relate the *Cena Cypriani* to a grotesque satire of the Spaniard Bachiarius on a banquet of the Emperor Julian the Apostate (Kirk, p. xv, names him as a Menippean satirist) in honour of the goddess Ceres. Lehmann, however, thinks neither view is fully correct and says that while it is true that the Veronese Bishop Zeno in one Easter sermon had advised his flock to satiate themselves with the Bible rather than with food and drink at Easter, and had gathered together all sorts of references in the Old and New Testaments to feasts of eating and drinking to colour his point, one witty fellow – possibly a 'Cyprian', but not the saint – had taken up Zeno's words and parodied them, and not to mock the sacred Word but, at the most, its devaluation by Zeno. Lehmann also notes that the work itself was

---

177 See, for instance, the *Monumenta Germaniae*, vol. IV, parts II & III, edited by Karl Strecker (Berlin, 1923); part II, pp. 857–900. (Lehmann is able to refer to this part in 1922 as it had first been published, and with his assistance, in 1914. The third part was only published together with the second in 1923, but, as in the 1914 volume, Lehmann's assistance with the volume is acknowledged in Strecker's prefatory comments to it.)

forgotten for some time before it was discovered again in the ninth century and that even then the Carolingian scholars did not regard it as blasphemous.[178]

Lehmann returns to the theory that the *Cena Cypriani* was used as a mnemonic when he writes that the old *Cena Cypriani* was popular as an amusing text for learning the names and attributes of biblical stories and characters, and also refers to the findings of another of Bakhtin's authorities on mediaeval parody, Francesco Novati, in his 'parody book',[179] that the old text had been expanded into an unequivocally jovial parody[180] in the second half of the ninth century by a Roman deacon named John and that there the *Cena Cypriani* is more of a 'burlesque entertainment' than in the earlier prose version.[181]

Further to describing the use of the *Cena Cypriani* as a burlesque, Lehmann notes (pp. 29–30) that Lapôtre believed that the poem was performed in the presence of Charles the Bald and the Pope in 876, and that, while the work as edited by Karl Strecker says only that the poet wishes that the Pope would let it be performed for him, an incomplete Epilogue seems to suggest that the old *Cena* had already found success at Charles' table. Lehmann then concludes this section (p. 34) by suggesting that while the *Cena Cypriani* prepared the way for other mediaeval parodies it was fairly unique in its time.

Following his discussion of works such as the *Cena Cypriani* Lehmann speaks of dividing parodies into (1) combative and triumphant parody, in which satire is the main aim and the comic the means to this end (used, for instance, against certain popes and

---

178 See Lehmann, p. 28. Lehmann also refers here to one strict and orthodox scholar named Hrabanus Maurus, who stressed the heuristic usefulness of the work as well as its ability to amuse, as being so entranced by the humorous charm of *Cena Cypriani* that he published a shortened version of it in 855 and dedicated it to King Lothar II. Bakhtin refers to Hrabanus Maurus when he refers to Rabanus Maurus in *Voprosy*, p. 437. (The name is translated as Raban Maur in *The Dialogic Imagination*, p. 74.)

179 See Francesco Novati, 'La Parodia Sacra nelle Letterature Moderne', in *Studi Critici et Letterari* (Turin, 1889), pp. 177–310.

180 Lehmann's term 'heitere Parodie' might also be translated as 'gay' or 'merry' parody and is related by him later, on pp. 136 ff., to ribald drinking songs and the like.

181 While the foot-note to Bakhtin's *Rabelais and his World*, p. 84 says of Novati, Ilvonen, and Lehmann that 'all three authors conceive medieval parody as something isolated and specific; they do not, therefore, disclose the organic link of this parody with the larger world of the culture of folk humor', they remain main sources together with such as Olga Freidenberg.

clerics)[182] and (2) humorous ... jovial and cheering parody (such as drinking songs to 'Saint Bacchus').[183] Having made this distinction Lehmann adds that even the second type may contain some satire, and that it is sometimes difficult to maintain hard-and-fast distinctions between the two types of satiric and humorous parody which he has defined.[184] Lehmann, as noted previously, had, however, also pointed out that many biblical parodies were satires of the misuse of the Bible by monks or other clergy, and that any liberation deriving from such parody was therefore liberation from the control of such people and their misuse of the sacred texts, rather than an attack on the latter themselves.

Lehmann's views on parody have also been described as having been of some influence. Wilhelm Horn, in his 1970 study of parody in Aristophanes,[185] has noted this in claiming that Lehmann's definition of parody was much used in his time. It was, for instance, taken up by Grellmann for his entry on parody in the first edition of the *Reallexikon der deutschen Literaturgeschichte*,[186] and for its division of parody into comic and critical,[187] although other aspects of Lehmann's descriptions of parody were later criticised by Liede in his article on parody for the second edition of the *Reallexikon* in the 1960s.[188]

Although directed specifically towards two particular types of early mediaeval parody Lehmann's views might also be said to have led Bakhtin and others to overlook several of the more ironic and meta-

182 See Lehmann, p. 43 on 'die streitende und triumphierende Parodie, bei der die Satire der Hauptzweck, das Komische Mittel zum Zweck ist'.
183 See Lehmann, ibid. on 'die humoristische ... heitere und erheiternde Parodie'.
184 See Lehmann, ibid. on his second type of parody: ' ... obwohl ich wohl weiß, daß auch sie Satire enthält und daß man bei der Unterscheidung zwischen satirischer und humoristischer Parodie zuweilen schwanken kann'.
185 See Wilhelm Horn, *Gebet und Gebetsparodie in den Komödien des Aristophanes* (Nuremberg, 1970), p. 35.
186 See H. Grellmann, 'Parodie', in *Reallexikon der deutschen Literaturgeschichte*, vol. 2, ed. P. Merker and W. Stammler (Berlin, 1926/28), pp. 630–53.
187 The division of ancient parody into comic and critical in Kleinknecht's *Die Gebetsparodie in der Antike* (Stuttgart and Berlin, 1937), pp. 13 ff., which was mentioned in chapter 1 as having been criticised by Lelièvre, is based on Grellmann's general division, and Kleinknecht has also discussed and taken up other aspects of Lehmann's work on mediaeval parody in his.
188 See Alfred Liede, 'Parodie', in *Reallexikon der deutschen Literaturgeschichte*, 2nd edn, vol. 3, edited by W. Kohlschmidt and W. Mohr (Berlin and New York, 1977), pp. 12–72; p. 12. (Liede's article had earlier been published as an unbound pamphlet in Berlin in 1966.)

fictional examples of parody which can be found in the literature of the later Middle Ages.[189] In addition to this point, not all other modern commentators on parody before Lehmann had found the *Cena Cypriani* to be of such great interest or value. Arthur Shadwell Martin's *On Parody*,[190] for instance, had earlier described the *Coena Cypriani* [or *Cena Cypriani*] as reproduced by E. du Méril (who is also referred to by Octave Delepierre in his 'Essai sur la Parodie'[191]), as 'a work of the third century, when art was at its very lowest ebb'. Martin had then gone on to describe parody as 'a plant of parasitical growth' which only flourishes 'as works become well-known in a community'.[192]

This last opinion, however, is not shared by Lehmann's reader Bakhtin in his account of the *Cena Cypriani*. Bakhtin continues his essay 'From the Prehistory of Novelistic Discourse' by referring to the *Cena Cypriani*, and in positive terms: 'At the very dawning of the Middle Ages there appeared a whole series of remarkable parodic works. Among them is the well-known *Cena Cypriani* or *Cyprian Feasts*, a fascinating gothic symposium.'[193] Bakhtin goes on to describe its contents as carnivalistic as well as parodic: 'The entire Bible, the entire Gospel was as it were cut up into little scraps, and these scraps were arranged in such a way that a picture emerged of a grand feast at which all the personages of sacred history from Adam and Eve to Christ and his Apostles eat, drink and make merry. In this work a correspondence of all details to Sacred Writ is strictly and precisely observed, but at the same time the entire Sacred Writ is transformed into carnival, or more correctly into Saturnalia. This is "pileata Biblia".'

Bakhtin notes further, as Lehmann had done, that the attitude of the *Cena Cypriani* to the Bible has been interpreted in many ways – from the innocence of an instructive mnemonic to 'blasphemous parody'. Bakhtin again adds his own terminology and assessment of the work to Lehmann's, however, when he goes on to describe it as 'a parodic travesty' and to distinguish the latter from the other roles attributed

---

189 Chaucer's treatment of the 'Tale of Sir Thopas' in his *Canterbury Tales* is an example.
190 See Arthur Shadwell Martin, *On Parody* (New York, 1896), p. 6.
191 See Octave Delepierre, 'Essai sur la Parodie', in *Philobiblon Society Miscellanies*, vol. XII (London, 1868–9), pp. 1–182; pp. 34 ff. Delepierre refers to Edelestand du Méril's account of the *Cena Cypriani* in his *Poésies populaires latines antérieures au douzième siècle* (Paris, 1843), 1 vol., p. 193.
192 See Martin, *On Parody*, p. 6.
193 See Bakhtin, *The Dialogic Imagination*, p. 70.

to the *Cena Cypriani* as a mnemonic: 'We mention these scholarly opinions only as an example. They testify to the complexity and ambiguity of the medieval treatment of the sacred word as another's word. *Cyprian Feasts* is not, of course, a mnemonic device. It is parody, and more precisely a parodic travesty.'[194] Having applied this latter more modern term of 'travesty' to the mediaeval parody, Bakhtin continues by criticising the application of what he understands to be a modern understanding of parody to the old: 'But one must not transfer contemporary concepts of parodic discourse onto medieval parody (as one also must not do with ancient parody). In modern times the functions of parody are narrow and unproductive. Parody has grown sickly, its place in modern literature is insignificant. We live, write and speak today in a world of free and democratized language; the complex and multi-leveled hierarchy of discourses, forms, images, styles that used to permeate the entire system of official language and linguistic consciousness was swept away by the linguistic revolutions of the Renaissance.'

Not only does Bakhtin generalise from examples such as the *Cena Cypriani* to mediaeval parody in general here, where, for example, works such as Chaucer's *Canterbury Tales* had contained parody of a more sophisticated meta-fictional and, in Bakhtin's terms, 'modern' kind, but he again neither seems to notice that his own preference for the term travesty in which the high is brought low is one for a modern (though less complex) post-Renaissance term, or that he might be applying some post-Renaissance concerns to the mediaeval through his use of it. Where Bakhtin might have joined his own more sophisticated, though still 'modern', stylistic analysis of parody to the analysis of the laughter of mediaeval or ancient parody with productive results, this, however, is not done.[195]

After referring to the variety of types of 'parodying and travestying of the sacred word' in mediaeval literature in his essay 'From the Prehistory of Novelistic Discourse',[196] Bakhtin attempts a stylistic analysis of parody and returns to his concept of the latter as dual-voiced, but again without relating the latter to any clear analysis of the production of laughter in the carnivalistic parody: 'Every type of

194 Ibid., p. 71.
195 Bakhtin's stylistic analysis of parody is described as 'modern' here because it has divided the complex, meta-fictional characteristics of parody from the comic.
196 See Bakhtin, *The Dialogic Imagination*, p. 75. Bakhtin also refers here to the comic beast epics.

parody or travesty, every word "with conditions attached", with irony, enclosed in intonational quotation marks, every type of indirect word is in a broad sense an intentional hybrid – but a hybrid compounded of two orders: one linguistic (a single language) and one stylistic. In actual fact, in parodic discourse two styles, two "languages" (both intra-lingual) come together and to a certain extent are crossed with each other: the language being parodied (for example, the language of the heroic poem) and the language that parodies (low prosaic language, familiar conversational language, the language of the realistic genres, "normal" language, "healthy" literary language as the author of the parody conceived it). This second parodying language, against whose background the parody is constructed and perceived, does not – if it is a strict parody – enter as such into the parody itself, but is invisibly present in it.'

Despite having begun with his carnivalistic linking of parody and travesty, Bakhtin has concentrated on parody and on its more formalistic aspects rather than on the travesty in this passage. Bakhtin maintains this emphasis when he continues: 'It is the nature of every parody to transpose the values of the parodied style, to highlight certain elements while leaving others in the shade: parody is always biased in some direction, and this bias is dictated by the distinctive features of the parodying language, its accentual system, its structure – we feel its presence in the parody and we can recognize that presence, just as we at other times recognize clearly the accentual system, syntactic construction, tempi and rhythm of a specific vulgar language within purely Latin parody (that is, we recognize a Frenchman or a German as the author of the parody). Theoretically it is possible to sense and recognize in any parody that "normal" language, that "normal" style, in light of which the given parody was created. But in practice it is far from easy and not always possible.'[197]

Bakhtin's analysis of parody in these paragraphs is one of the most extended in his work, and despite its limitations is still more sophisticated than many of the stylistic analyses made by the Russian formalists referred to earlier in this chapter. In addition to coming close to the point which is missing from both the formalists and his own work that the peculiar 'dual-codedness' of the parody allows it to renew and present that which it is parodying, Bakhtin develops his and Tynyanov's arguments for the dual-coded character of the parody:

197 Ibid., pp. 75–6.

'Thus it is that in parody two languages are crossed with each other, as well as two styles, two linguistic points of view, and in the final analysis two speaking subjects. It is true that only one of these languages (the one that is parodied) is present in its own right; the other is present invisibly, as an actualizing background for creating and perceiving. Parody is an intentional hybrid, but usually it is an intra-linguistic one, one that nourishes itself on the stratification of the literary language into generic languages and languages of various specific tendencies.'[198]

Bakhtin writes further on these 'stylistic hybrids' and their 'dialogization': 'Every type of intentional stylistic hybrid is more or less dialogized. This means that the languages that are crossed in it relate to each other as do rejoinders in a dialogue; there is an argument between languages, an argument between styles of language. But it is not a dialogue in the narrative sense, nor in the abstract sense; rather it is a dialogue between points of view, each with its own concrete language that cannot be translated into the other.' Bakhtin returns to speak specifically of parody: 'Thus every parody is an intentional dialogized hybrid. Within it, languages and styles actively and mutually illuminate one another.'

While Bakhtin proceeds in his essay to discuss again the parodic-travestying forms of the Middle Ages and their links with the carnival he still fails to give a clear explanation in it of the stylistic causes for the peculiarly comic effect of the parody which his concept of it as carnivalised literature has stressed. What Bakhtin appears in fact to have done in his stylistic analysis of parody in this instance is to have returned to the formalist analysis of its dual structure, and to have extended this, but without making reference to the particularly comic character of the 'travestying' forms of parody with which he, in contrast to the formalists, has become particularly concerned. Hence we have with Bakhtin's analysis of parody here an analysis of its formal (and 'intertextual') structure,[199] which, however, says little about those comic and other characteristics which he himself now wished to stress as being germane to it, and as being stronger in the mediaeval carnival than in the 'modern' parody discussed by the formalists.

198 Ibid., p. 76.
199 See also the following discussion of Julia Kristeva's extrapolations of the concept of the intertextual from Bakhtin.

It would also seem to be because of this modern disjunction in Bakhtin's theory of parody that some others who have followed him have stressed either one or the other aspect of his work – either his analysis of comic carnivalistic literature, or his analysis of dialogic (or 'intertextual') literary forms – but not the both at once, and have in this way continued the modern separation of the comic from the more meta-fictional and complex aspects of the parody. While Bakhtin has connected the mediaeval carnivalised literary forms which he discusses both here and in his *Rabelais and his World* of 1965 with other literary forms on the basis of their common dialogised character,[200] this connection also does not explain in any stylistic or formal detail the particularly ribald and comic aspects of carnivalised literature and its laughter which he has described elsewhere as being more important than the 'reduced' laughter of other modern literary forms.

Despite criticising the 'reduced' laughter of more modern writers, Bakhtin returns both to the ideas of formalists such as Shklovsky and Tynyanov on the role played by parody in the evolution of new literary forms and to some modern works in concluding his 'From the Prehistory of Novelistic Discourse' with a reference to how the parodic-travestying word had 'broken through all remaining boundaries' during the Renaissance,[201] and to how, in 'the great Renaissance novel – the novels of Rabelais and Cervantes', it 'revealed its full potential and began to play such a titanic role in the formulation of a new literary and linguistic consciousness'.[202]

In the first of the essays printed in *The Dialogic Imagination*, 'Epic and Novel', and the latest in time,[203] Bakhtin again recalls Shklovsky's comments on the rejuvenating function of parody in the novel, although he now runs together the concepts of parody and travesty as he has done in his discussions of carnivalistic parody, and without discussing the differences in age or meaning of the two terms: 'Parodic stylizations of canonized genres and styles occupy an essential place in the novel. In the era of the novel's creative ascendency – and even more so in the periods of preparation preceding this era – literature was flooded with parodies and travesties of all the high genres

---

200 Bakhtin writes with reference to mediaeval macaronic parody in *The Dialogic Imagination*, p. 78: 'In addition to Latin parody there also existed ... macaronic parody. This is an already fully developed, intentionally dialogized bilingual (and sometimes trilingual) hybrid.'

201 See Bakhtin, *The Dialogic Imagination*, p. 79.   202 Ibid., p. 80.

203 Ibid., pp. 3–40 and *Voprosy*, pp. 447–83.

(parodies precisely of genres, and not of individual authors and schools) – parodies that are the precursors, "companions" to the novel, in their own way studies for it. But it is characteristic that the novel does not permit any of these various individual manifestations of itself to stabilize. Throughout its entire history there is a constant parodying or travestying of dominant or fashionable novels that attempt to become models for the genre: parodies on the chivalric romance of adventure (*Dit d'aventures*, the first such parody, belongs to the thirteenth century), on the Baroque novel, the pastoral novel (Sorel's *Le Berger extravagant*), the Sentimental novel (Fielding, and *The Second Grandison* of Musäus) and so forth.'[204] Bakhtin concludes this passage in another echo of Shklovsky on the ability of the novel to renew itself through self-criticism: 'This ability of the novel to criticise itself is a remarkable feature of this ever-developing genre.'[205]

Bakhtin continues by relating parody in the novel to its 'double-voicedness' and 'heteroglossia' in a way not made explicit by Shklovsky, and by moving into an area of playful 'indeterminacy' which will prove to be of interest to some 'postmodernist' theorists: 'What are the salient features of this novelization of other genres suggested by us above? They become more free and flexible, their language renews itself by incorporating extraliterary heteroglossia and the "novelistic" layers of literary language, they become dialogized, permeated with laughter, irony, humor, elements of self-parody and finally – this is the most important thing – the novel inserts into these other genres an indeterminacy, a certain semantic openendedness, a living contact with unfinished, still-evolving contemporary reality (the openended present).'[206]

When Bakhtin goes on to again relate the novel to its 'folkloric' roots, he moves further, however, towards relating parody to the 'travestying' reduction of the high to the low: 'Precisely here, in popular laughter, the authentic folkloric roots of the novel are to be sought. The present, contemporary life as such, "I myself" and "my contemporaries", "my time" – all these concepts were originally the objects of ambivalent laughter, at the same time cheerful and

204 See Bakhtin, *The Dialogic Imagination*, p. 6.
205 Ibid. Bakhtin had, however, also written that 'any strict adherence to a genre begins to feel like a stylization', and 'a stylization taken to the point of parody, despite the artistic intent of the author'.
206 See Bakhtin, *The Dialogic Imagination*, pp. 6–7.

annihilating. It is precisely here that a fundamentally new attitude toward language and toward the world is generated. Alongside direct representation – laughing at living reality – there flourish parody and travesty of all high genres and of all lofty models embodied in national myth. The "absolute past" of gods, demigods and heroes is here, in parodies and even more so in travesties, "contemporized": it is brought low, represented on a plane equal with contemporary life, in an everyday environment, in the low language of contemporaneity.'[207]

Bakhtin also stresses the way in which the ancient forms of 'serio-comical' laughter, including Menippean satire, were concerned with 'demolishing' the distance between themselves and contemporary reality,[208] and goes on to say that one way in which such genres were able to abolish the distance between their subject-matter and contemporary reality was their use of laughter: 'Of special significance in this process of demolishing distance is the comical origins of these genres: they derive from folklore (popular laughter). It is precisely laughter that destroys the epic, and in general destroys any hierarchical (distancing and valorized) distance. As a distanced image a subject cannot be comical; to be made comical, it must be brought close.'[209]

When Bakhtin speaks next of laughter as being able to examine an object and to 'lay it bare' [*obnazhat'*] and 'expose it' he applies a concept like Shklovsky's 'laying bare of the device' not only to more primitive forms than the modern, post-Renaissance novel (Shklovsky has previously been seen to have applied the term 'obnazheniye priyoma', or 'laying bare of the device', to Sterne's revolutionary use of form in the opening of his essay on *Tristram Shandy* '[210]), but to the subjects of those forms,[211] and to a concept of laughter as both ridicule and carnivalistic 'uncrowning'.[212]

Bakhtin seems, however, to overlook the way in which the ridiculing genres work by way of distortion when he writes that Menippean satire is not only 'dialogic, full of parodies and travesties, multi-styles, and does not fear elements of bilingualism',[213] but able, therefore, to offer 'a realistic reflection of the socially varied and

---

207 Ibid., p. 21.   208 Ibid., pp. 21 ff.   209 Ibid., p. 23.
210 See, for instance, Lemon and Reis, p. 27.
211 Bakhtin, *The Dialogic Imagination*, p. 23, also speaks of demolishing fear and piety before an object and adds: 'Laughter is a vital factor in laying down that prerequisite for fearlessness without which it would be impossible to approach the world realistically.'
212 See Bakhtin, *The Dialogic Imagination*, pp. 23 ff.   213 Ibid., p. 26.

heteroglot world of contemporary life'.[214] While it could be said that Bakhtin is simply laying more stress on the hybrid rather than on the distortive nature of parody here, one other explanation for this apparent oversight may be found in the demands of the official socialist realist theories of the 1930s that art should be seen to reflect social reality.[215] Bakhtin also shows some awareness of the need to give an 'official' defence of his support for the comic when he refers to the authority of Marx in his *Rabelais and his World* while suggesting that comedy had gone into a decline with the rise of other dominant bourgeois ruling ideas in the seventeenth century,[216] although his theory of carnival goes on to suggest that its comedy can challenge all orthodoxies. While some more recent authors will be seen in the following chapter to have deliberately used parody in order to present their work as 'reflecting' the world, they have presented that world as having been itself distorted in a 'parodic' fashion.[217]

Whatever Bakhtin's reasons for emphasising the importance of folk humour and its ridiculing forms in the 1930s and later may have been, one major problem with the majority of Bakhtin's analyses is the maintenance of a concept of parody as carnivalistic folk mockery or ridicule together with extrapolations from that concept, and analyses of more complex parody works, where such a concept is inadequate for either the type of formal or stylistic parody involved, or the type of subject-matter it is supposed to reflect.

As seen already, Bakhtin is not alone in having the problem that his concept of parody as comic ridicule is inadequate for all types of parody. While he shares this problem with formalists like Shklovsky to some extent, he has exacerbated it by reducing their concepts of parody further to the burlesque and to its ridiculing uses in folk literature, and by sometimes describing parody as being on a par with travesty when discussing its carnivalistic forms, or, as in some of his other essays, as a 'parodic-travestying form'.

Having connected parody with both the older forms of carnivalistic parody and with Menippean satire in his essays of the 1930s and 1940s, Bakhtin was also to include both of those subjects in his

---

214 Ibid., p. 27.
215 See also Clark and Holquist, pp. 271–2. (It is after the official statements on socialist realism of 1932 onwards that Bakhtin's work concentrates on folk literature.) 216 See Bakhtin, *Rabelais*, p. 101.
217 See the following chapter's discussion of the 'parodic realism' found by Malcolm Bradbury in authors such as Martin Amis.

analysis of parody in his study of Dostoyevsky in the revised and expanded edition of his 1929 work on that author in 1963, but without revising or expanding his earlier stylistic analysis of parody specifically to cover his new subjects and all of their particular aspects. (One new note about carnival is added to the chapter on 'Discourse in Dostoyevsky' with reference to the introduction of 'conventionalized discourse, stylized or parodic' into 'the narration or principles of construction',[218] but does not apply the chapter's stylistic analysis of parody from 1929 to the carnival, or change that stylistic analysis to accommodate or explain the comic or 'laughing' aspects of the carnival.)

While Bakhtin has added new subject-matter to the examples of modern parody analysed by the formalists in introducing the carnivalistic as well as the Menippean in his later works, his failure to revise his earlier stylistic analysis of parody to accommodate these older and often more satiric as well as 'burlesque' forms of parody and their comedy means that his understanding of parody is presented on the one hand as a hostile but not explicitly comic clash of voices, and, on the other, as a form of burlesque or satiric ridicule in which laughter is present but not stylistically explained.

Bakhtin's *Problems of Dostoyevsky's Poetics* of 1963 also begins with a reference to the Russian formalists, when, in chapter 1 of that work, entitled 'Dostoyevsky's polyphonic novel and its treatment in critical literature', Bakhtin refers to the older Viktor Shklovsky's *Pro and Contra. Remarks on Dostoyevsky* of 1957[219] as being particularly interesting on the subject of Dostoyevsky,[220] and attributes to it a role in raising both the issue of the open-endedness of the polyphonic novel and that of its dialogic, and 'multi-voiced', character.[221]

When Bakhtin moves on to discuss the development of what he terms the 'serio-comical' or 'serious-smiling' genres in his 1963

218 See Bakhtin, *Problems*, p. 268, n. 23 to p. 227 ('These stylistic peculiarities too are all connected with the tradition of carnival and with reduced ambivalent laughter') and *Problemy*, 1963, p. 264.
219 See Bakhtin, *Problems*, pp. 38 ff. and *Problemy*, 1963, pp. 46 ff.
220 Despite Bakhtin's sympathy for some of Shklovsky's ideas here, the Glossary to Bakhtin's *Problems*, p. 319 says of Shklovsky that in his *Pro and Contra* he 'argued against Bakhtin's polyphony' and later [in 1970] 'contentiously reviewed' Bakhtin's book on Rabelais, where 'he took issue with several points: with Bakhtin's apparent willingness to see every conflict as "carnivalized", and with his insufficient attention to the historical aspect'.
221 See Bakhtin, *Problems*, pp. 38–9.

text,[222] he again introduces, however, the link between parody and carnival which is largely new to the early formalist studies of the parodic.[223] Not only had the early Russian formalists not paid very much attention to the history of parody, but, as seen, they had concentrated on its more modern literary appearances, rather than on its appearance in folk culture.[224] Bakhtin writes: 'What are the distinguishing characteristics of the genres of the serio-comical? For all their motley external diversity, they are united by their deep bond with *carnivalistic folklore*. They are all – to a greater or lesser degree – saturated with a specific *carnival sense of the world*, and several of them are direct literary variants of oral carnival-folkloric genres.'[225]

Where the formalists had attributed a renewing power to parody, Bakhtin now refers to how the carnivalistic renews and transforms the old: 'This carnival sense of the world possesses a mighty life-creating and transforming power, an indestructible vitality. Thus even in our time those genres that have a connection, however remote, with the traditions of the serio-comical preserve in themselves the carnivalistic leaven (ferment), and this sharply distinguishes them from the medium of other genres.' Bakhtin adds that he will call literature which has been 'influenced ... by one or another variant of carnivalistic folklore' *'carnivalized literature'*, and then goes on to describe these serio-comical genres as deliberately 'multi-styled' and 'hetero-voiced'.[226]

Unlike Shklovsky Bakhtin also connects the modern 'hetero-voiced' novel, including Cervantes' *Don Quixote* and Sterne's *Tristram Shandy*, to the tradition of Menippean satire in his 1963 work,[227] and

---

222 Ibid., p.106 and *Problemy*, 1963, p.122. The second edition of Liddell and Scott, p. 1631 says that σπουδογέλοιον ('spoudogeloion'), the Greek term to which Bakhtin refers here (see Bakhtin, *The Dialogic Imagination*, p. 21) means 'blending jest with earnest' and it has also been translated into English as 'jocoserious'.

223 As seen previously, the links made between parody and the ancient carnival and Menippean satire in Bakhtin's 1963 text are not made in that of 1929, but the link between parody and the ancient carnival is made in essays written by Bakhtin in the 1930s, and that between parody and Menippean satire may be found in essays from the 1940s on.

224 Shklovsky does refer to a 'mock requiem mass' in a folk drama about Emperor Maximilian and his son Adolf in his essay on the structure of the story and the novel (see Shklovsky, *O Teorii Prozy*, 1925 pp. 56–69; pp. 66 f. and Sher, pp. 52–71, p. 68). Shklovsky also quotes some of the drama in the versions of his essay on *Tristram Shandy* in his *O Teorii Prozy* (1929, p. 194, Sher, pp. 161 f.), but spends little further time on the subject.

225 See Bakhtin, *Problems*, p. 107.   226 Ibid., p. 108.

227 Ibid., pp. 112 ff.

comments on characteristics of the genre which Shklovsky had noted in Sterne's *Tristram Shandy* but had not connected to the Menippean tradition: 'The menippea is characterized by an *extraordinary freedom of plot and philosophical invention*.'[228] Shklovsky's depiction of parody in *Tristram Shandy* and other works as both destructive and creative will also be echoed by Bakhtin in his comments on the carnival, which Bakhtin will further describe as combining opposites of a great many different kinds.[229] Bakhtin even writes in his *Problems of Dostoyevsky's Poetics* of 1963 on carnival in a way which recalls some definitions of parody and travesty as combining the high and the low:[230] 'Carnival brings together, unifies, weds, and combines the sacred with the profane, the lofty with the low, the great with the insignificant, the wise with the stupid.'[231]

After giving a description of the 'dualistic ambivalent ritual' of 'crowning/decrowning' in the carnival,[232] Bakhtin speaks of the 'dualistic' character of the carnival in general: 'All the images of the carnival are dualistic; they unite within themselves both poles of change and crisis: birth and death (the image of pregnant death), blessing and curse (benedictory carnival curses which call simultaneously for death and rebirth), praise and abuse, youth and old age, top and bottom, face and backside, stupidity and wisdom. Very characteristic for carnival thinking is paired images, chosen for their contrast (high/low, fat/thin etc.) or for their similarity (doubles/twins) ... [and] the utilization of things in reverse.'[233]

It is also from this recognition of the dualistic character of such carnival types that Bakhtin goes on to speak of the ambivalence of the laughter produced by those forms: 'Deeply ambivalent also is carnival *laughter* itself. Genetically it is linked with the most ancient forms of ritual laughter. Ritual laughter was always directed toward something higher: the sun (the highest god), other gods, the highest earthly authority were put to shame and ridiculed to force them to *renew* themselves. All forms of ritual laughter were linked with death and rebirth, with the reproductive act, with symbols of the reproductive force.'[234]

228 Ibid., p. 114. 229 Ibid., pp. 123 ff.
230 As noted previously, Tomashevsky's 1925 *Teoriya Literatury* had also given such a definition when speaking of parody and travesty together.
231 See Bakhtin, *Problems*, p. 123. 232 Ibid., p. 124. 233 Ibid., p. 126.
234 Ibid., pp. 126 f.

While some editors, critics and translators of Bakhtin have failed even to mention parody in their discussions or indexing of Bakhtin's works, Bakhtin then moves on to speak specifically of the parody found in such carnivals, and to give one of several extended descriptions of it and its 'carnivalistic nature': 'Parody, as we have already noted, is an integral element in Menippean satire and in all carnivalized genres in general. To the pure genres (epic, tragedy) parody is organically alien; to the carnivalized genres it is, on the contrary, organically inherent. In antiquity, parody was inseparably linked to a carnival sense of the world. Parodying is the creation of a *decrowning double*; it is that same "world turned inside out".'[235]

Where, as previously seen, Tynyanov had found the ambivalence of parody to lie in its essential 'dual-structure', Bakhtin continues by again finding the reason for its ambivalence in its creation of a 'double' to more serious forms: 'For this reason parody is ambivalent. Antiquity parodied essentially everything: the satyr drama, for example, was originally the parodic and laughing aspect of the tragic trilogy that preceded it. Parody here was not, of course, a naked rejection of the parodied object. Everything has its parody, that is, its laughing aspect, for everything is reborn and renewed through death.'[236]

In his essay of 1940 Bakhtin had also described this parodic 'laughing aspect' as a 'parodic double' to more serious forms. Here he continues: 'In Rome, parody was an obligatory aspect of funeral as well as of triumphant laughter (both were of course rituals of the carnivalistic type). In carnival, parodying was employed very widely, in diverse forms and degrees: various images (for example, carnival pairs of various sorts) parodied one another variously and from various points of view; it was like an entire system of crooked mirrors, elongating, diminishing, distorting in various directions and to various degrees.' Bakhtin adds with especial reference to Dostoyevsky: 'Parodying doubles have become a rather common phenomenon in carnivalized literature.'

Despite this reference to the modern author Dostoyevsky, Bakhtin's next paragraph goes on to criticise what he terms modern 'formal' parody: 'In the narrowly formal literary parody of modern times, the connection with a carnival sense of the world is almost entirely

235 Ibid., p. 127.
236 Ibid., and see also the previous discussion of Bakhtin's 1940 essay, 'From the Prehistory of Novelistic Discourse'.

broken. But in the parodies of the Renaissance (in Erasmus, Rabelais, and others) the carnival fire still burned: parody was ambivalent and sensed its bond with death/renewal. Thus could be born in the bosom of parody one of the greatest and at the same time most carnivalistic novels of world literature: Cervantes' *Don Quixote*.'[237] Bakhtin gives no specific examples of this 'formal' modern parody here, but he has clearly excluded the work of both Cervantes and Dostoyevsky from it at this point.[238] Later Bakhtin adds that carnival continues to have some influence on contemporary literature, but that in most cases its influence is 'limited to the content of works and does not touch their generic foundation; that is, it is deprived of any genre-shaping power.'[239]

Bakhtin also comments on the importance of 'the carnival square' in this section of his work:[240] 'The main area for carnival acts was the square and the streets adjoining it. To be sure, carnival also invaded the home; in essence it was limited in time only and not in space; carnival knows neither stage nor footlights. But the central arena could only be the square, for by its very idea carnival *belongs to the whole people, it is universal, everyone* must participate in its familiar contact. The public square was the symbol of communal performance.' Bakhtin continues with reference again to the 'ambivalence' of carnival, and in terms which are reminiscent of Tynyanov's descriptions of the 'dual-planed' parody: 'In carnivalized literature the square, as a setting for the action of the plot, becomes two-leveled [dual-planed[241]] and ambivalent: it is as if there glimmered through[242] the actual square the carnival square of free familiar contact and communal performances of crowning and decrowning.'[243]

237 Ibid., p.128. Bakhtin also quotes Dostoyevsky as describing *Don Quixote* as 'the most profound and powerful work' 'in the world'.
238 In *Problems*, p. 165 Bakhtin does, however, speak of some of the laughter of Cervantes as being 'reduced' carnivalistic laughter.
239 See Bakhtin, *Problems*, p. 132. Bakhtin also speaks here of Socratic irony as being 'reduced carnival laughter'.
240 See also Bakhtin's 'Forms of Time and of the Chronotope in the Novel. Notes toward a Historical Poetics' in *The Dialogic Imagination*, pp. 159–60.
241 Bakhtin actually uses Tynyanov's word *plan*, or 'plane', here. See Bakhtin, *Problemy*, 1963, p. 148: 'dvuplanovoi'.
242 Bakhtin's term *skvoz* is similar to that used by Tynyanov to describe the way in which one plane glimmers through the other in the stylisation and, with more contrast, in the parody.
243 See Bakhtin, *Problems*, p. 128 where Bakhtin adds that other places like taverns can also take on this additional carnival-square significance.

Bakhtin's following comments on the carnival square and on what he sees to have been its role in mediaeval life also relate it to the way in which the carnival may be described as a parodying 'double' of normal life: 'It could be said (with certain reservations, of course) that a person of the Middle Ages lived, as it were, *two lives*: one was the *official* life, monolithically serious and gloomy, subjugated to a strict hierarchical order, full of terror, dogmatism, reverence, and piety; the other was *the life of the carnival square*, free and unrestricted, full of ambivalent laughter, blasphemy, the profanation of everything sacred, full of debasing and obscenities, familiar contact with everyone and everything. Both these lives were legitimate, but separated by strict temporal boundaries.'[244] Just prior to this passage Bakhtin had written that 'in the Middle Ages the vast comic and parodic literature in vernacular languages and in Latin was, one way or another, connected with festivals of the carnival type – with carnival proper, with the "Festival of Fools" with free "paschal laughter" (*risus paschalis*), and so forth',[245] and now goes on to note the way in which the carnival can bring the high low, and *'familiarise'* that which was distant without destroying all of it through its laughter: '... ambivalent carnival laughter burns away all that is stilted and stiff, but in no way destroys the heroic core of the image.'[246]

To some extent, and despite Bakhtin's claim that the laughter of carnival does not destroy the more valuable aspects of its targets, such statements on the way in which the carnivalistic may bring the high low are also based on the concept of parody as burlesque which has developed from the modern reduction of parody to a type of burlesque. Where, in those definitions, parody was often equated with the burlesque contrast of the low to the high, and travesty with the comparison of the high to the low, Bakhtin's concept of parody (like his use in other works of the term 'parodic-travestying forms') would seem to include both movements, but still to restrict and reduce them to the overall 'burlesque' technique of reducing the complex to a more simple contrast of opposites.[247]

---

244 Ibid., pp. 129 ff.   245 Ibid., p. 129.

246 Ibid., p. 133, and see also *Problems*, p. 139 on how something may be 'familiarised' by combination with an opposite or by being brought down to earth.

247 As seen previously, Tomashevsky's *Teoriya Literatury* of 1925, p. 209 had also spoken of parody as both the discussion of a high subject in low language, as in the burlesque 'or travesty', and the use of a high style for a low subject.

As noted earlier, Bakhtin's more stylistic and complex analyses of parody will not be directly applied to the laughter which he finds in the older forms of burlesque carnival parody (some of those stylistic analyses have been seen to have been developed in Bakhtin's 1929 text before he developed his interest in carnivalistic forms, and are not then changed or adjusted for the latter), although his selection of some modern examples of 'carnivalistic literature' can be said to have at least implicitly added some more complex functions to both the carnivalistic and to its parody.

One other form with which Bakhtin's 1963 text associates the carnivalistic and its parody, and which broadens the understanding of the latter's burlesque character to some extent because of the number and type of works to which Bakhtin applies it, is, again, the 'free and inventive' Menippean satire. Bakhtin also writes of the latter with reference to mediaeval parody in his 1963 book: 'Menippean elements are felt in the intensely carnivalized parodic and semi-parodic literature of the Middle Ages: in parodic visions from beyond the grave, in parodic "Gospel readings", and so forth.'[248]

It is interesting to note with reference both to Shklovsky's failure to connect the discontinuities and parody of *Tristram Shandy* with the Menippean tradition and to Bakhtin's broader understanding of the functions of the latter that Bakhtin then adds a 'Shklovskian' point about the productive nature of self-parody in the development of the novel to his analysis of the Menippean tradition that 'the mennipea – and this includes also its oldest antique forms – to some extent always parodies itself'.[249] Bakhtin continues that 'that is one of the generic characteristics of the menippea' and that 'this element of self-parody is one of the reasons for the extraordinary vitality of the genre'.[250]

Bakhtin also makes some changes to Tynyanov's analysis of Dostoyevsky's parody of Gogol in the former's *The Village of Stepanchikovo and its Inhabitants* when he connects its parody with the carnivalistic: 'The entire action of the tale is an uninterrupted series of scandals, eccentric escapades, mystifications, decrownings and crownings. The work is saturated with parodies and semiparodies, including

248 See Bakhtin, *Problems*, p. 136. And see also Kirk, pp. 226–7 on Bakhtin's accounts and uses of the Menippean tradition.
249 See Bakhtin, *Problems*, pp. 141–2.
250 Ibid., p. 142. Bakhtin also suggests here that Dostoyevsky might have been aware of older Menippean works, including Seneca's *Apocolocyntosis*.

a parody on Gogol's *Selected Passages from a Correspondence with Friends*; these parodies are organically linked with the carnival atmosphere of the tale as a whole.'[251]

For Bakhtin, however, not all modern carnivalistic literature laughs as loudly as the old carnival. With reference to this Bakhtin again speaks of 'reduced laughter',[252] or of the way in which the laughter in some 'carnivalized literature' is 'muffled' in more modern literary works: 'In the literature of the Renaissance, laughter is generally not reduced, but certain gradations of "volume" do, of course, exist even here. In Rabelais, for example, it rings out loudly, as is fitting on a public square. In Cervantes there is no longer that public-square intensity of sound, although in the first book of *Don Quixote* laughter is still quite loud, and in the second it is significantly (when compared with the first) reduced. This reduction is also linked with certain changes in the structure of the major hero's image, and with changes in the plot.'[253] Bakhtin continues with reference to the reduced laughter of irony: 'In carnivalized literature of the eighteenth and nineteenth centuries, laughter is as a rule considerably muffled – to the level of irony, humor, and other forms of reduced laughter.'[254]

Where Shklovsky had commented on the way in which Sterne was to lay bare the device of other fictions in not constructing his *Tristram Shandy* in the normal manner, but without reference to any Menippean or carnivalistic tradition, Bakhtin goes on to say that the carnival does not like conclusions and suggests that the affirmation of openness in Dostoyevsky's conclusions (to which Shklovsky had referred, but again without mentioning the carnivalistic tradition with which Bakhtin connects both Dostoyevsky and the 'open' conclusion) is also related to the *'purifying sense'* of ambivalent laughter'.[255] From here Bakhtin goes on to the stylistic analysis of parody given in his 1929 book, but, as noted previously, without making more than a brief reference back to these other carnivalistic and Menippean forms.[256]

Many of the points made in Bakhtin's earlier essays and books

251 Ibid., p. 163.   252 Ibid., pp. 164 ff.   253 Ibid., p. 165.

254 Ibid. Bakhtin, *Problems*, p. 166 also suggests, however, that Dostoyevsky's ironic parodies sometimes bring 'reduced laughter' 'to the surface'.

255 See Bakhtin, *Problems*, p. 166. One more recent open conclusion to a 'carnivalistic' novel is the ending of David Lodge's comic *Changing Places*. Lodge himself describes it as 'short-circuited' in his *Working with Structuralism. Essays and Reviews on Nineteenth- and Twentieth-Century Literature* (1981), (London, Boston, and Henley, 1986), p. 16.

256 See Bakhtin, *Problems*, chapter 5, 'Discourse in Dostoevsky', pp. 181 ff.

about the carnivalistic and the Menippean are repeated in Bakhtin's study of Rabelais and the Menippean and carnivalistic traditions in his *Rabelais and his World* of 1965, and together with some reference to the 'dialogical' character of Rabelais' novelistic work.[257]

Several of Bakhtin's statements about parody in his *Rabelais and his World* also repeat those already found in his other works. Thus Bakhtin's Introduction both names parody as one of the many forms belonging 'to one culture of folk carnival humor'[258] and stresses that 'the carnival is far distant from the negative and formal parody of modern times. Folk humor denies, but it revives and renews at the same time. Bare negation is completely alien to folk culture.'[259]

Despite criticising those analyses of laughter which have seen it as negative satire rather than as ambivalent Bakhtin indicates that his view of carnivalistic parody in this work will give value to its 'negative' reductive aspects. After referring to some mediaeval grammatical parodies which had brought their scholarly subject-matter down to the material level,[260] Bakhtin adds the very general statement: 'Not only parody in its narrow sense but all the other forms of grotesque realism degrade, bring down to earth, turn their subject into flesh ... Laughter degrades and materializes.'[261]

Other topics treated by Bakhtin in his Rabelais book already discussed in this chapter include those of laughter and the Menippean tradition, as well as the *Cena Cypriani*, although this is now described as 'the oldest grotesque parody'.[262] With regard to the *parodia sacra* Bakhtin wavers, as in other of his works, between descriptions of it as tolerated and as untolerated.[263]

In addition to describing parody again in terms of both parody and travesty,[264] Bakhtin depicts mediaeval parody as not being specifically negative but universal in its laughter, and, unlike those who have viewed the comic as something negative, separates mediaeval parody from a concern with only the negative side of things because its parody is supposed to have treated everything as comic: 'Medieval

257 See Bakhtin, *Rabelais and his World* (cited as 'Bakhtin, *Rabelais*'), translated by Helene Iswolsky (Cambridge, Mass. and London, 1968) from Bakhtin, *Tvorchestvo Fransua Rable* (Moscow, 1965).
258 See Bakhtin, *Rabelais*, p. 4.   259 Ibid., p. 11.   260 Ibid., p. 20.
261 Ibid. On Bakhtin, *Rabelais*, pp. 21 ff. Bakhtin goes on to repeat his earlier criticism of modern parody and to relate Cervantes' *Don Quixote* to the carnivalistic rather than to modern parody.   262 Ibid., p. 84.
263 Compare, for example, ibid., pp. 14 and 73 f.
264 See, for example, ibid., p. 74.

parody, especially before the twelfth century, was not concerned with the negative, the imperfections of specific cults, ecclesiastic orders, or scholars which could be the object of derision and destruction. For the medieval parodist everything without exception was comic. Laughter was as universal as seriousness; it was directed at the whole world, at history, at all societies, at ideology. It was the world's second truth extended to everything and from which nothing is taken away. It was, as it were, the festive aspect of the whole world in all its elements, the second revelation of the world in play and laughter.'[265]

Just prior to this passage Bakhtin had also stressed the importance of 'renewal on the material bodily level' in both mediaeval carnival and parody: 'All medieval parodical literature is recreative; it was composed for festive leisure and was to be read on feast days. It is, therefore, filled with the atmosphere of freedom and license. These gay parodies of the sacred were permitted on feast days, as was the *risus paschalis*, meat, and sexual intercourse. The parodies were filled with the same popular sense of the changing time and of renewal on the material bodily level. Here, too, is the prevailing logic of the ambivalent lower stratum.'[266]

Bakhtin's use of the mediaeval carnival and its laughter to explain the roots of the Rabelaisian laughter which is his particular subject in this book, and generalisation from the former to the mediaeval in general, again obscure, however, the presence in mediaeval literature of some more sophisticated examples of meta-fictional parody[267] as well as of irony.[268] While Bakhtin's *Rabelais and his World* adds to his other statements on parody in emphasising its laughter and comic aspects, this emphasis on the comic aspects of the parody is made with reference to its more burlesque, and now also grotesque, forms, and is again not connected in any thorough-going manner with Bakhtin's analyses of parody as a 'double-voiced' stylistic form.[269]

265 Ibid., p. 84. Ibid., p. 86 says of mediaeval parody in general that 'not a single saying of the Old and New Testaments was left unchallenged as long as it could provide some hint of equivocal suggestion that could be travestied and transposed into the language of the material bodily lower stratum'.
266 Ibid., p. 83. On p. 83 Bakhtin also goes on to connect mediaeval parody with school and university recreation.
267 See previous references to the 'Tale of Sir Thopas' in Chaucer's *The Canterbury Tales*.
268 See D. H. Green, *Irony in the Mediaeval Romance* (Cambridge, 1979).
269 Bakhtin's *Rabelais*, p. 415 describes the 'popular-festive language of the marketplace' as addressing a 'dual-bodied' world containing both death and

Bakhtin's contributions to the study of parody may be summarised as :

(1) Like the Russian formalist Tynyanov Bakhtin treats parody as a dual-structured device which can be compared and contrasted with stylisation.

(2) Like the Russian formalists Shklovsky and Tynyanov Bakhtin treats parody as a device which assists in literary evolution.

(3) Bakhtin goes further than Tynyanov in exploring the 'dual structure' of stylistic parody, but also emphasises more than Tynyanov the 'hostility' of the contrasting voices in the parody.

(4) In post-1929 works Bakhtin criticises the emphasis on what he terms modern parody and stresses the importance of carnivalistic forms of parody, but also describes some 'modern' works as carnivalistic, and uses a modern (in the sense of post-Renaissance) concept of parody as a burlesque or ridiculing 'double'.

(5) Advantages of Bakhtin's discussions of parody as a 'travestying' or burlesque form of folk art include their expansion of the range of parody works discussed by the Russian formalists and their stress on the importance of the comic elements which had been either eliminated, overlooked, or looked down upon by some formalist and other modern critics.

(6) Disadvantages of Bakhtin's understanding of parody as a 'travestying' or burlesque form of folk art include the further reduction of parody to the burlesque and to something written in opposition to another. (As noted previously, Tomashevsky for one had also briefly described the burlesque 'or travesty' as one type of parody in his 'Theory of Literature' of 1925.)

(7) One reason why Bakhtin's depictions of comic carnivalistic parody often reduce parody to the burlesque despite his more complex stylistic analyses of parody is that both analyses remain based on a largely negative modern view of parody as destructive or hostile to its target text.

(8) One other reason why Bakhtin's depictions of comic carnivalistic parody often reduce parody to the burlesque is that Bakhtin's stylistic and carnivalistic depictions of parody are developed separately from each other and are not then integrated in ways which might lead to their more negative aspects being changed.

renewal, but does not give any extended analysis of parody as dual-planed or dual-voiced.

(9) In addition to this last point, and in part because of it, Bakhtin's stylistic analyses of parody specifically lack an explanation of the way in which the laughter which Bakhtin sees to be central to the carnivalistic parody is produced in either it or the more complex parody with which Bakhtin's stylistic analyses deal, while carnivalistic parody is described by him as reducing the high to the low rather than as bringing the two together by way of the dual-structure of parody which is described in his more complex stylistic analyses.

(10) One other problem with both Bakhtin's descriptions of parody and with those of the Russian formalists discussed in previous pages has been their failure to analyse in any explicit detail how the dual structure of the parody preserves the parodied text within itself and how this not only contributes to the ambivalence of the parody towards the latter, but ensures the evocation and preservation of the parodied work beyond its demise.

Several different uses of the work of both the formalists and Bakhtin will be discussed in the following pages of both this chapter and the next. The first of these uses, which may also be said to have gone some way towards adding an appreciation of the ability of the parody text to evoke certain expectations from its readers by the quotation of another work, is that of the Constance reception theorists, Hans Robert Jauss and Wolfgang Iser.[270]

Reception theorists

One reference to the evocation of reader expectations in a literary work noted in the sections above has been by Viktor Shklovsky to Laurence Sterne's use of the device of plot retardation to create tension in the expectations of the audience for the continuation of the main action of the novel,[271] but few explicit comments on or references to the role played by quotation and imitation in parody in the evocation of reader expectations have been found in the works of either the Russian formalists or Mikhail Bakhtin.

It has, however, already been seen that writers from Aristotle onwards have described how comedy may be produced from the

---

270 The following discussion comments largely on the use and analysis of parody texts by Jauss and Iser. For a fuller description of reception theory see Robert C. Holub, *Reception Theory. A Critical Introduction* (London and New York, 1984).

271 See the earlier reference to the conclusion of the first part of Shklovsky's essay 'Literature Without a Plot', in *O Teorii Prozy*, 1925, pp. 165–6, or Sher, p. 192.

raising of expectations for X and the 'disappointment' of those expectations with the giving of something which is not-X, and this lesson may be used by anyone wishing either to investigate further the raising of reader expectations in the parody texts analysed by the formalists, or to relate the comic laughter produced by Bakhtin's carnivalistic parody to his stylistic analysis of parody as consisting of two texts or 'voices'.

The latter may be done, for instance, by adding the point not made by Bakhtin in his stylistic analyses of parody, that the parody does not just let the parodied text 'glimmer' through its own text or 'level' (to use Tynyanov's terms from his earlier discussions of parody and stylisation), but first sets up the text to be parodied (by imitation or partial quotation, or by way of other such devices) so that the reader will expect it, and then produces another version of it which the reader does not expect and which sets up some incongruous contrast or comparison with the original work. While this is only a very bare description of the various different ways in which a parodist may produce laughter from a reader, it may be said to be basic to most of the techniques used in parody, including the more carnivalistic types which Bakhtin has claimed to favour. (Even the mediaeval *Cena Cypriani*, which Bakhtin describes in his Rabelais book as one of the oldest grotesque parodies, works by setting up expectations for and reminiscences of the Bible which enable it to then contrast its comic distortions of the biblical stories with the latter, and to produce laughter from its audience because of their recognition of the discrepancy created between X and not-X.)

While he does not point to the gaps in formalist or Bakhtinian theory in the above manner, and retains a largely modern view of parody, Hans Robert Jauss has added an awareness of the role played by the raising of audience expectations in works such as *Don Quixote* to their findings which has gone some way toward helping us fill those *lacunae*.

One of the earliest texts in which Jauss both discusses the work of the Russian formalists and adds his awareness of the way in which a text may help establish and then subvert the expectations of its readers is in his 1967 address, *Literaturgeschichte als Provokation der Literaturwissenschaft*.[272] In it Jauss not only refers to the Russian

---

272 See Hans Robert Jauss, *Literaturgeschichte als Provokation der Literaturwissenschaft* (Constance, 1967), pp. 22 ff.

formalists and to their revolutionary emphasis on discontinuity, evolution, and the 'automation' of literary forms, but goes on to speak of the additional importance of understanding the role played by the evocation and destruction of the reader's horizon of expectations in literary works.

Jauss further recalls the Russian formalists when he generalises from parody texts to literary texts in general, and in a way which suggests that his general theory of reader reception has been influenced by the meta-fictional parody's foregrounding of that matter. In spite of referring to *Don Quixote* and to its evocation and destruction of the horizon of expectations of the reader of the knightly romance, Jauss, moreover, does not investigate the especial role played by parody in the evocation and destruction of reader expectations in that work, although he does allude, in contrast to some of his later essays on parody, to how the evocation and destruction of expectations in such texts need not only serve a critical purpose but may also produce new poetic effects.[273]

In a later essay, 'Über den Grund des Vergnügens am komischen Helden', published in a volume on comedy edited by Wolfgang Preisendanz and Rainer Warning in 1976, Jauss both goes further into the evocation and disappointment of expectations with more explicit reference to parody and speaks of Bakhtin's contributions to our understanding of comic forms.[274] Here Jauss points to the involvement of expectations in the reception of the parody[275] after referring to Theodor Verweyen's 1973 study of parody[276] and echoes Bakhtin's combinations of parody and travesty in writing that 'a parody or travesty can exploit the discrepancies between high and low on the level of either form or content in order to attack its object (which is mostly a text of authoritative standing) through critical imitation or to transform it into something new through an artistic heightening of the imitation'.[277]

---

273 See Jauss, 1967, pp. 33 ff. where he also refers to H.-J. Neuschäfer's *Der Sinn der Parodie im Don Quijote* (Heidelberg, 1963).

274 See Hans Robert Jauss, 'Über den Grund des Vergnügens am komischen Helden' in *Das Komische*, edited by Wolfgang Preisendanz and Rainer Warning (Munich, 1976), pp. 103–32.   275 See Jauss, 1976, p. 105.

276 See Theodor Verweyen, *Theorie der Parodie. Am Beispiel Peter Rühmkorfs* (Munich, 1973).

277 Translated from Jauss, 1976, pp. 104–5. Jauss is also referring in the last part of his sentence to a description of parody given by Erwin Rotermund in his *Die Parodie in der modernen deutschen Lyrik* (Munich, 1963).

This definition of parody by Jauss brings it together not only with travesty and with the definition of the latter as the comic imitation of the content of another work which brings the high low,[278] but with several modern definitions of parody which separate its critical and artistic functions, including Alfred Liede's definitions of parody. These various views of parody as critical or artistic are, moreover, not connected by any reference to the dual-codedness of the parody as suggested by Tynyanov or Bakhtin. Even when Jauss comes close to adding to their view of parody, when he goes on to refer to how Verweyen's analysis of parody has shown it to have set up not only the norms of an author, but those of their reception, he maintains a modernistic split between parody as criticism and parody as art.[279]

With reference to the figure of the comic hero with which he is particularly concerned in this essay, Jauss also stresses the critical or 'negating' functions of parody when he adds that 'in all these cases a comparison between the parody and that which is parodied is involved: the comic hero is not comic in himself, but, placed against a horizon of certain expectations, is comic in so far as he negates these expectations or norms'. Jauss continues by suggesting that the process of comparing expectations and their negation is central to the process of reception in this instance. While Jauss adds that 'whosoever does not know or recognise what a certain comic hero negates, does not need to find him comic', his description of the way in which a parody may set up expectations for its reader before negating them does recognise the process by means of which a parody may re-present that which is being parodied to the reader from within its own text. Jauss then goes on to suggest that the evocation of expectations means that the comic hero can be used to make conscious certain norms which can then be made fun of or made problematical, and that such parody can serve as a release from other authorities, or as a means of protesting against them, as well as a way of establishing new norms against the old.[280]

From this point[281] Jauss goes on to refer to Freud's discussion in the paragraphs on caricature, parody and travesty in his *Jokes and their*

---

278 Here Jauss may also be said to have taken over a definition of parody as the imitation of the form of another work which compares the low to the high and to have brought it together with the definition of travesty as the imitation of the content of a work which brings the high low.
279 See Jauss, 1976, p. 105.   280 Ibid., pp. 105–6.
281 Ibid., pp. 106 ff.

Relation to the Unconscious of 1905 of the way in which forms like parody can bring the high low.[282] Freud had followed his discussion of caricature by writing that '*parody* and *travesty* achieve the bringing low of something exalted in another way: by destroying the unity that exists between people's characters as we know them and their speeches and actions, by replacing either the exalted figure or their utterances by low ones', and had added that 'the same mechanism is also used for the *unmasking* [*die Entlarvung*], which ... comes into play where someone has seized dignity and authority by a deception and these have to be taken from him in reality'.[283]

Bakhtin might also be said to have shared some of Freud's views on parody, including that of it as a travestying form which brings the high low, as well as Freud's view of the carnival (both ancient and modern) as a time for the temporary release from regulation.[284] Jauss argues, however, that Bakhtin's analysis of Rabelais' 'grotesque hero' had presented a comic figure who does not just arise from a contrast with the ideal hero, and who represents a 'laughing with' rather than a 'laughing over'.[285] If Bakhtin may nonetheless be said to have understood the parody used by Rabelais as something which brings things low as in the carnival, Jauss' argument can at least itself be seen as an attempt to escape from the description of parody and other such forms as something which is only, or largely, negating and reductive. Because Jauss' overall presentation of parody explicitly stresses its negating functions, and tends to keep these separate from its artistic functions, it remains, however, within the problematic of the modern separation of parody into something which is either comic/negative or meta-fictional/artistic.

---

282 Ibid., p. 106.
283 See chapter 7 of Freud's *Der Witz und seine Beziehung zum Unbewußten*, in Sigmund Freud, *Gesammelte Werke*, ed. Anna Freud *et al.*, 17 vols. in 16 (London, 1940–52), vol. 6, pp. 229 f.; or *Jokes and their Relation to the Unconscious*, in *The Standard Edition of the Complete Psychological Works of Sigmund Freud*, translated and edited by James Strachey *et al.*, 24 vols. (London, 1953–74), vol. 8, p. 201.
284 See chapter 11 of Freud's *Massenpsychologie und Ich-Analyse* of 1921, in Freud, *Gesammelte Werke*, vol. 13, p. 147; or *Group Psychology and the Analysis of the Ego* in Strachey *et al.*, vol. 18, p. 131. Clark and Holquist, 1984, also comment on Mikhail Bakhtin's knowledge of Freud and other modern thinkers, while *Nicholas Bachtin. Lectures and Essays*, edited by A. E. Duncan-Jones (Birmingham, 1963), gives rare and interesting information on his brother Nicholas' interest in modern theorists, such as Freud, Kant and Nietzsche, as well as on his brother's knowledge of ancient thought.   285 See Jauss, 1976, pp. 106 ff.

Wolfgang Iser is another contemporary critic who has continued to refer to parody as something negative. His *Der implizierte Leser. Kommunikationsformen des Romans von Bunyan bis Beckett* of 1972 (translated as *The Implied Reader. Patterns of Communication in Prose Fiction from Bunyan to Beckett*) contains, for example, the statement that '*Tristram Shandy* is not to be explained through a merely parodistic, or even destructive intention'.[286] Like Jauss, Iser, however, has chosen general meta-fictional parodies for his analyses of the way in which the novel plays with the reader and their expectations.

In his work on the 'implied reader' in his *Der implizierte Leser* Iser deals, for example, with texts such as *Tristram Shandy* in which the author speaks of, and to, the reader, often with didactic purpose, or ironically to chide the reader for not taking an active enough part in the conversation between themself and the author suggested by the text.[287] In his 1976 work *Der Akt des Lesens. Theorie ästhetischer Wirkung* (translated as *The Act of Reading: A Theory of Aesthetic Response*) Sterne's conception of a literary text is further described as being 'like an arena in which reader and author participate in a game of the imagination'.

More recently still Iser has published a monograph on Sterne's *Tristram Shandy* which shows its suitability for his analysis of the way in which such meta-fictional texts may set up their own reader and their expectations within the text itself.[288] In it Iser defends *Tristram Shandy* from being called a muddle and follows Shklovsky in not only pointing to how Sterne was concerned with matters like the 'laying bare of the device' in its confused digressions, but in omitting to refer to the latter as one of the novel's Menippean characteristics: 'The strategy of interruption indicates the extent to which Sterne reflected through his narrator on narrative techniques. The strategy of digression, which structures the whole novel,

---

286 See Wolfgang Iser, *Der implizierte Leser. Kommunikationsformen des Romans von Bunyan bis Beckett* (Munich, 1972), pp. 98–9: 'die beim Wort genommene Ich-Form des *Tristram Shandy* [ist] nicht durch eine bloß parodistische oder gar destruktive Absicht allein zu erklären.'

287 Iser's *Der implizierte Leser* also deals with Fielding's *Joseph Andrews* and *Tom Jones* as well as with Smollett's *Humphrey Clinker* and Beckett and Joyce amongst others.

288 See Wolfgang Iser, *Sterne: Tristram Shandy* (1987), translated by David Henry Wilson (Cambridge, 1988).

is meant to lay bare the narrative fabric. Critics took note of this very early on, and it was of particular interest to the Russian formalists.'[289]

Like Shklovsky, Iser also makes little explicit acknowledgment of the role played by parody in the composition of Sterne's *Tristram Shandy* although he does discuss its humour in his 1988 work,[290] and does comment on how the parody in it has outlasted 'the context of its genesis': 'If ... Tristram's *Life* were written only as a counter to the success story contained in the *history*, then the latent parody would now have nothing but historical interest. But a parody that can outlast the context of its genesis must be more than a mere inversion of an inherited schema.'[291]

Earlier, in *The Implied Reader*, in its chapter on Fielding's *Joseph Andrews* and *Tom Jones*, Iser had also made the point that the parody can recall its target for its readers in the very act of distorting it.[292] As noted previously, Iser, however, had further referred to parody as something reductive in that work, as when, in speaking of *Tristram Shandy*, he had written that the extreme autobiographical form of that novel is not just to be explained as deriving from a 'a merely parodistic or even destructive intention', as, for example, a parody of Defoe's use of the autobiographical form in *Robinson Crusoe*.[293]

To sum up the contributions made by Jauss and Iser to the understanding of parody, it can be said that, despite the problems with their still modern concepts of parody referred to above, their analyses of general parody works such as Sterne's *Tristram Shandy* or Cervantes' *Don Quixote* have added to the analyses made of those

289 See Iser, 1988, p. 71. Iser refers to Shklovsky, 'A Parodying Novel: Sterne's *Tristram Shandy*', in *Laurence Sterne: A Collection of Critical Essays*, edited by J. Traugott, p. 69.
290 See Iser, 1988, pp. 106 ff. Prior to this section Iser had also stated, p. 105, that *Tristram Shandy* is 'the embodiment of what is virtually total play', that this gaming 'also renders subjectivity tangible' and that 'if what one is can only be played, then what one is, is inextricably equivocal. It is this equivocalness that gives rise to Sterne's humour.' 291 See Iser, 1988, p. 3.
292 Iser also refers here to E. H. Gombrich's discussion in chapter 4 of his *Art and Illusion* of the way in which an artist may 'correct' an image before being satisfied with its ability to 'match' that which is being portrayed, but acknowledges in his *Der Akt des Lesens*, p. 151, that Gombrich was speaking of mimetic rather than of parodic art in the passage in question.
293 Iser, *Der implizierte Leser*, p. 99. Iser, p. 299 also describes parody as expansive as well as reductive when discussing the parodies in Joyce's 'Oxen of the Sun' passage.

works by both the Russian formalists and Bakhtin. While, like their predecessors with their still modern and largely negative understandings of parody, they have not stressed the specifically parodic character of such works, or investigated their use of parody in depth, they can be said to have made an important contribution to the understanding of parody by pointing (with the help of Verweyen and others) to the way in which the authors of such works can conjure up the expectations of the reader for the parodied text, and to how those works can then not only 'imply', and play upon, the existence of the reader by such means, but ensure the reception of the parody work beyond its demise.

Structuralists and post-structuralists

The reception of the Russian formalists and of Mikhail Bakhtin has taken place in several different schools of literary criticism and analysis. While the following chapter will discuss how concerns of both the Russian formalists and Bakhtin have been extended by post-modernists of different varieties in recent years, this section will consider how some modern and 'late-modern' structuralist and post-structuralist theorists have developed ideas on the discontinuity, intertextuality and self-reflexivity of texts derived by the formalists from meta-fictional parody texts such as Sterne's, but have also maintained, and developed, a separation of the comic from the complex intertextual and meta-fictional aspects of parody. (As will be seen in the following sections and chapter, and in the summary given in chapter 6, there are several different 'late-modern' theories and uses of parody, ranging from those which separate the comic from the intertextual and concentrate on the latter, through those which condemn parody as being only comic ridicule, to others which extend the latter condemnation into further negative assessments and characterisations of parody.)

One of the earliest, and most influential, structuralist texts to discuss both the Russian formalists and Bakhtin was Julia Kristeva's essay 'Bakhtine, le mot, le dialogue et le roman' of 1966.[294] Kristeva

---

294 See Julia Kristeva, 'Le mot, le dialogue et le roman' (1966), in Julia Kristeva, Σημειωτική. Recherches pour une sémanalyse (Paris, 1969), pp. 143–73. (The essay was also published in *Critique* in 1967.) Its translation into English by Alice

had begun her introductory remarks by associating Bakhtin with the Russian formalists and by describing the theories of the latter as having been claimed as the source of what was then contemporary structuralist theory. In addition to describing Bakhtin as seeing carnivalistic discourse as breaking through the rules of censored speech, Kristeva had taken a special interest in Bakhtin's analysis of what she termed 'the intertextual'. Here Kristeva had spoken in particular of Bakhtin's 'discovery"that every text builds itself up as a mosaic of quotations, and that every text is the absorption and transformation of another text'. Kristeva concludes this paragraph by suggesting that in the place of the notion of intersubjectivity we have that of 'intertextuality', and that poetic language is read as a double language.[295] To Kristeva the Russian formalists were also occupied with the concept of 'linguistic dialogue',[296] although they had not made as much of this idea as had Bakhtin.[297]

Kristeva's interest in intertextuality has been taken up by many others in recent years and has been influential in the extension of the term intertextual from the works of comic parody studied by the Russian formalists and by Bakhtin to non-comic and non-parodic works in general. The way in which Kristeva's application of the term intertextual to the Russian formalists' and to Bakhtin's analyses of double-structured and double-voiced parody texts has come to be used to ignore the parodic and comic character of those texts may also be traced back to at least one apparently minor and to one more obviously major change to Bakhtin's theories made in her 1966 interpretation of them.

The minor change occurs when Kristeva adds the case of Kafka to the examples of the Menippean and 'polyphonic' novels listed by Bakhtin,[298] and the major when she decides that the category

---

Jardine, Thomas Gora and Léon S. Roudiez entitled 'Word, Dialogue and Novel' is reprinted from Kristeva, *Desire in Language: a Semiotic Approach to Literature and Art*, edited by Léon S. Roudiez (Oxford and New York, 1980) in *The Kristeva Reader*, edited by Toril Moi (Oxford, 1986), pp. 34–61.

295 See the first part of Kristeva's essay, 'le mot dans l'espace de textes', p. 146.

296 See part 2 of Kristeva's essay, 'le mot et le dialogue', pp. 147 ff.

297 Kristeva describes the carnivalistic as contributing to the intertextuality of the Menippean tradition and polyphonic novel, but separates modern parody from the carnivalistic in speaking of such parody as 'pseudo-transgression'.

298 Kristeva, p. 162. There are some parodic elements in Kafka's works, but Kristeva does not comment on these when adding him to Bakhtin's list of polyphonic novels, or provide evidence of why he should be included in the Menippean

of the carnivalistic should be treated as serious *rather* than as parody.[299]

Where Bakhtin had understood carnivalistic works such as the *Cena Cypriani* to be both comic parody and important, Kristeva has suggested that the interpretation of the word carnivalistic as connoting a comic parody has mystified the more tragic and revolutionary aspects of the carnival which she claims Bakhtin to have stressed. Despite the fact that Bakhtin had also used the word parody when discussing the more revolutionary functions of carnival, and had emphasised the importance of laughter in both, Kristeva continues: 'The laughter of the carnival is not simply parodic; it is not more comic than tragic, it is the two at the same time, it is, if one will – *serious*, and only in this way is its stage neither that of the law nor of the parody, but of its *other*.' Quoting not from Bakhtin but from Antonin Artaud, Kristeva adds that modern writing offers several flagrant examples of 'that generalised scene which is both *law* and the *other*, and on which laughter falls silent, because it is not parody, but *murder* and *revolution*.'[300]

As is the case in many 'late-modern' structuralist and post structuralist discussions, the overall emphasis in Kristeva's essay is on the intertextual and 'the serious' *rather* than on the parodic and the comic. In the first of the sentences translated above, Kristeva's reference to the laughter of the carnival being both comic and tragic is also made at the same time as she separates parody from the carnival and its serious aspects on the apparent, and modern, assumption that parody is only largely comic, and that its comedy cannot also be 'serious'. There is, hence, no key provided for understanding Bakhtin's appreciation of the complexity of parody and of the simultaneously destructive and constructive functions of its carnivalistic forms and their laughter, or the problems created by the lack of integration of his stylistic analyses of parody with his later analyses of carnivalistic parody. (Kristeva refers only briefly to Bakhtin's stylistic analyses of parody,[301] and seems to overlook his underplaying of the comic elements in parody in them as well as his comments on carnivalistic parody when condemning parody as being too comic for the

tradition. (Kirk's book on Menippean satire also makes no reference to Kafka in its Index.)

299 See Kristeva, ibid.   300 Ibid.
301 See Kristeva, p. 155, where she describes the author of the parody as introducing a signification opposed to that of the word of another.

carnivalistic.) While Kristeva's article was important in its time for bringing the work of Bakhtin to the attention of modern Western theorists it has also to be said that it did not do Bakhtin, or the understanding of the parodic character of the works with which Bakhtin was concerned, full justice with its interpretations.

It is necessary to make this point not only because some other editors and commentators on Bakhtin since Kristeva have continued to underplay the role of parody in his theories – and have either left it out of their indices or misinterpreted it as negative, parasitic, or trivial – but because several other late-modern commentators on parodic intertextuality have reduced parody to the intertextual by denying or overlooking the comic aspects of the parody.

Others who have followed Kristeva to write on both Bakhtin and intertextuality include the structuralist and Bakhtin commentator Tzvetan Todorov.[302] Todorov begins the chapter on intertextuality in his *Mikhail Bakhtin. The Dialogical Principle* of 1981[303] by saying that he will use Kristeva's term 'intertextuality' to discuss Bakhtin's concept of dialogism. While Kristeva had separated Bakhtin's concept of carnival from parody on the assumption that the latter is too comic, and had referred only briefly to Bakhtin's stylistic analyses of parody where the comic character of parody is not stressed, Todorov's use of the term 'intertextuality' to discuss Bakhtin's concept of dialogism leads him to discuss the stylistic parody which Bakhtin had described as a dialogic form under the overall category of the intertextual.[304] Although Todorov also refers here to Bakhtin's description of parody in his 'The Problem of the Text' of 1959–61 as a crude or 'rough-hewn' form of dialogism,[305] he further follows Bakhtin's stylistic analyses of parody in not discussing the comic as one of its distinguishing features[306] and hence contributes to the depiction of intertextual parody as non-comic.

One other student of the work of Bakhtin, and colleague of Jauss

302 It will also be seen that, following the 1967 publication of Kristeva's essay, Roland Barthes had spoken of both parody and dialogue with relation to the intertextual, but without explicitly taking any of those concepts back to Bakhtin's analyses.

303 See Tzvetan Todorov, *Mikhail Bakhtin. The Dialogical Principle* (1981), translated by Wlad Godzich (Minneapolis, 1984), p. 60.

304 See Todorov's discussion of parody in his chapter on 'Intertextuality', pp. 60–74.

305 See the earlier note on this work in the section on Bakhtin.

306 See Todorov, pp. 73–4.

and Iser, Renate Lachmann, has written on the development of the concept of intertextuality in an essay published in the early 1980s entitled 'Ebenen des Intertextualitätsbegriffs'.[307] Lachmann's essay opens by commenting upon the confused expansion of the concept of intertextuality in recent writings and names (p. 133) the more important examples of works on the subject as including Julia Kristeva's collection of essays *Séméiotiké [Σημειωτική]*. Recherches pour une sémanalyse, Paris, 1969 (in which she discusses Bakhtin and intertextuality) and her *Le Texte du roman*, Paris, 1970; J. Starobinski's *Les Mots sous le mots. Les Anagrammes de Ferdinand de Saussure*, Paris, 1971; *Poétique 27*, 1976; *Intertextuality. New Perspectives in Criticism*, ed. J. Parisier-Plottel/H.Charney, *New York Literary Forum 2*, New York, 1978; Michel Riffaterre, *Semiotics of Poetry*, Bloomington/London, 1978 and *La Production du texte*, Paris, 1979; and Gérard Genette's *Palimpsestes. La Littérature au second degré*, Paris, 1982. (Genette also discusses parody in some detail in his 1982 work, but his various typologies of parody, pastiche and travesty do not always reflect all the historical differences in the uses and understandings of those terms, while his most frequently quoted definition of parody as being, in general, a 'minimal transformation of a text', omits reference to its comic functions and to their many particular complexities as well as to other of its characteristics.)

Lachmann then goes on to say that many different terms have been used in the literature related to intertextuality, including 'subtext', 'hypotext', 'hypertext', 'anatext', 'paratext', 'intertext', 'transtext', 'text in text', and in union with words such as 'geno-', 'phenotext', 'metatext' and 'auto text'. (Lachmann herself adds the term 'implied text'.) For Lachmann one other aspect of this explosion of theory relates to the extension of the meaning of the concept and she asks if the latter should also be extended to name a general dimension of texts which she terms their 'Implikativität' (which can be translated as their ability to imply or suggest other texts); or should the concept be limited to describing texts, the structure of which has been affected by the interference of texts or elements of texts; or has the concept mainly a literary critical function, in that it can put into question existing concepts of literature such as uniqueness, isolation, structural totality, and 'system-likeness'. (Lachmann even goes on to say with

307 See Renate Lachmann, 'Ebenen des Intertextualitätsbegriffs' in *Das Gespräch*, ed. Karlheinz Stierle and Rainer Warning (Munich, 1984), pp. 133–8.

some irony that the theoreticians of intertextuality themselves represent a model of intertextuality in that the quoting, allusive, replicating interweaving of their theories appears to be producing a new type of literary discourse.)

Lachmann adds (p. 134) that it would be profitable to think through the subject further via the three perspectives of the 'text-theoretical', the 'text-descriptive' and the 'literary-' or 'cultural-critical'. With reference to the second category Lachmann suggests that it would also be a good idea to distinguish between the intended intertextuality which may be said to 'organise the surface of the text' and the latent intertextuality which 'does not disturb the surface of the intertext' but yet 'determines' the constitution of its meaning. Lachmann continues by noting that it would furthermore be useful to distinguish the intertextuality involved in the production of the text from that which has been termed 'reception intertextuality'.

Lachmann makes one brief reference to parody: 'In the last instance the problem of the constitution of the sense must be solved ... In the case of practices like the imbedding of foreign texts or text elements in the actual text (such as quotation, allusion, reminiscence etc.) or the interweaving of a number of foreign texts which belong to different poetics (heterogenisation, bricolage) or the repetition and opposition to a known text as replication, contrafact, parody etc., we are concerned neither with the evocation of an intact world of literary tradition, nor with the proof of unfathomable knowledge, which is sunk in the text as quotation, but with the semantic explosion, which happens when the texts touch, for the production of aesthetic and semantic difference [*Differenz*].' Lachmann adds to this already complex semantic explosion both that the intertextually organised text relates itself through a use of reference to other texts (Lachmann notes that such contact between texts may be described as a work of assimilation, transposition and transformation of foreign signs), and that concepts like 'palimpsest', 'anagram', 'overdetermination', and 'double-coding' suggest the latency, and presence, of a foreign text or its signs.

With reference to the use of the term 'double-coding' as a definer of the post-modern by Charles Jencks, and to the extension of it by some others to cover both what they call 'postmodern' intertextuality and parody, it is also interesting to note that Lachmann has spoken of double-coding with reference to 'intertextual' forms which include parody in this passage. Lachmann gives no particular meaning or source to explain her use of the term 'double-coding' ['*Doppel-*

kodierung'] but goes on to speak of the concept of 'double-coding' as a form of intertextuality in terms reminiscent of Bakhtin's discussions of stylistic parody, when she suggests that '"double-coding" means that the production of meaning is not programmed through the stock of signs of the given text, but points to that of another'.

While it is true that double-coding in parody may involve various degrees of foregrounding of another, parodied, text and its 'signs' there is, however, something of a problem with using the sentence just quoted from Lachmann for the further analysis of such double-coding. This problem resides in the fact that after the first part of Lachmann's sentence has spoken of the meaning in the text as not being programmed by the system of signs of 'the given text', Lachmann has moved on to speak of this meaning as referring to the text embedded or 'implied' in the other as if all of these things did not connect and were not all part of the given text and the 'programming' of its signs by the author. Even the 'double-coding' to be found in parody, where contrast between texts as well as integration is usually a part of the parodist's program, shows, however, that the choice to use two codes comes from the parody author, and that while the resulting parody text (or 'given' text) may point to the presence of another text embedded within it, it is the parodist who has reinterpreted the meaning of the embedded text, and given it its new functions, and implications, within the parody work as a whole. (Yet one other way of putting this is that in the double-coding found in parody the signs of the parodied text have been selected and added by the author of the parody or 'given text'.) The parodist may also recode elements of the parodied work to the extent that the latter is recreated as an integral part of the given text rather than simply quoted as a work 'foreign' to the parody. In either of these cases it will, moreover, be difficult to say that the meaning of the work as a whole comes from one or the other part of it rather than from the whole work as created by the author from its various parts.

Lachmann's sentence might have been clearer had she stayed further away from the intertextual trap of eliminating the author as the arbiter of meaning, and spoken of the author rather than of the parts of the 'given' work as the prime selector and controller of the work's overall sense. Lachmann does note, however, that we must recognise the existence of several different types of intertextuality – such as deconstructive or conservative, or Bakhtin's 'dialogic' – and that they may have different functions as well as different ways of producing meaning.[308] This differentiation of intertextuality, which at least implies some difference between intertextual authors, also goes some way towards returning the interpretation of Bakhtin's dialogicity to the specific meaning given it by him (in contrast to those who have run it together with other forms of intertextuality), and to suggesting that not all self-consciously intertextual literature is the same, and that not all literature or art is intertextual in the same sense. Despite these differentiations, and Lachmann's expert knowledge of Bakhtin, the recognition that parody is different from the other types of intertextuality which have been derived from the analysis of its examples by Bakhtin and others, and that it is different because of its peculiarly comic character, is not made explicit in this essay.[309]

Lachmann's other articles in the volume *Das Gespräch* in which this essay was published also reflect the concerns of the editors to concentrate on the subject of the dialogue ['das Gespräch'] and, like the essay described above, discuss both intertextuality and Bakhtin but without any significant reference to the parody with which the latter was concerned.[310] The editor Karlheinz Stierle's article 'Werk und Intertextualität'[311] even tends towards dismissing parody as a parasitic text with little value,[312] and it is necessary to return to another volume in this series, to *Das Komische*, edited by Wolfgang Preisendanz and Rainer Warning, and to Rainer Warning's contribution 'Elemente einer Pragmasemiotik der Komödie', to find a re-application of the category of intertextuality to parody itself.[313]

There Warning not only reapplies the category of intertextuality to parody, but also uses the term intertextuality in a similar way to that in which the formalists had used the term parody when describing the

308 See Lachmann, p. 138.
309 Some recognition of these differences was made, however, in Verweyen and Witting, 'Parodie, Palinodie, Kontradiktio, Kontrafaktur – Elementare Adaptionsformen in Rahmen der Intertextualitätsdiskussion', in *Dialogizität*, edited by Renate Lachmann (Munich, 1982), pp. 202–36, and is developed in their *Die Kontrafaktur: Vorlage und Verarbeitung in Literatur, bildender Kunst, Werbung und politischem Plakat* (Constance, 1987), pp. 22–53.
310 See Lachmann's 'Bachtins Dialogizität und die akmeistische Mythopoetik als Paradigma dialogisierter Lyrik' in *Das Gespräch*, pp. 489–515, and 'Zur Semantik metonymischer Intertextualität, *Das Gespräch*, pp. 517–23.
311 See Karlheinz Stierle, 'Werk und Intertextualität', in *Das Gespräch*, pp. 139–50.
312 See Stierle, p. 148.
313 See Rainer Warning, 'Elemente einer Pragmasemiotik der Komödie', in *Das Komische*, edited by Wolfgang Preisendanz and Rainer Warning (Munich, 1976), pp. 279–333.

latter as a device for alienation when he discusses both intertextuality and its parodic forms (p. 312) as methods of 'implicitly breaking through a fiction'. Warning also applies this description to the parody of tragedy such as that of Euripides in Aristophanes' *Peace*, and lists such cases of parodic 'intertextuality' with other types of inter-textuality such as 'self-quotation', the 'laying bare' [*Bloßlegung*] of stereotypical plot schemes, or of clichés, and the use of disguises or role exchanges in the comedy. Despite his discussion of parodic intertextuality, and use in it of formalist terminology, Warning's article omits, however, to trace back the derivation of either intertextuality or the idea of its 'laying bare of the device' to the Russian formalists' analyses of texts which were in the first place largely parodic.

Many others since have taken up the term intertextuality and applied it back to parody without commenting on the fact that it was largely from the analysis of parody works that the concept had been derived in the first place. While he also fails to trace the concept back through Kristeva's analyses of works by Bakhtin and the Russian formalists to works which were largely parodic, the critical discussion given by Raymond Tallis of intertextuality in his *Not Saussure. A Critique of Post-Saussurian Literary Theory* of 1988 fearlessly questions the emphasis placed on this concept in many recent literary analyses, as well as Roland Barthes' contributions, following Kristeva, to the way in which intertextuality has come to replace not only 'inter-subjectivity' in both structuralist and post-structuralist thought, but the idea of the authorial subject itself.[314]

Roland Barthes' 'From Work to Text' of 1971[315] had given the following description of intertextuality: 'The intertextual in which every text is held, it itself being the text-between of another text, is not to be confused with some origin of the text: to try to find the "sources", the "influence" of a work, is to fall in with the myth of filiation; the citations which go to make up a text are anonymous, untraceable, and yet already read: they are quotations without inverted commas.'

Earlier, Barthes' 'Death of the Author' essay of 1968[316] had alluded to the intertextuality of the text in statements such as its 'the text is

314 See Raymond Tallis, *Not Saussure. A Critique of Post-Saussurian Literary Theory* (London, 1988), pp. 42 ff.
315 See Roland Barthes, *Image-Music-Text*, translated by Stephen Heath (Glasgow, 1977), pp. 155–64; p. 160.   316 Ibid., pp. 142–8.

a tissue of quotations drawn from the innumerable centres of culture'.[317] Further to this, Barthes had described how this inter-textuality relates to the 'death of the author' with reference back to both dialogue and parody: ' ... a text is made of multiple writings, drawn from many cultures and entering into mutual relations of dialogue, parody, contestation, but there is one place where this multiplicity is focused and that place is the reader, not, as was hitherto said, the Author.'[318]

Where reception theorists such as Jauss and Iser have seen the parody's foregrounding of the reader and of their relation to the parody's 'intertexts' as explaining how authors can evoke and transform the expectations of the reader, Barthes writes that 'the reader is the space on which all the quotations that make up a writing are inscribed without any of them being lost' and that 'a text's unity lies not in its origin but in its destination'. Following this seductively metaphoric but questionable claim (not only does it posit a reader capable of taking all quotations in, but it also separates the author's construction of his or her work from its reception or 'destination'), Barthes concludes with the even more radical metaphor that 'the birth of the reader must be at the cost of the death of the Author'.[319]

Despite its problematical nature, Barthes' description of the 'death of the Author' has been echoed by several 'late-modern' 'post-structuralist' theorists, from Derrida to Foucault and to the American Althusserians, and, in the case of some of the latter at least, via the addition of some equally questionable 'Lacanian' theories of over-determination.[320]

Foucault's essay 'What is an Author?' of 1969[321] has also echoed Barthes' essay on the death of the author in concluding with the ironic question, 'What difference does it make who is speaking?', and many of his other works have stressed the 'literariness' and 'literary intertextuality' of discourse in general. The latter is also present in his

317 Ibid., p. 146.   318 Ibid., p. 148.   319 Ibid.

320 Fredric Jameson was still referring to these theories in his 'Postmodernism, or the Cultural Logic of Late Capitalism', in *New Left Review*, no. 146, July–August 1984, pp. 53–92; pp. 91 f., but they rest not only on individual theoretical steps which may be questioned but on the overall problem that they themselves are usually implicitly excluded (that is, without justification) from the over-determinations which they claim control others.

321 See *The Foucault Reader*, edited by Paul Rabinow (Harmondsworth, 1986), pp. 101–20; p. 120.

The Order of Things. An Archaeology of the Human Sciences, translated from his *Les Mots et les Choses. Une Archéologie des Sciences Humaines* of 1966,[322] where Foucault had written of Cervantes' *Don Quixote* that '*Don Quixote* is the first modern work of literature, because in it we see the cruel reason of identities and differences make endless sport of signs and similitudes; because in it language breaks off its old kinship with things and enters into that lonely sovereignty from which it will reappear, in its separated state, only as literature.'[323]

Foucault had begun his *The Order of Things* by noting that he had been inspired to write it by a story by the admirer of Cervantes and parodist Jorge Luis Borges: 'This book first arose out of a passage in Borges, out of the laughter that shattered, as I read the passage, all the familiar landmarks of my thought – *our* thought, the thought that bears the stamp of our age and our geography – breaking up all the ordered surfaces and all the planes with which we are accustomed to tame the wild profusion of existing things, and continuing long afterwards to disturb and threaten with collapse our age-old distinction between the Same and the Other.'[324]

Foucault had also concentrated in his *The Order of Things* on the predominance of discontinuity over continuity in the modern episteme[325] and had written further in his 1971 essay *The Discourse of Knowledge* that 'discourse must be treated as a discontinuous activity, its different manifestations sometimes coming together, but just as easily unaware of, or excluding each other'.[326]

While Foucault had not explicitly connected Cervantes' games with difference and discontinuity to parody in his *The Order of Things*, the latter work had led to an exchange of letters with the artist René Magritte,[327] in one of which[328] Magritte had referred to his *Perspective*:

322 See Michel Foucault, *The Order of Things. An Archaeology of the Human Sciences* (1966), translated by A. M. Sheridan Smith (London, 1970).
323 See Foucault, *The Order of Things*, pp. 48–9.   324 Ibid., p. xv.
325 A concept of 'discontinuity' is also briefly used in Roland Barthes' *Writing Degree Zero* (1953), translated by Annette Lavers and Colin Smith (London, 1967), pp. 54–5, and with reference to bricolage in his comments on Michel Butor's *Mobile*, in 'Littérature et Disconu' (first published in *Critique*, 1962), in Barthes, *Essais Critiques* (Paris, 1964), pp. 175–87.
326 See Foucault, *The Archaeology of Knowledge* (1969) translated by A. M. Sheridan Smith, and *The Discourse of Knowledge* (1971) (Appendix), translated by Rupert Sawyer (New York, Hagerstown, San Francisco, London, 1972), p. 229.
327 See Foucault, *This is not a Pipe*, translated and edited by James Harkness (Berkeley, Los Angeles and London, 1983), p. 58.
328 Magritte's letter of 4 June 1966, ibid.

Le Balcon de Manet, in which he replaces Manet's figures with coffins, and to other works in which human figures are replaced by coffins such as his *Perspective*: *Madame Récamier, de David* and *Perspective*: *Madame Récamier, de Gérard*, as 'parody'.

Foucault's essay 'Nietzsche, Genealogy, History' of 1971,[329] has used the term parody in its seventh section, moreover, to describe a view of history which is both 'directed against reality' and opposed to 'the theme of history as reminiscence or recognition'.[330] Foucault adds with reference to the other related types which he will discuss here: 'the second is dissociative, directed against identity, and opposes history given as continuity or representative of a tradition; the third is sacrificial, directed against truth, and opposes history as knowledge. They imply a use of history that severs its connection to memory, its metaphysical and anthropological model, and constructs a counter-memory — a transformation of history into a totally different form of time.'[331]

Foucault expands on the first 'parodic and farcical use' with borrowings from both Nietzsche on the decadence of the modern European and from Marx's *Eighteenth Brumaire* on the way in which history repeats itself as farce: 'The historian offers this confused and anonymous European, who no longer knows himself or what name he should adopt, the possibility of alternative identities, more individualized and substantial than his own. But the man with historical sense will see that this substitution is simply a disguise. Historians supplied the Revolution with Roman prototypes, romanticism with knight's armor, and the Wagnerian era was given the sword of a German hero — ephemeral props that point to our own unreality. No one kept them from venerating these religions, from going to Bayreuth to commemorate a new afterlife; they were free, as well, to be transformed into street vendors of empty identities. The new historian, the genealogist, will know what to make of this masquerade. He will not be too serious to enjoy it; on the contrary, he will push the masquerade to its limit and prepare the great carnival of time where masks are constantly reappearing. No longer the identification of our faint individuality with the solid identities of the past, but our "unrealization" through the excessive choice of identities — Frederick

---

329 See *The Foucault Reader*, edited by Paul Rabinow (Harmondsworth, 1986), pp. 76–100.
330 Ibid., p. 93.   331 Ibid.

of Hohenstaufen, Caesar, Jesus, Dionysus, and possibly Zarathustra. Taking up these masks, revitalizing the buffoonery of history, we adopt an identity whose unreality surpasses that of God, who started the charade. "Perhaps, we can discover a realm where originality is again possible as parodists of history and buffoons of God."'[332]

Not only has Foucault used the term parody in an apparently more positive way than Marx's use of it in the beginning of his *Eighteenth Brumaire* to describe the unwittingly farcical repetition of history, but he has also used it in a somewhat different way from the Nietzsche whom he quotes in this last sentence.

Foucault's reference is to Nietzsche's paragraph number 223 in his *Jenseits von Gut und Böse. Vorspiel einer Philosophie der Zukunft [Beyond Good and Evil. Prelude to a Philosophy of the Future]* of 1886 where Nietzsche had criticised the European lack of originality which had created the need for historical 'costumes' of various moral, religious or aesthetic kinds, and had concluded with the *ironic* point that it would only be as parodists that the European of whom he was speaking could become original: 'The European mixed man — a tolerably ugly plebeian, all in all — absolutely needs a costume: he needs history as the store-room of costumes. Admittedly he notices that none really suits him — he changes and changes. ... We are the first age which has been educated especially in the matter of costumes, I mean of morals, articles of faith, connoisseurship of art, and religions, prepared as no other age was, for a carnival of high style, for the most spiritual of carnival [*Fasching*] laughter and exuberance, for the transcendental height of the highest stupidity and Aristophanic world-mockery. Perhaps we shall discover here the realm of our *invention*, that realm where even we can still be original, if only as the parodists of world history and the clowns of god — perhaps so that, even when nothing else of today has a future, our *laughter* will have a future!'[333] Nietzsche's irony in this passage rests on the idea (which he shared with so many contemporaries) that parody was the opposite of originality, and that the carnivalistic laughter produced by it was a sign of its decadence and lack of future rather than of anything hopeful.

Foucault's reinterpretation of this parodic carnivalistic laughter into

---

332 Ibid., pp. 93–4.
333 Translated from *Nietzsche Werke. Kritische Gesamtausgabe*, ed. Giorgio Colli and Mazzino Montinari (Berlin, 1967 ff.), Abteilung VI/2, (1968), p.163.

something apparently more positive overrides Nietzsche's ironies.[334] Foucault's 'transformation' of Nietzsche's condemnation of parody only makes it more positive, however, in the sense that it now serves to celebrate, rather than to condemn, the reduction of the independence and reality of the human subject to its 'unrealisation' in the imitation of the ideas and beliefs of others. Hence this parody is carnivalistic and playful, but its purpose is just as negative as the carnivalistic celebration of masking which Nietzsche condemns. As with Foucault's description of Borges' laughter as 'a laughter which shatters', this parody is understood as being gay, but is also destructive.

Having transformed Nietzsche's use of the term parody into something which is in his eyes more positive, although its 'positiveness' rests in our acceptance of the loss of identity and reality which Nietzsche was bemoaning, Foucault continues with reference to Nietzsche's 'The Use and Abuse of History' by speaking of parody first as something consciously positive and critical and then as something unconscious: 'In this, we recognize the parodic double of what the second of the *Untimely Meditations* called "monumental history": a history given to reestablishing the high points of historical development and their maintenance in a perpetual presence, given to the recovery of works, actions, and creations, through the monogram of their personal essence. But in 1874, Nietzsche accused this history, one totally devoted to veneration, of barring access to the actual intensities and creations of life. The parody of his last texts serves to emphasize that "monumental history" is itself a parody. Genealogy is history in the form of a concerted carnival.'[335]

While some might wish to link the above passage from Foucault with Bakhtin's view of the carnival on the basis of Foucault's use of terms similar to his, the carnival constructed by Foucault from Nietzsche is one in which the masks rather than the human beings behind them are revealed as our reality. Bakhtin's view of the carnival cannot be equated with such 'post-structuralist' views, and neither can the Bakhtinian view of parody as contributing to the laughter of the carnival which brings the high back down to a human material level be compared with the more nihilistic playfulness of a concept of parody

---

334 Sander L. Gilman's *Nietzschean Parody. An Introduction to Reading Nietzsche* (Bonn, 1976), pp. 28 ff. also leaves these particular ironies unanalysed.
335 *The Foucault Reader*, p. 94.

used metaphorically to describe humans of all types as having been reduced to masks. (Although Kristeva had separated parody from Bakhtin's idea of carnival her 1966 essay had also spoken of the reduction of the subject to nothingness in the carnival and had described the 'anonymity of the author' 'that creates and sees itself created as self and other, as man and mask' which she claims occurs in the carnival as being reminiscent of Nietzsche's 'Dionysianism'.)

The negativity of Nietzsche's use of the concept of parody has been echoed by 'post-structuralists' of other varieties without it being reinterpreted into something even apparently positive. Jacques Derrida writes, for example, in a 1978 tract on Nietzsche: 'To use parody or the simulacrum as a weapon in the service of truth or castration would be in fact to reconstitute religion, as a Nietzsche cult for example, in the interest of a priesthood of parody interpreters. No, somewhere parody always supposes a naivety withdrawing into an unconscious, a vertiginous non-mastery. Parody supposes a loss of consciousness, for were it to be absolutely calculated, it would become a confession or a law table.'[336]

This largely negative view of parody, which can also be found in Baudrillard and in criticisms of post-modern parody and pastiche based on his writings, has not been made more positive by Gregory Ulmer's claim in his article, 'Of a Parodic Tone Recently Adopted in Criticism', that Derrida's overall tone may be described as 'parodic'.[337] While some classical rhetoricians had spoken of the pun and the parody together as forms of jest, Ulmer's concentration on Derrida's use of the pun reduces parody to it and to its more one-dimensional form, as when he states that 'the pun is now understood to be the structural principle of both parody-satire and allegory (modes that differ in tone – one devalorizes and the other valorizes – but which are structurally alike).'[338]

A predominantly one-dimensional, or negative, and, in this sense, typically, 'modern' view of parody will also be found in the writings

336 See Jacques Derrida, *Spurs. Nietzsche's Styles* (1978), translated by Barbara Harlow (Chicago and London, 1979), pp. 99–101.
337 See Gregory L. Ulmer, 'Of a Parodic Tone Recently Adopted in Criticism', *New Literary History*, vol. 13 (Spring 1982), no. 3, 'Theory: Parodies, Puzzles, Paradigms', pp. 543–60.
338 See Ulmer, p. 546, and see also the reference in chapter 1 to Hermogenes' depiction of parody as pun as a narrowing of the other meanings given to ⋆ ancient parody.

of other post-structuralist theorists taken up in recent years by some 'deconstructionist' post-modernists.

What the term 'deconstructionist' post-modernism designates, and how the views of such post-modernists differ from those of others who may be termed post-modern, is discussed next with reference to the subject of post-modern parody.

PART III

Post-modern parody

❖❖

Contemporary late-modern and post-modern theories and uses of parody

❖❖

The preceding chapter on modern (post-Renaissance) theories of parody has shown that the post-seventeenth-century definition of parody as burlesque has lived on with its negative connotations into this century, and has even affected theories dealing with more complex general parody works such as Cervantes' *Don Quixote* and Sterne's *Tristram Shandy*. In several modern and late-modern theories the failure of their authors to recognise the more positive and complex aspects of parody has also led them to treat books of general parody as meta-fictional, or as intertextual, but not as parody as such.

In this chapter some theorists who have been called 'postmodern' will further be seen to have explicitly separated parody from the comic in a late-modern fashion which extends the modern separation of the comic and the meta-fictional in parody. Before this issue can be examined, and the search for other, more 'post-modern' theories of parody begun, several distinctions have to be made between the types of post-modernist theories which have already been given that title.[1]

As a starting point a distinction will be maintained between what have been termed the 'deconstructionist' and 'double-coded' theories of post-modernism of the last two decades,[2] although some sharing of ideas between the two sets of theories will be seen to have developed in recent years as a result of ongoing debates and developments in the field. A diagrammatic summary of these theories and of the uses of the term post-modern which preceded them is also given in following

---

1 The word 'postmodern' has most often been used by 'deconstructionist' post-modernists following continental theory, while the hyphenated form of the word has been used by Charles Jencks and others, and is used here because it is also the more correct form in English.
2 See Charles Jencks, *What is Post-Modernism?* (London and New York, 1986), p. 6 and my *The Post-Modern and the Post-Industrial. A Critical Analysis* (Cambridge, 1991). Both concepts are also explained further in following sections.

pages in order to give some idea of the different negative and positive bases of the post-modernisms which are discussed in this chapter.[3]

One of the most difficult decisions which had to be made in constructing the following diagram concerned the choice of the two main category headings. Several alternatives to the Negative/Positive dichotomy which was chosen were considered, including 'Deconstructive/Constructive' as used by David Ray Griffin in his Introductions to the State University of New York Press Series in 'Constructive Postmodern Thought',[4] but a problem with these and other recent alternatives was that they could not be used to describe those uses of the term post-modern, such as, for example, those by Arnold Toynbee or Federico de Onis, which pre-dated the deconstructionist theories of the post-modern on which they have been partly based.[5] Other oppositions or pairs which have been used in the recent past, such as Hal Foster's 'neoconservative' and 'poststructuralist' 'postmodernisms' are also too restricted by virtue of their time- and theory-specific presuppositions to cover all the past uses of the term which have now been recorded.

Wolfgang Welsch even traces uses of the term post-modern back to the 1870s in his *Unsere postmoderne Moderne*,[6] to John Watkins Chapman's post-1870 use of the term post-modernism as described by Dick Higgins in his essay 'The Post-Cognitive Era: Looking for the Sense in it All' of 1976.[7] There Higgins writes that he could 'recall seeing it [the word "postmodern"] in an essay by the English salon painter Chapman who, around 1880, wanting to denounce the French impressionists but not wanting (horror!) to sound too conservative,

---

3 I should like to thank Charles Jencks for making suggestions regarding both the headings and categorisations of the theories for this summary. (Details of most theories named are given in my *The Post-Modern and the Post-Industrial* of 1991.)

4 See, for example, David Ray Griffin, William A. Beardslee and Joe Holland, *Varieties of Postmodern Theology* (New York, 1989), pp. xi–xiv; p. xii. (Griffin's alternative dichotomy of 'Eliminative/Revisionary' puts too much stress on the negative to be used here.)

5 Other problems with the deconstructive/constructive dichotomy – despite its many advantages – are that 'constructive' has associations in this century with modernist constructivist movements in both art and architecture while 'deconstructive' has recently been applied to the work of architects who have attempted to combine deconstructionist and constructivist theories.

6 See Wolfgang Welsch, *Unsere postmoderne Moderne* (1987), 2nd edn (Weinheim, 1988), pp. 12–13.

7 Higgins writes that his essay was first published in his *Two Essays Written on May 16, 1976* (New York, 1976).

used the term to describe himself and his friends'.[8] Higgins, however, provides no exact reference for Chapman's statement and, given that Chapman's work has been remembered for pre-Impressionist genre pieces with conventional genre painting titles such as 'The Mischievous Model' and 'Wooed but not Won', any use by him of the term post-modern can be suspected, until the arrival of evidence to the contrary, of having been a challenge to the innovations of the Impressionists, rather than a description of any other, more advanced innovation.[9]

The historically neutral dichotomy of Negative/Positive which was eventually chosen for the following summary has been used largely in order to describe the way in which some theories of the post-modern have moved from the negative function of describing the end or failings of modernism, or of other theories of the post-modern, to describing something more creative or innovative. Further to this, the dichotomy of Negative/Positive is intended to show the way in which the negative and positive conceptions, and uses, of post-modernism have sometimes interacted with each other in ways similar to the negative and positive poles of an electrical charge, to produce a variety of different views as well as certain continuous negative versus positive streams of thought.[10]

Some of the theorists who are listed in the left-hand, and 'negative', side of the diagram, are also shown as crossing into the right-hand column because their usage of the term has been in some way both 'positive' and 'negative'. While the following summary lists its examples in strict chronological order it is, however, not always the case that all users of the term have been aware of the usage of it which precedes their usage, or of other preceding usages. When the author of one particular use has been aware of usages before or beside theirs, it is also not necessarily the case that they have used the term post-

---

8 Welsch quotes this from Higgins, *A Dialectic of Centuries*, 2nd edn (New York and Vermont, 1978), p. 7.

9 Chapman's alleged use of the term post-modern is not included in the following summary because of lack of documentation for that use. The earliest use of the term given in the summary, by the 'Nietzschean' Pannwitz in 1917 to condemn the decadent, is documented by Welsch, pp. 12–13. (Canon Bernard Iddings Bell's use of the word Postmodernism after 1926 was aimed specifically at the theological Modernism of the time.)

10 The 'sceptical/affirmative' dichotomy used in some recent commentaries on post-modernism is similar to but still not as broad as the one chosen above.

modern in a similar fashion to another, or to mean the same or a similar reaction to the modern. It has, moreover, not just been the concepts of the 'modern' and its application, but the meanings of the prefix 'post' (as, for instance, either a break with or a continuation of the past) which have differed between uses of the term post-modern, and which have helped to create the variety of different meanings for that term which we now have.

An answer to the question of how and where the post-modern theories of parody described later in this chapter might fit into this diagram is suggested in the chapter's concluding section.

Concepts and theories of the post-modern: a summary

Negative	*Positive*

Prehistory: to the 1950s

RUDOLF PANNWITZ *Die Krisis der euro-päischen Kultur*, 1917: post-modern man ('der postmoderne Mensch') is out-wardly tough but inwardly decadent.

FEDERICO DE ONIS, *Antologia de la poesia espanola e hispanoamericana (1882-1932)*, 1934: 'postmodernismo' (1905–14) = a more prosaic or ironic modern alternative to decorative modernism.

ARNOLD J. TOYNBEE, *A Study of History*, 1939: Post-Modern = Post-1914 age.

DUDLEY FITTS' and H. R. HAYS' translation of de Onis' term 'postmodernismo', in Fitts' *Anthology of Contemporary Latin-American Poetry*, 1942, as 'post-Modernism' to describe the Latin-American poetry of both before and after Dario's death in 1916 which had reacted against the decorative excesses of symbolist modernism.

> BERNARD SMITH, *Place, Taste and Tra-dition*, 1945: 'post-Modernism' = a new 'social-realist' reaction to modernist ab-straction and 'l'art pour l'art' aesthet-icism.

JOSEPH HUDNUT, 'the post-modern house', 1945 and 1949: 'post-modern' = the ultra-modern, prefabricated house of the future, but one which still needs some soul to be added to its machinery.

Contemporary late-modern and post-modern theories and uses of parody

The post-modern seen as the modern in decline: 1950s to 1970s

ARNOLD J. TOYNBEE, *A Study of History* 1954 ff.: the 'post-Modern Age' (post 1875) will see the rise of a new 'post-Middle class' working class and new antinomian (and 'intellectually anarchic') sciences and religions.

(D. C. SOMERVELL foreshadows this usage of the term 'Post-Modern' by Toynbee, in D. C. Somervell, (ed.) *A Study of History by Arnold J. Toynbee,* 1946, p. 39.)

C. WRIGHT MILLS, *The Sociological Imagination,* 1959: a new 'post-modern period' will see the collapse of the modern age's Enlightenment ideals.

IRVING HOWE, 'Mass Society and Post-modern Fiction', 1959: the new mass society eliminates many of the moral and aesthetic bases of modernism and its classics.

HARRY LEVIN, *'What was Modernism?',* 1960: contrasts post-modern fiction and innovatory modernist literature.

The post-modern as the counter-culture of the 1960s or as innovation

NIKOLAUS PEVSNER, 'The Return to Historicism', 1961: describes a new 'post-modern' 'anti-rationalism' in architecture.

LESLIE FIEDLER, 'The New Mutants', 1965: 'post-Modernist' literature has an interest in new anti-rational counter-cultures.

NIKOLAUS PEVSNER, 'Architecture in Our Time. The Anti-Pioneers', 1966–7: uses 'post-modern style' to describe a new expressionism and extremism in architecture, new 'eclecticism', and 'contradiction of form and function'.

AMITAI ETZIONI, *The Active Society. A*

Theory of Societal and Political Processes, 1968: includes descriptions of post-World War Two [post-industrial] transformations of the technologies of communication, knowledge and energy, and of hope for new values.

LESLIE FIEDLER, 'Cross the Border – Close the Gap', 1969, describes 'Post-Modernist literature' (including science fiction and Westerns) as 'closing the gap' between high and popular culture and expanding the popular.

IHAB HASSAN, *The Dismemberment of Orpheus: Toward a Postmodern Literature* & 'POSTmodernISM: A Paracritical Bibliography', 1971: 'postmodernism' is irrational, indeterminate, anarchic, but also 'participative'.

The post-modern as critique or criticised vs the post-modern as critique and innovation: 1970s onwards

CHARLES JENCKS, 'The Rise of Post Modern Architecture', 1975: uses the term 'Post-Modern' to describe a new 'hybrid' movement different from the Modern Movement in architecture.

DANIEL BELL, *The Cultural Contradictions of Capitalism,* 1976: includes a critical description of the interest of post-modernist writers in new anti-rational counter-cultures.

CHARLES JENCKS, *The Language of Post-Modern Architecture,* 1977 ff.: describes the positive aspects of 'Post-Modern' architecture's mixing of the Modern with other codes. (Jencks uses the term 'double-coding' for this from 1978 on.)

ROBERT STERN, 'At the Edge of Modernism', 1977: 3 principles of post-modern architecture are 'Contextualism', 'Allusionism', and 'Ornamentalism'.

MICHAEL KOEHLER, '"Postmodernismus": Ein begriffsgeschichtlicher Überblick', 1977: 'postmodernism' is dated from 1970 and contrasted with both modernism and 'late modernism'.

JEAN-FRANÇOIS LYOTARD, *The Postmodern Condition*, 1979: describes the 'postmodern' as the questioning of the 'meta-narratives' of modernity.

CHARLES JENCKS, *Late-Modern Architecture*, 1980: tables and analyses differences between the 'Modern', the 'Late-Modern' and the 'Post-Modern'.

ROBERT STERN, 'The Doubles of Post-Modern', 1980: distinguishes between, (1) a 'schismatic' post-modernism that argues for a break with Western Humanism and a continuity with modernism, and (2) a 'traditional' post-modernism that argues for a break with modernism and a return to Western Humanism, especially the Romantic tradition.

PAOLO PORTOGHESI, 1980: contributes to the exhibition of post-modern architecture in the Venice Biennale of 1980 under the title of 'The Presence of the Past', and defends post-modern 'historicism'.

JOHN BARTH, 'The Literature of Replenishment', 1980: suggests post-modernist literature can add something new to the modern.

JÜRGEN HABERMAS, 'Modernity – An Incomplete Project', 1980: criticises both the post-modernist architecture shown in the Venice Biennale of 1980 as turning its back on the 'project of modernity' and 'neo-conservatives' who put the blame for the problems of modernity onto cultural modernism.

JEAN BAUDRILLARD, 'On Nihilism', 1981: describes post-modernity as the 'destruction of meaning'.

Parody: ancient, modern, and post-modern

ALAN WILDE, *Horizons of Assent. Modernism, Postmodernism, and the Ironic Imagination*, 1981: gives a largely deconstructionist post-modernist account of irony as 'multiplicity, randomness, contingency, and even absurdity'.

UMBERTO ECO, 'Postscript to *The Name of the Rose*', 1983: the post-modern is the ironic revisiting of the 'already said' in an age of lost innocence.

JEAN-FRANÇOIS LYOTARD, 'Answering the Question: What is Postmodernism?', 1982: develops the concept of the 'postmodern sublime' but suggests that post-modernist architecture has thrown out the experimental elements of modernism and developed its capitalist aspects.

PAOLO PORTOGHESI, *Postmodern. The Architecture of the Postindustrial Society*, 1982: suggests that the term 'postmodern' allows us 'temporarily to put together and compare different traditions arising from a common dissatisfaction with that group of equally heterogeneous things called modernity'.

HAL FOSTER, *Postmodern Culture*, 1983: distinguishes between a 'postmodernism of resistance' and a 'postmodernism of reaction', and criticises the latter.

FREDRIC JAMESON, 'Postmodernism and Consumer Society', in Foster 1983: uses the term 'postmodernism' to attack post-modernist architecture as part of the culture of capital, and projects a Baudrillardian concept of modern parody onto the pastiche of post- modern architecture.

CRAIG OWENS, 'The Discourse of Others: Feminists and Postmodernism', in Foster, 1983: suggests that the (Lyotardian) 'postmodern' refining of sensitivity to difference and increased tolerance of incommensurability is matched by feminist concerns for the same.

FREDRIC JAMESON, 'Postmodernism, or the Cultural Logic of Late Capitalism',

1984: projects the term 'postmodernist' onto John Portman's late-modern Bonaventure Hotel, & continues to criticise post-modernism as in 1983.

ANDREAS HUYSSEN, 'Mapping the Postmodern', 1984: includes development of ideas such as that found in Fiedler that 'postmodernism' attempts to cross the modernist divide between high and low art, and suggests that post-modernism has both to be criticised and to be accepted as a new force.

HAL FOSTER,'(Post)Modern Polemics', 1984: develops notion that there are two forms of 'postmodernism': 'neoconservative' (humanist) 'postmodernism' and 'post structuralist' 'postmodernism', but that both assume some death, or 'deconstruction', of the subject.

HEINRICH KLOTZ, *The History of Postmodern Architecture*, 1984: describes postmodern architecture as 'fiction as well as function', amongst other things.

CHARLES JENCKS, *What is Post-Modernism?*, 1986: defends the Post-Modern in architecture and criticises Hassan, Lyotard, Jameson, and Foster for giving descriptions of the 'Late-Modern' rather than of the 'Post-Modern'.

CHARLES JENCKS, *Post-Modernism: The New Classicism in Art and Architecture*, 1987: defines the emergent canons for Post-Modern Classicism as a public mode of art and architecture.

IHAB HASSAN, *The Postmodern Turn*, 1987: includes old essays and new criticisms of Lyotard and Jameson as well as critical extensions of his own categories.

WOLFGANG WELSCH, *Unsere postmoderne Moderne*, 1987: discusses the term post-modern from its early uses onwards.

DICK HEBDIGE, *Hiding in the Light: On Images and Things*, 1988: gives a largely 'deconstructionist' account of postmodernism in several media.

RICHARD KEARNEY, *The Wake of Imagination* , 1988: characterises post-modernism as being concerned with the 'loss of the imagination', but echoes Jameson's negative characterisations of post-modern pastiche.

E. ANN KAPLAN, 'Feminism/Oedipus/Postmodernism: the Case of MTV', in Kaplan, *Postmodernism and its Discontents*, 1988: takes Baudrillard and his followers as representative of existing 'post-modernism' and criticises their attempts to abolish difference while also positing the need for another (allegedly still utopian) type of post-modernism, which (following Owens) will fight for 'difference without opposition'.

PETER FULLER, *Theoria*, 1988: develops his earlier criticisms of both deconstructionist and double-coded post-modernism and suggests a more ideal post-modernism which would take up the Ruskinian value of 'theoria'.

DAVID RAY GRIFFIN, 1988 ff., distinguishes deconstructive from constructive post-modernism and extends discussion of the latter.

LINDA HUTCHEON, *A Poetics of Postmodernism*, 1988: discusses post-modernism as 'double-coded' and as 'historiographic', but also uses these categories to run some 'deconstructionist' post-modernist examples and criteria together with those of 'double-coded' post-modernism.

DAVID HARVEY, *The Condition of Postmodernity*, 1989: includes extension of Hassanian and Jamesonian concepts of the 'postmodern' to analyse the latter as late-capitalist flux.

STEVEN CONNOR, *Postmodernist Culture. An Introduction to Theories of the Contemporary*, 1989: gives a broad account of post-modernist theory which, however, sometimes applies the categories of deconstructionist post-modernism to double-coded post-modernism and *vice versa*.

JIM COLLINS, *Uncommon Cultures*, 1989: criticises more anarchic theories of post-modernism as well as monolithic modernist views and defends post-modernist eclecticism, intertextuality, heterogeneity, and their relations to mass and local cultures.

DAVID KOLB, *Postmodern Sophistications*, 1990: discusses the role played by irony and related forms in post-modern architecture, but with some criticism of the latter.

CHARLES JENCKS, 'Post-Modernism between Kitsch and Culture', 1990: discusses some new developments in Post-Modern architecture and warns against a degeneration into kitsch.

CHARLES JENCKS, 'Post-Modern Triumphs in London', 1991: includes new discussion of the carnivalistic in Post-Modern architecture.

As Charles Jencks has pointed out in his works on post-modernism in architecture and in general, many of the 'deconstructionist' theories of post-modernism described above, such as Hassan's and Lyotard's, have been based on 'late-modern' beliefs of post-structuralist theory which contrast and conflict with his understanding of post-modernism as double-coding the modernist 'code' with some other 'code'.[11] Jencks reinforces this point in the 1991 revised and enlarged edition of his *The Language of Post-Modern Architecture* of 1977 when he writes that Hassan's use of the term 'postmodernism' in 1971 was positive in contrast to some earlier negative uses of it, but was used by Hassan to mean 'what I and other critics will mean by Late- or Ultra-Modernism – that is the Modernism of extreme Avant-Gardism, Deconstruction, silence and Minimalism'.[12]

Some of the 'late-modern' characteristics to be found in the 'deconstructionist' theories of post-modernism discussed below include the more nihilistic understanding of carnival which has been found already in Foucault and which may be contrasted with Bakhtin's celebration of the ancient and mediaeval carnival which is taken up by some post-modern rather than late-modern theorists; the reduction of

---

11 See, for instance, Charles Jencks, *What is Post-Modernism?*, pp. 6 ff.
12 See Charles Jencks, *The Language of Post-Modern Architecture* (1977), 6th revised enlarged edn (London, 1991), p. 20, where Jencks also excludes Fiedler's uses of the term from the more negative.

parody to something empty of meaning as in Derrida or Baudrillard which may be seen as carrying over earlier modern understandings of parody as something negative; and the equation of parody with play when it equates it with that which is destructive or anarchistic.

Deconstructionist and other late-modern theories of the post-modern and parody

The term 'deconstructionist' is used here, as in the preceding summary, to describe those theories of the post-modern which have been based on principles about the 'indeterminacy' or 'relativity' of meaning, or on the prescriptive need for meanings to be made more 'indeterminate', and include the theories of both the early Ihab Hassan and of Jean-François Lyotard. (Derrida, despite descriptions of his work as 'postmodernist' by others, has not yet associated himself with the term post-modernism, and it is not his theories in particular which are referred to when the term deconstructionist is used with reference to theories of the post-modern, although there are, as indicated above, some connections which can be made, and some common 'late-modern' aspects to both.) In some, if not all, of the theories of the post-modern which are called deconstructionist in this chapter there is also an emphasis on what may be described as an anarchistic attitude towards selected canons and theories of modernism, as well, however, as some unlabelled borrowings from both those and other modernist canons.

As shown in the summary above, Leslie Fiedler's 'The New Mutants' of 1965[13] had already included a description of 'post-Modernist' literature's interest in new anti-rational counter-cultures,[14] while his 'Cross the Border − Close the Gap', of 1969[15] had described 'Post-Modernist literature' (including science fiction and Westerns) as 'closing the gap' between high and popular culture to expand the popular. Both deconstructionist and double-coded theories of post-modern have taken up Fiedler's phrase of 'closing the gap' in some way or another. Of the latter theorists, Charles Jencks, for example, has spoken of post-modern architecture as being able to bridge the

13 See Leslie A. Fiedler, *A Fiedler Reader* (New York, 1977), pp. 189–210.
14 See also Frank Kermode's discussion of Fiedler's essay in his 'Modernisms Again. Objects, Jokes and Art', in *Encounter*, vol. 26, no. 4, April 1966, pp. 65–74.
15 See Leslie A. Fiedler, *A Fiedler Reader*, pp. 270–94.

gap between the classical and the popular by the 'double-coding' of each, although he has also warned of the reduction of such gaps to 'crude compromises'.[16] Fiedler's initial association of post-modernism with new anti-rational counter-cultures, has, however, been taken over by deconstructionist post-modernists *rather* than by the second group of theorists.[17]

Ihab Hassan has been but one 'deconstructionist' theorist of post-modernism to take up Fiedler's early use of the term 'post-modernist' and has included some of the other anarchic characteristics given to post-modernism in Fiedler's early essay in his early table of differences between 'Modernism' and 'Postmodernism' of 1971. In Hassan's 1971 table[18] 'Modernist' 'Dehumanization' is contrasted, for instance, with 'Postmodernist' 'Antielitism, antiauthoritarianism' and 'diffusion of the ego' and with art which has become 'communal', 'optional' and 'anarchic'. In addition to making these extensions of Fiedler, Hassan contrasts 'Modernist' 'Antinomianism' with 'Postmodernist' 'counter cultures', and even though the concepts of the antinomian and the counter-cultural are not necessarily exclusive of each other.

Fiedler's counter-cultures are in fact also 'antinomian' in the sense that they oppose traditional belief in a 'Law of God'. Prior to Fiedler's use of the term 'counter-culture', Arnold J. Toynbee had already used the term 'antinomianism' to describe the growth of something different from the modern and its traditional beliefs, and this might even be said to have influenced Fiedler's use of his term. Toynbee had written, for instance, in volume IX, chapter 11 of his *A Study of History* of the 'Antinomianism of Late Modern Western Historians' (their 'repudiation of the Belief in a "Law of God"') as leading not only to the 'post-Modern' scientific obsession with the laws of Nature,[19] and to the establishment of the new sciences of Psychology, Anthropology, Political Economics and Sociology, but to the encouragement of 'post-Western' religions.[20] While Toynbee had used the terms 'late

16 See Charles Jencks, *The Language of Post-Modern Architecture*, 6th edn, 1991, pp. 165 ff.
17 Daniel Bell's criticisms of post-modernism were also based on his understanding of it from Fiedler as denoting counter-culture.
18 See Hassan, 'POSTmodernISM: A Paracritical Bibliography', in Hassan, *The Postmodern Turn. Essays in Postmodern Theory and Culture* (Ohio, 1987), pp. 25–45; pp. 40–44.
19 See Arnold J. Toynbee, *A Study of History*, vol. 9, pp. 173 ff.
20 Ibid., pp. 185 ff.

Modern' and 'post-Modern' interchangeably in parts of this chapter, as when speaking of 'an intellectually anarchic late Modern and post-Modern Age',[21] and to describe developments which can now be looked back upon as late-modern extensions of the modern, Fiedler's 1960s description of the anarchic counter-cultures of his time can also be described as 'late-modern' rather than as 'post-modern'.

Hassan echoes Toynbee's belief as well as Fiedler's in the rise of 'intellectual anarchy' in most of his other 'late-modern' categories of the post-modern, though with little, if any, of the criticism to be found in Toynbee's uses of the term. (Hassan's reference to the rise of 'Counter Western "ways" or metaphysics' at the conclusion of his paragraph which lists 'counter cultures' as opposed to modernist 'antinomianism' is also to a phenomenon which both Toynbee and Fiedler had described as typical of their new ages.) Many of Hassan's categories may furthermore be said to be derived from the modern world and its literature, which (as Hassan's application of the term 'Antinomianism' to 'Modernism' suggests) was itself anti-hierarchical in some ways, while his emphasis on the increased relation of his 'Postmodernist' categories to the irrational and the chaotic can be described as a 'late-modern' extension of the modern. When classified under 'Postmodernism' by Hassan, and together with a mixture of modern and late-modern forms including 'radical irony, self-consuming play, entropy of meaning, comedy of the absurd, black humour, slapstick, camp, and negation', parody is described as 'insane' in what can further be characterised as a 'late-modern' manner.[22]

Hassan's 1971 list of modernist and 'postmodernist' characteristics also gives an additional description of parody as a 'postmodernist' form which opposes 'Modernist Experimentalism'[23] and places it in the category of 'Postmodernism' together with a mixture of modern and late-modern forms which include 'open, discontinuous, improvisational, indeterminate, or aleatory structures', 'simultaneism, fan-

21 Ibid., p. 189.
22 See Hassan, *The Postmodern Turn*, pp. 40–4. As will be seen presently, Fiedler too had sometimes used the term parody in a largely negative and modern fashion, although he had also demonstrated an understanding of some of its more positive characteristics.
23 Lyotard also criticises post-modernist architecture for its treatment of modernist experimentalism in his 'Answering the Question: What is Postmodernism?', translated by Régis Durand, in Lyotard, *The Postmodern Condition: A Report on Knowledge* (Manchester, 1984), p. 71.

tasy, play, humour, happening', and 'increasing self-reflexiveness, intermedia, the fusion of forms, the confusion of realms'. While all of these forms are described as 'postmodernist', they remain, however, separate, and comic parody and meta-fiction are not explicitly brought together as representing any new post-modernist understanding of parody as being both comic and meta-fictional.

Hassan concludes his description of the post-modernist characteristics referred to above with a reference to Susan Sontag's essay 'Against Interpretation' of 1964. Sontag, however, had not only *not* mentioned the post-modern in that essay but had been speaking specifically of *modern* art, and of its abstract modernist (and experimental) forms, and of how they had rejected the forms of interpretation which had treated other works as consisting of 'items of content'. Since Jencks and some theorists of post-modernism other than Hassan have described post-modernist art as a *return to content*, and the post-modernist restoration of decoration and meaning in architecture as a *revolt against modernist abstraction*, the description of Sontag's argument as 'post-modern' has become even more open to questioning.

Sontag had also included both decorative art and parody in the types of art which she saw as representing the modernist flight from the interpretation which imposed content on art works, and had done so on the basis of an understanding of decoration and parody which differs from Jencks' understanding of them as forms of encoding which add new meaning and content to the modern. Sontag writes, for example: 'Interpretation, based on the highly dubious theory that a work of art is composed of items of content, violates art. It makes art into an article for use, for arrangement into a mental scheme of categories. Interpretation does not, of course, always prevail. In fact, a great deal of today's art may be understood as motivated by a flight from interpretation. To avoid interpretation, art may become parody. Or it may become abstract. Or it may become ("merely") decorative. Or it may become non-art.'[24]

To concentrate on Sontag's reference to parody, it might be suggested first of all that little definite can be said about it given the brevity of its appearance in this argument. If parody is not interpretation in Sontag's sense (she has also described interpretation

---

24 See Susan Sontag's essay 'Against Interpretation', in Sontag, *Against Interpretation and Other Essays* (1966), (New York, 1978), p. 10.

as a concealed translation on her page 5 and as a concealed alteration of that which it interprets on her page 6), her use of its name seems, however, to be at least to some extent similar to those modern and late-modern depictions of parody as lacking in both intention and in its own content which we can find from Nietzsche and Derrida onwards through Baudrillard to his 'postmodernist' (or, rather, anti-post-modernist) followers.[25] While the bases for Sontag's rejection of interpretation in modern art and parody are different from those of the writers named above, it may still be asked whether her view of parody as a flight from interpretation is an accurate, useful, or 'post-modern' attribute for it.

Even if that flight from interpretation could be understood in the light of the conclusion of Sontag's penultimate paragraph as being a meta-fictional alternative which would show 'how the art-work is what it is' rather than what it says (Sontag writes there that 'the function of criticism should be to show *how it is what it is*, even *that it is what it is*, rather than to show *what it means*'[26]), most meta-fictional parody has been seen to show 'how' *as well as* 'that'. In addition to restricting parody to the demonstration of the form *rather* than the content of a work (as in some earlier 'modern' descriptions of parody), there is no mention in Sontag's essay of the particular comical or critical functions of parody. Sontag's concept of parody could, however, only be 'post-modern', in the sense being arrived at in this work, if her understanding of it were more clearly to go beyond both the late-modern description of it as non-intentional and the modern depiction of it as *either* meta-fictional *or* comic.

Hassan also is not clear as to why, in his use of Sontag's essay, he has chosen her term 'against interpretation' as being particularly post-modern. He himself had suggested, as seen previously, that the post-modern was more self-reflexive, and interpretative, in this sense at least, than modern art.

Hassan's emphasis on self-reflexivity is, moreover, in conflict with Fiedler's explicit separation of post-modernism from the self-reflexivity which he saw to be typical of many modernist works, made when he claimed in his 1969 essay 'Cross the Border – Close the Gap' that the new [post-modernist] age was 'distrustful of self-protective irony

---

25 This point is explained further in following sections.
26 Sontag, p. 14. Sontag concludes: 'In place of a hermeneutics we need an erotics of art'.

and too great self-awareness'.[27] Hassan's contrasting description of increasing self-reflexiveness as a characteristic of the post-modern has, nonetheless, and together with his tendency to define post-modernism in terms of works and categories which others have described as modernist, both ensured modernist self-reflexive meta-fiction a place in the canons of many other theories of the post-modern, and given a broader and less formalistic meaning to the meta-fiction described by Sontag.

For some other theorists of post-modernism the re-canonisation of modernist meta-fiction as post-modernist has also meant that a new form of post-modernist meta-fiction has had to be found to distinguish it from other modernist meta-fictions. While David Lodge has described post-modern fiction as both more discontinuous and meta-fictional than modern meta-fiction in various of his critical works,[28] Linda Hutcheon has suggested that the term 'historiographical meta-fiction' should be used to characterise post-modern meta-fiction.[29]

The term 'historiographical meta-fiction' has the advantage for Hutcheon that she is then able to suggest further links between that which she has designated as being post-modernist meta-fiction and the post-modernist architecture which has been described by Jencks as 'double-coding' other historical styles with the modern style. Hutcheon, however, not only glosses over some very real differences between these two sets of practices in bringing them together in this way, but is only able to link 'historiographic' post-modern meta-fiction and post-modern architecture with its double-coding of the modern with other 'historic' codes or styles because her understanding of the term 'historiographic' means that it does not refer to 'factual' history (of architecture or of any other form or area of human life), but to history understood in a very general way as being, like fiction, yet another form of discourse.[30]

---

27 Fiedler, p. 272.
28 See, for example, Lodge, *Working with Structuralism. Essays and Reviews on Nineteenth- and Twentieth-Century Literature* (1981) (London, Boston, Henley, 1986), p. 14 on post-modernism and discontinuity, and his *After Bakhtin: Essays on Fiction and Criticism* (London, 1990), p. 43 on post-modernism and meta-fictionality.
29 See Hutcheon, *A Poetics of Postmodernism* (London and New York, 1988).
30 Hutcheon's suggestion that parody is post-modern because of its ability to renew and look back to other historical works also obscures the fact that most parody does this.

Whether the self-referentiality of meta-fiction can be carried over from fiction to architecture without the differences between the two fields being taken into account is also as questionable as is the stretching of the term 'historiographic' to cover all the different uses of historical discourse and architectural style in each. Heinrich Klotz has written that 'the architecture of postmodernism is referential, not self-referential',[31] and even works such as Oswald Mathias Ungers' *Deutsches Architekturmuseum*, Frankfurt am Main (1980–1983) and its 'house within a house' can be understood to illustrate or *refer* to self-referentiality rather than to describe and practise it in the same manner as the verbal or written arts.

The question of how the various post-modernist understandings of meta-fiction relate to parody and to its peculiarly comic character is one which will be discussed again presently.

Hassan's later essay on post-modernism, 'The Question of Postmodernism', published 1980,[32] also discusses Fiedler's 1969 argument that post-modernism had 'closed the gap' between high and pop culture,[33] but does not name parody in the list of characteristics for post-modernism which Hassan sets up against modernism in it. While it does repeat other elements with which parody was listed in 1971, such as play, anarchy, and happening, these, moreover, are listed together with some new but still largely 'deconstructive' forms such as 'Antiform (disjunctive, open)', 'Decreation/Deconstruction', 'Text/Intertext', and 'Antinarrative'.[34]

Later still, in his 'Pluralism in Postmodern Perspective' of 1986,[35] Hassan does make, however, several references to Bakhtin,[36] and includes parody under the category of post-modernist 'Hybridization'. Although parody is at first listed together with what Hassan describes as other forms of the 'mutant replication of genres', such as travesty and pastiche, Hassan also goes on to give a more positive view of both it and pastiche as constructive when he writes that 'cliché and plagiarism ("playgiarism", Raymond Federman punned), parody and

31 See Heinrich Klotz, *The History of Postmodern Architecture* (1984), translated by Radka Donnell (Cambridge, Mass. and London, 1988), p. 421.
32 Published in Harry R. Garvin (ed.), *Romanticism, Modernism, Postmodernism*, Bucknell Review, vol. 25, no. 2 (London and Toronto, 1980), pp. 117–26.
33 Hassan, 1980, p. 118. (Hassan, p. 117 also mentions Toynbee's use of the term post-modern.) 34 Ibid., p. 123.
35 See Hassan, *The Postmodern Turn*, pp. 167–87.
36 See Hassan's discussions of irony and carnivalisation in *The Postmodern Turn*, pp. 170–1.

pastiche, pop and kitsch, enrich re-presentation'.[37] After stating that 'in this view, image or replica may be as valid as its model (the *Quixote* of Borges' Pierre Menard)', and 'may even bring an *"augment d'être"'*, Hassan continues: 'This makes for a different concept of tradition, one in which continuity and discontinuity, high and low culture, mingle not to imitate but to expand the past in the present. In the plural present, all styles are dialectically available in an interplay between the Now and the Not Now, the Same and the Other. Thus, in postmodernism, Heidegger's concept of *"equitemporality"* becomes really a dialectic of equitemporality, an intertemporality, a new relation between historical elements, without any suppression of the past in favor of the present – a point that Fredric Jameson (1983) misses when he criticizes postmodern literature, film, and architecture for their ahistorical character, their *"presentifications"*.'[38]

Hassan's criticism of Fredric Jameson in this passage also appears to be indicative, together with his description of parody as something constructive as well as destructive, of a heightened sensitivity to the type of pastiche and parody described in the 'double-coded' theories of post-modernism developed by Charles Jencks from Robert Venturi's work on the 'complexity' and 'contradiction' of recent architecture.[39] While he makes no specific mention of parody in his following segment on carnivalisation, Hassan's references to Bakhtin show some appreciation of the ambivalence of forms related to parody, and even though many of these are still described via Hassan's older terms for post-modernism such as 'indeterminacy' and the 'absurd'. Although Hassan's characterisation of Bakhtin's carnival as embracing 'indeterminacy, fragmentation, decanonization, and selflessness' as well as 'hybridization' is reminiscent of Foucault's more nihilistic interpretation of carnival, it too is joined by some more positive characteristics: '*Carnivalization*. The term, of course, is Bakhtin's, and it riotously embraces indeterminacy, fragmentation, decanonization, selflessness, irony, hybridization, all of which I have already adduced. But the term also conveys the comic or absurdist ethos of postmodernism, anticipated in the *"heteroglossia"* of Rabelais and Sterne, jocose prepostmodernists.'[40]

---

37 Ibid., p. 170.   38 Ibid., pp. 170–1.
39 Hassan also lists both Charles Jencks and Robert Venturi in the 'pell-mell' list of post-modernists which he gives in his *The Dismemberment of Orpheus: Toward a Postmodern Literature* (1971), 2nd edn (Wisconsin and London, 1982), p. 260.
40 See Hassan, *The Postmodern Turn*, p. 171.

Hassan's description of Rabelais and Sterne as 'jocose prepost-modernists' is also interesting for its stress on both the 'heteroglossia' and the comical nature of their works, although no mention is made of their use of parody, and the comedy in question is again associated with the modernist category of the absurd rather than with the elements with which Bakhtin had associated it. Like several other commentators on Bakhtin and post-modernism, Hassan also appears to refer to Bakhtin's descriptions of the reduction of hierarchies in the carnival as the wholesale relativisation of those levels when he goes on to speak of 'carnivalization' as entailing the 'gay relativity' of things.[41] It might be noted, however, and with reference to other deconstructionist post-modernists who have seen the relativisation of truth as well as of good and evil argued for in Bakhtin, that Bakhtin had generally been more specific about the nature of the relativisation which he was describing with relation to the carnival's bringing of the high low, and had, for instance, specifically mentioned 'the *joyful relativity* of all structure and order, of all authority and all [hierarchical] position' in his *Problems of Dostoyevsky's Poetics*.[42]

In 'post-modernist' contradistinction to late-modernist 'Nietz-schean' relativism, Leslie Fiedler has described the relativisation of hierarchies in post-modernism in his essay 'Cross the Border – Close the Gap' as a relativisation of high and low which still allows one to speak of good and bad. After describing Pop Art and its ability to subvert hierarchies ('Pop Art is, whatever its overt politics, subversive: a threat to all hierarchies insofar as it is hostile to order and ordering in its own realm'),[43] Fiedler continued: 'What the final intrusion of Pop into the citadels of High Art provides, therefore, for the critic is the exhilarating new possibility of making judgments about the "goodness" and "badness" of art quite separated from distinctions between "high" and "low" with their concealed class bias.'

Fiedler, however, had also spoken of how the destructiveness of parody might be put to use in closing the gap between the high and the low – the elite and the popular – by bringing the high low: 'There is, however, no doubt in the minds of most other writers whom the

41 Douglas Kellner suggests that Jean Baudrillard uses a similar term in his *L'Échange symbolique et la mort* of 1976. See Kellner, *Jean Baudrillard. From Marxism to Postmodernism and Beyond* (Oxford and Cambridge, 1989), p. 93.
42 See Bakhtin's *Problems*, p. 124. (Bakhtin also specifically mentions the relativisation of the hierarchical aspects of language in his *Problems*, p. 107 and of 'official' truth in his *Rabelais*.)   43 Fiedler, p. 287.

young especially prize at the moment that their essential task is to destroy once and for all — by parody or exaggeration or grotesque emulation of the classic past, as well as by the adaptation and "camping" of Pop forms just such distinctions and discriminations. But to turn High Art into vaudeville and burlesque at the same moment that Mass Art is being irreverently introduced into museums and libraries is to perform an act which has political as well as aesthetic implications ... an act which closes a class, as well as a generation gap.'[44]

Fiedler also describes a classical work of literature brought low as becoming 'something closer to travesty than emulation',[45] but had earlier indicated in more general terms that comic parody had already played some positive role in the development of the genre of the novel which might be repeated in the post-modern: 'The New Novel must be anti-art as well as antiserious. But this means, after all, that it must become more like what it was in the beginning, more what it seemed when Samuel Richardson could not be taken quite seriously, and what it remained in England (as opposed to France, for instance) until Henry James had justified himself as an artist against such self-declared "entertainers" as Charles Dickens and Robert Louis Stevenson: popular, not quite reputable, a little dangerous — the one his loved and rejected cultural father, the other his sibling rival in art.'[46]

Although this last statement on parody might be described as 'proto-post-modernist' because of its recognition of the re-creative as well as comic aspects of parody, Fiedler's overall view of parody is still 'late-modern' in its attribution of a negative and destructive function to parody,[47] and is not yet 'post-modern' enough to have explicitly rejected this aspect of the modern understanding of parody, or to have explicitly linked the comic and meta-fictional functions of that form. (Fiedler also uses the term parody in an ambivalent manner in referring to the popularity of 'the Western' as meaning that 'its sentimentality ... has come to possess our minds so completely that it can now be mitigated without essential loss by parody, irony — and even critical analysis'. But although Fiedler seems here to be describing the critical powers of parody as being less destructive, this latter phenomenon is

44 Ibid., pp. 286–7.
45 Ibid., p. 279. On p. 286 Fiedler also uses the term burlesque in a negative way.
46 Ibid. p. 276.
47 Fiedler's 1965 essay 'The New Mutants', in Fiedler, pp. 203–4, had also used the word parody in a largely negative sense in discussing Edward Albee's *Who's Afraid of Virginia Woolf*.

explained as deriving more from the strength of popularity of the Western than from any ambiguous relationship of parody to its target.[48])

Hassan had continued his description of carnivalisation with a mixture of Bakhtinian and deconstructionist post-modernist categories: 'Carnivalization further means "polyphony", the centrifugal power of language, the "gay relativity" of things, perspectivism and performance, participation in the wild disorder of life, the immanence of laughter.'[49] Hassan adds: 'Indeed, what Bakhtin calls novel or carnival – that is, antisystem – might stand for postmodernism itself, or at least for its ludic and subversive elements that promise renewal. For in carnival, "the true feast of time, the feast of becoming, change, and renewal", human beings, then as now, discover "the peculiar logic of the 'inside out' (à l'envers), of the 'turn-about', ... of numerous parodies and travesties, humiliations, profanations, comic crownings and uncrownings. A second life".'[50]

Some aspects of Bakhtin's work on the carnival have recently been taken up into the theories of 'double-coded' post-modernism by Charles Jencks, who has also welcomed Hassan's more recent work as representing something of a development away from his earlier more 'deconstructionist' theories of post-modernism. Prior to this, Hassan's more deconstructionist theories had, however, not only been of some influence on other theorists of the post-modern and on their understandings of parody as play, but had been both overtaken by, and sometimes confused with, Fredric Jameson's transformation of Jean Baudrillard's more negative understanding of modern parody into a much quoted criticism of post-modernist pastiche as a 'blind' or 'blank' form of parody.

Jean Baudrillard has often been described in recent works of criticism and theory as a 'postmodernist', and even though he himself had rarely used this term up until his most recent works, and has in those works specifically criticised that which others have termed post-modern. Douglas Kellner also admits in his *Jean Baudrillard. From Marxism to Postmodernism and Beyond* that Baudrillard has not used the term post-modernism in his own work to a great extent, and, apart from answering some questions on it in his 'Interview: Game with Vestiges' of 1984, where he describes it as 'playing with the pieces',

48 Fiedler, p. 278.   49 Hassan, *The Postmodern Turn*, p. 171.
50 Ibid. Hassan is quoting from Bakhtin's *Rabelais and his World*, pp. 10–11.

had discussed it at length only in his 'On Nihilism' of 1981.[51] More recently, Mike Gane has referred to Baudrillard's critical comments on post-modernity in his *Cool Memories* of 1987, and concluded that Baudrillard should even be regarded as an 'anti-postmodernist'.[52]

These facts, and the related fact that Baudrillard is often speaking specifically of modernist phenomena in the works which others have referred to as 'postmodernist', are also relevant to assessing the way in which his descriptions of modern parody as blind, blank or empty have been taken over by Jameson and by those following him in their critical descriptions of post-modern pastiche as blind or blank.[53] As will be seen below, the application of Baudrillard's characterisations of modern art and of its use of parody to that which is termed 'postmodern pastiche', also means that the problems of modernity and of its capitalist elements, as characterised by Baudrillard, have been projected onto the post-modern and onto its use of pastiche without total explanation or justification.

One use of the term parody by Baudrillard which is of particular relevance to understanding the tenor of Fredric Jameson's use of the term 'blank parody' in his descriptions of 'postmodern' pastiche is to be found in Baudrillard's essay 'Gesture and Signature: Semiurgy in Contemporary Art' in which modern art is described as being both critical in appearance and yet in collusion with the contemporary world. Baudrillard writes of this art: 'It plays with it, and is included in the game. It can parody this world, illustrate it, simulate it, alter it; it never disturbs the order, which is also its own.' [54] A similarly mixed and ultimately self-contradictory account of parody, which describes it both as being potentially politically useful and as having 'the

51 See Douglas Kellner, *Jean Baudrillard. From Marxism to Postmodernism and Beyond* (Oxford and Cambridge, 1989), pp. 116–18.
52 See Mike Gane, *Baudrillard's Bestiary. Baudrillard and Culture* (London and New York, 1991), pp. 159–60.
53 Baudrillard's comments on the post-modern as a nihilistic game with meaning in his 'On Nihilism' of 1981 (see *On the Beach*, 6, Spring 1984, pp. 38–9) also extend his descriptions of the modern rather than present the post-modern as something new or more hopeful.
54 See Jean Baudrillard, *For a Critique of the Political Economy of the Sign* of 1972, translated by Charles Levin (St. Louis, 1981), p. 110. Baudrillard also writes here that 'art no longer contests anything if it ever did' and Thomas Docherty's suggestion in his *After Theory. Postmodernism/Postmarxism* (London and New York, 1990), p. 118 that Baudrillard can be used to argue for a parody which can challenge reality would be better applied to Foucault.

tepidity of simile', had, moreover, previously been published by one of Baudrillard's sources, Marshall McLuhan, in his and Wilfred Watson's *From Cliché to Archetype* of 1970.[55]

Baudrillard had also written in his 'The Orders of Simulacra' of 1975, with reference to the duplication of images in modern pictures such as Andy Warhol's, of a parody which is both 'non-intentional' and 'blind': 'Today, when the real and the imaginary are confused in the same operational totality, the esthetic fascination is everywhere. ... A kind of non-intentional parody hovers over everything, of technical simulation, of indefinable fame to which is attached an esthetic pleasure, that very one of reading and of the rules of the game. Travelling of signs, the media, of fashion and the models, of the blind and brilliant ambiance of the simulacra.'[56] Baudrillard continues: 'And so art is everywhere, since artifice is at the very heart of reality. And so art is dead, not only because its critical transcendence is gone,[57] but because reality itself, entirely impregnated by an aesthetic which is inseparable from its own structure, has been confused with its own image.'[58] Later, in his *America* of 1986, Baudrillard uses the word parody in an apparently more ambivalent manner to describe the culture of America and its 'parody' of other cultures as both the 'mirror of *our* [Europe's] decadence' and as 'hyperreal in its vitality',[59] but again with the suggestion that such parody lacks intentionality.

Baudrillard had written further in his 'The Precession of Simulacra'[60] that 'simulation is master, and nostalgia, the phantasmal parodic rehabilitation of all lost referentials, alone remain',[61] and had earlier depicted parody, in contrast to Foucault's characterisation of Cervantes' *Don Quixote*, as something which cancels out difference.[62] When Baudrillard speaks of parody in an apparently 'differentiative'

55 See Marshall McLuhan and Wilfred Watson, *From Cliché to Archetype* (New York, 1970), pp. 167–70. (Although Baudrillard criticises McLuhan's praise for modern technology and culture he still uses McLuhan's work to help define his targets.)
56 See Jean Baudrillard, 'The Orders of Simulacra' (1975), translated by Philip Beitchman in *Simulations*, translated by Paul Foss, Paul Patton, Philip Beitchman (New York, 1983), pp. 83–159, p. 150.   57 Ibid., p. 151.
58 Ibid., p.152. Baudrillard concludes this passage: ' ... The principle of simulation wins out over the reality principle just as over the principle of pleasure.'
59 See Jean Baudrillard, *America*, translated by Chris Turner (London and New York, 1988), p. 104.
60 See Baudrillard, 'The Precession of Simulacra', translated by Paul Foss and Paul Patton in Jean Baudrillard, *Simulations*, pp. 1–79.
61 Ibid., p. 72.   62 Ibid., p. 40.

manner in his 'The Orders of Simulacra' with reference to a cook who had created a 'mini-world' out of concrete, it is, moreover, with an echo of Nietzsche which can be said to have mixed the latter's concept of a 'will to power' with Nietzsche's view of parody as something which was its opposite, but which fails to find such parody in action: 'Nothing here of a Luciferan revolt, or a will-to-parody, or of a desire to espouse the cause of naive art.'[63]

The term parody has also been used by Baudrillard to characterise both destruction and a lack of intentionality when referring to the public's reactions to Renzo Piano's and Richard Rogers' Paris Pompidou Centre in his 1977 essay 'The Beaubourg-Effect'. There Baudrillard writes: 'Thus a type of parody, of oversimulation in response to the simulation of culture: the masses, meant only to be cultural livestock, are always transformed into the slaughterers of a culture of which Beaubourg is just the shameful incarnation.'[64]

Baudrillard's analysis of the 'Beaubourg' has been echoed by Fredric Jameson in his 1984 criticism of John Portman's Bonaventure Hotel in the essay 'Postmodernism, or the Cultural Logic of Late Capitalism'.[65] Baudrillard had not criticised the 'Beaubourg' as a post-modern building,[66] and both it and John Portman's Bonaventure Hotel are either late-modern or modern rather than post-modern buildings for architectural historians such as Charles Jencks and Heinrich Klotz.[67] Despite this, Jameson has criticised the latter building as both 'late capitalist' and 'post-modernist', and attributed to it, and to the 'post-modern', some of the problems attributed to the Beaubourg by Baudrillard.[68]

---

63 See Baudrillard, 'The Orders of Simulacra', pp. 83–159; p. 91.
64 See Jean Baudrillard, 'The Beaubourg-Effect: Implosion and Deterrence' (1977), in *October*, Spring 1982, pp. 3–13; p. 7.
65 See Fredric Jameson, 'Postmodernism, or the Cultural Logic of Late Capitalism' in *New Left Review*, no. 146, July-August 1984, pp. 53–92; pp. 80 ff.
66 Baudrillard's later question, in Baudrillard, *America* (1986), translated by Chris Turner (London and New York, 1988), p. 59, as to whether the Bonaventure Hotel is post-modern, might be seen as having been produced by Jameson's 1984 description of the hotel as such.
67 See Charles Jencks, *The Language of Post-Modern Architecture* (revised enlarged edn, London, 1978), p. 35; Jencks, *Late-Modern Architecture and Other Essays* (London and New York, 1980), p. 15; and Heinrich Klotz, *The History of Postmodern Architecture*, p. 63.
68 Jameson takes the term 'late-capitalist' from Ernest Mandel, who had not applied it to post-modern architecture. Lyotard's 'Answering the Question: What is

But why call Portman's building post-modern? A brief look at the Bonaventure Hotel will show us that its high-tech and high-gloss structure has little to do with the pastiche which Jameson has condemned as post-modern. As suggested previously, Jameson's characterisations of pastiche also echo, however, Baudrillard's descriptions of the non-intentional modern parody which he claims have filled the 'hyperspaces' of the modern. Jameson is unable to use his condemnation of pastiche to condemn the Bonaventure Hotel as post-modern, because it does not use pastiche in any obvious manner, but does use Baudrillard's characterisations of modernity as 'hyperreal' and as 'hyperspace' to criticise what he calls the post-modernist space of the hotel. Yet not only had Baudrillard been describing works of architecture which architectural historians such as Charles Jencks have named late-modern because of their extension of the modernist use of space, as well as of other modern features,[69] but the extension of modernist space in Portman's Bonaventure Hotel is still not 'Post-Modern' rather than 'Late-Modern' according to Jencks' criteria.[70]

In addition to characterising that which he calls the 'hyperspace' of the Bonaventure Hotel as 'postmodern' in a manner which others have been able to describe as arbitrary as well as misleading,[71] Jameson, as already indicated, had separately condemned the post-modern use of pastiche as 'blind' parody in his *New Left Review* article 'Postmodernism, or The Cultural Logic of Late Capitalism' of 1984.[72]

This criticism of post-modern pastiche, which echoes and extends

Postmodernism?' of 1982, p. 76, had, however, spoken of the post-modern 'in Jencks' sense' and capitalism together.

69 See, for example Jencks' comments on the Pompidou Centre in his *What is Post-Modernism?*, p. 36: 'The Modernist emphasis on structure, circulation, open space, industrial detailing and abstraction is taken to its Late-Modern extreme, although again often mis-termed Post-Modern.'

70 See Jencks on Portman's building in Jencks, *The Language of Post-Modern Architecture* (revised enlarged edn, 1978), p. 35 and Jencks, *Late-Modern Architecture and Other Essays*, p. 15.

71 See also the criticisms made of Jameson's analysis of the Bonaventure Hotel by David Shumway in Douglas Kellner (ed.), *Postmodernism/Jameson/Critique* (Washington, 1989), p. 192 and by Mike Gane, on his pp. 143 ff.

72 And see Jameson, 'The Politics of Theory: Ideological Positions in the Postmodernism Debate' (1984), in Fredric Jameson, *The Ideologies of Theory: Essays 1971–1986. Volume 2: The Syntax of History* (London, 1988), p. 105, where Jameson writes that the 'complacent play of historical allusion and stylistic pastiche (termed "historicism" in the architecture literature) is a central feature of postmodernism more generally'.

Baudrillard's descriptions of modern parody as unintentional, while overtly but loosely referring to Adorno's criticisms of Stravinsky's use of older musical forms,[73] is based on an earlier but similar criticism of pastiche as 'blank' parody in Jameson's 'Postmodernism and Consumer Society' in Hal Foster's collection of essays on the post-modern of 1983.[74] (Jameson's criticisms of the Russian formalists in his *The Prison-House of Language* of 1972 had not included any extended discussion of their concepts of parody and his earlier *Marxism and Form* of 1971 had run pastiche and parody together in moving from Adorno's criticisms of Stravinsky to speak of 'the theoretical justification for the use of such pastiche and parody' by Thomas Mann, 'for whom the act of speaking with irony through a dead style permits speech in a situation where it would otherwise be impossible'.[75])

Jameson's earlier essay on post-modernism begins its discussion of post-modernist pastiche by describing both pastiche and parody as involving 'the imitation or, better still, the mimicry of other styles and particularly of the mannerisms and stylistic twitches of other styles'.[76] Later Jameson will also refer to the humour of parody as being absent from pastiche, and use this as a reason for describing the latter as a more 'blank' form of parody, and even though pastiche has never necessarily involved humour as has parody. Firstly, however, Jameson claims that a peculiarity of parody has been that it 'capitalizes on the uniqueness of ... styles and seizes on their idiosyncrasies and eccentricities to produce an imitation which mocks the original'. Jameson continues with further emphasis on the relationship of parody to

73 See Jameson, 'Postmodernism, or the Cultural Logic of Late Capitalism', pp. 64 f. While the section of Adorno's (1949) work to which Jameson alludes condemns developments which Jameson criticises as being typical of pastiche, it does not use that term, and in 1962 Adorno uses the word pastiche to describe a more undermining use of older forms by Stravinsky.

74 See *The Anti-Aesthetic. Essays on Postmodern Culture*, edited by Hal Foster (Port Townsend, Washington, 1983); republished as *Postmodern Culture* (London, 1985).

75 See Jameson, *Marxism and Form. Twentieth-Century Dialectical Theories of Literature* (Princeton, 1974), p. 34. Despite distinguishing between 'postmodern' pastiche and 'modern' parody, Jameson's 'Postmodernism, or the Cultural Logic of Late Capitalism', p. 64 also takes the origins of pastiche back to both Thomas Mann and Adorno, and without explaining why this does not make pastiche 'modern' as well as 'postmodern'.

76 See Fredric Jameson, 'Postmodernism and Consumer Society', in Foster, *Postmodern Culture* (London, 1985), pp. 111–25; p. 113.

ridicule: 'I won't say that the satiric impulse is conscious in all forms of parody. In any case, a good or great parodist has to have some secret sympathy for the original, just as a great mimic has to have the capacity to put himself/herself in the place of the person imitated. Still, the general effect of parody is – whether in sympathy or with malice – to cast ridicule on the private nature of these stylistic mannerisms and their excessiveness and eccentricity with respect to the way people normally speak or write. So there remains somewhere behind all parody the feeling that there is a linguistic norm in contrast to which the styles of the great modernists can be mocked.'[77]

The disappearance of shared norms is also the moment at which Jameson claims modern parody is made 'impossible' and the 'blanker' form of 'postmodern' pastiche takes over: 'That is the moment at which pastiche appears and parody has become impossible. Pastiche is, like parody, the imitation of a peculiar or unique style, the wearing of a stylistic mask, speech in a dead language: but it is a neutral practice of such mimicry, without parody's ulterior motive, without the satirical impulse, without laughter, without that still latent feeling that there exists something *normal* compared to which what is being imitated is rather comic. Pastiche is blank parody, parody that has lost its sense of humor: pastiche is to parody what that curious thing, the modern practice of a kind of blank irony is to what Wayne Booth calls the stable and comic ironies of, say, the 18th century.'[78]

To Jameson the disappearance of the norms to which modernism was accustomed has accompanied the 'death' of the individual subject,[79] and this idea is also suggested in his description of the 'blank' character, or, rather, lack of character, of pastiche and its 'nostalgic' rehabilitation of the past:[80] 'Hence, once again, pastiche: in a world in which stylistic innovation is no longer possible, all that is left is to imitate dead styles, to speak through the masks and with the voices of the styles in the imaginary museum.'[81] Jameson continues:

77 Ibid., pp. 113–14.   78 Ibid., p. 114.
79 See ibid., pp. 114–15, and Jameson, 'Postmodernism, or the Cultural Logic of Late Capitalism', p. 64.
80 Jameson also echoes Baudrillard's statement in his 'The Precession of Simulacra', p. 72 that 'Simulation is master, and nostalgia, the phantasmal parodic rehabilitation of all lost referentials, alone remain' in his criticism of the nostalgia produced by the use of pastiche in his 'Postmodernism and Consumer Society', pp. 116 ff.
81 Hassan also mentions Malraux's *musée imaginaire* or 'imaginary museum' in his *The Postmodern Turn*, p. 177.

'But this means that contemporary or postmodernist art is going to be about art itself in a new kind of way; even more, it means that one of its essential messages will involve the necessary failure of art and the aesthetic, the failure of the new, the imprisonment in the past.'[82] Here too, and on the basis of his own late-modernist post-structuralist and Marxist presuppositions, rather than on those of the post-modern architecture and its uses of pastiche which he is attacking, Jameson criticises the post-modern as being both 'nostalgic' about the past and as 'schizophrenic, as well as being a part of a capitalistic 'consumer society'.[83]

As stated previously, in chapter 2, architectural history has seen many different uses of pastiche, but has also been able to offer a largely neutral definition of it as the transference of a design or design element from one work or medium into another. In contrast to such descriptions of pastiche as a device for the translation and re-use of other design elements, Jameson has burdened it with his own particular metaphors of nostalgia and schizophrenia, and criticisms of them,[84] and has, in addition, followed some other modern commentators on pastiche, from areas concerned with the more individual and 'original' production of art or literary works, in condemning it as something derivative and as antipathetic to the modernist experimentation which both he and Lyotard have defended against the post-modernist architecture supported by Jencks.

Jameson writes of post-modern pastiche in language which is similar to that of his 1983 article in his 1984 essay, 'Postmodernism, or The Cultural Logic of Late Capitalism', but with the addition of the adjective 'blind' to his description of pastiche as a 'blank' form of parody:[85] 'Parody finds itself without a vocation; it has lived, and that strange new thing pastiche slowly comes to take its place. Pastiche is, like parody, the imitation of a peculiar mask, speech in a dead language: but it is a neutral practice of such mimicry, without any of parody's ulterior motives, amputated of the satiric impulse, devoid of laughter and of any conviction that alongside the abnormal tongue you have momentarily borrowed, some healthy linguistic normality still exists. Pastiche is thus blank parody, a statue with blind eyeballs:

82 Jameson, 'Postmodernism and Consumer Society', pp. 115–16.
83 See ibid., pp. 116 ff.
84 Jameson also uses these terms differently from Jencks.
85 See Jameson, 'Postmodernism, or The Cultural Logic of Late Capitalism', p. 65.

it is to parody what that other interesting and historically original modern thing, the practice of a kind of blank irony, is to what Wayne Booth calls the "stable ironies" of the 18th century.'[86]

Despite the fact that Jameson's descriptions of pastiche as both post-modern and blind give an idiosyncratic and a misleading view of their subject,[87] they have been taken up by several other commentators on the post-modern. One of these, Hal Foster, the editor of the volume in which Jameson had first written of post-modern pastiche in the above manner, writes, for instance, in his later essay '(Post)Modern Polemics' that 'the use of pastiche in postmodern art and architecture deprives styles not only of specific context but also of historical sense: husked down to so many emblems, they are reproduced in the form of partial simulacra. In this sense, "history" appears reified, fragmented, fabricated – both imploded and depleted (not only a history of victors, but a history in which modernism is bowdlerized). The result is a history-surrogate, at once standard and schizoid.'[88]

Foster even attacks pastiche as 'relativistic' when he goes on to write of that which he has termed 'neoconservative postmodernism', and of that which he has described as its 'privileging' of both style and a return to history: 'Thus the postmodern zeitgeist. Yet nearly every postmodern artist and architect has resorted, in the name of style and history, to pastiche; indeed it is fair to say that pastiche is the official style of this postmodernist camp. But does not the eclecticism of pastiche (its mix of codes) threaten the very concept of style, at least as the singular expression of an individual or period? And does not the relativism of pastiche (its implosion of period signs) erode the very ability to place historical references – to think historically at all? To put it simply, this Postmodern Style of History may in fact signal the disintegration of style and the collapse of history.'[89]

It is also ironic, given that Jencks has been careful to distinguish his support for the pluralism of styles achieved by much post-modernist use of pastiche from the relativism of such as Lyotard, and confusing,

86 Ibid. (Jameson has also eliminated the adjective 'comic' from his 1983 reference to Wayne Booth's description of 'the stable and comic ironies of ... the 18th century'.)
87 For one thing, pastiche is not as new as Jameson suggests.
88 See Hal Foster, *Recodings. Art, Spectacle, Cultural Politics* (Washington, 1985), pp. 121–36; p. 123. Jameson had also described the culture of post-modernism as 'schizophrenic' in his 1984 essay.
89 Foster, *Recodings*, p. 127.

that Foster should describe such pastiche as relativistic here.[90] Apart from the fact that Jencks' descriptions of pastiche have seen it working for the creation of pluralism rather than of relativism, pastiche, like parody, is a device which is not in itself 'relativistic', or 'blind', in the senses applied to it by Jameson and Foster, but a device which may be put to a variety of uses by those applying it in their work.

Like Foster, whose concept of 'neoconservative postmodernism' also follows ideas set out by Habermas which conflict to some extent with those set up by Jameson, several other commentators on the post-modern have used Jameson's negative depiction of post-modern pastiche or eclecticism together with an eclectic mixture of related and unrelated concepts. Dick Hebdige, for instance, has followed Jameson in characterising post-modernism as 'pastiche' and as 'the "hyperspace" of the new architecture' in his *Hiding in the Light: On Images and Things*,[91] but has also spoken of bricolage in the same breath as pastiche, where some have defined bricolage as denoting a meaningful assemblage of parts in contrast to the meaninglessness attributed by Jameson to pastiche.

(Although the term 'bricolage' has been used in some other recent criticism as a synonym for pastiche to denote the assemblage of different texts or objects in an art work, it has not necessarily been used together with the negative concept of pastiche concocted by Jameson, and even though the word 'bricolage' was formerly a largely negative word for the work of the tinkerer or amateur. Most dictionaries defined it as 'pottering about, doing odd jobs'. Its present use by cultural theorists and by art critics following them which can be taken back to Claude Lévi-Strauss' application of it to myth in his *La Pensée Sauvage* (*The Savage Mind*) of 1962 generally refers to some meaningful, if limited, assemblage of given materials.)

In addition to speaking of bricolage and pastiche in the same breath without explicit reference to the different assessments given in recent years of their meanings, Hebdige has run parody and pastiche together where Jameson had explicitly separated them. Where Jameson had described the death of parody and its replacement by

---

90 Jencks has relegated Foster and those anthologised by him to the camp of 'Nothing Post-Modernists' in his *What is Post-Modernism?* of 1986, p. 30.

91 See Dick Hebdige, *Hiding in the Light : on Images and Things* (London and New York, 1988), p. 195. Hebdige goes on to describe post-modernity as 'modernity without the hopes and dreams which made modernity bearable'.

pastiche as accompanying the 'death' of the modernist individual subject, Hebdige has further characterised both pastiche and parody in terms of intertextuality and the 'Barthesian' understanding of the latter as implying the 'death' of the author:[92] 'The rhetorical tropes which form the literary-artistic-critical means for effacing the traces of teleology are parody, simulation, pastiche and allegory. All these tropes tend to deny the primacy or originary power of the "author" as sole source of meaning, remove the injunction placed upon the (romantic) artist to create substance out of nothing (i.e., to "invent", be "original") and confine the critic/artist instead to an endless "reworking of the antecedent" in such a way that the purity of the text gives way to the promiscuity of the inter-text and the distinction between originals and copies, hosts and parasites, "creative" texts and "critical" ones is eroded (i.e., with the development of meta-fiction and paracriticism). In parody, pastiche, allegory and simulation what tends to get celebrated is the *accretion* of texts and meanings, the *proliferation* of sources and readings rather than the isolation, and deconstruction of the single text or utterance. None of these favoured tropes (parody etc.) offers the artist a way of speaking from an "authentic" (that is [after Barthes, Derrida and Foucault] imaginary) point of pure presence (romanticism). Nor do they offer the critic a way of uncovering the "real" or intended meaning or meanings buried in a text or a "phenomenon" (hermeneutics).'[93]

Later Hebdige does, however, offer a more positive view of pastiche which differs from Jameson's view of postmodern pastiche as something normless and blind: 'As semiotics gets increasingly annexed by the advertising and marketing industries, information and knowledge begin to circulate outside the old parameters on the other side of the established institutional circuits: in the fast forward, rewind and slow motion functions of domestic video machines, in the pause button on a walkman audio cassette. Once rescued from the aura of despair which surrounds them in the original passages, pastiche and collage in this context shed their entropic connotations and become the means through which ordinary consumers can not only appropriate new technologies, new media skills to themselves, but can learn a new principle of assemblage, can open up new meanings and affects. Pastiche and collage can be valorised as forms which enable

92 Hebdige, p. 147 also quotes Barthes as describing parody as 'dislocation'.
93 Hebdige, p. 191.

consumers to become actual or potential producers, processors and subjects of meaning rather than the passive bearers of pregiven "messages".[94]

Many past users of pastiche have of course utilised it in such deliberate ways (which is why Charles Jencks has been able to speak of the 'radical eclecticism' rather than of the 'blindness' of those post-modern architects who have used pastiche to double-code the modern with some other code), although some have used it in the more derivative and less critical manner which has led to it being disparaged by some modern critics as uninventive. It has, however, taken a considerable time for many to return to a more rational insight into the way pastiche may be controlled by its users for a variety of both inventive and not so inventive purposes, and some had still not completed the journey at the time this text was being written.

Jameson's negative view of post-modern pastiche may also be said to have been applied back to parody, and the latter divided into 'modern' and 'postmodern' forms, in Michael Newman's 'Revising Modernism, Representing Postmodernism', where it is claimed that 'the difference between modernist and postmodernist parody' is a shift from 'a strong to a weak form of nihilism'.[95] Although Newman makes no specific mention of Jameson's views of pastiche in this section of his essay,[96] he relates his description of parody to the question of norms just as Jameson had related his description of post-modern pastiche to the death of modernist norms, and characterises post-modern parody as parody in which belief in the impossibility of norms contrasts with the modernist challenge to norms.[97]

Several other descriptions of parody and pastiche as nihilistic, weak, chaotic, superficial, or negative have echoed not only the 'late-modern' views of such as Baudrillard and Jameson on parody and pastiche respectively, but also the negativity of the modern view of parody which those late-modern theories have extended. (One other critic to give a 'late-modern' extension of the modern view of parody as the distortion of its targets was Pierre Macherey, when he wrote in his *A Theory of Literary Production* of 1966 that 'we have defined

94 Ibid., p. 211.
95 See Michael Newman's 'Revising Modernism, Representing Postmodernism: Critical Discourses of the Visual Arts', in *ICA Documents*, nos. 4/5 (London, 1986), pp. 32–51; p. 48.
96 Newman discusses Jameson elsewhere in his essay, as, for instance, on its pp. 49–50.   97 Ibid., p. 48.

literary discourse as parody, as a contestation of language rather than a representation of reality. It distorts rather than imitates.'[98])

Even given Jameson's contrast of modern parody to post-modern pastiche as to a weaker form based on 'normlessness' and on the 'death' of the individual subject, his own definition of parody as ridicule harbours the modern conception of parody as something negative which has been seen to have been echoed by other late-modernist views of parody such as Baudrillard's. While Newman, like Hutcheon, excludes the comic from his definition of parody, he also retains the negativity which was associated with the definition of parody as ridicule in many of the modern definitions given of it in the past.[99]

Despite the essentially 'late-modern' negativity of Jameson's descriptions of pastiche and of its post-modern practitioners, and the modern character of his view of parody, many analyses and characterisations of parody and pastiche based on those descriptions have appeared under the guise of either being 'postmodernist', or of being concerned with the depiction of the 'postmodern', and are to be found in works of the social sciences on anthropology, sociology, and urban planning, as well as in writings on literature and the arts.

In, for example, a discussion of post-modern ethnography published in a 1988 edition of *Current Anthropology*, Michael M. J. Fischer, George E. Marcus and Stephen A. Tyler describe post-modernism as 'the deconstructive, parodic, entropic dissolution of power',[100] while in sociology Zygmunt Bauman has been but one to have taken over Jameson's description of post-modernism as characterised by eclecticism and pastiche.[101] In geography and urban studies David Harvey has extended categories suggested by both Jameson and Hassan,[102] while M. J. Dear's article 'Postmodernism and Planning' of

---

98 See Pierre Macherey, *A Theory of Literary Production* (1966), translated by Geoffrey Wall (London, Henley, Boston, 1978), p. 61.

99 Newman, p. 48 also refers to Linda Hutcheon's definition of parody as 'repetition with critical distance, which marks difference rather than similarity' (from Hutcheon 1985, p. 6).

100 See *Current Anthropology*, volume 29, number 3, June 1988, pp. 405–35, p. 426.

101 See, for example, Zygmunt Bauman's *Legislators and Interpreters: On Modernity, Postmodernity and Intellectuals* (Oxford and Cambridge, 1987), p. 130.

102 See David Harvey, *The Condition of Postmodernity* (Oxford, 1989). Edward Soja's *Postmodern Geographies. The Reassertion of Space in Critical Social Theory* (London and New York, 1989) also expresses some sympathy with Jameson's analyses of post-modernism.

1986 has not only taken over Jameson's descriptions of both pastiche and hyperspace as 'postmodern', but has also transformed a remark made by Jencks in his *The Language of Post-Modern Architecture* about 'unintended pastiche' into a much more ambiguously general and negative reference to 'degenerate pastiche'.[103]

Richard Kearney has also echoed Jameson's negative views of post-modern pastiche when writing in his *Wake of the Imagination* (p. 4) of post-modern parody and pastiche together that 'in many postmodern works the very distinction between artistic-image and commodity-image has virtually faded. The practice of parody and pastiche, while it frequently intends to subvert the *imaginaire* of contemporary 'late capitalist' society, often ends up being co-opted or assimilated.'[104]

Kearney had preceded this general claim with the equally general 'Baudrillardian' statements (p. 3) that 'postmodernism undermines the modernist belief in the image as an *authentic* expression. The typically postmodern image is one which displays its own artificiality, its own pseudo-status, its own representational depthlessness', and (p. 4) that 'like every commodity of our mass communications society, the postmodern image has itself become an interchangeable consumer item, a pseudo-imitation which playfully celebrates its pseudonymity, parades its own superficiality and derivitiveness'.

Kearney uses the language of Baudrillard himself on his following page in making the further generalisation that 'even the most dissident imaginations appear to be swallowed into the "ideology of the simulacrum" which prevails in our consumer age'.[105] Despite a claim made by Kearney towards the end of his book (p. 360) that the deconstructionists should not have the last word, and that we should attempt to restore the imagination in some way,[106] his view of both the post-modern and of parody remains dominated by their categories and pessimism.

103 See M. J. Dear, 'Postmodernism and Planning', in *Environment and Planning D: Society and Space*, vol. 4, 1986, pp. 367–84. Dear refers to Jencks' p. 88 on his pp. 370–2.

104 See Richard Kearney, *Wake of the Imagination. Ideas of Creativity in Western Culture* (London, 1988).

105 Kearney goes on to refer to Jameson, and the language of this quotation is also that of a text used by both Baudrilland and Jameson, of Guy Debord's *La Société du spectacle* (Paris, 1967), translated as *Society of the Spectacle* in 1970 (Detroit, 1983).

106 Kearney also echoes Hassan's description of the post-modern imagination as 'disestablished' in other sections of his book.

In a chapter entitled 'The Parodic Imagination', Kearney also includes a discussion of Derrida in which the terms post-modern and parody are both loosely applied to Derrida's statements,[107] and gives a late-modern characterisation of post-modern parody as a restrictive and imitative rather than creative form (p. 291): ' ... we can no longer ask the question: *how does one escape from parody*? There is no escape. The imagination which is deconstructed into a parody of itself abandons all recourse to the metaphysical opposition between inner and outer. There is no way out of the cave of mirrors, for there is nothing *outside* of writing. Or, in Derrida's own phrase, there is no *hors-texte*. As an endless mimicry of itself, the text cannot be transcended in the direction of some extra-textual *beyond*.'

After discussing the Beaubourg or Pompidou Centre as a parody of 'the high-tech functionalism of modern architecture',[108] instead of as the example of a late-modern celebration of the latter which it is, Kearney is unable, however, to decide whether 'the parody' found in post-modern architecture is a part of the problems of modern technological society or a 'subversion' of it.[109]

A somewhat less pessimistic view of post-modern pastiche, but one which nonetheless associates it with both 'façadism'[110] and with Jameson's 1984 description of it as 'blind', is provided by A. S. Byatt in her Booker-Prize-winning novel *Possession*. After pages of imitation and pastiche of nineteenth-century prose and verse Byatt's characters are described as looking up 'at the bland or blind face' of a house called 'BETHANY': '"It's a good restoration job," said Maud. "It makes you feel funny. A simulacrum."' Byatt's characters continue their conversation by associating all with the 'postmodern': '"It would have been sootier. It would have looked older. When it was younger."'; '"A postmodern quotation – ".'[111]

The question of where this echo of Jameson's denigration of the pastiche of post-modern architecture as 'blind' leaves Byatt's own use

<hr/>

107 Other sections of Kearney's chapter 7 also use the term parody loosely or with relation to statements in which the term itself was not used.
108 See Kearney, p. 338. Kearney also follows Jameson in describing the 'Bonaventura Hotel' [*sic*] as 'postmodern'.   109 See Kearney, p. 339.
110 'Façadism' describes the attachment to a building of another front or façade. Jencks' descriptions of post-modern pastiche present it, by contrast, as having 'double-coded' the modern and its lack of decoration with other styles and messages in a variety of different ways.
111 See A. S. Byatt, *Possession* (London, 1990), pp. 210–11.

of pastiche is not directly answered, or addressed, by any of her characters, although they are also not made to condemn such pastiche as explicitly as the appearance of Jameson's terms suggest they might, and Byatt's own 'postmodern' use of pastiche gives the echo of those terms an ironic rather than a condemnatory role. Byatt's reflections on the problems of a post-modernism which is sometimes all too self-reflective further suggest that her concept of the post-modern is ultimately one in which it is self-consciously meta-fictional,[112] and that both pastiche and parody are understood in her novel as being hyper-reflective and as partners to a kaleidoscopic irony rather than as 'blind'.

This is also suggested when Byatt writes of her characters Roland and Maud: "They spoke peacefully, and with a kind of parody of ancient married agreement of "we" or "us". ... Somewhere in the locked-away letters, Ash had referred to the plot or fate which seemed to hold or drive the dead lovers. Roland thought, partly with precise postmodernist pleasure, and partly with a real element of superstitious dread, that he and Maud were being driven by a plot or fate that seemed, at least possibly, to be not their plot or fate but that of those others. And it is probable that there is an element of superstitious dread in any self-referring, self-reflexive, inturned postmodernist mirror-game or plot-coil that recognises that it has got out of hand, that connections proliferate apparently at random, that is to say, with equal verisimilitude, apparently in response to some ferocious ordering principle, not controlled by conscious intention, which would of course, being a good postmodernist intention, *require* the aleatory or the multivalent or the "free", but structuring, but controlling, but driving, to some – to what? – end.'[113]

Byatt continues to recount what might be called a 'deconstruc-tionist' view of post-modernism (Hassan contrasts 'Postmodernist' 'aleatory structures' as well as parody to 'Modernist' 'Experi-mentalism' in 1971), but with an author's interest in the possibilities which that view provides for added meta-fictionality and self-awareness rather than despair: 'Coherence and closure are deep human desires that are presently unfashionable. But they are always

112 Like both David Lodge's *The British Museum is Falling Down* and Umberto Eco's *Name of the Rose* Byatt's *Possession* also uses the 'meta-fictional' device of the searching for and finding of a lost manuscript.
113 See Byatt, pp. 421–2.

both frightening and enchantingly desirable. "Falling in love", characteristically, combs the appearances of the world, and of the particular lover's history, out of a random tangle and into a coherent plot. Roland was troubled by the idea that the opposite might be true. Finding themselves in a plot, they might suppose it appropriate to behave as though it was that sort of plot. And that would be to compromise some kind of integrity they had set out with.'[114]

Despite several other recent descriptions of both parody and pastiche as being particularly post-modern, it has been seen, however, that pastiche is just as modern a term as is parody, and that parody also has a more ancient heritage.

Jameson in particular has been wilful in his redefinition of pastiche as post-modern, although his description of it as a kind of blank parody which has lost both its satirical bite and its humour might be said to have at least described the traditionally non-comic character of much pastiche.

When Jameson's descriptions of post-modern pastiche are applied to post-modern parody by others such as Hebdige, Newman, or Kearney, we are, however, shown a late-modern understanding of parody as something which is not necessarily comic, which, as such, cannot serve the description of parody as well as it can serve the description of pastiche.

In addition to the problems referred to previously, Jameson's own depiction of the pastiche with which much post-modernist architecture has been associated has reduced it to something negative as well as to something humourless, and has said little of the function both it and parody have been given in post-modernist architecture as a means not just to the rehabilitation of the past,[115] but to the 'double-coding' of the modern with other styles.

Double-coded post-modernism and parody

In contrast to Fredric Jameson, the architectural historian and critic Charles Jencks has described the 'Post-Modern' as a 'double-coding' of the 'Modern' with some other style, and as one which therefore preserves something of the 'Modern' while both adding to it and

---

114 Ibid., p. 422.
115 As seen previously, Jameson had also criticised post-modernist architecture for its nostalgia.

going beyond it in some meaningful way.[116] One 'Post-Modern' work, James Stirling and Michael Wilford and Associates' New Württemberg State Gallery at Stuttgart of 1977–84, uses elements, for example, of both modern and late-modern architecture as well as references to numerous other older and ancient styles. Here pastiche may also be ironic, and even parodic, as illustrated by the ironic reference to the fallen stones of a ruined classical temple in the use made by Stirling and Associates of fallen blocks to create ventilation for the car park of the new gallery.[117]

Jencks has listed thirty characteristics to distinguish the 'Modern', 'Late-Modern'[118] and 'Post-Modern' styles of architecture,[119] of which the eclecticism to which pastiche contributes is but one of the 'stylistic variables' of the 'Post-Modern'.[120] Other stylistic variables of the 'Post-Modern' include 'hybrid expression'; 'complexity'; 'variable space with surprises'; 'conventional and abstract form'; 'semiotic articulation'; 'variable mixed aesthetic depending on context; expression of content and semantic appropriateness toward function'; 'pro-organic and applied ornament'; 'pro-representation'; 'pro-metaphor'; 'pro-historical reference'; 'pro-humour', and 'pro symbolic'. Jencks' inclusion of 'pro-humour' in the stylistic variables of the Post-Modern is contrasted with the anti-humour of the 'Modern' and the unintended humour of the 'Late-Modern', and may also be said to have been important, together with his descriptions of double-coding, and of other variables of the 'Post-Modern' architecture described in his works, in distinguishing his concept of post-modernism from most other uses of the term, from de Onis, Toynbee, Smith, Hudnut and Pevsner onwards.

116 Jameson has also given a misleading description of Jencks' post-modernism as 'anti-modernist' in the diagram in his 1984 essay, 'The Politics of Theory: Ideological Positions in the Postmodernism Debate', p. 110.
117 See, for instance, Jencks, *What is Post-Modernism?*, 1986, p. 16.
118 For Jencks the 'Late-Modern' and the 'Post-Modern' in architecture run concurrently from the 1960s onwards.
119 Jencks has published his table of differences between the Modern, Late-Modern, and Post-Modern in his *Late-Modern Architecture and Other Essays* (London and New York, 1980), p. 32, and in his 'Essay on the Battle of the Labels Late-Modernism vs Post-Modernism', in *Architecture and Urbanism* (Tokyo), January Extra Edition, 1986, pp. 209–36; p. 213.
120 Jencks, 1980, p. 32 also lists several 'Ideological' definers and 'Design Ideas' of the 'Post-Modern'. And see also Jencks' *What is Post-Modernism?*, 3rd revised enlarged edn (London and New York, 1989), p. 60 for a more recent comment on how pastiche is only one of many definers of the post-modern in architecture.

One other statement by Jencks on the post-modern eclecticism to which pastiche has contributed can be found in his article 'Post-Modernism and Eclectic Continuity' of 1987. Like many other of his statements on the subject, this article stresses the way in which eclecticism may contribute to complexity and unity as well to contrast and contradiction. Jencks also writes there: 'The contrast of discontinuous styles is not the only valid approach for expressing complex urban realities. One can also adopt an integrated grammar that has eclectic fragments absorbed into its unity. Both approaches acknowledge varying tastes and differing functions, but what could be called "eclectic continuity" stresses the urban ensemble.'[121]

In addition to stressing the importance of seeing post-modern architecture as involving both contradiction and complexity, as Robert Venturi had put it in his *Complexity and Contradiction in Architecture* of 1966 (one of Jencks' early publications was his review of Venturi's *Complexity and Contradiction in Architecture*, in a special edition of *Arena. Architectural Association Journal*, June 1967, on 'Meaning in Architecture'[122]), Jencks' 'Post-Modernism and Discontinuity' of 1987 both discusses Venturi's ideas[123] and offers some criticisms of the concept of discontinuity favoured by Lyotard.[124] Here too Jencks explicitly goes beyond the modern and late-modern canonisation of discontinuity: 'We are thus left with the conclusion that discontinuity is a legitimate, if limited, strategy for art and architecture in a pluralist age, one that expresses our "contradictions" and "inconsistencies", as Venturi and Stirling insist. But it is a necessarily incomplete method until it is supplemented by a symbolic programme or some unifying plot.'[125]

For Jencks both pastiche and parody may be described as methods

---

121 See Charles Jencks, 'Post-Modernism and Eclectic Continuity' in *Architectural Design*, vol. 57, nos 1–2, 1987, Profile 65, *Post-Modernism and Discontinuity* (London, 1987), p. 25.

122 See *Arena. Architectural Association Journal*, vol. 83, no. 913, June 1967, pp. 4–5.

123 Jencks refers to Venturi's work in his 'Post-Modernism and Discontinuity', in *Architectural Design*, vol. 57, nos. 1–2, 1987, Profile 65, *Post-Modernism and Discontinuity* (London, 1987), pp. 5–8; pp. 5 ff.

124 See Jencks, 'Post-Modernism and Discontinuity', p. 6.

125 Jencks, 'Post-Modernism and Discontinuity', p. 8. Jencks' stress on the importance of finding both complexity and meaning in architecture can be found in works as early as his 1967 review of Venturi's *Complexity and Contradiction in Architecture*, and his essay 'Semiology & Architecture', in his and George Baird's *Meaning in Architecture* (London, 1969), pp. 11–25.

for 'double-coding' the modern with other codes and their messages in a way which can add some of the symbolic and other meanings which contribute to such a symbolic, and complex, programme.[126] Jameson's criticisms of post-modern pastiche, and other modern and late-modern condemnations of parody as mere ridicule, have led Jencks to describe 'parody, nostalgia and pastiche' as 'the lesser genres with which Post-Modernism is equated by its detractors' in his *Post-Modernism. The New Classicism in Art and Architecture* of 1987,[127] but Jencks himself has continued to comment on the many different positive functions which pastiche has been given in post-modern art and architecture. Further to this, and apart from some other passing references to more negative modern uses of the term,[128] Jencks has explicitly praised parody in his *The Language of Post-Modern Architecture*, when writing in one early passage, which will be returned to presently, that 'one of the virtues of parody, besides its wit, is its mastery of cliché and convention, aspects of communication which are essential to Post-Modernism'.[129]

Unlike Jameson, Jencks has also had no problem in finding a combination of pastiche and satire in post-modernist paintings such as Carlo Maria Mariani's *The Constellation of Leo*, also called 'The School of Rome', of 1980–1.[130] Not only is Mariani's painting a pastiche, in the sense of a compilation, of motifs from several other works, but it is also 'post-modern' in that its ironic and satirical pastiche is of both modern neo-classical and modernist art. These works include Raphael's *School of Athens*, the *Parnassus* of 1761 in the Villa Albani, Rome, by the admirer of Raphael Anton Raffael Mengs, several other neo-classical works, Tischbein's portrait of Goethe in the Campagna of 1786, and the modernist Magritte's two disembodied 'shoe-feet' in his painting *The Red Model* of 1935.[131] When Magritte's 'shoe-feet' are

126 Jencks' contribution to his and Nathan Silver's *Adhocism. The Case for Improvisation*, (London, 1972) also contains some positive evaluations of both bricolage and pastiche. (See Jencks' pp. 16–17 on bricolage and pp. 23 ff. on 'The prescient wit of art'.)
127 See Jencks, *Post-Modernism. The New Classicism in Art and Architecture* (London, 1987), p. 338.
128 As, for instance, in Jencks, *The Language of Post-Modern Architecture*, 6th edn, 1991, p. 165.
129 See Jencks, *The Language of Post-Modern Architecture* (revised enlarged edn, 1978), p. 93.
130 See Charles Jencks, *What is Post-Modernism?*, 1986, pp. 24 and 27.
131 This work is illustrated in Suzi Gablik, *Magritte* (London, 1970), ill. 89, p. 111.

evoked in the similarly placed disembodied feet of a classical statue, modernism is also 'double-coded' with other periods via the use of pastiche, and the art of the 'modern' or of 'now'[132] itself made a part of history.[133]

In addition to illustrating the art of post-modern pastiche, Mariani's reconstructions of modern art may be seen as contributing to a post-modern parody of modernism which has added both humour and a new meta-artistic commentary to the modern by joining, or 'pastiching', its masterpieces together in incongruous but also meta-artistic ways.

Charles Jencks' concept of pastiche may furthermore be said to have allowed him to see it used in a work which is not only parodic, but which he has described as containing satire,[134] because pastiche for him is not as 'normless' as Jameson has described it to be. For Jencks, for whom (in contrast to Jameson) the individual subject is alive and well, pastiche may also be part of a 'radical eclecticism' which sees the architect making choices of both a radical and a meaningful kind.[135] While Jean-François Lyotard's 1982 article, 'What is Postmodernism?' had condemned the post-modern architecture favoured by Jencks as both capitalist and as a product of a philosophy of 'anything goes' eclecticism,[136] Jencks' concept of pastiche has set it up as something which may be used to criticise as well as to celebrate and to add to the past in a variety of specifically different, and meaningful, ways.[137]

132 The word 'modern' derives from one for 'now' or 'today' and has been defined as meaning 'of the present'.

133 Jameson refers to Magritte's 'shoe-foot' as 'postmodern' in his *Postmodernism, or, the Cultural Logic of Late Capitalism* (London and New York, 1991), p. xv, but reveals the 'late-modern' categories behind this claim when writing, p. 10, that 'Magritte, unique among the surrealists, survived the sea change from the modern to its sequel, becoming in the process something of a postmodern emblem: the uncanny, Lacanian foreclusion, without expression.'

134 See Jencks on Mariani's 'School of Rome', in Jencks, *What is Post-Modernism?*, 1986, pp. 24 ff.

135 See, for example, Jencks, *The Language of Post-Modern Architecture*, revised enlarged edn, 1978, p. 128, and the conclusion of Jencks' 'The Bank as Cathedral and Village', in *Architectural Design*, vol. 58, nos. 11–12, 1988, Profile 76, *New Directions in Current Architecture* (London, 1988), pp. 77–9; p. 79.

136 See Jean-François Lyotard, 'Answering the Question: What is Postmodernism?', p. 76.

137 Jencks also argues that 'nostalgia' can be radical in his 'Peter Eisenman. An *Architectural Design* Interview by Charles Jencks', in *Architectural Design*, vol. 58, nos. 3–4, 1988, Profile 72, *Deconstruction in Architecture* (London, 1988), pp. 49–61; p. 54.

The phrase 'anything goes' is problematical, moreover, in that if 'anything goes' then even its opposite 'anything does not go' must also be true. Despite this fact, and the use of it for more light-hearted topics by Cole Porter and others,[138] the phrase has been used with both great seriousness, and with little recognition of its problems, by those following Lyotard who have wished to condemn the use of pastiche in post-modern art, architecture, and literature as a feckless or meaningless compilation of styles.

The post-modern pastiche described by Jencks is, however, not just the pastiche of 'anything', but is, more specifically, the pastiche of the modern with another code which will add something which the modern has lacked. One of the precepts of the modern style challenged by post-modernist architects has been an antipathy to decoration, and pastiche has also enabled the post-modernist architect to return something of the decoration which the modernists had removed. Again, however, post-modern pastiche of the type which Jencks has praised has not just been decoration, but has been a re-coding of the modern with both the idea that decoration is something positive, and with another stylistic code and its 'messages'.

Jencks has used the term 'code' to describe the styles of architecture because he sees them as sending out meanings or messages in a manner similar to the messages sent out in language or in other such communications between human subjects, and this should also show how different his concept of pastiche as a 'double-coding' of styles is from Jameson's concept of it as an empty or blind form of the parody of the past.

Despite the specific character of Jencks' use of the term double-coding (Jencks' description of post-modernism as 'double-coded' also represents a means to transforming the Modern Movement's preference for only one – 'international' – code rather than for a pluralism of styles and their 'messages'), its interpretation has been made more general by some commentators who have tried to match it with terms like Bakhtin's 'double-voicedness'. Not only, however, can such generalisations reduce the specific meaning of each term, but Bakhtin's use of the word 'double-voiced' to describe an opposition of 'hostile' voices in parody can distort the meaning of Jencks'

138 P. G. Wodehouse began writing the script for *Anything Goes* with Guy Bolton in 1934, but was soon describing his contribution to it as having been reduced to two lines. See his *Performing Flea. A Self-Portrait in Letters* of 1953 (Harmondsworth, 1961), p. 91.

understanding of post-modern pastiche and parody as a 'double-coding' of the modern which is made in positive rather than hostile ways.

Linda Hutcheon has also tried to connect Charles Jencks' concept of post-modern double-coding with the double-coded structure of parody as such in her *A Theory of Parody. The Teachings of Twentieth-Century Art Forms* of 1985, and despite the fact that such dual-coding is basic to all types of parody, from the ancient onwards.[139] Following Hutcheon, Matei Calinescu wrote in his *Five Faces of Modernity* of 1987[140] that 'the enjoyment offered by postmodern art (architecture included) comes in the form of a broadly defined parodic practice, in which some commentators have discerned a more general characteristic of our cultural times. It has thus been suggested that the new "reconstructive" treatment of the past, parodic or otherwise, shows a marked preference for "double coding" (Jencks, and with different implications, Hutcheon), really for multiple coding or even "over-coding" (Scarpetta).'[141] Calinescu continues by pointing out that 'in actuality, of course, the issue of postmodernism in architecture is much more complex and messy than I have made it out to be for purposes of expository convenience and brevity', but despite this awareness and his reference to some differences between the usages of Hutcheon and Jencks of the term 'double-coding' does not explicitly point to all of the significant differences between parody and the double-codings of the post-modern which are run together in Hutcheon's text.[142]

The differences between parody and its double-codings and those of post-modernism in general, or architectural post-modernism in particular, are, however, as important as their similarities. Not only, for instance, may the post-modern architect 'double-code' the modern style with another without any of the satire characteristic of some uses of parody, but he or she may do it without irony, or without comedy of any kind. While this last factor should demonstrate at least one

---

139 When I described parody as consisting of two codes in my *Parody//Meta-Fiction* of 1979 I did not describe that particular 'dual-coding' as being essentially or exclusively 'post-modern', and still would not do so given that such 'dual-coding' is common to all types of parody.

140 See Matei Calinescu, *Five Faces of Modernity* (Durham, 1987).

141 Calinescu, *Five Faces of Modernity*, p. 285.

142 In a review of Hutcheon's 1985 text, entitled 'Parody and Intertextuality', in *Semiotica* 65, nos. 1/2 (1987), pp. 183–90, Calinescu does, however, question Hutcheon's equation of parody and intertextuality, and asks for further distinctions to be made between such terms.

difference between the device parody and the 'post-modern' which will help to keep the two separate (parody is, as seen, also a device which has been used in both ancient and modern forms prior to the post-modern era), Hutcheon is one of those critics who have reduced the traditional linkages of parody with comedy, so that the distinguishing peculiarity of parody as a *comic* form of 'double-coding' has conveniently gone missing by the time she identifies parody with the post-modern via their apparently common use of the double or dual code. (Hutcheon even misrepresents Householder on the presence of humour in parody when she translates his already questionable suggestion that, given another word was attached to the term for parody by the scholiasts 'when the presence of humor or ridicule is to be made plain', 'the notion of humor' was not regarded by them as 'essentially present in the word',[143] into the much more sweeping, and misleading, claim that 'in classical uses of the word parody, humor and ridicule were not considered part of its meaning'.[144])

One of Hutcheon's reasons for her separation of parody from the comic is her laudable, if not novel, criticism of the reduction of parody to the negative and one-dimensional form of ridicule with which the modern definition of parody as burlesque has been associated.[145] Her virtual elimination of the comic from parody[146] (which she can then go on to equate with other non-comic intertextual forms and with that which she terms post-modernist meta-fiction) may be described, however, as a 'late-modern' reaction to the modern description of parody as burlesque comedy which has divided parody from the comic rather than reunited the latter with the parody's more complex intertextual aspects. This reaction is 'late-modern' rather than 'post-modern', because when it suggests that if parody is burlesque comedy, *pace* the modern description of it as such, then the general parody of Sterne and Cervantes and their progeny is meta-fictional parody *rather*

---

143 See Householder, p. 8 and the criticisms of these claims in chapter 1.

144 See Hutcheon, 1985, p. 51. Michele Hannoosh's recent study of Laforgue and parody, entitled *Parody and Decadence*, which was seen too late to be mentioned further in this text, also comments on Hutcheon's misunderstanding of both this and some other issues in notes to its chapter 1.

145 As seen in chapter 1, Householder had also sought to separate the ancient understanding of parody as ridicule from the more modern kind, but this point is not explored by Hutcheon in her references to him.

146 See Hutcheon, *A Theory of Parody*, 1985. (Hutcheon also refers interchangeably to ridicule and humour when criticising the definition of parody as comic.)

than comic parody, it extends rather than rejects and overcomes the modern division of the complex and the comic in parody.[147]

While some late-modern views of comedy have extended the modern description of it and its forms as ridicule by emphasising its power to criticise or deconstruct authority,[148] some late-modern theorists of parody following Hutcheon who have denied it its comic functions have also implicitly extended its critical and ridiculing functions in attributing to it new and often unrealistic political powers.

Yet others who have discussed parody in recent years without stressing its essentially comic character include several other critics who have attempted to equate it with meta-fiction, or with what are described as self-reflective intertextual forms.[149] Amongst these critics Brian McHale describes parody as 'a form of self-reflection and self-critique, a genre's way of thinking critically about itself',[150] but does not explicitly mention its particularly comic character in his definitions of it. The comic character of parody is also not stressed as being important in McHale's criticism of Christine Brooke-Rose's application of the term parody and of Bakhtin's distinction between parody and stylisation to Thomas Pynchon's novel *V* in her *A Rhetoric of the Unreal* of 1981. Rather, McHale 'improves' upon Bakhtin's distinction by writing that 'in a stylization, the dominant of the original (the model being stylized) is preserved, while in parody it is not'.[151]

Whether this formulation improves upon Bakhtin's descriptions of parody must be questioned, however, given, for one thing, its failure to make reference to the comic aspects and functions of the parody which were so vital to the carnivalistic forms which Bakhtin suggested were of greater importance than its more modern examples. As seen previously, Bakhtin's distinction between parody and stylisation had itself failed to stress the comic character of parody emphasised

---

147 Many of Hutcheon's descriptions of parody also reduce it to a very general concept of 'difference'.

148 See, for instance, Jerry Aline Flieger, *The Purloined Punch Line. Freud's Comic Theory and the Postmodern Text* (Baltimore and London, 1991).

149 Wendy Steiner, to whose 'Intertextuality in Painting', in *American Journal of Semiotics*, vol. 3, no. 4 (1985), pp. 57–67, Hutcheon, 1988, p. 140 refers, also shares Hutcheon's 'late-modern' view of parody when suggesting on p. 64 of her article that the mere evocation and 'undercutting' of the meaning of one work in another may be described as parody and that humour is something separate from the latter.

150 See Brian McHale, *Postmodernist Fiction* (New York and London, 1987), p. 145.

151 See McHale, p. 21.

elsewhere in his work. A response to McHale given in Christine Brooke-Rose's chapter 'Illusions of Parody' of her *Stories, Theories and Things* of 1991 is critical of the confused uses made of the term parody in McHale and other recent writers, but also fails to investigate the comic as well as complex character of parody, the acknowledgment of which could help to make their uses of the term less confused.[152]

Confusion abounds however. For example, even if Mikhail Bakhtin has come to be described by some critics in recent years as post-modern because of his use of terms such as 'double-voicedness', a 'double-voicedness' or 'double-coding' alone will not make something post-modern, just as it will not make something parody if the comic juxtaposition of texts is not present. To argue that because parody is double-coded and the post-modern is double-coded, then parody is post-modern, as some others have done in recent years, not only makes the further confusion of failing to distribute the middle term, as in the more obviously false but similar syllogism of 'all cats are four-legged, all dogs are four-legged, therefore all cats are dogs',[153] but also fails to tell us as much as we need to know about the differences between the post-modern and parody.

The problem of such confusions has been touched upon by some others in recent times. David Kolb, for instance, writes in his *Postmodern Sophistications. Philosophy, Architecture, and Tradition* with regard to irony: 'There are many kinds of double reference and self-awareness. Too many critics and philosophers class every kind of doubling as irony. This collapses a wide variety of attitudes and stances into one opposition between simple inhabitation and ironic distance.' Kolb continues by relating this to architectural criticism: 'The result in architectural criticism has been to run together wit, humor, parody, playfulness, self-awareness, self-consciousness, irony, and the like.'[154]

Contrary to David Kolb's criticisms of architectural critics, which

152 See Christine Brooke-Rose, *Stories, Theories and Things* (Cambridge, 1991), pp. 191–203.

153 The middle terms, 'double-coded' and 'four-legged', need to be distributed in premise form as, say: 'some four-legged animals are cats', or 'some double-codings are post-modern'.

154 See David Kolb, *Postmodern Sophistications. Philosophy, Architecture, and Tradition* (Chicago and London, 1990), p. 133. Kolb also discusses the use of parody on his p. 140 but follows Hutcheon in underestimating its comic functions. He does, however, point in a critique of Hutcheon p. 143 to how parody is not alone in its ability to either 'double' or 'contest' codes.

relates more to some of their interpreters (or, rather, misinterpreters) than to themselves, Charles Jencks at least has not only separated irony, parody, and pastiche in his discussions of their usage in post-modern architecture, but has suggested that it is specifically the double-coding of the modern with some other code, where the modern becomes both a part of the post-modern and the object which the latter is transforming, which makes sense of the post-modern building being called 'post-modern'.

For Charles Jencks, the post-modern is also something which both follows the modern[155] and replaces its concentration on single codes and on messages of an 'either-or' variety with statements of 'both-and'.[156] Even if parody is 'double-coded' by virtue of its combinations of at least two texts and their messages, this argument suggests that parody too will not necessarily be 'post-modern' unless it has transcended the 'modern' use or understanding of parody as *either* meta-fiction *or* burlesque comedy.

Parody regained? Post-modern parody in theory and practice

Charles Jencks' own discussions of parody also show him to have developed a concept and use of parody which goes beyond the modern reduction of it to *either* comedy *or* meta-fiction and which preserves rather than distorts its essential characteristics by seeing it as *both* comic *and* 'double-coded'.

Such a development may be found in both his earlier work on post-modern architecture, when he describes parody as involving wit as well as a 'mastery of cliché and convention' in his *The Language of Post-Modern Architecture*,[157] and in his more recent extension of Bakhtin's concept of carnivalisation in his articles 'The Carnival: Grotesque and Redeemable' and '25 Carnivalesque Buildings' of 1991.[158]

155 Charles Jencks writes in his *What is Post-Modernism?*, 3rd edn, 1989, p. 65 that 'to be "post" means to be "beyond"', and, in this sense at least, to be 'more modern [in the sense of up-to-date] than Modern'.

156 Both Charles Jencks and Robert Venturi have described those statements which go beyond the modernist reductions which their ideal architectures have transcended as 'both-and' statements. See Jencks, *The Language of Post-Modern Architecture* (revised enlarged edn, 1978), p. 87.

157 See Jencks, *The Language of Post-Modern Architecture* (revised enlarged edn, 1978), p. 93.

158 See Charles Jencks, 'The Carnival: Grotesque and Redeemable', in *Architectural Design* vol. 61, nos. 5–6, 1991, Profile 91, *Post-Modern Triumphs in London* (London, 1991), pp. 78–9 and '25 Carnivalesque Buildings', ibid., pp. 80–93.

Jencks' way of describing the 'Post-Modern' has itself been characterised as a mixture of wit and complexity, and it has also been seen how, in 1980, he had listed 'pro-humour' as one of the stylistic variables of post-modern architecture.[159]

In the passage in his *The Language of Post-Modern Architecture* referred to above, Jencks had also spoken of both the humour and creative nature of parody in a way which, despite its concurrent use of the term travesty for the use by the architects in question of what may be called a more late-modern understanding of parody, was in advance of many others at the time in recognising that a central function of parody was not just its wit, but its ability to pull other factors together: ' ... This caricature, or parody of serious culture, of course undermines its pretensions, as the unconscious travesty devalues it. But the subversion is only momentary, a short space of time before the latent humour asserts itself and establishes the travesty as a new level of culture. Monta, Watanabe, Shirai, and to a certain extent Isozaki and Takeyama, are using travesty as a kind of mirror-image genre of cultural confusion, and if it's practised long enough, it may have the unintended consequence of uniting a fragmented society. One of the virtues of parody, besides its wit, is its mastery of cliché and convention, aspects of communication which are essential to Post-Modernism.'[160]

In a lively discussion of Ian Pollard's commercialisations of high Post-Modernist architecture, Jencks also speaks in his more recent 'The Carnival: Grotesque and Redeemable', in a caption to Pollard's *Ramesses II* (model kit), of the 'parody and pastiche of high culture sources from Nouvel, Pei and Egypt, applied to another shed building'.[161] Jencks adds with an awareness of the complexity of the ironies involved that 'the thin peels and juxtapositions are Stirling-esque and essentially Post-Modern: they create an ornament which is both didactic and amusing, decoration which tells you it is a sign of a sign.'

159 This also goes further than others who have described post-modernism as ironic but have not necessarily stressed its humour. And see also Achille Bonito Oliva's *Transavantgarde International* (Milan, 1982), p. 62 on the irony of the art he has called 'transavantgarde'.

160 Jencks, *The Language of Post-Modern Architecture* (revised enlarged edn, 1978), p. 93. Jencks' preceding paragraph also speaks of parody as 'hybridisation', which is a word which is sometimes used interchangeably with 'dual-coding' in this and other works after 1978.

161 See Charles Jencks, 'The Carnival: Grotesque and Redeemable', p. 78.

Elsewhere, in an article written for the *The Times Saturday Review* of 22 June 1991, and entitled 'Metropolitan Post Marks', Jencks further applies the concept of the carnivalistic to some recent post-modern building, including one by Ian Pollard and another by one of Pollard's 'sources', James Stirling, and uses the term parody in doing so: 'The "carnivalesque" in post-modern literature is the crossing of boundaries, the break-down of all categories of class, sex and genre that occurs in any carnival worthy of the name. Architecturally, this breaks out in the gold-rush city run up overnight, the Docklands. Everybody pretends to hate it but, like bad taste and chaos, it resists treatment. The master of this mixed genre is Ian Pollard, who at *Homebase, W14,* parodies several "high-styles" – Egyptian, high-tech and James Stirling's Stuttgart. There, Stirling was parodying several "low-styles", so the result is a double-crossing of boundaries, and some amusing details.'[162]

As with Jencks' earlier claim in this article that 'like literature which is post-modern, it seeks to affirm and question at the same time, and this double coding gives it a common style',[163] there is some linkage here, in his use of the concept of the carnivalistic, with the concerns of post-modern literary criticism. Many writers on the latter, however, have differed from Jencks in taking Bakhtin's carnival on board their 'postmodernisms' for the sake of its more anarchic elements.

Other apparent similarities between Jencks' concept of carnivalisation and Bakhtin's have also to be studied for their differences, and Bakhtin's modern concepts, and reduction of parody to ridicule, contrasted with Jencks' more post-modern views of it and of its architectural uses. As seen previously, even one of Bakhtin's descriptions of ambiguous dialogicity had harboured a concept of hostility between codes which is not easily made compatible with Jencks' concept of post-modern double-coding.

Other apparent similarities between their ideas should also not obscure their differences. Bakhtin, for example, has emphasised the importance of the carnival square to the carnival and to its 'democratising' functions, and Jencks has spoken of the importance of the idea of the public realm or *res publica* to post-modern architects

---

162 See Charles Jencks, 'Metropolitan Post Marks', in *The Times Saturday Review* (22 June 1991), pp. 15–17; p. 17. Jencks also discusses the 'witch-like' roofscape of *Minster Court, E3* as well as *Meridian Gate, E14* which he describes as producing 'the very image of yuppietown gone bust'.

163 Jencks, 'Metropolitan Post Marks', p. 15.

interested in expanding both the communicative competence and democratic character of their buildings.[164] Jencks, however, has also described this with a particular reference to architecture not made by Bakhtin, as happening through the multiplication of the architect's codes and through their consultation with their clients, as well as through the building of new public spaces along the lines of the classical *agora* or public square.

With reference still to the similarities and differences to be found in Bakhtin's concept of the carnival and in Jencks' presentation of post-modernism, Jencks, like Leslie Fiedler, has made a call to 'close the gap' between high and low, when speaking of the way in which post-modernism can mix styles from both realms,[165] but has, as mentioned earlier, also warned against the degeneration of such mixtures to 'crude compromise'.[166] The closing of the gap between high and low in much of the post-modern architecture praised by Jencks does not just involve the bringing down of the high from its pedestal (as is the case in the traditional carnival), but the raising of the low or the popular to some higher, more complex level.

The failure to raise the low to any higher, or more complex, or meaningful level is one reason for some of Jencks' recent criticisms of the Disney headquarters in Burbank, California, designed by Michael Graves.[167] While some of the aspects of that building – such as its use of the seven dwarfs as caryatids – might be seen as parody as well as pastiche, they are, like some carnivalistic humour, not parody or pastiche of the most complex or uplifting (at least in the sense of 'intellectually uplifting') kind.

This problem may also be said to have arisen because the two traditional functions of parody of being both beside and against its

164 See again Jencks, *The Language of Post-Modern Architecture*, and Charles Jencks and Maggie Valentine, 'The Architecture of Democracy. The Hidden Tradition', in *Architectural Design*, vol. 57, nos. 8–10, Profile 69, *The Architecture of Democracy* (London, 1987), pp. 9–25.
165 Like Fiedler, 1969, p. 287 ('most importantly of all, it [post-modernism] implies the closing of the gap between artist and audience, or at any rate, between professional and amateur in the realm of art'), one other of the gaps which Jencks has seen post-modern architecture close is that between professional and amateur through its attempts to increase the participation of clients in the design process.
166 See, for instance, Jencks, *The Language of Post-Modern Architecture*, 6th edn, 1991, pp. 165 ff. and Jencks, 'Post-Modernism between Kitsch and Culture', in *Architectural Design*, vol. 60, nos. 9–10, 1990, Profile 88, *Post-Modernism on Trial* (London, 1990), pp. 24–35.   167 Ibid.

target are not evenly or productively balanced. Hence, while the caryatidic dwarfs parodistically imitate the more classical caryatid, they carry out this function with much empathy with the world of Disney, but with little 'double-coding' of the classical.

Jencks writes with especial reference to the 'dwarf' caryatids on Graves' building that 'though in Disney terms it might be an improvement on "Cinderella's Castle" ... seen in terms of the developing Post-Modern tradition of ornament and symbolism, some of the work is regressive'.[168] After commenting that this phase in Graves' work has been called "hokey-tecture", 'because its tongue-in-cheek fakery is so knowing', he adds that while 'the attempt, as in kitsch, is to succeed through excess', 'when it is this calculating and obvious one wonders'.

While Jencks also notes in a caption to an illustration of Graves' 'seven dwarfs' caryatids that Michael Eisner, who commissioned it, had said '"When I come to work I want to smile"', and that the dwarfs' leader, Dopey, 'smiles back', he concludes that 'Dopey, the central dwarf caryatid – a mere nineteen-foot midget – looks for the moment only like Dopey', and that 'unlike Michael Graves' earlier sketches for sculpture – notably "Portlandia" for the Portland Building' – there is 'no ambiguity, abstraction and transformation of the image'.[169]

In that Jencks' recent discussions of carnivalistic post-modern architecture suggest it to be both parodic and complex when done well, his concept of carnivalistic parody can also be said to represent a transformation of the modern reduction of parody to *either* the burlesque *or* the meta-fictional into a much more complex post-modern '*both-and* statement' which makes parody *both* comic *and* complex, and to be, as such, a 'post-modern' transformation of Bakhtin's more modern separations of those parts.

One other writer admired by Jencks,[170] the novelist and semiotician Umberto Eco, has also made some further changes to, and 'post-modernisations' of, both Bakhtin and the carnivalistic in his 1980 novel *Il Nome della Rosa*.[171] In addition to interweaving references to and from Bakhtin into its story of the search for Aristotle's 'lost' work on comedy, Eco has referred both to Aristotle's lost work on comedy

168 See Charles Jencks, *The Language of Post-Modern Architecture*, 6th edn, 1991, p. 172.   169 Ibid.

170 Jencks has also written admiringly of both David Lodge and John Barth in his recent work.

171 Translated by William Weaver in 1983 as *The Name of the Rose* (London, 1984).

and to Bakhtin and his theory of carnival in his essays 'The Comic and the Rule'[172] and 'The Frames of Comic "Freedom"' and has suggested some adjustments to Bakhtin's theory of carnival in those works.[173]

Eco has also referred in his latter essay to the out-dated nature of the parody in the *Cena Cypriani* praised by Bakhtin and suggested meta-fictional parodies such as Cervantes' *Don Quixote* to be more complex as well as both comic and humorous.[174] (Eco expands on Pirandello's already arbitrary twentieth-century distinction between the comic and the humorous to suggest that where comedy and carnival do not really transgress the rule, but reinforce and remind us of it, humour, in being 'metasemiotic', can both 'cast in doubt other cultural codes' and show us 'the structure of our own limits'. Eco's comments on Cervantes' parody suggest, however, that even when comedy and humour can be separated by such an artificial distinction they are to be found together in such meta-fictional comic works.) When Eco the novelist uses some of Bakhtin's account of the *Cena Cypriani* in the dream of the young monk Adso in *The Name of the Rose*,[175] he furthermore gives the older parody a new and complex comic/humorous meta-fictional role within his novel by substituting his character of the abbot for the king of the original story and by adding other characters from his book such as its 'villain', the laughter-hating monk, 'Jorge of Burgos'. This Jorge's name has already parodistically turned the parody loving author Jorge Luis Borges into his opposite earlier in Eco's novel, and Adso's carnivalistic dream of the *Cena Cypriani* not only turns the laughter-hating monk Jorge back into a jester,[176] in the manner of the carnival's turning of the world upside-down which shows that world to have been the wrong way up,[177] but evokes the original Jorge's more meta-fictional and ironic uses of parody.[178]

172 See Eco, 'The Comic and the Rule' (1980), in Eco, *Travels in Hyperreality. Essays*, translated by William Weaver (London, 1986), pp. 269–78.

173 See, for example, Eco, 'The Frames of Comic "Freedom"', in *Carnival!*, edited by Thomas A. Sebeok (Berlin, New York, Amsterdam, 1984), pp. 1–9; p. 6. (Eco also refers to Bakhtin's essay on chronotopes in his 1984 essay, 'Casablanca: Cult Movies and Intertextual Collage', in his *Travels in Hyperreality*, pp. 197–211; p. 200.)

174 See Eco, 'The Frames of Comic "Freedom"', pp. 6 ff.

175 See Eco, *The Name of the Rose*, pp. 427 ff.   176 Ibid., p. 428.

177 See also Eco, 'The Frames of Comic "Freedom"', p. 2 on this device.

178 Eco's 'Postscript to *The Name of the Rose*' (see Eco, 'Reflections on *The Name of the Rose*' (1983), trans. William Weaver (1984) (London, 1985), pp. 71 f.) also makes reference to essays in which John Barth discusses Borges' use of

Eco's novel is also about the ban put on laughter by the monk Jorge of Burgos and the latter's censorship of the lost volume of Aristotle's *Poetics* on comedy,[179] and it will be, moreover, a copy of the *Cena Cypriani* which Eco's detective-hero, the English monk William of Baskerville, will find bound together with the lost, and banned, volume of Aristotle on comedy in the great library which Jorge of Burgos controls. The third work with which these two are bound is described as an Egyptian work of the third century AD which 'attributes the creation of the world to divine laughter' (see Bakhtin's *Rabelais*) and Eco's own 'manuscript' is divided into seven days.

There are many other literary references to be found in Eco's *Name of the Rose* before this union of the *Cena Cypriani* with Aristotle is described in it. In addition to its allusion through the name of its hero 'William of Baskerville' to Conan Doyle's detective novel *The Hound of the Baskervilles*, as well as to its own lightly parodistic use of the detective novel form,[180] Eco's use of the name of the modern writer Jorge Luis Borges for the laughter-hating monk Jorge of Burgos ironically plays upon Borges' love for detective stories,[181] as well as on what might be described as Borges' 'proto-post-modernist' understanding of parody as both comic and meta-fictional.[182] More will be said of such 'proto-post-modernist' understandings of parody, and of why they are not yet wholly 'post-modern', presently. Because Borges' overall understanding of parody derives more from works such as Cervantes', rather than from a direct challenge to the

    parody. (See, for example, Barth, 'The Literature of Exhaustion' (1967), in Malcolm Bradbury (ed.), *The Novel Today. Contemporary Writers on Modern Fiction* (Manchester and Totowa, N. J., 1977); pp. 70–110.)

179 Aristotle's lost work on comedy has also been 'reconstructed' by Lane Cooper in his *An Aristotelian Theory of Comedy with an Adaptation of the Poetics and a Translation of the 'Tractatus Coislinianus'* (Oxford, 1924).

180 Eco's use of the detective novel, which has his hero searching for the truth in the library of the abbey, can also be said to reflect on how parody can be used to create a situation where (as with Eco's novel) readers must become detectives to uncover the meaning of all its references.

181 Patricia Waugh's *Metafiction. The Theory and Practice of Self-Conscious Fiction* (London and New York, 1984), p. 84 refers to Borges' 'inversion' of the detective story in his 'Death and the Compass' of 1964.

182 *The Hound of the Baskervilles* is also referred to in both Borges' and Bioy-Casares' comically and meta-fictionally parodic *Six Problems for Don Isidoro Parodi*, published as the work of 'Bustos Domecq', and their *Chronicles of Bustos Domecq*. (Eco refers to this fake Domecq in pp. 197 ff. of his 'Fakes and Forgeries', in Eco, *The Limits of Interpretation* (Bloomington and Indianapolis, 1990).)

modern reduction of parody to either comedy or meta-fiction, it can, however, already be said that it is difficult to categorise it as post-modern in all of the senses being given that word here, and may better be described as pre- and proto-post-modern.[183]

Further to making its more general reference to Borges through the name of Jorge of Burgos, Eco's novel recalls Borges' story, 'The Library of Babel',[184] of a 'library' which contains all books and their variations ever written, as well as Borges' comic and meta-fictional writings on *Don Quixote*, and recollection in them of Cervantes' description of the attempts to burn his 'hero's' library.[185] Here too Eco may be seen to be involved in some ironic and parodistic turning of his sources on their head, for where Cervantes had described the attempts of Don Quixote's niece to have all the romances burnt which have turned her uncle's mind away from reality, and which Cervantes is in the process of parodying, Eco describes the burning of the library in his novel as a result of Jorge of Burgos' attempt to ban such comedy and its laughter.

Bakhtin too had been an admirer of Cervantes' *Don Quixote*, and Bakhtin's even stronger interest in Rabelais and in his 'carnivalistic' writings may remind us that we can find a description of a library in which almost every title is a grotesque parody of the serious in Rabelais' *Gargantua and Pantagruel* where the 'library of Saint Victor's' which Pantagruel visits in Paris is described as containing all sorts of ribald and parodic titles such as the *Bigua salutis*, 'The Props of Salvation', and the *Bragueta juris*, 'The Codpiece of the Law'.[186]

Eco's novel may only recall such sources to the reader through the train of associations which his meta-fictional and 'intertextual' references to them evoke. (Cervantes had also used the scene in which Don Quixote's niece attempts to have burned all the romances which have turned her uncle's mind to list the works he is parodying in his novel.) But it still shows us through these and other meta-fictional

---

183 Both of these terms are discussed again in following pages.

184 See Borges, 'The Library of Babel', in Jorge Luis Borges, *Labyrinths. Selected Stories and Other Writings*, edited by D. A. Yates and J. E. Irby (Harmondsworth, 1976), pp. 78–86.

185 See Borges', 'Pierre Menard, Author of the *Quixote* ' in Borges, *Labyrinths*, pp. 62–71; p. 70 and Miguel de Cervantes, *Don Quixote*, Part I, chapter 6. Eco's essay 'The Comic and the Rule', p. 276, also refers to Cervantes' *Don Quixote* and to its scene in the library.

186 See François Rabelais, *The Histories of Gargantua and Pantagruel*, translated by J. M. Cohen (1955), (Harmondsworth, 1963), Book 2, chapter 7, pp. 186 ff.

references how meta-fictionality and comic/humorous parody can join to counter the modern reduction of the latter and its laughter to mockery or ridicule in which Bakhtin too had participated with his praise of 'parodic-travestying' forms such as the *Cena Cypriani*.

When Eco refers to Aristotle on comedy he also refers to a description of comedy which initially depicts it as showing men to be worse than they are with respect to 'the ridiculous' or 'the laughable'. As noted previously, Aristotle, in his *Poetics*, chapter 2, had stated after referring to Hegemon of Thasos, 'the first writer of parodies', and to others, that comedy shows persons in a worse light than they are, while tragedy shows them to be better, and had, in *Poetics*, chapter 5, spoken specifically of the ridiculous or 'the laughable' as the subject of comedy.[187]

As suggested above, Eco's own humour/comedy is itself more like that of the ironic and self-reflexive brand of humour of his hero the English monk William of Baskerville than either the carnivalistic comedy of the *Cena Cypriani* which is initially held up as a counter to the repressiveness of Jorge of Burgos' censorship of the comic, or the comedy which is reduced to dealing with the ridiculous. William's helper, the Germanic Adso, writes regarding William's ironic comments on relics: 'I never understood when he was jesting. In my country, when you joke you say something and then you laugh very noisily, so everyone shares in the joke. But William laughed only when he said serious things, and remained very serious when he was presumably joking.'[188]

The apparent conflict between these descriptions of the comic is, however, to at least some extent resolved in Eco's descriptions of the cathartic functions of comedy which are said to have been propounded in the 'lost' book of Aristotle's *Poetics* which William finally 'uncovers'. There we not only hear an echo of the reconstruction of Aristotle in the *Tractatus Coislinianus*, where the 'Aristotelian' notion of comedy is presented as a form of dramatic 'imitation', which 'by means of pleasure and laughter effects the purification of the corresponding passions',[189] and one of Bakhtin's mention of the

187 Although the more correct translation of Aristotle's words might be 'the laughable', Eco's text (see Eco, *Il Nome della Rosa* (Milan, 1990), p. 471) will describe Aristotle as having spoken of the ridiculous.
188 Eco, *The Name of the Rose*, p. 425.
189 See Lane Cooper, p. 224 and H. J. Rose, *A Handbook of Greek Literature. From Homer to the Age of Lucian* (1934), 4th edn, revised, and corrected (London and

'*purifying sense* of ambivalent laughter',[190] but we also see Eco relate this catharsis to our freeing from the ridiculous.[191] This last point is suggested when William 'translates' the first page of Aristotle's lost work on comedy: 'In the first book we dealt with tragedy and saw how, by arousing pity and fear, it produces catharsis, the purification of those feelings. As we promised, we will now deal with comedy (as well as with satire and mime) and see how, in inspiring the pleasure of the ridiculous [*del ridicolo*], it arrives at the purification of that passion.'[192]

If Eco's novel can be said to have celebrated the cathartic purging of the ridiculous in and through comedy in this passage, and to have itself used meta-fictional as well as comic devices to develop this point, it may also be said to have transcended the modern reduction of the comic to a ridiculing treatment of the ridiculous.[193]

In speculating on how Aristotle would have defined comedy in his missing work on that subject Lane Cooper had also suggested the idea that where the cure effected by the cathartic action of tragedy on the emotions of fear and pity was homeopathic, the cure wrought by comedy as the opposite of tragedy would be 'allopathic' – that is, using the opposite rather than the same emotions.[194] Eco's characterisation of the catharsis of comedy as homeopathic rather than allopathic has allowed him, by contrast, both to speak of the ridiculous itself as being purged in such a catharsis, and to come closer to giving a 'post-modern' depiction of parody as the freeing of an author from another through 'homeopathic' rather than through more hostile 'allopathic' means than had Cooper's more 'modern' understanding of the comic.

In addition to suggesting the 'post-modern' idea that the ridiculous be purged by cathartic means of a complex rather than a one-dimensional, hostile, and negative character – and *through* rather than

New York, 1964), p. 400 on this aspect of the *Tractatus*. (Eco mentions the *Tractatus Coislinianus* in his 'The Frames of Comic "Freedom"', p. 1.)

190 See Bakhtin, *Problems of Dostoevsky's Poetics* (Manchester, 1984), p. 166.
191 See Eco, *The Name of the Rose*, p. 468 and Eco, *Il Nome della Rosa*, p. 471.
192 Ibid. The rest of this passage refers, as has Bakhtin in his *Rabelais*, p. 68, to Aristotle's *On the Soul* as claiming that 'of all living creatures only man is endowed with laughter', but also mentions the 'buffo' and vulgar elements in the ridiculous which is to be purified.
193 Eco's depiction of comic catharsis also goes beyond Medley's presentation of satiric ridicule as cathartic of other foibles in Fielding's *The Historical Register for the Year 1736.*   194 See Lane Cooper, p. 67.

without the comic – Eco has achieved his particular transformation of the modern reduction of the comic to the ridiculing of the ridiculous[195] by discussing the carnivalistic and its comedy through the more complex form of the meta-fictional and self-reflexive novel so that in it the understanding of the comic and the use of self-reflexive literary forms are brought together rather than separated.[196]

In contrast to Eco's 'post-modern' extension of Bakhtin's descriptions of the carnival and its comic functions, and to Eco's 'post-modern' awareness of parody's complex and positive self-reflective as well as humorous functions, not all who have linked Bakhtin to post-modernism have interpreted his still modern views on comedy and parody in a positive post-modern manner.

In addition to Hassan's 'deconstructionist' characterisation of Bakhtin, Gilles Lipovetsky in his 'La Societé humoristique' in his *L'Ère du vide. Essais sur l'individualisme contemporain*, of 1983 has described the post-modern as being characterised by a Bakhtinian type of grotesque comedy[197] and by an 'ineluctable parody' which exists 'independently of our intentions'.[198] Clearly this description of parody is, however, and like Jameson's characterisations of post-modern pastiche, much more like the normless and unintentional parody described by Derrida and Baudrillard (and like the unintended parody created by a poetaster or 'would-be' but incompetent writer) than the intentional parody spoken of by Bakhtin.[199]

Amongst other contemporary writers who have suggested the power of laughter to be potentially positive, and that it may accompany parody in its 'meta-fictional' analyses and reconstructions of fiction, are David Lodge and Malcolm Bradbury. Reference has already been made to some of their literary works, and to both their

---

195 Eco's own earlier 'Diario Minimo' parodies are, while comic, also generally less complex and 'post-modern' than those in his 1980 novel.

196 Although Bakhtin's interest in the carnivalistic has been described as post-modern by some, the carnivalistic as such is, as noted previously, a relatively crude form of unreflexive and ridiculing comedy, and is different in this last respect from the meta-fictional parody which has been espoused by both 'postmodern' and 'post-modern' writers in general in recent times.

197 See Lipovetsky, *L'Ère du vide. Essais sur l'individualisme contemporain* (Paris, 1983), chapter 5, pp. 153 ff.   198 Ibid., p. 173.

199 Lipovetsky, p. 160, also writes of 'postmodern' humour, after writing on his p. 155 of the grotesque realism described by Bakhtin, that the tone is morose, vaguely provocative, given in the vulgar, and ostensibly as the emancipation of language, of the subject, and of sex.

comic and meta-fictional uses of parody, and both may be said to have described parody in recent theoretical works in a way which reflects their 'post-modern' uses of it for both comic and meta-fictional purposes.

David Lodge, for instance, has suggested such a characterisation of parody as both comic and meta-fictional in his discussions of Bakhtin in his *After Bakhtin. Essays on Fiction and Criticism* of 1990.[200] Lodge's introduction to this collection of essays further matches some concerns of Jencks when it praises Bakhtin for giving 'an account of value and an account of communication' as recommended by I. A. Richards:[201] 'Bakhtin's theory has both these essential components and has therefore given new hope to literary critics who were beginning to wonder whether there was a life after post-structuralism.'[202]

Lodge (p. 7) also reveals that one particular passage in Bakhtin had explained to him why he was 'a novelist rather than a poet' and 'why, as a novelist, I have been drawn to pastiche, parody and travesty – often of the very kind of discourse I produce in my capacity as an academic critic'. The passage quoted by Lodge from Bakhtin concludes: '"For the prose artist the world is full of other people's words, among which he must orient himself and whose speech characteristics he must be able to perceive with a very keen ear. He must introduce them into the plane of his own discourse, but in such a way that this plane is not destroyed. He works with a very rich verbal palette."'[203]

Lodge's first chapter of his *After Bakhtin. Essays on Fiction and Criticism*, 'The novel now. Theories and practices', also comments (p. 22) both on Bakhtin's concept of the polyphonic novel, as first formulated in his *Problems of Dostoyevsky's Art* of 1929, and on how Bakhtin had traced its roots back to the 'parodying-travestying' forms of the carnival: 'What then seemed to him to be a unique innovation of Dostoevsky's [Dostoyevsky's] – the way in which the Russian novelist allowed different characters to articulate different ideological

200 See David Lodge, *After Bakhtin. Essays on Fiction and Criticism* (London, 1990).
201 See I. A. Richards, *Principles of Literary Criticism* (London and New York, 1930), p. 25. Richards refers to parody on his p. 247 with reference to its ability to unmask 'pseudo-tragedy': 'Parody easily overthrows it, the ironic addition paralyses it.' (Jencks also refers to Richards on both irony and value in his 1967 review of Venturi, p. 5.)   202 See Lodge, *After Bakhtin*, p. 4.
203 Quoted by Lodge from *Problems of Dostoevsky's Poetics*, edited by Caryl Emerson, (Manchester, 1984), p. 201.

positions in a text without subordinating them to his own authorial speech – he later came to think was inherent in the novel as a literary form. In the revised and much expanded version of the Dostoevsky book, *Problems of Dostoevsky's Poetics* (1963), and in the essays collected in English under the title, *The Dialogic Imagination*, he traced its genealogy back to the parodying-travestying genres of classical literature – the satyr play, the Socratic dialogue and the Menippean satire – and to that carnival folk-culture which kept the tradition alive through the Middle Ages and up to the Renaissance.'

Lodge adds (pp. 23–4), despite Bakhtin's criticisms of modern parody, and in an extension of Bakhtin's words to other complex as well as 'contradictory' forms, that Bakhtin's theory of the novel also applies well to more recent works, including 'the carnival face-pulling, the parodying and travestying of academic discourse in *Lucky Jim*; the invented polyglossia, the *skaz* energy and vitality, the *Notes from the Underground* subversiveness of *A Clockwork Orange*; the disconcerting hybridization of *The French Lieutenant's Woman*'. Lodge concludes this chapter (p. 24): 'As for my own contribution to contemporary British fiction, I must leave the Bakhtinian reading of that to others. I will only say that I have found Bakhtin's theory of the novel very useful when challenged to explain how I can write carnivalesque novels about academics while continuing to be one myself.'[204]

Lodge has succeeded in this chapter of his *After Bakhtin* in applying Bakhtin's two, still somewhat separated, analyses of the double-voiced character of the parody and of the laughter of the 'parodying-travestying' forms of the carnival to contemporary works, and further references to parody in Lodge's *After Bakhtin* essays emphasise how the meta-fictional or dialogic parody and the comic are connected rather than separated in his view of them. Lodge (p. 39) also quotes from Bakhtin's 'Epic and the Novel' in his second chapter, 'Mimesis and diegesis in modern fiction', before again relating Bakhtin's description of carnivalistic parody to the more modern: '"any and every straightforward genre, any and every direct discourse – epic, tragic, lyric, philosophical – may and indeed must have itself become the object of representation, the object of a parodic, travestying

---

204 Lodge's *Paradise News. A Novel* also evokes Bakhtin's descriptions of the carnival as both playful and grotesque in its description of the carnivalesque transportation of various of its characters around Heathrow, in Lodge, *Paradise News. A Novel* (London, 1991), p. 17.

'mimicry'. It is as if such mimicry rips the word away from its object, disunifies the two, shows that a given straightforward generic word – epic or tragic – is one-sided, bounded, incapable of exhausting the object; the process of parodying forces us to experience those sides of the object that are not otherwise included in a given genre or a given style. Parodic-travestying literature introduces the permanent corrective of laughter, of a critique of the one-sided seriousness of the lofty direct word, the corrective of reality that is always richer, more fundamental and most importantly *too contradictory and heteroglot* to be fitted into a high and straightforward genre." '[205] Lodge adds: 'Bakhtin might have been writing about [Joyce's] *Ulysses* in that passage. In fact, he was writing about the fourth play of classical Greek drama, the satyr play, which traditionally followed the tragic trilogy and mocked its grandeur and seriousness. And he notes in passing that "the figure of the 'comic Odysseus', a parodic travesty of his high epic and tragic image, was one of the most popular figures of satyr plays, of ancient Doric farce and pre-Aristophanic comedy, as well as of a whole series of minor comic epics". Bloom has an ancient genealogy.'

Joyce's *Ulysses* could also be described as a modern meta-fictional extension of the ancient idea of *parodia* as a comic mock Homeric epic and had earlier been acknowledged by Lodge as having provided some inspiration for his comic and meta-fictional novel *The British Museum is Falling Down* of 1965.[206] As Lodge explains in the 1980 'Afterword' to his novel, the latter contains not only an imitation of Molly Bloom's interior monologue from Joyce's *Ulysses* but at least nine other passages 'of parody or pastiche'.[207] Lodge's 'An Afterword' itself names Joseph Conrad, Graham Greene, Ernest Hemingway, Henry James, James Joyce, Franz Kafka, D. H. Lawrence, Fr. Rolfe (Baron Corvo), C. P. Snow, and Virginia Woolf as the authors 'mimicked' in these passages. These parodies and pastiches also echo Joyce's 'Oxen of the Sun' parodies in his *Ulysses*, in which expertise is shown in the imitation of other styles, and in which the older practice of parodying a collection of authors in which the parodist pretends that several different poets have written on one particular topic in their own particular styles, as made popular by Horace and James Smith in their *Rejected Addresses* of 1812 and in the numerous

205 Lodge has quoted from Bakhtin, *The Dialogic Imagination*, p. 55.
206 See Lodge, 'An Afterword', in Lodge, *The British Museum is Falling Down* (1965), (Harmondsworth, 1983), pp. 163–74; p. 171.   207 Ibid., p. 168.

anthologies of verse parody which followed them,[208] is made more meta-fictional by the subject-matter of all being that of the novel in which they are embedded.

Lodge's use in his 'Afterword' of 1980 of the terms 'allusion' and 'mimicry' as well as 'parody' and 'pastiche' to describe the 'Oxen of the Sun' passages in his novel is significant, moreover, in that those passages often seem not only to imitate Joyce's parodic passages, but to imitate rather than to parody the other authors in question. (Lodge himself comments on the understated nature of the earlier examples of parody in his 1965 novel in the 'Afterword' to it, p. 170.) Although some irony is produced from Lodge's imitation of these authors in the middle of his own narrative, there is clearly less of the deliberate incongruity which makes Malcolm Bradbury's parodies in his *Who Do You Think You Are?* of 1976, or Lodge's own later works, so explicitly comic and parodic.

If Lodge's early parody/pastiches are not all as demonstrably parodic or as comic as are his later works (or as comic as the satire and humour in his earlier ones), they may be said, nonetheless, to have laid some of the ground-work for the more comic use of parody in works such as his *Changing Places* and *Small World*. Lodge's development of the interrelationship of the comic and the complex in such works of parody – and naming of them as parody rather than as something else in his later critical writings – further makes his understanding of parody 'post-modern' in contrast to those modern and late-modern theorists of parody who have acknowledged only *either* the meta-fictional *or* the comic aspects of the parody involved in such works.

The two criteria of the meta-fictional and the comic mentioned above as being necessary for a 'post-modern' understanding of parody are, however, not by themselves sufficient for determining the question of whether a use of parody is 'post-modern' in the sense being developed here. Larry McCaffery's suggestion that 'it is a commonplace to note that *Tristram Shandy* is a thoroughly post-modern work in every respect but the period in which it is written'[209] also points to the problem of whether we should call Sterne's novel 'post-modern' according to the description of 'post-modern parody'

208 Jerrold and Leonard's *A Century of Parody and Imitation* also begins with the *Rejected Addresses* of Horace and James Smith.
209 See Larry McCaffery (ed.), *Postmodern Fiction. A Bio-Bibliographical Guide* (New York and London, 1986), p. xv.

as both meta-fictional and comic given above, or whether even more recent, early twentieth-century 'meta-fictional and comic' authors such as Joyce might be called 'post-modern'. Given that the definition of post-modern parody being worked out here entails seeing the concept of parody go beyond the more limited modern understanding of it as *either* meta-fictional *or* comic, the answer to all of these questions must, however, be 'no'.

One way of explaining this answer is that even though Joyce's and Sterne's novels contain elements of the meta-fictional as well as the comic, they do not suggest that what they are doing is a deliberate transformation of the modern restriction of parody to '*either* the meta-fictional *or* the comic', and could not do so fully given the further development of that view after their composition.[210] While the use of parody for both the meta-fictional and the comic in such works can be described as 'pre-post-modern', the preceding arguments may be summarised as suggesting that only works or theories of parody may be described as 'post-modern' which have (1) overcome both (a) the modern reduction of parody to *either* the meta-fictional *or* the comic, and (b) the modern understanding of the comic as something negative,[211] and (2) followed the 'modern' period and its works in time, and with some conscious transformation of modernist principles.

Both of these criteria (which were also applied in preceding discussions to the work of Charles Jencks and Umberto Eco) can be applied to David Lodge's writings from at least the 1970s onwards, although the question of to what extent Lodge's earlier works may be called post-modern requires, as suggested previously, a slightly different answer. This is so because even though Lodge's *The British Museum is Falling Down* of 1965 uses parody for both comic and meta-fictional purposes, and to deal with the 'anxiety of influence' of the modern novel on its author (see Lodge's 'Afterword' to it of 1980, pp. 168 ff.), it can be argued that it still imitates Joyce and his parody in a 'pre-' or 'proto-post-modern' manner, rather than goes beyond Joyce's modernism or that of the other writers imitated in it in any

210 One other reason for not calling works such as Sterne's *Tristram Shandy* and Joyce's *Ulysses* 'post-modern' is that they are 'modern' in other aspects apart from their use of parody.

211 As seen previously, the modern denigration of parody as comic follows to at least some extent from the equation of parody with less complex forms such as the burlesque and from the subsequent separation of parody from its more complex meta-fictional and re-creative functions.

clearly 'post-modern' way. By contrast, Lodge's later novels, such as *Small World* and its comic re-use of works ranging from the legends of the Grail to Oscar Wilde's already parodic *The Importance of Being Earnest* and to structuralist and post-structuralist theory, treat their modern sources in what can be said to be both a clearly comic and a clearly innovatory intertextual parodistic manner.

While the lines between the pre-post-modern and the post-modern which are drawn above might be said to be fine ones, Lodge's critical writings of the 1980s and later also comment more explicitly on both the humour of works such as Joyce's and the mixture of the comic and the dialogic in parody. Lodge explicitly connects laughter and the dialogic, and with reference to Joyce's parody, when he continues the second chapter in his *After Bakhtin* by writing there (p. 40) that 'according to Bakhtin, the two crucial ingredients in the Rabelaisian project, which made the novel possible, were *laughter* – the mockery of any and every type of discourse in the folk-carnival tradition, and what he called "polyglossia", the "interanimation of languages", such as obtained between Latin and the vernaculars at the Renaissance', and that 'laughter and the interanimation of languages were also the vital ingredients of *Finnegans Wake*'.

Putting aside for the moment the fact that Joyce himself was not post-modern in the sense that he did not explicitly challenge the modernism of which he was a part, Lodge's stress on the inter-connection of the dialogic and the comic here can be said to have presented a view of Joyce which is much more 'post-modern' than either those which have emphasised only one or the other of these, or of other, aspects of Joyce's work[212] or the views suggested by his own earlier mimicry of Joyce. Lodge's overall understanding and use of parody can, moreover, be characterised as post-modern (and differentiated from the modern by more than either the meta-fictional or the 'diegetic'[213]), because it clearly goes beyond the modern separation of the meta-fictional and the comic. Lodge speaks in both chapter 4 and chapter 5 of his *After Bakhtin* of Bakhtin as having distinguished parody from stylisation as a form where the style is used for purposes

---

212 Joyce's *Finnegans Wake* is, for instance, for Hassan in 1971 a 'crucial' work in the development of the post-modern from the modern because of the radical disjunctions of Joyce's prose. (See Hassan, *The Postmodern Turn*, p. 29.)

213 Lodge suggests in his *After Bakhtin*, p. 84 that the opposition between *mimesis* and *diegesis* which he has used in earlier chapters and essays cannot be used to describe the 'double-voicedness' of which Bakhtin has spoken.

'opposite to or incongruous with the intentions of the original',[214] but also gives an explicitly comic, and meta-literary, example of such parody in his chapter 5 (p. 84) in referring to Fielding's *Jonathan Wild* and its 'parody of heroic biography'. (And see the reference to Fielding's *Joseph Andrews* in the entry entitled 'Intertextuality' in Lodge's recent *The Art of Fiction*. Some earlier comments by Lodge on Kingsley Amis, in the last essay of Lodge's *Language of Fiction* of 1966, refer both to Amis' debt in *Lucky Jim* to Fielding's understanding of 'the Ridiculous' and to the more meta-fictional elements of Amis' later novels, but without commenting specifically on the more meta-fictional and parodic aspects of Fielding.)

Malcolm Bradbury is another contemporary writer and theorist who has developed a concept and use of parody which clearly show the latter to be able to be both meta-fictional and comic.[215] In the parodies published in his *Who Do You Think You Are? Stories and Parodies* of 1976 the styles of the authors being parodied are not only imitated and then exaggerated, but are suddenly confronted with comically incongruous comments and interpolations.[216] In a parody of the opening of C. P. Snow's Cambridge novels, in the story 'An Extravagant Fondness for the Love of Women' in the aforementioned collection, Snow's habit of having his character Lewis Eliot recount the details of his rooms to the reader is suddenly turned into a meta-fictional and parodic comment on that habit itself.[217] In addition to being used to parody other modern authors, including Iris Murdoch, Muriel Spark and Lawrence Durrell, and in even more comic and incongruous ways, this technique of imitating and then changing the texts in hand in some unexpected, out-of-place, and comic, manner is used to bring C. P. Snow's Lewis Eliot together with Kingsley Amis' Jim Dixon in the story 'An Extravagant Fondness for the Love of Women' so that a type of 'double parody' of both authors is created.

Earlier Bradbury had provided a match for Dixon's drunken parody of the academic public lecture, in Kingsley Amis' *Lucky Jim* of 1954,[218] in his parody of Carey Willoughby's 'angry young man' lecture in

---

214 See Lodge, *After Bakhtin*, p. 60 and p. 84.
215 Bradbury, however, is also aware that not all parody is meta-fictional, as can be seen, for example, from p. 51 of his review article 'An Age of Parody. Style in the Modern Arts', in *Encounter*, vol. 55, no. 1 (July 1980), pp. 36–53.
216 See Malcolm Bradbury, *Who Do You Think You Are? Stories and Parodies* (1976), (London, 1988), pp. 147–221.   217 Ibid., pp. 155–63; p. 157.
218 See Kingsley Amis, *Lucky Jim* (Harmondsworth, 1977), pp. 221–7.

Eating People is Wrong of 1959.[219] While there are significant, and also comic, differences between these two texts, in that, for example, Bradbury's bellicose but milk-drinking Willoughby could be said to be both more sober and less conscious of the parody being used to constitute his speech than Amis' drunken Jim, and provides a caricature of both author and hero,[220] the parody of Willoughby's angry young man lecture is similar to Amis' parody of the academic lecture in being both overridingly comic and satiric rather than primarily meta-fictional.

Although there are some other ironic meta-fictional comments in Bradbury's 1959 novel,[221] it is largely in his works of the late 1970s and after that parody is used in both a clearly comic and a meta-fictional manner.[222] Even Bradbury's *Why Come to Slaka?* of 1986 which is an hilarious parody of certain travel guides is, in addition, meta-fictional in that it parodies the naive use of legends and other literary forms in such guides and refers to characters from Bradbury's *Rates of Exchange* of 1983, which itself contains several comic meta-fictional parodic moments.

As well as using parody in both a meta-fictional and comic way in his *Who Do You Think You Are?* of 1976 and above-named fictions Bradbury has commented upon the meta-fictional and comic aspects of parody in his more recent theoretical works,[223] and has used parody to have some fun with several fashionable modern and late-modern literary concepts and theories in other of his works of comic fiction. One of the best examples of the latter available at the date at which this text was completed was *My Strange Quest for Mensonge.*

---

219 See Bradbury, *Eating People is Wrong* (London, 1978), pp. 224 ff.

220 Bradbury has warned against comparing the works too closely in the 'Afterword' to the later printings of his *Eating People is Wrong* but there are several other deliberate (and comic) references to Amis' *Lucky Jim* in it, including one on p. 243 to Jim's burning of Welch's bed-linen, made through Treece's cogitations on the dangers of inviting angry young men (and authors) to stay.

221 Bradbury's *Eating People is Wrong* also contains a comic meta-fictional comment (on its p. 86) on people who write satirical novels about universities, and some other comic references to the dangers of being made a character in such works.

222 In addition to its meta-fictional 'Author's Note', Bradbury's *The History Man* of 1975 contains a memorable satiric parody of a university departmental meeting, a 'meta-fictional' comment on which is to be found in Bradbury's *Unsent Letters* (London, 1989), p. 163.

223 See especially Bradbury's second article entitled 'An Age of Parody. Style in the Modern Arts', in Bradbury, *No, Not Bloomsbury* (London, 1987), pp. 46–64.

Structuralism's Hidden Hero. With a Foreword/Afterword by Michel Tardieu (Professor of Structuralist Narratology, University of Paris) translated by David Lodge of 1987.[224]

Mensonge, as the title has been abbreviated, is full of parodies of structuralist and post-structuralist theory, from Roland Barthes' 'Death of the Author' and Foucault's 'What is an Author?' through to the many self-conscious, though often uncritical, commentaries on the same, as well as of their Bibliographies, Indices, Forewords, Afterwords, and, in the case of its paperback edition, publishers' blurbs, and covers.[225] Here parody is not only used to foreground the way in which the book is made (as, say, in *Tristram Shandy* where even the end pages of the book are reproduced in the midst of the text),[226] but is, ironically, also used to satirise the overuse and misuse of what are in fact some of its own 'post-Sternean' contributions to the modern and post-modern understanding of the role of the author, text, reader, and 'intertext' in the literary work.

Bradbury is well aware of both the intertextual character of parody[227] and of the popularity of the concept of intertextuality with some contemporary late-modern or 'postmodern' critics, and has been able to do much with the ironic possibilities created by those two facts. In, for example, the final chapter of his *Unsent Letters* of 1988, 'The Nympholept's Tale', Bradbury not only parodies the naive discovery, or, rather, 'construction', of a literary source for a well-known work (Nabokov's *Lolita*), but also parodies the popularity of theories of intertextuality while ironically using both parodies to set up his own complex and comic set of intertextual references: 'so advanced and sophisticated has our critical and scholarly profession become – and it is no doubt in part thanks to V.'s [Nabokov's] own influence that it has

---

224 Bradbury's *Doctor Criminale*, which appeared in 1992 after the completion of the above text, also contains an ironic reference to the fictional character of Mensonge as well as references to several other living authors and their creations.

225 See Malcolm Bradbury, *My Strange Quest for Mensonge. Structuralism's Hidden Hero. With a Foreword/Afterword by Michel Tardieu (Professor of Structuralist Narratology, University of Paris) translated by David Lodge* (London, 1989).

226 Bradbury's *Why Come to Slaka? A Guidebook and a Phrasebook translated into English by Dr. F. Plitplov (Dozent Extraordinarius, Universitet Dvarfim Borism). Introduction by Dr. A. Petworth* of 1986 (London, 1987) is also parody from its front to its back cover.

227 Bradbury also speaks of parody and the intertextual together on p. 54 of his essay 'An Age of Parody' in his *No, Not Bloomsbury*.

done so – that we no longer need such proofs to be able to establish a significant connection between the two books. We do, after all, have the happy concept of "intertextuality". And intertextuality – as you well know, Charles [Bradbury's fictional interlocutor in this piece is, in ironic intertextual fashion, Nabokov's fictional Charles Kinbote], if you keep up with these things, and I have no doubt you do – proves that all texts are related to all other texts. Indeed not only does it demonstrate the universality of that pattern of allusion, quotation, cross-reference, parody and parallelism which has always kept us scholars in business and research grants; it also shows philosophically that authors do not write writing at all, but that writing writes authors. So cunning are the ways of intertextuality that we need no evidence to show that V. did actually open the pages of Carter's book, let alone wrote it in the first place, in order to prove that he was influenced by it. Many a book has been a proven influence on a later author without his ever having taken the trouble actually to read it.'[228]

One equally comic as well as complex, and intertextual, example of a parodistic use of theories of intertextuality is to be found in *Mensonge* when David Lodge is able to 'translate' a 'Foreword/ Afterword' to that work by one of his own characters from *Small World*, the 'Parisian theorist Michel Tardieu'. Lodge then adds further fuel and irony to the structuralist/post-structuralist debate on the absence of authors, and to its parodistic treatment by Bradbury, by pointing to the similarities between the names of Bradbury and Oscar Wilde's fictional Bunbury from *The Importance of Being Earnest* which Lodge himself has previously evoked in parodistic fashion in his *Small World. An Academic Romance* of 1984.[229]

One recipe for intertextuality given by Brian McHale in his *Postmodernist Fiction*[230] also provides a guide for an understanding of Lodge's and Bradbury's parodistic foregrounding of the late-modern and post-modern canonisation of intertextuality in *Mensonge*. McHale writes: 'It has become commonplace since Eliot's "Tradition and the individual talent", and even more so since the French structuralists' work on intertextuality, to picture literature as a field or, better, a network whose nodes are the actual texts of literature. By this account,

228 See Bradbury, *Unsent Letters*, p. 225.
229 See *Mensonge*, p. 91. (Oscar Wilde's *The Importance of Being Earnest* is parodistically evoked by Lodge in *Small World* with the 'loss' of the Pabst twins in a Gladstone bag by Miss Maiden.)
230 See Brian McHale, *Postmodernist Fiction*, pp. 56–7.

an intertextual space is constituted whenever we recognize the relations among two or more texts, or between specific texts and larger categories such as genre, school, period. There are a number of ways of foregrounding this intertextual space and integrating it in the text's structure, but none is more effective than the device of "borrowing" a character from another text – "transworld identity", Umberto Eco has called this, the transmigration of characters from one fictional universe to another.'[231]

Lodge's 'small world' in the novel of that name might also be described as a 'transworld' in the 'Econian' sense that it borrows characters from other fictional works, such as Wilde's Miss Prism, as well as from the sometimes more real world of textual theory.[232] In addition to practising this 'transmigration of characters' in *Mensonge* via both parody and self-parody, Lodge's character Tardieu is able to parody Bradbury's parodic and ironic 'Aujourd'hui, mes amis, et aussi les anglais, nous sommes tous de nécessité structuralistes' in a way which not only makes another joke out of Bradbury's,[233] but which also plays on the fiction created in Bradbury's text (as elsewhere) that he and Lodge are one and the same person.[234]

Mensonge must not, however, be done the injustice of explaining away all of its multivalent levels of humour in the generally 'monologic' and non-incongruous prose of criticism – and especially as Bradbury has written (if with some irony) that 'because translation itself is, as Saussure has shown, impossible, a deviant misreading, I should prefer myself not to be quoted by anyone'.[235] Given this statement is ironic in several ways (for one thing, Bradbury himself has

231 McHale, pp. 56–7. McHale opens his *Postmodernist Fiction*, p. xii with a reference to David Lodge's *The Modes of Modern Writing* of 1977 as providing a typology of 'postmodernist' strategies, such as contradiction, discontinuity, randomness, excess, and short circuit, 'by which postmodernist writing seeks to avoid having to choose either of the poles of metaphoric (modernist) or metonymic (antimodernist) writing'. Many of these categories can, however, be described as late-modern rather than 'post-modern', and Jencks has also suggested in his *Late-Modern Architecture* of 1980, p. 32 that post-modern architecture has been 'pro-metaphor' where modern architecture was not.
232 Later Eco also speaks of fictional worlds as being 'small worlds' in another sense in his *The Limits of Interpretation*, pp. 64–82.
233 See *Mensonge*, pp. 4 and 89.
234 Bradbury also speaks in his 'Wissenschaft File', in his *Unsent Letters* (1988), (London, 1989), p. 13, on the subject of whether he and David Lodge are the same, as 'the vexed issue of the well-known writer "Bodge"'.
235 *Mensonge*, p. 67.

just 'translated' Saussure, so that we cannot be sure if what he says about what 'Saussure' says about translation being a deviant reading is correct or not), we might still offer some explanation of such humour in the more 'monologic' language of criticism, but without suggesting that such an explanation can replace its subject, or recreate the same incongruities and their comic effects.

While differences between the more monological, and (generally) less incongruous, analysis of humour in criticism and the more dialogical and incongruous aspects of fictional humour provide some explanation as to why the former cannot usually be as comic as the latter, they cannot justify, however, the elimination of both the analysis and recognition of humour from the account of parody given in recent years by some 'late-modern' analysts of that subject.

At least one other point which can be made about Bradbury's and Lodge's parodistic games with the theories of intertextuality referred to previously is that they show, if indirectly, how much humour has disappeared from the structuralist and post-structuralist use of the categories derived by the Russian formalists from parody. One can ask, for instance, if Bradbury, or Lodge, could have had so much fun with structuralist and post-structuralist theory,[236] and with the canonisation of categories such as intertextuality by such theories, if so many proponents of the latter had not taken themselves so seriously in contrast to their sources in the first place, and underplayed the role of comic parody in the genesis of their own theories for so long. The fact that some structuralist and post-structuralist categories have a lot to do with the lessons taught by parody texts about intertextuality, incongruity and self-reflexivity – without all of their proponents realising either this point, or that parody had added some humour to the analysis of such categories – may also help to explain the ripeness of those categories for parody and irony.

Bradbury himself might be said to have alluded to this problem when he writes with a double dose of irony after commenting on both the general problems of quoting another and on the problem of quoting one like 'Mensonge' who claims that 'the entire book itself is a quote from a quote' that 'I have tried to retain the spirit of Mensonge's eccentric and complex style, which has sometimes been

---

236 In his *Nice Work* of 1988, Lodge also comments ironically on the difficulty of having a literary theorist as a character who does not believe in 'the concept of character'. See Lodge, *Nice Work* (Harmondsworth, 1989), p. 39.

compared with Jonathan Swift, though in fact his work lacks Swift's sunny benevolence and optimism'.[237] Bradbury continues with his own particular type of incongruous wit, in which one statement is followed by its opposite, or by an ironically concealed opposite message, to refer to the way in which such wit has been included in the canons of structuralist and post-structuralist theories if with an emphasis on its intertextual, rather than its comic aspects: 'But there is a style of incongruous wit which some have regarded as the distinctive Mensongian signature, enabling us to identify when he is writing, even when he may not be.'

Charles Jencks has also written of the recanonisation of intertextuality by some 'postmodernist' critics, and with some irony, that '"intertextuality", the cliché of Post-Modern literature, shows that where there are too many texts there is no author'.[238] As with Bradbury's ironic investigations of the interrelationship of the disappearance of the author with the growth of intertextuality, it should, however, be remembered that this hypothesised connection between the growth of intertextuality and the diminishing of authorial power can be traced back to Barthes' interconnections of intertextuality with the phrase the 'death of the Author', and that before him Kristeva had derived the concept of the intertextual from her reading of the Russian formalists and from Bakhtin where it can be traced back to the analyses by them of works of general parody such as *Tristram Shandy* and *Don Quixote* in which the parodic (and comic) juxtaposition of texts was understood by them to have foregrounded what is now termed the intertextuality of literature in general. Unlike both Jencks and Bradbury, many modern and late-modern followers of Barthes and Kristeva have, as seen previously, also followed the latter's reduction of the comic in such forms of intertextuality, and failed to understand either the derivation of the latter concept from the parodic works analysed by the Russian formalists and by Bakhtin, or the comic nature of those works.

Like many good parodists Bradbury, however, has shown sympathy for his subjects, and has written with good-humoured irony in *Mensonge* of the philosophical revolution brought about by struc-

---

237 See *Mensonge*, p. 67.
238 Jencks, 'Post-Modernism and Discontinuity', in *Architectural Design*, vol. 57, nos. 1–2, 1987, Profile 65, *Post-Modernism and Discontinuity* (London, 1987), pp. 5–8; p. 8.

turalism and deconstruction that 'it is proving beyond doubt that we find ourselves in the age of the floating signifier, when word no longer attaches properly to thing, and no high bonding glues can help us. It discloses to us a world of parody and pastiche, query and quotation; and having shown us all this, it teaches us how to enjoy it.'[239]

Bradbury had also described parody itself as a 'floating signifier' in the second version of his 1980 essay 'An Age of Parody. Style in the Modern Arts' when writing that it 'belongs with the floating free of the signifier and the crisis of nomination' and that it 'claims the ludic freedom of a writing beyond nomination',[240] and Lodge's suggestion, in his 'Afterword' to *Mensonge*, that 'Bradbury/Bunbury' has himself become 'a free-floating signifier' has extended Bradbury's humorous treatment of that phrase even further.

To see parody now being defined by others without reference to its comic effect or structure, or even with explicit elimination of the comic, and through the structuralist and post-structuralist theories of intertextuality which were based on the analysis of comic parody in the first place,[241] is, however, to be led to wonder how far such seriousness can be taken before *it* becomes comic.[242] As Bradbury notes in his letter to the all-too-serious Dr Wissenschaft in 'The Wissenschaft File' of his *Unsent Letters*, with reference to Wissenschaft's queries regarding his work: 'Yes, of course, my novels are complex textual monads, philosophical reflections, tales of human tragedy, novels of pain. But to be frank they are quite heavily infested with satirical intentions, humoristic practices, and the like. In fact, to be entirely open with you – not something I do often when there are critics about – they are comic novels, and certain pages here and there are intended to produce a physiological comic reflex, which in Britain we call laughter.'[243]

239 Bradbury, *Mensonge*, p. 5.
240 See Bradbury, *No, Not Bloomsbury*, pp. 46–64; p. 62.
241 See, for example, Hutcheon 1985 and 1988. Hutcheon, 1985, criticises aspects of Gérard Genette's depictions of parody, but also writes, p. 21, that what is good about his definition of parody as a 'minimal transformation of a text' in his *Palimpsestes* of 1982 is 'its omission of the customary clause about comic or ridiculing effect'.
242 Hutcheon's elimination of comedy from parody in her 1985 *A Theory of Parody* even allows her on its p. 6 to allow Euripides' tragic *Medea* to be described as parody because it replaces 'the traditional male protagonist with a woman, and a woman who was an outsider ...'.
243 Bradbury, *Unsent Letters* (1988), (London, 1989), p. 11.

Bradbury also refers (p. 12) to Aristotle's unfinished work on comedy in answer to Wissenschaft's query (p. 3) of 'if your books are funny, please tell me where, and send me your ontology of the comedic and your theoretiks of the humorous, and how you like to compare yourself with Aristotle, Nietzsche, Bergson and Freud': 'My relationship with Aristotle, Nietzsche, Freud and Bergson has been for some time a vexed question, and my lawyer advises me it could well be subject to litigation. So I will comment only briefly. As I understand it, Aristotle never completed his work on comedy, being overcome with a paroxysm of something. He did, however, argue that comedy is an inverted tragedy, or a tragedy written upside down, and this is the way I have always tried to write my books.' Bradbury continues by practising the art of incongruously turning the serious upside down in at least a metaphoric manner: 'On the matter of Nietzsche, I have, to be frank, tried to avoid him as much as possible, and I believe he has taken the same attitude towards me.'

The later essay by Bradbury entitled 'An Age of Parody. Style in the Modern Arts' also has much to say on both parody and post-modernism rather than on Nietzsche. Bradbury, however, does follow the more Nietzschean Hassan to some extent in his depictions of post-modernism, as when he speaks of 'the arts of both modernism and postmodernism' as 'troubled by silences and absences, a consciousness of lost meanings and lost coherences, feelings of absurdity and nothingness'.[244] Despite this apparent despair, Bradbury's 'A Professorial Dilemma' turns such ironic insights into more (non-Nietzschean) comedy: 'Evidently we are caught up in one of those strange paradoxes of relationship between a so-called fiction and a so-called reality that bedevil all aspects of life in the postmodern world, and indeed keep some of us in royalties as well.'[245]

Irony is also described as a characteristic of the post-modern by Bradbury, as when, for instance, he speaks in his second 'An Age of Parody' essay of 'the newest philosophies of the Death of the Subject and the randomness of signs, the endless sense that style and sense have become collage, that nothing has a single and unicultural

---

244 Bradbury, *No, Not Bloomsbury*, p. 48. Bradbury's earlier, 1980, discussion of parody in *Encounter* also shows him to be aware of the existence of several different theories of post-modernism when he writes, p. 42: 'In fact there are many post-modernisms, as there were many modernisms, and they imply many different historiographies.'

245 Bradbury, *Unsent Letters*, p. 163.

meaning', and adds that 'culture is seen as synchronic, history as change, and both become part of a politics of performance, self-knowing and ironic, by which we enact as much substance as we care to have, and reserve the right to invest ourselves differently tomorrow'.[246] Bradbury continues by referring to the eclecticism of post-modern architecture: 'Our postmodern buildings declare themselves as constructs of random, eclectic quotation, where any reference can be relevant, form not following function, but building fancy into it.'

Bradbury had also used the idea of post-modernism as eclecticism in his novel *The History Man* in his description of a Kirk party: 'The downstairs of the house looks like a vast museum of costume, as if all the forms and styles of the past have been made synchronic and here, in Howard's own house, have converged, and blurred; performers from medieval mystery plays, historical romances, dramas of trench warfare, proletarian documentaries, Victorian drawing-room farces play simultaneously in one eclectic, post-modern collage that is a pure and open form, a self-generating happening.'[247] Post-modernism is presented as being both eclectic and a happening in the Hassanian sense here,[248] although Bradbury has been more explicit than Hassan about the way in which post-modernism has carried devices such as parody over from modernism when discussing these topics in his essay 'Modernisms/Postmodernisms' for Ihab and Sally Hassan's *Innovation/Renovation. New Perspectives on the Humanities* of 1983.[249]

In the same year as that essay appeared, Bradbury published his *The Modern American Novel*, and again commented on the extension of the modernist use of parody in contemporary culture: 'Whether or not postmodernism is the dominant or "appropriate" style of the age may be questionable; what is certain is that formal and epistemological questions crucial to fiction's nature are being articulated in writers who have extended certain fundamental preoccupations of modernism – notably with fiction as play, game, parody, forgery, and fantasy – and added new challenges to the notion that art is referential and formally

---

246 Bradbury, *No, Not Bloomsbury*, p. 51.
247 Bradbury, *The History Man*, p. 82.
248 As noted earlier, Hassan also mentions Malraux's *musée imaginaire* in his *The Postmodern Turn*, p. 177.
249 See Bradbury, 'Modernisms/Postmodernisms', in *Innovation/Renovation. New Perspectives on the Humanities*, edited by Ihab Hassan and Sally Hassan (Wisconsin and London, 1983), pp. 311–27.

coherent. In their works the stable text disappears; the fiction becomes meta-fictional; the writer is invited into novels in novel ways.'[250] Bradbury had previously referred to the way in which much modern parody was meta-fictional when writing on that subject in his 1980 review article for *Encounter*,[251] and this 1983 text further suggests parody to be able to be both a part of a movement which favours meta-fiction and a positive, creative form.[252]

Bradbury has also turned to the carnivalistic and to John Barth's essay 'The Literature of Replenishment',[253] in which Barth had again referred to parody as a means to the renewal of older forms,[254] in his later essay on parody: 'Like the manners of our lives, the arts suggest the present as a playful mood of carnival, and Barth speaks also of the "literature of replenishment", reinvigorated by random freedoms.'[255] While Bradbury concludes his preceding sentence with the apparently less optimistic phrase that 'fullness and emptiness seem much the same thing, circling round a vacated centre',[256] he takes up the idea later in his essay that parody has moved into the centre from the margins when he writes, if with some irony, that 'it can indeed be argued that parody has moved from the margins to the centre, even as the centre, in the form of unified culture or authenticated and firmly authored facts, departs'.[257]

Bradbury goes on to define parody with reference to its older

250 Bradbury, *The Modern American Novel* (Oxford and New York, 1983), p. 163.
251 Bradbury had also referred to the many different types of parody which have existed since ancient through modern to post-modern times in his *Encounter* article on parody of 1980.
252 See Bradbury, *The Modern American Novel*, p. 164.
253 See John Barth, 'The Literature of Replenishment. Postmodernist Fiction', in *The Atlantic* vol. 245, no.1 (January 1980); pp. 65–71.
254 See also Barth's earlier essay 'The Literature of Exhaustion' of 1967.
255 Bradbury, *No, Not Bloomsbury*, p. 51.
256 Bradbury concludes the paragraph, 'we no longer believe we are in an era of reality', and refers p. 52 to Christopher Lasch's *The Culture of Narcissism* of 1978 as seeing the '"irony of an increasing self-consciousness" expressing itself as weariness in "postmodern" art'.
257 See Bradbury, *No, Not Bloomsbury*, pp. 54–5. Charles Jencks, *Post-Modernism. The New Classicism in Art and Architecture* (London, 1987), pp. 349 f., has spoken of the way in which the modernist idea that 'things fall apart; the centre cannot hold', which is quoted by Bradbury and MacFarlane from Yeats in their *Modernism 1890–1930* (Harmondsworth, 1976), p. 26, and echoed by Hassan in his 1971 essay on 'postmodernism' (Hassan, *The Postmodern Turn*, p. 40), has been replaced by the 'Post-Modernist' idea that 'things fall together, and there is no centre, but connections'.

definitions in terms of form and content as 'an ironic renegotiation of the relationship between style and substance, so that the stylistic presentation passes into the foreground and the content is minimalised to the background, this often having a comic effect', and adds that parody both 'perpetuates and destroys'. After several other comments of interest, not all of which can be mentioned again here, Bradbury summarises his remarks on parody in a passage which also summarises the history of parody in recent times: 'So it seems clear that in our century parodic activity has vastly increased, moved, in art and literature, in practice and theory, from the margins to the centre, and become a primary level of textual or painterly representation. An essential part of our art is an art of mirrorings and quotations, inward self-reference and mock-mimesis, of figural violation and aesthetic self-presence, which has displaced and estranged the naive-mimetic prototypes we associate with much nineteenth-century writing and challenged its habits of direct *vraisemblance*, orderly narrative, and dominant authorial control.'[258]

More lately still Bradbury has suggested that some recent uses of parody by Richard Carver, Don DeLillo, and Martin Amis have been part of attempts to reflect the world as one which is 'out of joint', and that such usages of parody might be termed 'parodic realism'.[259] As seen previously, Charles Jencks had written in his *The Language of Post-Modern Architecture* that some architects have used travesty as a 'kind of mirror-image genre of cultural confusion',[260] and Ihab Hassan's 'late-modern' concept of parody as insane may further be taken to have assumed that such parody in some way reflects the insanity of the 'postmodern' world around it which Hassan has emphasised in his earlier writings.

Patricia Waugh's *Metafiction. The Theory and Practice of Self-Conscious Fiction* of 1984 has also stated (p. 82) with reference to meta-fiction that the detective-story plot 'is useful for exploring readerly expectation because it provides that readerly satisfaction which attaches to the predictable', and has added (p. 83), in an echo of Hassan's depiction of the post-modern, that 'in the post-modern

---

258 Bradbury, *No, Not Bloomsbury*, p. 60.
259 Malcolm Bradbury suggested this in a comment to the publisher on a draft for this book.
260 See Jencks, *The Language of Post-Modern Architecture* (revised enlarged edn, 1978), p. 93.

period, the detective plot is being used to express not order but the irrationality of both the surface of the world and of its deep structures'.

Martin Amis' *London Fields*, which both uses parody in its detective cum crime plot and alludes to Cervantes' *Don Quixote* while retaining little of the cheerfulness of the latter,[261] even refers, while describing itself as 'plagiarized from real life',[262] to the difficulty of depicting all the discontinuities of the modern city: 'The people in here, they're like London, they're like the streets of London, a long way from any shape I've tried to equip them with, strictly non-symmetrical, exactly lop-sided – far from many things, and far from art.'[263]

Bradbury had also gone on to relate parody in a Hassanian manner both to a 'deferring indeterminacy' and to 'the opening of spaces and fractures, that is the mark alike of a modern writing and a modern post-essentialist philosophy' in his second 'An Age of Parody' essay.[264] In contrast, however, to the less cheerful 'late-modern' uses of parody described above and to modern reductions of parody to ridicule,[265] Bradbury ultimately affirms his other recent uses and descriptions of parody as both comic and complex when he concludes his essay with the statement that 'parody is not simply a crisis of language, but a major form of creative play and artistic self-discovery which can give us a joyously experimental and comic art'.[266]

Post-modernism and parody: conclusion

Bradbury's, Lodge's, Eco's, and Jencks' reaffirmations of the laughter of parody have all been 'post-modern' in returning some recognition of the comic or humorous aspects of parody to it,[267] and together with

261 'Late-modern' uses of parody such as Martin Amis' may be said to have matched some late-modern theories of it in their reduction of its comicality, but, like those theories, cannot eliminate the comic altogether without their parody becoming something else.

262 See Martin Amis, *London Fields* (1989), (Harmondsworth, 1990), p. 467.

263 Ibid., p. 463.   264 See Bradbury, *No, Not Bloomsbury*, p. 62.

265 Even when referring to parody as imitation and forgery in *No, Not Bloomsbury*, p. 63 Bradbury describes it as at once entering deep into texts and 'skating buoyantly' along their surfaces in a way which conjures up both its complexity and its humour.   266 Ibid., p. 64.

267 Apart from Eco, 'comic' and 'humorous' have been used interchangeably by most of the twentieth-century writers discussed above.

an understanding of its more complex, intertextual, meta-fictional or 'double-coded' characteristics and potential.[268]

While ancient concepts and uses of parody related it to applications which were both meta-fictional and comic, but without the theories of the meta-fictional and the intertextual developed in this century to explain and extend that function, modern theories of parody have seen it reduced to the burlesque, so that, while its use in meta-fiction continued, it was largely unrecognised as parody there. Continuing this modern division of the comic or burlesque parody from the meta-fictional or general parody, late-modern theories of parody from the 1960s and after have tended to emphasise either the powerlessness or the nihilistic character of its comic factors, or its meta-fictional or intertextual aspects, but not both the comic understood as something positive and the meta-fictional or the intertextual at the same time.

What have been called post-modern theories of parody in this work (of, for instance, Bradbury, Lodge, Eco, and Jencks) return to it, at the very least, both its humour and its meta-fictional complexity, and in contrast to the modern separation of the meta-fictional parody from the comic. While some critics have treated Eco, Bradbury and Lodge as 'post-modern' because their work has been described as meta-fictional, and in a late-modern manner which emphasises the meta-fictional or the intertextual at the expense of the comic, this book has discussed their uses and concepts of parody as post-modern because they have presented parody as encompassing in a positive manner *both* the meta-fictional *and* the comic, and because this view of it both follows and goes beyond the modern restriction and reduction of parody to only one or the other of those two forms. [269]

The preceding summary of the post-modernist understanding of parody as both comic and meta-fictional may not seem to have travelled very far from the ancient understanding and use of it in works which were both comic and meta-fictional, and ambivalent towards their targets, such as Aristophanes' *Frogs*. It has on the way to becoming 'post-modern', however, also picked up the modernist

---

268 Other English-language writers who could be named as post-modern include John Barth. One other artist with a post-modern understanding of parody is the Australian Peter Tyndall.

269 *Parody//Meta-Fiction* also presented a 'post-modern' view of parody as both meta-fictional and comic in contrast to modern reductions of parody to the burlesque, but, like the present work, did not restrict parody as such to 'the comic plus meta-fiction'.

extension of its use in meta-fictional works such as Cervantes' *Don Quixote* and Sterne's *Tristram Shandy,* and others, which, with their modern literary experiences and philosophies, have made of it an even more sophisticated tool of literary analysis, 'archaeology', and 'intertextual' re-creation within the literary text than even Aristophanes' many different, and ingenious, uses of it were able to show it to be in 'ancient' times.[270]

In becoming 'post-modern' through the rejection and revision of the modern reduction of parody to *either* meta-fiction *or* comedy, and in favour of an understanding of parody as a much more complex combination and development of both the meta-fictional and the comic and their related forms, the parody 'regained' in the post-modern depictions of it described in the preceding section might even be said to have 'double-coded' the modern with the ancient. Despite such 'post-modern' understandings of parody, few of the theorists or writers discussed above have been quite as positive as Charles Jencks has been about the post-modern as such. One reason for this, moreover, is that some of the ideas which they and others have explicitly dealt with or described as post-modern have been of a more 'late-modern' and negative variety than those which Jencks has described as 'Post-Modern'.[271]

As seen in the preceding section, the rehabilitation of parody as both comic and meta-fictional may itself, however, be described as 'post-modern', and can as such be added to those positive affirmations of the post-modern which are already listed in the category entitled 'The post-modern as critique … vs the post-modern as critique and innovation: 1970s onwards' in the summary of descriptions of the post-modern given in the beginning of this chapter. Such a category might be entitled 'Post-modern theories of parody', be dated 'from the 1970s onwards', and be described as 'Post-modern parody understood as *both* comic *and* meta-fictional or complex. (Bradbury, Eco, Jencks, Lodge, *et al.*).'[272] How this type of parody compares with other –

270 The 'post-modern' views of parody discussed in the preceding section have also been much more complex than the descriptions of parody found in extant ancient texts.

271 This applies, for example, to Eco's 'Reflections on *The Name of the Rose*' as well as to some of Bradbury's early and more Hassanian (though often also ironic) descriptions of the post-modern.

272 The word complex is chosen to cover Jencks' various post-modern descriptions of parody as well as others which might arise and which could be termed 'post-modern' according to all of the criteria described in preceding pages.

ancient, modern, and late-modern – theories and uses of that device is
summarised in the chapters which follow.[273]

273 With reference to Joseph A. Dane's recent claims regarding the problems of
positing a parody tradition, it has been seen not only that it is not true that
ancient parody usage and definition was not influential in later uses of parody,
but that tradition clearly shows an interaction of parody definition and usage
which has produced both a variety of uses and definitions and a common base
by means of which parodies can be recognised and defined as such.

PART IV

❖❖

Parody: past and future

❖❖

5

General review of past theories and uses of parody

Preceding chapters have shown that while it has been possible to identify several different basic characteristics of parody (see chapters 1 and 2) there have been a variety of modern, late-modern, and post-modern theories and uses of that device.

To summarise the differences between the modern, late-modern, and post-modern theories of parody discussed in the last two chapters it can be said first of all that despite the example of works of general parody such as *Don Quixote* and *Tristram Shandy* in which parody is both comic and meta-fictional, many modern (post-Renaissance to twentieth century) theories and uses of it have reflected both the post-sixteenth-century definition of it as ridicule and the post-seventeenth-century definition of it as burlesque.

While the nineteenth century was given the title 'the age of parody' from the collections of burlesque verse which flourished during it, it has been seen that more complex works of modern parody such as Cervantes' *Don Quixote* or Sterne's *Tristram Shandy* were not always named parody by modern and 'late-modern' theorists interested in their complex aspects and that some modern and late-modern theorists have discussed the intertextuality of parodic works without acknowledging the importance of their comic elements.

With reference to the post-modern theories of parody discussed in the last chapter, the contemporary late-modern theorists referred to there can also be said to have taken over from the modern and late-modern theories just mentioned a view of parody which is *either* comic *or* meta-fictional, but which is not necessarily both at the same time, and to have sometimes extended the negativity of the modern understanding of comic parody as ridicule.

In contrast to these theorists, several others have been described as developing a 'post-modern' view of parody which goes beyond the modern reduction of it to either the comic or the meta-fictional. Here the ancient parody which was 'lost' to so many modern commentators through their reduction of it to the burlesque has also been 'regained', and has been combined with the modern in a manner which has created a new and even more complex understanding of parody than was seen in previous centuries.

Despite this post-modern development and restoration to parody of some of the characteristics taken from it by modern and late-modern commentators, parody remains at its most basic a device which, not forgetting its particular characteristics of an ambivalent dual structure and comic character, may be used for several different purposes and in several different ways. Hence, while some post-modern theories and uses of parody have overcome the modern and late-modern reduction of it to *either* the comic *or* the meta-fictional, the 'post-modern' understanding of parody would itself have to be seen to be restricting parody to only some of its aspects if it were ever to reduce the parody to *only* the meta-fictional and the comic, and obscure the fact, already recognised by at least some of the practitioners and theorists of post-modern parody discussed in the conclusion of chapter 4, that parody can be used in a variety of different ways and for both meta-fictional and non-meta-fictional comic purposes.

Because the post-modern uses and descriptions of parody discussed in the final pages of the preceding chapter have both revived and extended the complex and creative aspects of parody, there may be less chance now than in the past that its many different functions will be overlooked or reduced. The continuing use of the word parody by modern and late-modern critics emphasising only one or the other of its critical or meta-fictional aspects means, however, that some awareness of the problems surrounding the definition of parody in the past must still be used in assessing its contemporary uses and definitions.

6

❖❖❖❖❖❖❖❖❖❖❖❖❖❖❖❖❖❖❖❖❖❖❖❖❖❖❖❖❖❖❖❖❖❖❖❖❖❖

Summary of past theories and uses of parody

❖❖❖❖❖❖❖❖❖❖❖❖❖❖❖❖❖❖❖❖❖❖❖❖❖❖❖❖❖❖❖❖❖❖❖❖❖❖

The following is a brief summary of the main types of understandings and uses of parody which have been discussed in previous chapters or mentioned in their notes. (Where one type of understanding or use of parody is repeated in the same period, as, say, burlesque or ridicule, this is not necessarily listed again.)

In addition to listing the uses and understandings of parody under the broad headings of the ancient, modern, and the post-modern which have served as headings for the preceding parts of this book, the following summary will use the category of the 'late-modern' to describe the extension of certain attitudes from the modern uses and understandings of parody. As suggested in earlier chapters, the 'late-modern' extension of the modernist view of parody as *either* metafictional *or* comic, and of the modern assessment of the comic as something negative or destructive, may also be found in various forms in the works of some of today's 'late-modern' authors and critics who have been termed 'postmodernist' by either themselves or by others. When such a 'late-modern' view of parody is found, it will, as previously, be classified as 'late-modern' rather than as 'post-modern'.[1]

Contemporary literature and theory have also shown that the late-modern and post-modern views of parody described below are co-existent from at least the 1970s onwards, and that the 'late-modern' may be found in earlier years, from at least the mid-1960s on. This chronology differs slightly from Charles Jencks' chronology of the 'Late-Modern' and the 'Post-Modern' in architecture where the two are seen as running concurrently from the 1960s onwards, but does not exclude the possibility, as suggested in chapter 4, that individual

---

1 As suggested previously, some of these 'late-modern' theories may also be questioned as to whether they fully describe parody when they eliminate its comic aspects.

works such as David Lodge's *The British Museum is Falling Down* of 1965 or Malcolm Bradbury's early novels could be described as having been 'proto-post-modern' in their use of parody as a device which is to at least some extent both comic and meta-fictional. (Leslie Fiedler's suggestion of 1969 that parody is re-creative as well as comic has also been described as 'proto-post-modern' in chapter 4, but Fiedler's other comments on parody as destructive have restricted his overall use of the term to the 'late-modern' rather than to the 'post-modern'.)

The existence of both late-modern and post-modern theories and uses of parody, together with continuing modern theories and uses, from at least the 1970s onwards further shows that when a theory comes from the 1970s or after, it will not necessarily mean that it is post-modern rather than late-modern or modern. As suggested previously, it will only be *post*-modern if it both challenges and overcomes the modern and late-modern reduction of parody to *either* meta-fiction *or* the comic, and understands the latter to be something positive.[2]

Ancient uses and definitions

παρῳδία/*parodia* = used by the time of the fourth century BC to describe the comic imitation and transformation of an epic verse work (as applied to Hegemon, fifth century BC, by Aristotle in the fourth), and is then extended to cover further forms of comic quotation or imitation in literature by Aristophanic and other scholiasts and to cover examples in speech by the rhetoricians. (Quintilian's first century AD definition of *parode* as 'a name drawn from songs sung in imitation of others, but employed by an abuse of language to designate imitation in verse or prose' was, however, and despite his association of *parodia* with wit, to lead some other rhetoricians and scholars to misleadingly define parody as being largely a form of imitation.)

Παρατραγῳδεῖν/*paratragodein* or *paratragoedia* = the parody of dramatic tragedy, used for comic 'meta-fictional' as well as satiric purposes (e.g. Aristophanes).

---

2 The word 'intertextual' has also been included in the following summary of post-modern uses and theories of parody in order to point to some of the differences between their more advanced theoretical bases and earlier uses and understandings of parody as both a meta-fictional and comic form.

Modern uses and definitions (post-Renaissance onwards)

Parody = the inversion of another song which turns it into the ridiculous (J. C. Scaliger, 1561).

Parody = the 'turning of a verse by altering some words' (John Florio, 1598, following earlier scholars writing after Quintilian).

Parody = meta-fictional, critical, and comic – as practised in works such as *Don Quixote* (1605–15) or *Tristram Shandy* (1759–67). (Both these works suggest that parody may criticise and renew other literary works as well as reflect in comic or ironic fashion on the possibilities and limits of fiction from within a fictional frame, but apart from providing models for other parodists from Fielding to Joyce, do not lead to definitions of parody as both meta-fictional and comic until later. As suggested in chapter 4, they themselves cannot yet be called post-modern because they and their authors do not explicitly challenge the major modern reductions of parody to either the comic or the meta-fictional, and because they contain elements which make them 'modern' rather than post-modern according to other criteria.)

Parody – the imitation of verses which makes them 'more absurd' (Ben Jonson, 1616).

Parody = burlesque (as in Joseph Addison's 1711 discussion of burlesque where *Don Quixote* is taken as an example of one type of burlesque and Lucian's Aristophanic works of another, and in later explicit definitions of parody as such).

Parody = criticism of falsity (Fuzelier, 1738).

Parody = a changing of another work and a method of criticising the false; applications of which range from comic fancy through the satiric to the malignant reduction of an original to the ridiculous (Isaac D'Israeli, 1823).

Parody = lack of originality and its laughter the laughter of despair (Nietzsche, 1886).

Parody = parasitical (Martin, 1896).

Parody = (burlesque) ridicule of a useful, critical kind (Stone, 1914).

Tristram Shandy and *Don Quixote* display discontinuity of plot and character development (Shklovsky, 1921).

Parody = a (sometimes comic) device for 'laying bare the device' (Shklovsky, 1920s).

Parody = double-planed (Tynyanov, 1921).

Parody = double-voiced (Bakhtin, 1929 ff.).
Carnivalistic parody = also comic travesty (Bakhtin, 1929 ff.).
Parody = high burlesque (Bond, 1932, *et al.*).
Parody = artistic imitation *or* critical *or* agitatory (Liede, 1966).
Works such as *Don Quixote* foreground and refunction the 'horizon of expectations' evoked from the reader and changed by an author (Jauss, 1967).
Parody = negative but works such as *Tristram Shandy* foreground the 'implied reader' (Iser, 1972).

Late-modern uses and definitions (1960s onwards)

Parody = against interpretation (Sontag, 1964).
Don Quixote = the first modern work of literature because in it the certainty of similitude is replaced by difference, and Borges' laughter is a 'laughter that shatters' (Foucault, 1966).
Parody = contestation and distortion (Macherey, 1966).
Parody = comic (and modern parody = 'pseudo-transgression'), but carnival (re Bakhtin) = 'serious' transgression (and contributes to the dialogic or 'intertextual' Menippean and polyphonic traditions) (Kristeva, 1966).
Parody = critical of reality (Foucault, 1971).
Parody = insane (Hassan, 1971).
Parody = lack of power, intentionality, and difference (Baudrillard, 1972 ff.).
Parody = non-mastery (Derrida, 1978).
Parody = intertextual but sometimes also crude (Todorov, following Bakhtin and Kristeva on Bakhtin, 1981).
Parody = a 'minimal transformation of a text' (Genette, 1982).
Parody = modern and satiric; pastiche ('blank parody') = post-modern and normless (Jameson 1983 ff.).
Parody = repetition with difference but need not also be comic (Hutcheon, 1985 ff.).
Parody = nihilistic (Newman, 1986).
Parody can be used to suggest an insane/discontinuous world (Martin Amis, 1990).

Post-modern uses and definitions (1970s onwards)

Parody = meta-fictional/intertextual + comic (Bradbury, 1970s ff.).

Summary of past theories and uses of parody

Parody = meta-fictional/intertextual + comic (Lodge, 1970s ff.).
Parody = complex + comic (Jencks, 1977 ff.).
Parody = meta-fictional/intertextual + comic/humorous (Eco, 1980).

7

The future of parody: some concluding comments

As suggested in preceding chapters, the variety of different uses and descriptions given parody over the ages – from the ancient, through the modern, to the post-modern – has shown it to be a form rich in complexity as well as in contradiction. That the restriction of parody to the latter more negative term, or to related terms, in some modern and late-modern theories and uses of it has now been superseded by a 'post-modern' understanding of both its complex meta-fictional and comic aspects may mean that it will be given some even more complex and positive functions in the future. If these new and more complex functions can be assessed and extended without distorting the established character or history of parody, then parody should also be able both to maintain a place in the centres of literary awareness from which it was excluded in the past by those who did not, or could not, appreciate either its heritage or potential because of previous distortions or misunderstandings of its history and functions and to assist those centres towards new and interesting developments. That it has already contributed much to the development of modern and post-modern literature and art has been recognised more and more in recent years. That it could make further such contributions should not be denied now that some of the many different and complex reasons for its creative powers can be described and those descriptions used for the development of new creative works and insights.

Bibliography

Addison, J., *The Spectator*, 5 vols., vol. 2, ed. D. F. Bond. Oxford, 1965.

Adorno, Theodor Wiesengrund, *Gesammelte Schriften*, ed. Rolf Tiedemann. Frankfurt on Main, 1973 ff.

Aeschylus, 2 vols., trans. Herbert Weir Smyth (1922). London and Cambridge, Mass., 1963.

Albertsen, L. L., 'Der Begriff des Pastiche', *Orbis Litterarum*, 26, 1971, pp. 1–8.

Aldrich, Keith, 'The Imitative Nature of Roman Satire', in François Jost (ed.), *Proceedings of the 4th Congress of the International Comparative Literature Association*, 1964, 2 vols. The Hague, 1966, vol. 2, pp. 789–96.

Alter, Robert, *Fielding and the Nature of the Novel*. Cambridge Mass., 1968.

Partial Magic. The Novel as a Self-Conscious Genre. Berkeley, Los Angeles, London, 1975.

Amis, Kingsley, *Lucky Jim* (1954). Harmondsworth, 1977.

Amis, Martin, *London Fields* (1989). Harmondsworth, 1990.

Aristophanes, *Aristophanes*, trans. Benjamin Bickley Rogers (1924). London and Cambridge, Mass., 1968, 3 vols.

The Wasps, The Poet and the Women, The Frogs, trans. David Barrett (1964). Harmondsworth, 1971.

Aristotle, *Rhetorica*, trans. W. Rhys Roberts; *De Poetica*, trans. Ingram Bywater, in *The Works of Aristotle*, ed. W. D. Ross, vol. XI. Oxford, 1924.

The Poetics, trans. W. Hamilton Fyfe (1927 and 1932). Cambridge, Mass. and London, 1973.

On the Soul, trans. W. S. Hett (1936). London and Cambridge, Mass., 1964.

Athenaeus, *The Deipnosophists*, 7 vols., trans. Charles Burton Gulick. London and Cambridge, Mass. 1941.

Aytoun, W. E., *Stories and Verses*. Edinburgh, 1964.

Baker, Kenneth (ed.), *Unauthorized Versions. Poems and their Parodies*. London, 1990.

Bakhtin, Michael M., *Problemy Tvorchestva Dostoyevskogo*. Leningrad, 1929.

Tvorchestvo Fransua Rable. Moscow, 1965.

Problems of Dostoevsky's Poetics (1963), trans. R. W. Rotsel. Ann Arbor Michigan, 1973.

Voprosy Literatury i Estetiki. Moscow, 1975.

Problemy Poetiki Dostoyevskogo (1963). Moscow, 1979.

Estetika Slovesnogo Tvorchestva, ed. Sergey Averintsev and Sergey Bocharov. Moscow, 1979.

The Dialogic Imagination: Four Essays, ed. Michael Holquist, trans. Caryl Emerson and Michael Holquist. Austin and London, 1981.

Problems of Dostoevsky's Poetics (1963), ed. and trans. Caryl Emerson. Manchester and Minnesota, 1984.

Rabelais and his World (1965), trans. Helene Iswolsky. Cambridge, Mass. and London, 1968.

Speech Genres and Other Late Essays, trans. Vern W. McGee, ed. Caryl Emerson and Michael Holquist (from M. M. Bakhtin, *Estetika Slovesnogo Tvorchestva*). Austin, 1986.

Barth, John, 'The Literature of Exhaustion' (1967), in Malcolm Bradbury (ed.), *The Novel Today. Contemporary Writers on Modern Fiction*. Manchester and Totowa, N. J., 1977, pp. 70–110.

'The Literature of Replenishment. Postmodernist Fiction', in *The Atlantic*, 245/1, January 1980, pp. 65–71.

Barthes, Roland, *Writing Degree Zero* (1953), trans. Annette Lavers and Colin Smith. London, 1967.

Essais Critiques. Paris, 1964.

Image-Music-Text, trans. Stephen Heath. Glasgow, 1977.

Baudrillard, Jean, 'Gesture and Signature: Semiurgy in Contemporary Art', in *For a Critique of the Political Economy of the Sign* (1972), trans. Charles Levin. St Louis, 1981.

'The Beaubourg-Effect: Implosion and Deterrence' (1977), in *October*, Spring 1982, pp. 3–13.

Simulations, trans. Paul Foss, Paul Patton, Philip Beitchman. New York, 1983.

'Interview: Game with Vestiges', in *On the Beach*, 5, Winter 1984, pp. 19–25.

'On Nihilism' (1981), in *On the Beach*, 6, Spring 1984, pp. 38–9.

'The Ecstasy of Communication', in *Postmodern Culture* (1983), ed. Hal Foster. London 1985, pp. 126–34.

America (1986), trans. Chris Turner. London and New York, 1988.

Cool Memories (1987), trans. Chris Turner. London, 1990.

Bauman, Zygmunt, *Legislators and Interpreters: On Modernity, Postmodernity and Intellectuals*. Oxford and Cambridge, 1987.

Beare, William and Robert P. Falk, 'Parody', in A. S. Preminger (ed.), *Princeton Encyclopaedia of Poetry and Poetics*, enlarged edn. London, 1975, pp. 600–2.

Becker, Erik, 'Parodie und Plagiat', in *Plagiat. Schriftenreihe der Internationalen Gesellschaft für Urheberrecht*, 14, 1959, pp. 42–50.

Beckett, Samuel and others, *Our Exagmination Round his Factification for Incamination of Work in Progress* (1929). London, 1972.

Bloom, Harold, *The Anxiety of Influence: A Theory of Poetry*. New York, 1973.

'The Necessity of Misreading', *Georgia Review*, 29, 1975, pp. 267–88.

Bibliography

Blumauer, Aloys, *Virgils Aeneis travestirt* (1783 ff.), in *Aloys Blumauer's gesammelte Schriften*, neueste Gesammt-Ausgabe in 3 Theilen, erster Theil. Stuttgart, 1862.

Bond, Richmond P., *English Burlesque Poetry, 1700–1750*. Cambridge, Mass., 1932.

Bonito Oliva, Achille, *Transavantgarde International*. Milan, 1982.

Booth, Wayne C., 'The Self-Conscious Narrator in Comic Fiction before *Tristram Shandy*', in *PMLA*, 67, March 1952, pp. 163–85.

The Rhetoric of Fiction (1961). Chicago and London, 1970.

A Rhetoric of Irony. Chicago and London, 1974.

Borges, Jorge Luis, *Labyrinths. Selected Stories and Other Writings*, ed. D. A. Yates and J. E. Irby. Harmondsworth, 1976.

and Adolfo Bioy-Casares, *Six Problems for Don Isidoro Parodi* (1942), trans. Norman Thomas di Giovanni. London, 1981.

Chronicles of Bustos Domecq (1967), trans. Norman Thomas di Giovanni. London, 1982.

Bradbury, Malcolm, *Eating People is Wrong* (1959). London, 1978.

Stepping Westward (1965). London, 1979.

Possibilities. Essays on the State of the Novel. London, Oxford, New York, 1973.

The History Man (1975). London, 1977.

Who Do You Think You Are? Stories and Parodies (1976). London, 1988

(ed.), *The Novel Today. Contemporary Writers on Modern Fiction*. Manchester and Totowa, N. J., 1977.

(ed. with James McFarlane), *Modernism 1890 1930*. Harmondsworth, 1979.

'An Age of Parody. Style in the Modern Arts', in *Encounter*, 55/1, July 1980, pp. 36–53.

'Modernisms/Postmodernisms', in *Innovation/Renovation. New Perspectives on the Humanities*, ed. Ihab Hassan and Sally Hassan. Wisconsin and London, 1983, pp. 311–27.

The Modern American Novel. Oxford and New York, 1983.

Rates of Exchange (1983). London, 1987.

Why Come to Slaka? A Guidebook and a Phrasebook translated into English by Dr. F. Plitplov (Dozent Extraordinarius, Universitet Dvarfim Borism). Introduction by Dr. A. Petworth (1986). London, 1987.

(ed. with Sigmund Ro), *Contemporary American Fiction*. London, 1987.

No, Not Bloomsbury. London, 1987.

My Strange Quest for Mensonge. Structuralism's Hidden Hero. With a Foreword/Afterword by Michel Tardieu (Professor of Structuralist Narratology, University of Paris) translated by David Lodge (1987). London, 1989.

Unsent Letters (1988). London, 1989.

(with Richard Ruland), *From Puritanism to Postmodernism. A History of American Literature*. London and New York, 1991.

Doctor Criminale. London, 1992.
Brooke-Rose, Christine, *A Rhetoric of the Unreal. Studies in Narrative and Structure, Especially of the Fantastic*. Cambridge, 1981.
Stories, Theories and Things. Cambridge, 1991.
Buckingham, George Villiers, 2nd Duke of, *The Rehearsal*, ed. D. E. L. Crane. Durham, 1976.
Burden, Robert, *John Fowles, John Hawkes, Claude Simon: Problems of Self and Form in the Post-Modernist Novel; a Comparative Study*. Würzburg, 1980.
Byatt, A. S., *Possession*. London, 1990
Calinescu, Matei, 'Parody and Intertextuality', in *Semiotica*, 65/1–2, 1987, pp. 183–90.
Five Faces of Modernity. Durham, 1987.
(ed. with Douwe Fokkema), *Exploring Postmodernism*. Amsterdam and Philadelphia, 1987.
Canetti, Elias, *Die Blendung* (1935). Frankfurt on Main, 1965.
Auto-da-Fé, trans. C. V. Wedgwood (1946). Harmondsworth, 1965.
Carey, Henry, *Chrononhotenthologos*. London, 1734.
Cecil, David (ed.), *Max Beerbohm*. London, 1970.
Cervantes, Miguel de, *The Adventures of Don Quixote* (1605–15), trans. J. M. Cohen (1950). Harmondsworth, 1964.
Chambers, Robert William, Jr, *Parodic Perspectives: A Theory of Parody*. Dissertation, Indiana, 1974.
Chaucer, Geoffrey, *The Complete Poetry and Prose of Geoffrey Chaucer*, ed. John H. Fisher. New York etc., 1977.
Christensen, Inger, *The Meaning of Metafiction. A Critical Study of Selected Novels by Sterne, Nabokov, Barth and Beckett*. Bergen, Oslo, Tromsø, 1981.
Christiansen, Broder, *Philosophie der Kunst*. Hanau, 1909.
Clark, Katerina and Michael Holquist, *Mikhail Bakhtin*. Cambridge, Mass. and London, 1984.
Clinton-Baddeley, V. C., *The Burlesque Tradition in the English Theatre After 1660*. London, 1952.
Cocking, J. M., *Proust. Collected Essays on the Writer and his Art*. Cambridge, 1982.
Coffey, Michael, *Roman Satire*. London, 1976.
Collins, Jim, *Uncommon Cultures. Popular Culture and Post-Modernism*. New York and London, 1989.
Connor, Peter, *Horace's Lyric Poetry: The Force of Humour*. Berwick, Victoria, 1987.
Connor, Steven, *Postmodernist Culture: An Introduction to Theories of the Contemporary*. Oxford and New York, 1989.
Cooper, Lane, *An Aristotelian Theory of Comedy with an Adaptation of the Poetics and a Translation of the 'Tractatus Coislinianus'*. Oxford, 1924.
Cornford, F. M., *The Origin of Attic Comedy*. Cambridge, 1914.
Cotton, C., *Scarronides: or, Virgile Travestie. A Mock-Poem. Being the First Book of Virgils Æneis in English, Burlésque*. London, 1664.

Bibliography

Courtney, E., 'Parody and Literary Allusion in Menippean Satire', in *Philologus*, 106, 1962, pp. 86–100.

Crews, Frederick C. *The Pooh Perplex. A Freshman Casebook* (1963). New York, 1965.

Cross, Wilbur D., *The Life and Times of Laurence Sterne*. New Haven, 1925.

Cuddon, J. A., *A Dictionary of Literary Terms* (1977), revised edn. London, 1979.

Culler, Jonathan, *Structuralist Poetics*. London, 1975.

Cunningham, J. S. (ed.), *Pope. The Rape of the Lock*. Oxford, 1966.

D'Israeli, Isaac, *Curiosities of Literature*, 3 vols. London, 1791–1817.

'Parodies', in Isaac Disraeli, *Curiosities of Literature*, Second Series (1823), 14th edn, 3 vols. London, 1849, vol. 2, pp. 504–11.

Dane, Joseph A., *Parody. Critical Concepts Versus Literary Practices, Aristophanes to Sterne*. Norman, 1988.

Davidson, Israel, *Parody in Jewish Literature*. New York, 1907.

Davis, J. L., 'Criticism and Parody', in *Thought*, 26, 1951, pp. 180–204.

Dear, M. J., 'Postmodernism and Planning', in *Environment and Planning D: Society and Space*, 4, 1986, pp. 367–84.

Debord, Guy, *Society of the Spectacle* (1967). Detroit, 1983.

Delepierre, Joseph Octave, 'Essai sur la Parodie', in *Philobiblon Society Miscellanies*, vol. XII. London 1868–9, pp. 1–182 (reprinted as *La Parodie chez les Grecs, chez les Romains et chez les modernes*. London, 1870).

Derrida, Jacques, *Spurs. Nietzsche's Styles* (1978), trans. Barbara Harlow. Chicago and London, 1979.

Dionysius of Halicarnassus. *The Critical Essays*, 2 vols., trans. Stephen Usher. Cambridge, Mass. and London, 1985.

Docherty, Thomas, *After Theory. Postmodernism/Postmarxism*. London and New York, 1990.

Donaldson, Ian, *The World Upside Down. Comedy from Jonson to Fielding*. Oxford, 1970.

'"The Ledger of the Lost-and-Stolen Office": Parody in Dramatic Comedy', in Margaret A. Rose (ed.), *Parody. A Symposium, in Southern Review*, 13/1, Adelaide, March 1980, pp. 41–52.

Dostoyevsky, Fyodor, *Notes from Underground, The Double*, trans. Jessie Coulson. Harmondsworth, 1972.

Dover, K. J., *Aristophanic Comedy*. Berkeley and Los Angeles, 1972.

Dryden, John, *Of Dramatic Poesy and Other Critical Essays*, 2 vols., ed. George Watson. London and New York, 1962.

Dübner, Friedrich (ed.), *Scholia Graeca in Aristophanem, cum prolegomenis grammaticorum*. Paris, 1843.

Duckworth, George E., *The Nature of Roman Comedy. A Study in Popular Entertainment*. New Jersey, 1952.

Duncan-Jones, A. E. (ed.), *Nicholas Bachtin. Lectures and Essays*. Birmingham, 1963.

Eco, Umberto, *Il Nome della Rosa* (1980). Milan, 1990.

The Name of the Rose, trans. William Weaver (1983). London, 1984.

'Reflections on *The Name of the Rose*' (1983), trans. William Weaver (1984). London, 1985.

'The Frames of Comic "Freedom"', in *Carnival!*, ed. Thomas A. Sebeok. Berlin, New York, Amsterdam, 1984, pp. 1–9.

Travels in Hyperreality. Essays, trans. William Weaver. London, 1986

The Limits of Interpretation. Bloomington and Indianapolis, 1990.

Eidson, John Olin, 'Parody', in Joseph T. Shipley (ed.), *Dictionary of World Literature. Criticism, Forms, Technique.* London, 1945, pp. 423–4.

'Parody', in Joseph T. Shipley (ed.), *Dictionary of World Literary Terms. Forms, Techniques, Criticism* (1943), new enlarged and completely revised edn. London, 1970, pp. 231–2.

Eikhenbaum, Boris M., *Literatura: Teoriya, Kritika, Polemika* Leningrad, 1927.

'The Theory of the "Formal Method"', in Lee T. Lemon and Marion J. Reis (eds.), *Russian Formalist Criticism: Four Essays.* Lincoln, Nebraska, 1965, pp. 99–139.

'O. Henry and the Theory of the Short Story', trans. I. R. Titunik, in L. Matejka and K. Pomorska (eds.), *Readings in Russian Poetics: Formalist and Structuralist Views.* Cambridge, Mass., 1971, pp. 227–70.

The New Encyclopædia Britannica, 15th edn (1974). Chicago etc., 1991.

Epistolæ Obscurorum Virorum. The Latin text with an English rendering, notes, and an historical introduction by Francis Griffin Stokes. London, 1909.

Erasmus of Rotterdam, *Praise of Folly and Letter to Martin Dorp* (1515), trans. Betty Radice. Harmondsworth, 1971.

Erlich, Victor, *Russian Formalism. History–Doctrine* (1955), 3rd edn. New Haven and London, 1981.

(ed.), *Twentieth-Century Russian Literary Criticism.* New Haven and London, 1975.

Euripides, in 4 vols., trans. Arthur S. Way (1912). London and Cambridge, Mass., 1966.

Evans, James E., *Comedy: An Annotated Bibliography of Theory and Criticism.* Metuchen, N. J. and London, 1987.

Federman, Raymond (ed.), *Surfiction. Fiction Now and Tomorrow.* Chicago, 1975.

Feibleman, James K., *In Praise of Comedy. A Study of its History and Practice.* New York, 1970.

Fiedler, Leslie A., *A Fiedler Reader.* New York, 1977.

Fielding, Henry, *The Tragedy of Tragedies, or the Life and Death of Tom Thumb the Great. With the Annotations of H. Scriblerus Secundus.* London, 1731.

Don Quixote in England. A Comedy. London, 1734.

The Historical Register for the Year 1736. London, 1737.

An Apology for the Life of Mrs. Shamela Andrews. In which, the many notorious Falshoods and Misrepresentations of a Book called Pamela Are exposed and refuted. By Mr Conny Keyber. London, 1741.

Joseph Andrews (1742), ed. Martin C. Battestin. Oxford, 1967.

(with the Rev. Mr Young) *'Plutus, the God of Riches. A Comedy'* from *Aristophanes*. London, 1742.

The History of the Life of the Late Mr. Jonathan Wild the Great. London, 1743.

The History of Tom Jones. A Foundling. London, 1749.

Flieger, Jerry Aline, *The Purloined Punch Line. Freud's Comic Theory and the Postmodern Text*. Baltimore and London, 1991.

Florio, John, *Worlde of Wordes, Or Most Copious and exact Dictionarie in Italian and English*. London, 1598.

Fokkema, Douwe and Hans Bertens (ed.), *Approaching Postmodernism*. Amsterdam and Philadelphia, 1986.

Foster, Hal (ed.), *The Anti-Aesthetic. Essays on Postmodern Culture*. Port Townsend, Washington, 1983; republished as *Postmodern Culture*. London, 1985.

Recodings. Art, Spectacle, Cultural Politics. Washington, 1985.

Foucault, Michel, *The Order of Things. An Archaeology of the Human Sciences* (1966), trans. A. M. Sheridan Smith. London, 1970.

The Archaeology of Knowledge (1969), trans. A. M. Sheridan Smith, and *The Discourse of Knowledge* (1971) (Appendix), trans. Rupert Sawyer. New York, Hagerstown, San Francisco, and London, 1972.

'What is an Author?' (1969), in Paul Rabinow (ed.), *The Foucault Reader*. Harmondsworth, 1986, pp. 101–20.

'Nietzsche, Genealogy, History' (1971), in Paul Rabinow (ed.), *The Foucault Reader*. Harmondsworth, 1986, pp. 76–100.

This is not a Pipe (1973), trans. and ed. James Harkness. Berkeley, Los Angeles and London, 1983.

Fowles, John, *The French Lieutenant's Woman* (1969). London, 1987.

Freidenberg, Olga, *Poetika Suzheta i Zhanra*. Leningrad, 1936.

'The Origin of Parody', in H. Baran (ed.), *Semiotics and Structuralism*. New York, 1976, pp. 269–83.

Freud, Sigmund, *Gesammelte Werke*, ed. Anna Freud *et al.*, 17 vols. in 16. London, 1940–52.

The Standard Edition of the Complete Psychological Works of Sigmund Freud, trans. and ed. James Strachey *et al.*, 24 vols. London, 1953–74.

Freund, Winfried, *Die literarische Parodie*. Stuttgart, 1981.

Fuzelier, Louis, *Les Parodies du Nouveau Théâtre Italien* (1738). Geneva, 1970, 2 vols.; vol. 1, pp. XIX–XXXV.

Gablik, Suzi, *Magritte*. London, 1970.

Gane, Mike, *Baudrillard's Bestiary. Baudrillard and Culture*. London and New York, 1991.

Garrad, Ken, 'Parody in Cervantes', in Margaret A. Rose (ed.), *Parody. A Symposium*, in *Southern Review*, 13/1, Adelaide, March 1980, pp. 21–9.

Gellius, Aulus, *The Attic Nights of Aulus Gellius*, 3 vols., trans. John C. Rolfe (1927). Cambridge, Mass. and London, 1961.

Genette, Gérard, *Palimpsestes. La Littérature au second degré*. Paris, 1982.

Gibbons, Stella, *Cold Comfort Farm* (1932). Harmondsworth, 1977.

Gilman, Sander L., *The Parodic Sermon in European Perspective. Aspects of*

Liturgical Parody from the Middle Ages to the Twentieth Century. Wiesbaden, 1974.

Nietzschean Parody. An Introduction to Reading Nietzsche. Bonn, 1976.

Goethe, Johann Wolfgang von, 'Über die Parodie bei den Alten' (1824), in Goethe, *Sämtliche Werke,* Jubiläums-Ausgabe, 40 vols., ed. E. v. d. Hellen *et al.* Stuttgart and Berlin, 1902–7, vol. 37, pp. 290–3.

Gombrich, E. H., *Art and Illusion. A Study in the Psychology of Pictorial Representation* (1959), 4th edn. London, 1972.

Gottsched, Joh. Chr., *Versuch einer critischen Dichtkunst* (1742). Darmstadt, 1962.

Grannis, V. B., *Dramatic Parody in Eighteenth Century France.* New York, 1931.

Green, D. H., *Irony in the Mediaeval Romance.* Cambridge, 1979.

Grellmann, H., 'Parodie', in P. Merker and W. Stammler (eds.), *Reallexikon der deutschen Literaturgeschichte,* vol. 2. Berlin, 1926/28, pp. 630–53.

Griffin, David Ray, William A. Beardslee, and Joe Holland, *Varieties of Postmodern Theology.* New York, 1989.

Grimm, Jacob and Wilhelm, *Deutsches Wörterbuch.* Leipzig, 1889.

Habermas, Jürgen, 'Modernity – An Incomplete Project', in Hal Foster (ed.), *Postmodern Culture.* London, 1985, pp. 3–15.

Hamm, Jean-Jacques (ed.), 'La Parodie: Théorie et Lectures', *Études littéraires,* 19/1, Spring-Summer 1986.

Hannoosh, Michele, *Parody and Decadence. Laforgue's Moralités légendaires.* Columbus, 1989.

Hanslik, R., 'Parodie', in C. Andresen, H. Erbse, O. Gignon, K. Schefold, K. F. Stroheker and E. Zinn (eds.), *Lexikon der alten Welt.* Zürich und Stuttgart, 1965, pp. 2224–6.

Hardy, Barbara, 'Parody', in S. H. Steinberg (ed.), *Cassell's Encyclopaedia of Literature,* 2 vols. London, 1953, vol. 1, pp. 404–7.

Harris, Max (ed.), *Ern Malley's Poems.* Adelaide, 1971.

Harter, K. E., 'A Russian Critic and *Tristram Shandy* ', in *Modern Philology,* 52, 1954, pp. 92–9.

Harvey, David, *The Condition of Postmodernity.* Oxford, 1989.

Hassall, Anthony, 'Fielding and the Novel as Parody', in Margaret A. Rose (ed.), *Parody. A Symposium,* in *Southern Review,* 13/1. Adelaide, March 1980, pp. 30–40.

Hassan, Ihab, *The Dismemberment of Orpheus: Toward a Postmodern Literature* (1971), 2nd edn. Wisconsin and London, 1982.

'The Question of Postmodernism', in Harry R. Garvin (ed.), *Romanticism, Modernism, Postmodernism,* Bucknell Review, 25/2. London and Toronto, 1980, pp. 117–26.

The Postmodern Turn. Essays in Postmodern Theory and Culture. Ohio, 1987.

Hebdige, Dick, *Hiding in the Light : On Images and Things.* London and New York, 1988.

Heine, Heinrich, *Sämtliche Werke,* ed. Ernst Elster (1890), 7 vols., 2nd, revised, printing. Leipzig and Vienna, 1893.

Bibliography

Hempel, Wido, 'Parodie, Travestie und Pastiche', in *Germanisch-Romanische Monatsschrift*, neue Folge, 15, 1965, pp. 150–76.

Higgins, Dick, *A Dialectic of Centuries. Notes Towards a Theory of the New Arts*, 2nd edn. New York and Vermont, 1978.

Highet, Gilbert, *The Anatomy of Satire*. Princeton, 1962.

Holquist, Michael, *Dialogism. Bakhtin and his World*. London, 1990.

Holub, Robert, C., *Reception Theory. A Critical Introduction*. London and New York, 1984.

Home, Henry (Lord Kames), *Elements of Criticism* (1762), 3rd edn (with additions and improvements), 2 vols. Edinburgh and London, 1765.

Homer, *The Odyssey*, 2 vols., trans. A. T. Murray (1919). London and Cambridge, Mass., 1966.

The Iliad, 2 vols., trans. A. T. Murray (1924). London and Cambridge, Mass., 1971.

Hope, Edward William, *The Language of Parody. A Study in the Diction of Aristophanes*. Dissertation (1905), Baltimore, 1906.

Horn, Wilhelm, *Gebet und Gebetsparodie in den Komödien des Aristophanes*. Nuremberg, 1970.

Householder, Fred W., Jr, 'ΠΑΡΩΙΔΙΑ', in *Classical Philology*, 39/1, January 1944, pp. 1–9.

Hutcheon, Linda, *A Theory of Parody. The Teachings of Twentieth-Century Art Forms*. New York and London, 1985.

A Poetics of Postmodernism. History, Theory, Fiction. New York and London, 1988.

The Politics of Postmodernism. London and New York, 1989.

Huyssen, Andreas, *After the Great Divide. Modernism, Mass Culture and Postmodernism*. Indiana, 1986 and London, 1988.

Ilvonen, Eero, *Parodies de thèmes pieux dans la poésie française du moyen age*. Paris, 1914.

Iser, Wolfgang, *Der implizierte Leser. Kommunikationsformen des Romans von Bunyan bis Beckett*. Munich, 1972.

Der Akt des Lesens. Theorie ästhetischer Wirkung. Munich, 1976.

'Das Komische: Ein Kipp-Phänomen', in Wolfgang Preisendanz and Rainer Warning (ed.), *Das Komische*. Munich, 1976, pp. 398–402.

Sterne: Tristram Shandy (1987), trans. David Henry Wilson. Cambridge, 1988.

Jameson, Fredric, *Marxism and Form. Twentieth-Century Dialectical Theories of Literature* (1971). Princeton, 1974.

The Prison-House of Language. A Critical Account of Structuralism and Russian Formalism (1972). Princeton, 1974.

'Postmodernism and Consumer Society', in Hal Foster (ed.), *Postmodern Culture* (1983). London, 1985, pp 111–25.

'Postmodernism, or the Cultural Logic of Late Capitalism' in *New Left Review*, 146, July-August 1984, pp. 53–92.

The Ideologies of Theory: Essays 1971–1986. Volume 2: The Syntax of History. London, 1988.

Bibliography

'Postmodernism and Consumer Society', in *Postmodernism and its Discontents*, ed. E. Ann Kaplan. London and New York, 1988, pp. 13–29.

Postmodernism, or, the Cultural Logic of Late Capitalism. London and New York, 1991.

Janko, Richard, *Aristotle on Comedy. Towards a Reconstruction of Poetics II.* London, 1984.

Jantz, H. 'Kontrafaktur, Montage, Parodie: Tradition und symbolische Erweiterung', in Werner Kohlschmidt and Herman Meyer (eds.), *Tradition und Ursprünglichkeit. Akten des III. Internationalen Germanistenkongresses 1965 in Amsterdam*. Bern and Munich, 1966, pp. 53–65.

Jauss, Hans Robert, *Literaturgeschichte als Provokation der Literaturwissenschaft*, Konstanzer Universitätsreden, 3, ed. Gerhard Hess. Constance, 1967.

'Über den Grund des Vergnügens am komischen Helden', in Wolfgang Preisendanz and Rainer Warning (eds.), *Das Komische*. Munich, 1976, pp. 103–32.

Jencks, Charles, Review of Robert Venturi, *Complexity and Contradiction in Architecture*, in *Arena. Architectural Association Journal*, 83/913, June 1967, pp. 4–5.

Meaning in Architecture, edited with George Baird. London, 1969.

Adhocism. The Case for Improvisation, with Nathan Silver. London, 1972.

'The Rise of Post Modern Architecture', in the *Architectural Association Quarterly*, 7/4, October/December 1975, pp. 3–14.

'A Genealogy of Post-Modern Architecture', in *Architectural Design*, Profile 4. London, 1977, pp. 269–71.

The Language of Post-Modern Architecture. London, 1977; 2nd revised enlarged edn, London, 1978; 3rd revised enlarged edn, London, 1981; 4th revised enlarged edn, London, 1984; 5th revised enlarged edn, London, 1987; 6th revised enlarged edn, London, 1991.

'Why Post-Modernism?' in 'Post-Modern History', in *Architectural Design* 48/1, Profile 10. London, 1978, pp.11–26 & 43–58.

Late-Modern Architecture and Other Essays. London and New York, 1980.

'Towards Radical Eclecticism', in *Architecture 1980. The Presence of the Past. Venice Biennale*, ed. Gabriella Borsano. New York, 1980, pp. 30–7.

(ed.) *Post-Modern Classicism – The New Synthesis*. London, 1980.

Current Architecture. London, 1982.

Towards a Symbolic Architecture. The Thematic House. London, 1985.

'Essay on the Battle of the Labels Late-Modernism *vs* Post-Modernism', in *Architecture and Urbanism*, January Extra Edition, *Charles Jencks*. Tokyo, 1986, pp. 209–36.

What is Post-Modernism? London and New York, 1986; 2nd revised enlarged edn, London and New York, 1987; 3rd revised enlarged edn, London and New York, 1989.

Post-Modernism. The New Classicism in Art and Architecture. London, 1987.

'Post-Modernism and Discontinuity', in *Architectural Design*, 57/1–2, 1987; Profile 65, *Post-Modernism and Discontinuity*. London, 1987, pp. 5–8.

'Post-Modernism and Eclectic Continuity', in *Architectural Design*, 57/1–2, 1987; Profile 65, *Post-Modernism and Discontinuity*. London, 1987, p. 25.

and Maggie Valentine, 'The Architecture of Democracy. The Hidden Tradition', in *Architectural Design*, 57/8–10; Profile 69, *The Architecture of Democracy*. London, 1987, pp. 9–25.

'Deconstruction: The Pleasure of Absence', in *Architectural Design*, 58/3–4, 1988; Profile 72, *Deconstruction in Architecture*. London, 1988, pp. 17–31.

'Peter Eisenman. An *Architectural Design* Interview by Charles Jencks', in *Architectural Design*, 58/3–4, 1988; Profile 72, *Deconstruction in Architecture*. London, 1988, pp. 49–61.

'The Battle of High-Tech: Great Buildings with Great Faults', in *Architectural Design*, 58/11–12, 1988; Profile 76, *New Directions in Current Architecture*. London, 1988, pp. 19–39.

'The Bank as Cathedral and Village', in *Architectural Design*, 58/11–12, 1988; Profile 76, *New Directions in Current Architecture*. London, 1988, pp. 77–9.

Architecture Today. London, 1988.

'Death for Rebirth', in *Architectural Design*, 60/9–10, 1990; Profile 88, *Post-Modernism on Trial*. London, 1990, pp. 6–9.

'Post-Modernism between Kitsch and Culture', in *Architectural Design*, 60/9–10, 1990; Profile 88, *Post-Modernism on Trial*. London, 1990, pp. 24–35.

'The Carnival: Grotesque and Redeemable' in *Architectural Design*, 61/5–6, 1991; Profile 91, *Post-Modern Triumphs in London*. London 1991, pp. 78–9.

'25 Carnivalesque Buildings' in *Architectural Design*, 61/5–6, 1991; Profile 91, *Post-Modern Triumphs in London*. London, 1991, pp. 80–93.

'Metropolitan Post Marks', in *The Times Saturday Review*, 22 June 1991, pp. 15–17.

(ed.), *The Post-Modern Reader*. London and New York, 1992.

Jerrold, Walter and R. M. Leonard (eds.), *A Century of Parody and Imitation*. Oxford, 1913.

Johnson, Philip and Mark Wigley, *Deconstructive Architecture*. New York, 1988.

Jonson, Ben, *The Complete Plays of Ben Jonson*, ed. G. A. Wilkes. Oxford, 1981 ff.

Joyce, James, *Ulysses* (1922). Harmondsworth, 1968.

Finnegans Wake (1939). New York, 1965.

Jump, John D., *Burlesque*. London, 1972.

Kant, Immanuel, *Kants Werke. Akademie-Textausgabe* (1902 ff.). Berlin, 1968.

Anthropology from a Pragmatic Point of View, trans. Mary J. Gregor. The Hague, 1974.

Kant's Critique of Aesthetic Judgement, trans. James Creed Meredith. Oxford, 1911.

Kaplan, E. Ann, 'Feminism/Oedipus/Postmodernism: The Case of MTV', in

Bibliography

E. Ann Kaplan (ed.), *Postmodernism and its Discontents*. London and New York, 1988, pp. 30–44.

Karrer, Wolfgang, *Parodie, Travestie, Pastiche*. Munich, 1977.

Kayser, Wolfgang, *Das Groteske. Seine Gestaltung in Malerei und Dichtung.* Oldenburg and Hamburg, 1957.

Kearney, Richard, *The Wake of Imagination. Ideas of Creativity in Western Culture.* London, 1988.

Keeble, T. W., *The Burlesque of Mythology in Seventeenth-Century Poetry in Spain*. Dissertation, London, 1948.

Kellner, Douglas, *Jean Baudrillard. From Marxism to Postmodernism and Beyond.* Oxford and Cambridge, 1989.

(ed.), *Postmodernism/Jameson/Critique*. Washington, 1989.

Kermode, Frank, 'Modernisms Again. Objects, Jokes and Art', in *Encounter*, 26/4, April 1966, pp. 65–74.

Kiremidjian, G. David, *A Study of Modern Parody. James Joyce's Ulysses, Thomas Mann's Doctor Faustus* (Dissertation, Yale, 1964). New York and London, 1985.

'The Aesthetics of Parody', *Journal of Aesthetics and Art Criticism*, 28, 1969, pp. 231–42.

Kirk, Eugene, P., *Menippean Satire: An Annotated Catalogue of Texts and Criticism*. New York, 1980.

Kitchin, George, *A Survey of Burlesque and Parody in English*. London, 1931.

Kleinknecht, Hermann, *Die Gebetsparodie in der Antike*. Stuttgart and Berlin, 1937.

Klotz, Heinrich, *The History of Postmodern Architecture* (1984), trans. Radka Donnell. Cambridge, Mass. and London, 1988.

Knoche, Ulrich, *Roman Satire* (1949), trans. E. S. Ramage. Indiana, 1976.

Kolb, David, *Postmodern Sophistications. Philosophy, Architecture and Tradition.* Chicago, 1990.

'Postmodern Sophistications', in *Architectural Design*, 60/9–10, 1990; Profile 88, *Post-Modernism on Trial*. London, 1990, pp. 13–19.

Koller, Hermann, 'Die Parodie', in *Glotta*, 35/1–2, 1956, pp. 17–32.

Kranz, Walther, 'Paratragödie', in Konrat Ziegler (ed.), *Paulys Real-Encyclopädie der classischen Altertumswissenschaft*, neue Bearbeitung. Stuttgart, 1949, vol. XVIII/4, 1410–12.

Kreissmann, B., 'Pamela-Shamela. A Study of the Criticisms, Burlesques, Parodies and Adaptations of Richardson's "Pamela"', *University of Nebraska Studies*, New Series, 22, May 1960.

Kristeva, Julia, 'Le mot, le dialogue et le roman' (1966), in Julia Kristeva, Σημειωτική. *Recherches pour une sémanalyse*. Paris, 1969, pp 143–73.

'Word, Dialogue and Novel', trans. Alice Jardine, Thomas Gora and Léon S. Roudiez (1980), in Toril Moi (ed.), *The Kristeva Reader*. Oxford, 1986, pp. 34–61.

Kuhn, Hans, 'Was parodiert die Parodie?', in *Neue Rundschau*, 85/4, 1974, pp. 600–18.

Lachmann, Renate (ed.) *Dialogizität*. Munich, 1982.

Bibliography

'Ebenen des Intertextualitätsbegriffs', in Karlheinz Stierle and Rainer Warning (eds.), *Das Gespräch*. Munich, 1984, pp. 133–8.

'Bachtins Dialogizität und die akmeistische Mythopoetik als Paradigma dialogisierter Lyrik', in Karlheinz Stierle and Rainer Warning (eds.), *Das Gespräch*. Munich, 1984, pp. 489–515.

'Zur Semantik metonymischer Intertextualität', in Karlheinz Stierle and Rainer Warning (eds.), *Das Gespräch*. Munich, 1984, pp. 517–23.

Lalli, Giovanni Battista, *Eneide travestita*. Rome, 1633.

Lampe, G. W. H., *A Patristic Greek Lexicon*. Oxford, 1961–8.

Leavis, F. R., *The Great Tradition* (1948). Harmondsworth, 1967.

Lee, Charles and D. B. Wyndham Lewis, *The Stuffed Owl. An Anthology of Bad Verse* (1930). London, 1963.

Lehmann, Paul, *Die Parodie im Mittelalter*. Munich, 1922.

(ed.), *Parodistische Texte. Beispiele zur lateinischen Parodie im Mittelalter*. Munich, 1923.

Pseudo-Antike Literatur des Mittelalters. Leipzig and Berlin, 1927.

Lelièvre, F. J., 'The Basis of Ancient Parody', in *Greece and Rome*, Series 2, 1/2, June 1954, pp. 66–81.

Lemon, Lee T. and Marion J. Reis (eds.), *Russian Formalist Criticism: Four Essays*. Lincoln, Nebraska, 1965.

Levi-Strauss, Claude, *La Pensée Sauvage*. Paris, 1962.

Lichtenberg, Georg Christoph, *Vermischte Schriften. Neue vermehrte, von dessen Söhnen veranstaltete Original-Ausgabe*, 14 vols. Göttingen, 1844–53.

Liddell, Henry George and Robert Scott (eds.), *A Greek-English Lexicon*, revised by Sir Henry Stuart Jones with the assistance of Roderick McKenzie and others. Oxford, 1983.

Liede, Alfred, 'Parodie' (1966), in W. Kohlschmidt and W. Mohr (eds.), *Reallexikon der deutschen Literaturgeschichte*, 2nd edn, vol. 3. Berlin and New York, 1977, pp. 12–72.

Lipovetsky, Gilles, *L'Ère du vide. Essais sur l'individualisme contemporain*. Paris, 1983.

Lodge, David, *The British Museum is Falling Down* (1965). Harmondsworth, 1983.

Language of Fiction. Essays in Criticism and Verbal Analysis of the English Novel (1966), 2nd edn. London, Boston, Melbourne, Henley, 1984.

Changing Places. A Tale of Two Campuses (1975). Harmondsworth, 1987.

Working with Structuralism. Essays and Reviews on Nineteenth- and Twentieth-Century Literature (1981). London, Boston, Henley, 1986.

Small World. An Academic Romance (1984). Harmondsworth, 1986.

Nice Work (1988). Harmondsworth, 1989.

After Bakhtin: Essays on Fiction and Criticism. London, 1990.

Paradise News. A Novel. London, 1991.

The Art of Fiction. Harmondsworth, 1992.

Loveridge, Mark, *Laurence Sterne and the Argument against Design*. London, 1982.

Lucian, *Satirical Sketches*, trans. Paul Turner. Harmondsworth, 1961.

Lucie-Smith, Edward, *The Thames and Hudson Dictionary of Art Terms.* London, 1984.

Ludwich, A., *Die Homerische Batrachomachia des Karers Pigres nebst Scholien und Paraphrase.* Leipzig, 1896.

Lyotard, Jean-François, *Driftworks,* ed. Roger McKeon. New York, 1984. *The Postmodern Condition: A Report on Knowledge* (1979), trans. Geoff Bennington and Brian Massumi, and 'Answering the Question: What is Postmodernism?' (1982), trans. Régis Durand. Manchester, 1984.

McCaffery, Larry (ed.), *Postmodern Fiction. A Bio-Bibliographical Guide.* New York and London, 1986.

MacDonald, Dwight (ed.), *Parodies, An Anthology from Chaucer to Beerbohm – and After.* London, 1960.

McHale, Brian, *Postmodernist Fiction.* New York and London, 1987.

McLuhan, Marshall and Wilfred Watson, 'Parody', in *From Cliché to Archetype.* New York, 1970, pp. 167–170

McMahon, A. P., 'On the Second Book of Aristotle's *Poetics* and the Source of Theophrastus' Definition of Tragedy', in *Harvard Studies in Classical Philology,* 28, 1917, pp. 1–46.

MacQueen-Pope, W. J., 'Burlesque', in S. H. Steinberg (ed.), *Cassell's Encyclopaedia of Literature,* 2 vols. London, 1953, vol. 1, pp. 72–3.

Maas, Paul, 'Parodos (παρῳδός)', in Konrat Ziegler (ed.), *Paulys Real-Encyclopädie der classischen Altertumswissenschaft,* neue Bearbeitung. Stuttgart, 1949, vol. XVIII/4, 1684–5.

Macherey, Pierre, *A Theory of Literary Production* (1966), trans. Geoffrey Wall. London, Henley, Boston, 1978.

Madius, V., *De ridiculis,* in V. Madius and B. Lombardus, *In Aristotelis librum de poetica communes explanationes.* Venice, 1550, pp. 301–27.

Mann, Thomas, *Gesammelte Werke.* Frankfurt on Main, 1960.

Markiewicz, Henryk, 'On the Definitions of Literary Parody', in *To Honor Roman Jakobson. Essays on the Occasion of his Seventieth Birthday,* 3 vols., vol. 2. The Hague, 1967, pp. 1264–72.

Martin, Arthur Shadwell, *On Parody.* New York, 1896.

Marx, Karl, *The Eighteenth Brumaire of Louis Bonaparte* (1852). Moscow, 1977.

Matejka, L. and K. Pomorska (eds.), *Readings in Russian Poetics: Formalist and Structuralist Views.* Cambridge, Mass., 1971.

Medvedev, P. N/M. M. Bakhtin, *The Formal Method in Literary Scholarship. A Critical Introduction to Sociological Poetics,* trans. Albert J. Wehrle. Baltimore and London, 1978.

Meredith, George, *An Essay on Comedy and the Uses of the Comic Spirit* (1877). Westminster, 1897.

Méril, Edelestand du, *Poésies populaires latines antérieures au douzième siècle.* Paris, 1843.

Meyer, Herman, *Das Zitat in der Erzählkunst. Zur Geschichte und Poetik des europäischen Romans* (1961), 2nd revised edn. Stuttgart, 1967.

Minogue, Valerie, 'The Uses of Parody: Parody in Proust and Robbe-Grillet',

Bibliography

in Margaret A. Rose (ed.), *Parody. A Symposium*, in *Southern Review*, 13/1. Adelaide, March 1980, pp. 53–65.

Mitsdörffer, W., *Die Parodie Euripideischer Szenen bei Aristophanes*. Dissertation, Berlin, 1943.

Mollett, J. W., *An Illustrated Dictionary of Words used in Art and Archaeology*. London, 1883.

Monumenta Germaniae, vol. iv/ii & iii, ed. Karl Strecker. Berlin, 1923.

Monro, David Hector, *Argument of Laughter*. Melbourne, 1951.

Muecke, Douglas, C., *The Compass of Irony*. London, 1969.

Irony. London, 1970.

Irony and the Ironic. London, 1982.

Muecke, Frances, 'Playing with the Play: Theatrical Self-Consciousness in Aristophanes', in *Antichton*, 11, 1977, pp. 52–67.

Murray, Augustus T., *On Parody and Paratragoedia in Aristophanes with Especial Reference to his Scenes and Situations*. Berlin, 1891.

Murray, Gilbert, *A History of Ancient Greek Literature* (1897), 3rd edn. London, 1907.

Aristophanes. A Study. Oxford, 1933.

Murray, Peter and Linda, *A Dictionary of Art and Artists* (1959). Harmondsworth, 1960.

Neuschäfer, Hans-Jörg, *Der Sinn der Parodie im Don Quijote*. Heidelberg, 1963.

Newman, Michael, 'Revising Modernism, Representing Postmodernism: Critical Discourses of the Visual Arts', in *ICA Documents*, 4/5. London, 1986, pp. 32–51.

Nietzsche, Friedrich, *Nietzsche Werke. Kritische Gesamtausgabe*, ed. Giorgio Colli and Mazzino Montinari. Berlin, 1967 ff.

Novati, Francesco, 'La Parodia Sacra nelle Letterature Moderne', in *Studi Critici et Letterari*. Turin, 1889, pp. 177–310.

Oxford English Dictionary. Oxford, 1933; 2nd edn. Oxford, 1989.

Plato, *Philebus*, trans. Harold N. Fowler (1925). London and Cambridge, Mass., 1962.

Pöhlmann, Egert, 'ΠΑΡΩΙΔΙΑ', in *Glotta*, 50/3–4, 1972, pp. 144–56.

Pollard, Arthur, *Satire*. London, 1970.

Potts, L. J., *Comedy* (1949). London, 1966.

Preisendanz, Wolfgang and Rainer Warning (eds.), *Das Komische*. Munich, 1976.

Priestman, Judith, *The Age of Parody. Literary Parody and Some Nineteenth-Century Perspectives*. Dissertation, University of Kent at Canterbury, 1980.

Quintilian, *Institutio Oratoria*, 4 vols., trans. H. E. Butler. London and Cambridge, Mass., 1960.

Rabelais, François, *The Histories of Gargantua and Pantagruel*, trans. J. M. Cohen (1955). Harmondsworth, 1963.

Rau, Peter, *Paratragödia. Untersuchungen einer komischen Form des Aristophanes*. Munich, 1967.

Bibliography

Raven, D. S., *Poetastery and Pastiche. A Miscellany*. Oxford, 1966.

Richards, I. A., *Principles of Literary Criticism*. London and New York, 1930.

Richardson, Mrs Herbert, *Parody*, The English Association Pamphlet No. 92, August 1935. London, 1935.

Riewald, J. G., 'Parody as Criticism', in *Neophilologus*, 50, 1966, pp. 125–48.

Riffaterre, Michel, 'Intertextual Representation: On Mimesis as Interpretive Discourse', in *Critical Inquiry*, 11, 1984, pp. 141–62.

Riha, Karl, *Cross-Reading und Cross-Talking. Zitat-Collagen als poetische und satirische Technik*. Stuttgart, 1971.

Roberts, David, *Kopf und Welt*, trans. Helge und Fred Wagner. Munich and Vienna, 1975.

Röhrich, Lutz, *Gebärde–Metapher–Parodie*. Düsseldorf, 1967.

Rose, H. J., *A Handbook of Greek Literature. From Homer to the Age of Lucian* (1934), 4th edn, revised, and corrected. London and New York, 1964.

Rose, Margaret A., *The Functions of Biblical Language in the Poetry of Heinrich Heine. Conventional and Parodic Uses of the Bible and of Biblical Language*. Dissertation, Monash University, Victoria, Australia, 1973.

'Carnival and *Tendenz*: Satiric Modes in Heine's *Atta Troll. Ein Sommernachtstraum*', *AUMLA* 43, May 1975, pp. 33–49.

Die Parodie: Eine Funktion der biblischen Sprache in Heines Lyrik. Meisenheim on Glan, 1976.

Reading the Young Marx and Engels. Poetry, Parody and the Censor. London and Totowa, N. J., 1978.

Parody//Meta-Fiction. An Analysis of Parody as a Critical Mirror to the Writing and Reception of Fiction. London, 1979.

(ed.), *Parody. A Symposium* (1976), in *Southern Review*, 13/1. Adelaide, March 1980. (Translated by Susumu Shimaoka as *The Structure of Parody*. Tokyo, 1989.)

'Defining Parody', introductory essay to *Parody. A Symposium, Southern Review*, 13/1. Adelaide, March 1980, pp. 5–20.

'The Second Time as Farce: History Understood as Fiction', in Leonard Schulze and Walter Wetzels (eds.), *Literature and History*. Lanham, New York and London, 1983, pp. 27–35.

'Die Parodie als Bild der Rezeption und Produktion des Textes', in *Akten des VI. IVG Kongresses. Basel 1980*, ed. H. Rupp and H-G. Roloff. Bern, 1981, pp. 397–400.

'Parody Revisited', in *Comic Relations. Studies in the Comic, Satire and Parody*, ed. P. Petr, D. Roberts and P. Thomson. Frankfurt on Main, Bern and New York, 1985, pp. 187–92.

'Parody and Post-Structuralist Criticism', in *Jahrbuch für internationale Germanistik*, 18/1, 1986, pp. 96–101.

'Parody/Post-Modernism', in *Poetics*, 17, 1988, pp. 49–56.

'Postmodernistskaya Imitatsiya', trans. G. A. Sokolov, in *Iskusstvo*, 8, 1990, pp. 44–8.

'Post-Modern Pastiche', in *British Journal of Aesthetics*, 31/1, January 1991, pp. 26–38.

Bibliography

The Post-Modern and the Post-Industrial. A Critical Analysis. Cambridge, 1991.

'Defining the Post-Modern', in Charles Jencks (ed.), *The Post-Modern Reader.* London and New York, 1992, pp. 119–36.

Rotermund, Erwin, *Die Parodie in der modernen deutschen Lyrik.* Munich, 1963.

Gegengesänge. Lyrische Parodien vom Mittelalter bis zur Gegenwart. Munich, 1964.

Rutherford, W. G. (ed.), *Scholia Aristophanica,* 3 vols. London, 1896.

Ryle, Gilbert, *The Concept of Mind* (1949). Harmondsworth, 1966.

Salingar, Leo, *Shakespeare and the Traditions of Comedy.* Cambridge, 1974.

Sallier, l'Abbé, 'Discours sur l'origine et sur le caractère de la Parodie', *Histoire de l'Academie Royal des Inscriptions et Belles Lettres,* vol. VII. Paris, 1733, pp. 398–410.

Scaliger, J. C., *Poetices libri septem.* Lyons, 1561.

Scarron, Paul, *Typhon ou la Gigantomachie. Poëme Burlesque.* Paris, 1644.

Le Virgile Travesty en vers Burlesques (1648–53). Paris, 1653.

Schlegel, August Wilhelm, *Kritische Schriften und Briefe,* 6 vols., ed. E. Lohner. Stuttgart, Berlin, Cologne, Mainz, 1962–74.

Schlegel, A. W. and Fr. (eds.), *Athenaeum.* 1798–1800. Stuttgart, 1960.

Schlegel, Friedrich, *Sämmtliche Werke,* 10 vols. in 5. Vienna, 1822–5.

Schlesinger, A. C., 'Indications of Parody in Aristophanes', in *Transactions of the American Philological Association,* 67, 1936, pp. 296–314.

'Identification of Parodies in Aristophanes', in *American Journal of Philology,* 58, 1937, pp. 294–305.

Schmidt, Siegfried, J., *Texttheorie. Probleme einer Linguistik der sprachlichen Kommunikation.* Munich, 1973.

Literaturwissenschaft als argumentierende Wissenschaft. Munich, 1975.

Schneegans, Heinrich, *Geschichte der grotesken Satire.* Strassburg, 1894

Scholes, Robert, *The Fabulators* (1963). Oxford, 1967.

Shakespeare, William, *The Complete Works,* new edn, ed. P. Alexander. London and Glasgow, 1951.

Sharpe, Tom, *Porterhouse Blue* (1974). London, 1983.

Sheldon, Richard Robert, *Viktor Borisovic Shklovsky: Literary Theory and Practice, 1914–1930.* Dissertation, Michigan, 1966.

Shepperson, A. B., *The Novel in Motley: A History of the Burlesque Novel in English* (1936). New York, 1967.

Sheridan, Richard, Brinsley, *The Major Dramas of Richard Brinsley Sheridan. The Rivals, The School for Scandal, The Critic,* ed. George Henry Nettleton. Boston, 1906.

Shimaoka, Susumu, 'The Spirit of Parody: the *Salomé* of Jules Laforgue', in *Bulletin of General Education Faculty of Ibaraki University,* 11, March 1979, pp. 35–50.

'Notes on *Tradition and the Individual Talent*: T. S. Eliot and his Relational Way of Thinking', in *Bulletin of General Education Faculty of Ibaraki University,* 14, March 1982, pp. 43–50.

Shipley, John Burke, 'Satire', in Joseph T. Shipley (ed.), *Dictionary of World*

Literary Terms. Forms, Techniques, Criticism (1943), new enlarged and completely revised edn. London, 1970, pp. 286–90.

Shklovsky, Viktor, *'Tristram Shendi' Sterna i Teoriya Romana*. Petrograd and Moscow, 1921.

Rozanov. Petrograd, 1921.

'Evgenii Onegin'. (Pushkin i Stern), in *Ocherki po Poetike Pushkina*. Berlin, 1923, pp. 199–220.

O Teorii Prozy. Moscow and Leningrad, 1925.

O Teorii Prozy, 2nd edn. Moscow, 1929.

Khudozhestvennaya Prosa. Razmishleniya i Razbori. Moscow, 1959.

'Art as Technique', in Lee T. Lemon and Marion J. Reis (eds.), *Russian Formalist Criticism: Four Essays*. Lincoln, Nebraska, 1965, pp. 3–24.

'Sterne's *Tristram Shandy*: Stylistic Commentary', in Lee T. Lemon and Marion J. Reis (eds.), *Russian Formalist Criticism: Four Essays*. Lincoln, Nebraska, 1965, pp. 25–57.

'A Parodying Novel: Sterne's *Tristram Shandy*', trans. W. George Isaak, in John Traugott (ed.), *Laurence Sterne. A Collection of Critical Essays*. Englewood Cliffs, N. J., 1968, pp. 66–89.

A Sentimental Journey. Memoirs, 1917–1922 (1923), trans. Richard Sheldon. Ithaca and London, 1970.

'The Mystery Novel: Dickens's *Little Dorrit*', trans. Guy Carter, in L. Matejka and K. Pomorska (eds.), *Readings in Russian Poetics: Formalist and Structuralist Views*. Cambridge, Mass., 1971, pp. 220–6.

'The Connection between Devices of *Syuzhet* Construction and General Stylistic Devices', trans. Jane Knox, in Stephen Bann and John E. Bowlt (eds.), *Russian Formalism: A Collection of Articles and Texts in Translation*. Edinburgh, 1973, pp 48–72.

'Pushkin and Sterne: *Eugene Onegin*', trans. M. Holquist, in Victor Erlich (ed.), *Twentieth-Century Russian Literary Criticism*. New Haven and London, 1975, pp. 63–80.

Theory of Prose (1929), trans. Benjamin Sher with an introduction by Gerald L. Bruns. Illinois, 1990.

Shlonsky, Tuvia, 'Literary Parody. Remarks on its Method and Function', in François Jost (ed.), *Proceedings of the 4th Congress of the International Comparative Literature Association, 1964*, 2 vols. The Hague, 1966, vol. 2, pp. 797–801.

Shumway, David R., 'Jameson/Hermeneutics/Postmodernism', in Douglas Kellner (ed), *Postmodernism/Jameson/Critique*. Washington, 1989, pp. 172–202.

Smith, Dane Farnsworth, *Plays About the Theatre in England From 'The Rehearsal' in 1671 to the Licensing Act in 1737; or, The Self-Conscious Stage and its Burlesque and Satirical Reflections in the Age of Criticism*. Oxford, 1936.

Soja, Edward W., *Postmodern Geographies. The Reassertion of Space in Critical Social Theory*. London and New York, 1989.

Sontag, Susan, *Against Interpretation and Other Essays* (1966). New York, 1978.

Squire, Sir John Collings (ed.), *Apes and Parrots. An Anthology of Parodies.* London, 1928.

Stackelberg, Jürgen von, *Literarische Rezeptionsformen. Übersetzung. Supplement. Parodie.* Frankfurt on Main, 1972.

Stearn, Gerald Emanuel (ed.), *McLuhan: Hot and Cool.* Harmondsworth, 1968.

Steinecke, W., *Das Parodieverfahren in der Musik.* Kiel, 1934.

Steiner, Wendy, 'Intertextuality in Painting', in *American Journal of Semiotics,* 3/4, 1985, pp. 57–67.

Stephanus, Henricus, *Thesaurus Graecae Linguae.* 5 vols., Geneva, 1572. *Parodiae Morales.* Geneva, 1575.

Sterne, Laurence, *The Life and Opinions of Tristram Shandy, Gentleman* (1759–67), ed. Graham Petrie. Harmondsworth, 1967.

Stierle, Karlheinz, 'Werk und Intertextualität', in Karlheinz Stierle and Rainer Warning (eds.), *Das Gespräch.* Munich, 1984, pp. 139–50.

Stone, Christopher, *Parody.* London, 1914.

Striedter, Jurij, 'Zur formalistischen Theorie der Prosa und der literarischen Evolution', in Jurij Striedter (ed.), *Texte der Russischen Formalisten,* vol. 1. Munich, 1969, pp. IX–LXXXIII.

Strohschneider-Kohrs, Ingrid, *Romantische Ironie in Theorie und Gestaltung.* Tübingen, 1960.

Tallis, Raymond, *Not Saussure. A Critique of Post-Saussurian Literary Theory.* London, 1988.

Todorov, Tzvetan, 'Some Approaches to Russian Formalism', trans. Bruce Merry, in Stephen Bann and John E. Bowlt (eds.), *Russian Formalism: A Collection of Articles and Texts in Translation.* Edinburgh, 1973, pp. 6–19.

Mikhail Bakhtin. The Dialogical Principle (1981), trans. Wlad Godzich. Minneapolis, 1984.

Tomashevsky, Boris, *Teoriya Literatury.* Leningrad, 1925. *Teoriya Literatury. Poetika.* Moscow and Leningrad, 1927.

'Thematics', in Lee T. Lemon and Marion J. Reis (eds.), *Russian Formalist Criticism: Four Essays.* Lincoln, Nebraska, 1965, pp. 61–95.

Toynbee, Arnold J., *A Study of History by Arnold J. Toynbee,* ed. D. C. Somervell. London, 1946.

A Study of History, vols. 1–6, London, 1939, and vols. 7–10, London, 1954.

'Art: Communicative or Esoteric?', in Edward F. Fry (ed.), *On the Future of Art.* New York, 1970, pp. 3–19.

Trachtenberg, Stanley (ed.), *The Postmodern Moment. A Handbook of Contemporary Innovation in the Arts.* Westport, Connecticut and London, 1985.

Traugott, John (ed.), *Laurence Sterne. A Collection of Critical Essays.* Englewood Cliffs, N. J., 1968.

Tynyanov, Yuriy N., *Dostoyevsky i Gogol'* (k Teorii Parodii) (1921). Letchworth, 1975.

Problema Stikhotvornogo Yazyka (1924). The Hague, 1963.

Bibliography

Arkhaisty i Novatory (1929). Munich, 1967.

'On Literary Evolution', translated by C. A. Luplow, in L. Matejka and K. Pomorska (eds.), *Readings in Russian Poetics: Formalist and Structuralist Views*. Cambridge, Mass., 1971, pp. 66–78.

'Dostoevsky and Gogol', in Victor Erlich (ed.), *Twentieth-Century Russian Literary Criticism*. New Haven and London, 1975, pp. 102–16.

'O Parodii', in Yuriy N. Tynyanov, *Poetika, Istoriya Literatury, Kino*. Moscow, 1977, pp. 284–310.

The Problem of Verse Language (1924), ed. and trans. Michael Sosa and Brent Harvey. Michigan, 1981.

Ulmer, Gregory L., 'Of a Parodic Tone Recently Adopted in Criticism', in *New Literary History*, 13/3, Spring 1982, 'Theory: Parodies, Puzzles, Paradigms', pp. 543–60.

Van Ghent, Dorothy, *The English Novel. Form and Function*. New York, 1953.

Venturi, Robert, *Complexity and Contradiction in Architecture*. New York, 1966.

Verweyen, Theodor, *Theorie der Parodie. Am Beispiel Peter Rühmkorfs*. Munich, 1973.

Verweyen, Theodor and Gunther Witting, *Die Parodie in der neueren deutschen Literatur. Eine systematische Einführung*. Darmstadt, 1979.

'Parodie, Palinodie, Kontradiktio, Kontrafaktur – Elementare Adaptionsformen in Rahmen der Intertextualitätsdiskussion', in Renate Lachmann (ed.), *Dialogizität*. Munich, 1982, pp. 202–36.

Die Kontrafaktur: Vorlage und Verarbeitung in Literatur, bildender Kunst, Werbung und politischem Plakat. Constance, 1987.

Virgil, 2 vols., trans. H. Rushton Fairclough, rev. edn. London and Cambridge, Mass., 1967.

Volosinov, V. N., *Freudianism. A Marxist Critique*.(1927), trans. I. R. Titunik, ed. in collab. with Neal H. Bruss. New York, San Francisco, London, 1976.

Wales, HRH, the Prince of, *A Vision of Britain*. London, 1989.

Warning, Rainer, 'Elemente einer Pragmasemiotik der Komödie', in Wolfgang Preisendanz and Rainer Warning (eds.), *Das Komische*. Munich, 1976, pp. 279–333.

Watson, E. Bradlee, 'Burlesque', in Joseph T. Shipley (ed.), *Dictionary of World Literature. Criticism, Forms, Technique*. London, 1945, pp. 79–80.

'Burlesque', in Joseph T. Shipley (ed.), *Dictionary of World Literary Terms. Forms, Techniques, Criticism* (1943), new enlarged and completely revised edn. London, 1970, p. 35.

Waugh, Patricia, *Metafiction. The Theory and Practice of Self-Conscious Fiction*. London and New York, 1984.

Weisstein, Ulrich, 'Parody, Travesty and Burlesque. Imitation with a Vengeance', in François Jost (ed.), *Proceedings of the 4th Congress of the International Comparative Literature Association*, 1964, 2 vols., vol. 2. The Hague, 1966, pp. 802–11.

Welsch, Wolfgang, *Unsere postmoderne Moderne* (1987), 2nd edn. Weinheim, 1988.

Welsford, Enid, *The Fool. His Social and Literary History* (1935). London, 1968.

West, Francis, *Gilbert Murray. A Life*. London and New York, 1984.

Wilde, Alan, *Horizons of Assent: Modernism, Postmodernism, and the Ironic Imagination*. Baltimore, 1981.

Wilde, Oscar, *The Importance of Being Earnest*, in *Complete Works of Oscar Wilde*, introduced by Vyvyan Holland (1948), new edn. London and Glasgow, 1969.

Wimsatt, W. K., 'The Criticism of Comedy', in W. K. Wimsatt, *Hateful Contraries. Studies in Literature and Criticism*. Kentucky, 1965, pp. 90–107.

Wodehouse, P. G., *Right Ho, Jeeves*. London, 1922.

The Code of the Woosters (1937). London, 1990.

Performing Flea. A Self-Portrait in Letters (1953). Harmondsworth, 1961.

Jeeves and the Feudal Spirit (1954). London, 1990.

Woodhouse, S. C., *English-Greek Dictionary. A Vocabulary of the Attic Language*. London, 1932.

Worcester, David, *The Art of Satire* (1940). New York, 1960.

Index

absurdity, the absurd, 9, 10, 27, 32, 33, 37, 66, 85, 202, 208, 213, 214, 267, 281
Addison, Joseph, 10, 49, 57ff., 61, 66, 67, 86, 281
Adorno, Theodor W., 221
Aeschylus, 19, 29, 34
Aesopian language, 30
agora, see public square
Albee, Edward, 215
Albertsen, L. L., 73, 75
Aldrich, Keith, 81
alienation device, 79, 104, 109, 114, 117, 120, 184
Alter, Robert, 105
alteration, 10, 27f., 49, 210, 281
ambiguity, ambivalence, 8, 29, 41, 47, 48, 49, 50, 51, 52, 78, 79, 83, 87, 88, 90, 128ff., 152, 156, 159, 161, 162, 163, 164, 166, 167,170, 213, 246
Amis, Kingsley, 93, 254, 259 f.
Amis, Martin, 2, 158, 270, 271, 282
ancient parody, 1, 2, 5ff., 42, 54, 55, 57, 59ff., 63, 64, 65, 67, 83, 86, 91, 113, 143, 144, 145, 146, 147, 152, 157, 162, 238, 239, 269, 272, 273, 274, 277f., 279, 280, 281, 284
archaeology of texts, 90, 273
Ariosto, Ludovico, 128
Aristophanes, 2, 6, 15, 18f., 20, 22, 24, 29, 34, 36, 47f., 49, 50, 55, 59, 64, 67, 83, 86, 91, 142, 150, 185, 189, 272, 273, 280
Aristophanic scholiasts, 15, 18, 19, 20, 21, 22, 25, 42, 64, 280
Aristotle, 6, 7, 9, 11, 13, 18, 19, 20, 34, 57f., 66f., 170, 246ff., 267, 280
Aristoxenus, 20

Athenaeus of Naucratis, 7, 9, 11f., 15f., 20, 23, 25, 61, 144
Aytoun, W. E., 71f.

Bachiarius, 148
Bachtin, Michail, see Bakhtin, Mikhail
Bachtin, Nicholas, 174
Bakhtin, Mikhail, 2, 124, 125ff., 171, 172, 173, 174, 177, 178ff., 181, 183f., 185, 190, 205, 212, 213, 214, 216, 237f., 240f., 242, 244f., 246ff., 252, 253ff., 258, 265, 282
Bakhtin, Nikolai, see Bachtin, Nicholas
Barth, John, 201, 246, 247, 269, 272
Barthes, Roland, 180, 185f., 187, 226, 261, 265
bathos, 69
Batrachomyomachia, 12f., 14f., 60, 61, 63, 143, 145
Battle of the Frogs and the Mice, see *Batrachomyomachia*.
Battle of the Giants, see *Gigantomachia*.
Baudrillard, Jean, 2, 191, 201, 202, 204, 206, 210, 214, 216ff., 221, 222, 227, 228, 229, 252, 282
Bauman, Zygmunt, 228
Baxtin, Mikhail, see Bakhtin, Mikhail
Baxtin, Nikolai, see Bachtin, Nicholas
Beaumarchais, Pierre-Augustin Caron de, 114
Beckett, Samuel, 175
Beerbohm, Max, 24
Beigesang, 46, 48, 49, 50, 139f.
Bell, Bernard Iddings, 197
Bell, Daniel, 200, 207
Bely, Andrei, 120
Beroalde de Verville, François, 106
Bible, the, 43ff., 120, 147ff., 165, 168, 171

306

Index

Index

Hassan, Ihab, 2, 200, 203, 204, 205, 206, 207ff., 222, 228, 229, 231, 252, 258, 267, 268, 269, 270, 271, 273, 282
Hawkes, John, 95
Hays, H. R., 198
Hebdige, Dick, 2, 203, 225f., 232
Hegemon of Thasos, 7, 11f., 14, 15, 16, 19, 58, 250, 280
Heine, Heinrich, 43ff.
Hemingway, Ernest, 255
Hempel, Wido, 74
Henry, O., see Porter, William Sydney
Hermippus of Athens, 16
Hermogenes, 24, 191
heteroglossia, 130, 133f., 136ff., 156, 160, 213, 214, 254, 255, 258
  see also dialogic, double-voiced parody, and polyglossia
Higgins, Dick, 196f.
hilarodia, 15
Hipponax of Ephesus, 15, 16, 43, 61
hoax, 69ff., 74
Holquist, Michael, 125f., 140
Holub, Robert C., 170
Home, Henry, Lord Kames, 62f.
Homer, 10, 11, 12, 13, 14, 16, 17, 59, 60, 61, 120, 145, 146, 255
  see also Homeric rhapsodists
Homeric rhapsodists, 9, 10, 11, 27, 145
Horace, 9, 81
Horn, Wilhelm, 17, 18, 49, 64, 150
Householder, Fred W., Jr, 7ff., 19, 20ff., 42, 47f., 54, 64, 239
Howe, Irving, 199
hudibrastic, 56ff.
Hudnut, Joseph, 198, 233
humour, 15, 18, 20, 22ff., 31ff., 34f., 36, 37, 38, 42, 45, 55, 61, 78f., 85, 97, 120, 142, 149, 150, 156, 158, 167, 176, 208, 209, 221, 222, 232, 233, 236, 239, 240, 241, 243, 245, 247ff., 256, 258, 263, 264, 265, 266, 267, 271, 272, 283
  sense of, 31f., 37
  lack of sense of, 31, 37, 264ff.
Hutcheon, Linda, 80, 98, 211, 228, 238ff., 241, 266, 282
Hutten, Ulrich von, 70
Huyssen, Andreas, 203

hybridisation, 131, 134f., 136, 141, 153f., 155, 212, 213, 233, 243

Ibsen, H., 111
Ilvonen, Eero, 149
imitation, 6, 7, 8, 10, 11, 12, 14, 15, 18, 21, 22, 23, 29ff., 36f., 38, 43, 44, 45ff., 49, 53, 54, 55, 56, 58, 61f., 64, 66, 67, 68, 69, 70, 71, 72, 73, 74, 75, 76, 77, 78, 79, 80, 81, 82, 83, 93, 94, 95, 96, 106, 107, 112, 143, 145, 146, 147, 170, 171, 172, 173, 190, 213, 221, 222, 223, 228, 229, 230, 246, 250, 255, 256, 257, 258, 259, 270, 271, 280, 281, 282
incongruity, 21, 29ff., 37, 38, 42, 45, 52, 56, 61f., 64, 69, 73, 78, 79, 88, 114, 116, 122, 124, 126, 127, 171, 236, 256, 259, 263, 264, 265, 267
intertextuality, 1, 6, 28, 68, 71, 90, 99, 103, 107, 108, 111, 112, 113, 114, 117, 154, 155, 177, 178ff., 195, 205, 226, 238, 239, 240, 249, 258, 259, 261ff., 272, 273, 277, 280, 282, 283
  see also quotation
irony, 2, 23, 30, 35, 36, 37, 42, 43, 47, 48, 51, 59, 61, 69, 70, 71, 78, 79, 83, 84, 86, 87ff., 91, 92, 93, 94, 95, 96, 97, 107, 109, 112, 117, 128, 134, 139, 142, 145, 150, 153, 156, 163, 166, 168, 175, 189f., 198, 202, 205, 208, 210, 212, 213, 215, 221, 222, 224, 231, 233, 235, 238, 241, 242, 243, 247, 248, 249, 250, 253, 256, 260, 261, 262, 263, 264, 265, 267, 269, 273, 281
Iser, Wolfgang, 2, 170, 175ff., 186, 282
Isozaki, Arata, 243
Ivanov, V. V., 125

James, Henry, 215, 255
Jameson, Fredric, 2, 186, 202, 203, 204, 213, 216, 217, 219, 220ff., 225, 226, 227, 228, 229, 230, 231, 232, 233, 235, 236, 237, 252, 282
Janko, Richard, 34
Jauss, Hans Robert, 2, 170, 171ff., 175, 186, 282
Jefferson, D. W., 106
Jencks, Charles, 2, 77, 182, 195, 200,

Index

201, 203, 205, 206, 209, 211, 213,
216, 219, 220, 223, 224, 225, 227,
229, 230, 233ff., 238, 242ff., 253,
257, 262, 265, 269, 270, 271, 272,
273, 279, 283
Jerrold, Walter, 39
joco-serious, 160
    see also serio-comical
Johnson, Philip, 77
Johnson, Samuel, 10
Jonson, Ben, 10, 69, 281
Joyce, James, 34, 38, 47, 71, 105, 175,
    176, 255, 256, 257, 258, 281
Julian the Apostate, 148
Jump, John, 55ff., 62
Juvenal, 81

Kafka, Franz, 178, 179, 255
Kallimachos, see Callimachus
Kames, Lord, see H. Home
Kant, Immanuel, 32f., 34, 50, 111, 174
Kaplan, E. Ann, 204
Karrer, Wolfgang, 62f., 73
Kaverin, V., 110
Kayser, Wolfgang, 133
Kearney, Richard, 204, 229f., 232
Kellner, Douglas, 214, 216f.
Kermode, F., 206
Kersey, John, 57
Kirk, Eugene, P., 85f., 105ff., 148, 165,
    179
Kitchin, George, 69
Kleinknecht, H., 23, 150
Klotz, Heinrich, 203, 212, 219
Koehler, Michael, 200
Kolb, David, 205, 241f.
Koller, Hermann, 49
Kranz, W., 18
Kratinos, see Cratinus
Kristeva, Julia, 154, 177ff., 181, 185,
    191, 265, 282
Kuhn, Hans, 68

Lachmann, Renate, 181ff.
Lalli, G., 55
Lapôtre, 148, 149
Lasch, Christopher, 269
late-modern parody, 1, 2, 6, 28, 47, 68,
    94, 95, 103, 113, 116, 125, 177ff.,
    195, 205ff., 235, 239f., 243, 256,

261, 262, 264, 265, 270, 271, 272,
274, 277, 278, 279f., 282, 284
late-modern 'postmodernism', see post-
    modernism, deconstructionist
laughable, the, 9, 11, 20, 23, 58, 66,
    250
laughter, 9, 20, 23, 24, 25, 32, 34, 36,
    46, 52, 62, 63, 66, 67, 81, 88, 112,
    131, 141f., 145, 146, 152, 155, 156,
    157, 159, 161, 162, 163, 164, 166,
    167, 168, 170, 171, 174, 179, 187,
    189f., 222, 223, 247, 248, 249, 250,
    251, 252, 254, 255, 258, 266, 271,
    282
    see also comedy, humour, and the
    laughable
Lawrence, D. H., 255
laying bare of the device, 82, 83, 105,
    109, 110, 112, 115, 115ff., 117, 121,
    126, 138f., 157, 166, 175, 185, 281
    see also playing with and renewal of
    the device
Leavis, F. R., 1, 105
Lee, Charles, 69
Lehmann, Paul, 31, 147ff., 151
Lelièvre, F. J., 7, 8ff., 12, 13, 17, 22,
    23f., 47f., 64, 78
Lemon, Lee T., 108
Leonard, R. M., 39
Lesage, Alain René, 132
Leskov, N. S., 115
levelling, 65
    see also burlesque, carnival,
    'carnivalesque' or 'carnivalistic'
    architecture, literature and parody,
    crossing borders, closing gaps, and
    travesty
Levin, Harry, 199
Lévi-Strauss, Claude, 225
Lewis, D. B. Wyndham, 69
Lichtenberg, G. Chr., 77f.
Liddell and Scott, 5, 7, 12, 49, 160
Liede, Alfred, 30f., 64f., 150, 173, 282
Lipovetsky, Gilles, 252
literary evolution, see evolution,
    literary
Lodge, David, 2, 71, 95f., 124f., 166,
    211, 231, 246, 252, 253ff., 261, 262,
    263, 264, 266, 271, 272, 273, 280,
    283

311

Index

Index

montage, 72
Monumenta Germaniae, 148
Motte, Houdard de la, 26f.
Muecke, D. C., 48, 87
Muecke, F., 36
Murdoch, Iris, 259
Murray, A. T., 18
Murray, Gilbert, 12ff., 16, 24, 29
Murray, Linda and Peter, 72
Musäus, Johann Karl August, 137, 156
mystery stories, 110, 131
   see also detective stories

Nabokov, V., 261f.
Neuschäfer, Hans-Jörg, 172
Newman, Michael, 227, 228, 232, 282
Nicochares, 11, 58
Nietzsche, Friedrich, 174, 188ff., 197,
   210, 214, 219, 267, 281
nostalgia, 218, 222, 223, 232, 235, 236
Nouvel, Jean, 43
Novati, Francisco, 149

obnazheniye priyoma, see 'laying bare of
   the device'
Obscure Men, Letters of, 70f.
Oenonas, 15, 20
'O. Henry', see Porter, William Sydney
Onis, Federico, de, 196, 198, 233
Owens, Craig, 202, 204
Oxford English Dictionary, 5, 7, 20, 48,
   49, 68, 72, 73f., 75, 80
Ozell, John, 58

Pannwitz, Rudolph, 197, 198
para (παρά), 7, 8, 9, 46, 48f., 51, 54,
   245f.
paratragedy (paratragoedia),
   paratragodein (παρατραγῳδεῖν), 18,
   280
παροδε (πάροδή), 7
parode (παρῳδή), 8, 11f., 18, 19, 22, 23,
   29, 30, 70, 280
parodeo (παρῳδέω), 10, 15, 19, 21, 42
parodia (παρῳδία), 5, 6, 7, 8, 9, 10, 11f.,
   15, 16, 17f., 19, 20, 21, 22, 23, 29,
   30, 42, 48f., 50, 55, 64, 255, 280.
parodia sacra, 147ff., 160, 164, 167, 168,
   247f.
   see also Bible

parodic doubles, 145, 146, 162, 164,
   169, 190
parodic realism, 48, 158, 270f.
parodic stylisation, 130, 131, 132, 133,
   135, 136, 155, 156
parodic-travesty, 144ff., 147, 151f., 153,
   154, 155, 158, 164, 250, 253, 254,
   255
parodoi (παρῳδοί), 7, 10, 11, 19, 145
   see also parodos (παρῳδός)
parodos (πάροδος), 7
parodos (παρῳδός), 7, 8, 11, 14, 19
parody, passim, and see also ancient
   parody, 'carnivalesque' or
   'carnivalistic' parody, double
   parody, double-coded parody,
   double-planed parody, double-voiced
   parody, general parody, grotesque
   parody, late-modern parody,
   macaronic parody, mediaeval parody,
   modern parody, parodia sacra,
   parodic doubles, parodic realism,
   parodic stylisation, parodic-travesty,
   post-modern parody, pre- and proto-
   post-modern parody, and self-parody
pastiche, 2, 52, 71, 72ff., 77, 94, 181,
   191, 202, 204, 212, 213, 216, 217,
   220ff., 230f., 233ff., 242, 245, 253,
   255, 256, 266, 282
Paul, Jean, see Richter, Johann Paul
   Friedrich
Pei, I. M., 243
pekoral, 21, 37, 68f.
persiflage, 53, 68
Persius, 81
Petronius, 85, 86
Pevsner, Nikolaus, 199, 233
Phillips, Edward, 57
Piano, Renzo, 219, 220, 230
Picasso, Pablo, 78, 105
Pigres, 12
Pirandello, Luigi, 247
phlyakography, 15
plagiarism, 32, 69, 75, 106f., 212, 271
planes, see double-planed parody
Platen, August von, 144
Plato, 50, 66f.
Plautus, 20
play, playfulness, 31, 33, 36, 47, 94,
   109, 117, 121, 133, 147, 156, 168,

313

Index

Röhrich, Lutz, 46
Rolfe, Fr (Baron Corvo), 255
romance, the, 39, 41, 59, 84, 91, 114,
    124, 137, 140, 141, 156, 172, 249,
    268
Rose, H. J., 12f., 16
Rotermund, Erwin, 79, 172
Rozanov, Vasily V., 113, 118, 122
Rühmkorf, Peter, 172
Russian formalists, 2, 79, 82f., 93,
    103ff., 125ff., 130f., 132, 133, 136,
    138, 139, 140, 142, 146, 153, 154,
    155, 156, 157, 158, 159, 160, 161,
    162, 163, 164, 165, 166, 169, 170,
    171, 172, 175f., 177, 178, 184f., 221,
    264, 265, 281
Rutherford, W. G., 20
Ryle, Gilbert, 99

Salingar, Leo, 28
Sallier, l'Abbé, 11
satire, 2, 6, 12, 16, 17, 20, 28, 29, 30,
    36, 37, 42, 48, 49, 51, 53, 56, 60, 61,
    62, 65, 68, 70, 71, 77, 78, 79, 80ff.,
    88, 89f., 91, 95. 96, 98, 115, 141,
    148, 149, 150, 159, 167, 191, 222,
    223, 232, 235, 236, 238, 251, 256,
    260, 261, 266, 280, 281, 282
see also Menippean satire and satura.
satura, 80f., 106
saturnalia, Roman, 147, 151
satyr play, 145, 146, 162, 254, 255
Scaliger, J. C., 9, 10, 11, 145, 281
Scarron, Paul, 27, 55, 59, 143, 144
Schlegel, August Wilhelm, 50
Schlegel, Friedrich, 50, 88
Schlesinger, A. C., 18
Schmidt, Siegfried J., 40
Schneegans, Heinrich, 62, 133
scholia, see scholiasts
scholiasts, 15, 18, 19, 20, 21, 22, 25,
    42, 64, 239, 280
see also grammarians
Scottish 'Spasmodics', 72
Seaman, Owen, 26
self-parody, 88, 91f., 156, 165, 263
Seneca, 65, 85, 86, 165
serio-comical, 157, 159, 160
Shaftesbury, the third Earl of, see
    Cooper, Anthony Ashley

Shakespeare, William, 69
Sharpe, Tom, 44f.
Sheldon, Richard, 108, 112
Sher, Benjamin, 104, 120
Sheridan, R. B., 84
Shipley, John Burke, 80f.
Shirai, Seiichi, 243
Shklovsky, Viktor, 79, 103ff., 115, 116,
    117, 118, 119, 120, 121, 123f., 126,
    131, 132, 133, 136, 138, 139, 140,
    142, 155, 156, 157, 158, 159, 160,
    161, 165, 166, 169, 170, 175, 176,
    281
Shlonsky, Tuvia, 82f.
Shumway, David, 220
silloi, sillos, 17
simulation, 29ff., 49, 69, 78, 217, 218,
    219, 222, 224, 226, 229, 230
see also imitation
skaz, 126, 127, 128, 134, 254
Sklovskij, Victor, see Shklovsky, Viktor
slapstick, 208
Smith, Bernard, 198, 233
Smith, Horace and James, 24, 255f.
Smollett, Tobias, 131, 132, 137, 175
Snow, C. P., 255, 259
socialist realism, 140, 158
Socratic irony, see irony
Soja, Edward W., 228
Somervell, D. C., 199
Sontag, Susan, 209ff., 282
Sopater (Sopatros), 15
Sorel, Charles, 156
Sotades of Maroneia, 14
Spitzer, Leo, 128
spoudogeloios (σπουδογέλοιος), see serio-
    comical
Squire, John, 41
Starobinski, J., 181
Steinecke, W., 7
Steiner, Wendy, 240
Stephanus, Henricus, see Stephen,
    Henry
Stephen, Henry (Henricus Stephanus, or
    Henri Estienne), 10, 11
Stern, Robert, 200, 201
Sterne, Laurence, 6, 43, 47, 85, 92, 96,
    103ff., 113, 114, 115, 131, 132, 133,
    134, 136, 137, 139, 141, 157, 160,
    161, 165, 170, 175f., 195, 213, 214,

Index